D1236430

THE STUDIA PHILONICA ANNUAL
Studies in Hellenistic Judaism

Program in Judaic Studies
Brown University
BROWN JUDAIC STUDIES

Edited by

Shaye J. D. Cohen, Ernest S. Frerichs, Calvin Goldscheider

Editor for Studia Philonica: Shaye J. D. Cohen

Number 299

THE STUDIA PHILONICA ANNUAL
Studies in Hellenistic Judaism

edited by
David T. Runia

THE STUDIA PHILONICA ANNUAL
Studies in Hellenistic Judaism

Volume VI

1994

EDITOR:
David T. Runia

ASSOCIATE EDITORS:
Alan Mendelson
David Winston

BOOK REVIEW EDITOR:
Gregory E. Sterling

Scholars Press
Atlanta, Georgia

THE STUDIA PHILONICA ANNUAL
Studies in Hellenistic Judaism

The financial support of
C. J. de Vogel Foundation, Amsterdam
Leiden University
Coe College, Cedar Rapids, Iowa
University of Notre Dame
is gratefully acknowledged

ISBN: 0-7885-0030-9

Printed in the United States of America
on acid-free paper

THE STUDIA PHILONICA ANNUAL

STUDIES IN HELLENISTIC JUDAISM

The Studia Philonica Annual accepts articles for publication in the area of Hellenistic Judaism, with special emphasis on Philo and his *Umwelt*.

Contributions should be sent to the Editor, Prof. D. T. Runia, Rijnsburgerweg 116, 2333 AE Leiden, The Netherlands. Please send books for review to the Book Review Editor, Prof. G. E. Sterling, Dept. of Theology, University of Notre Dame, Notre Dame, IN 46556, U.S.A.

Contributors are requested to observe the 'Instructions to Contributors' located at the end of the volume. Articles which do not conform to these instructions cannot be accepted for inclusion.

CONTENTS

ARTICLES

REVIEW ARTICLES

BOOK REVIEW SECTION

Philonic Nomenclature

DAVID T. RUNIA

to David Winston[*]

Introduction

It is one of the commonplaces of modern Philonic scholarship that Philo is known under two names, Philo Alexandrinus (or Philo of Alexandria) and Philo Judaeus (or Philo the Jew). As an example we may adduce Valentin Nikiprowetzky's magisterial monograph *Le commentaire de l'Écriture chez Philon d'Alexandrie*, which was written as a kind of Prolegomena to the reading and study of Philo.[1] It commences with two introductory chapters on Philo's Hellenic and Judaic background which are pointedly given the titles Philo Alexandrinus and Philo Judaeus respectively.[2] It would certainly be a very interesting exercise to examine how these two titles have been used in Philonic scholarship during the past century and a half. But that is not my aim in this essay. What I want to do is to look at the background of these and other titles, which, as we shall see, in certain (but not all) respects go as far back as antiquity. The subject of my enquiry is Philonic nomenclature. I wish to examine the labels which are given to Philo in our ancient sources in order to signify him as the historical and literary personage which he was.

By way of introducing our topic, it will be worthwhile briefly to look at Philo's actual name. Φίλων (usually *Philo* when transcribed into Latin)[3] is one of the more common personal names in the Greek-speaking

---

[*] This piece of research was suggested by a conversation I had with David Winston in Washington in November 1993, when we were attending the Philo Seminar as part of the annual AAR/SBL meeting. David asked me whether Jerome was the first to call Philo 'Judaeus'. I said I thought this was correct, but could not say for certain. At almost the same time as this article will appear in print, David will withdraw from active teaching duties at the Graduate Theological Union in Berkeley, where he has been Professor of Hellenistic and Jewish studies for nearly 30 years. By means of this article I would like to wish him a blessed and fruitful period of retirement.

[1] See the remarks at *SPhA* 1 (1989) 6, and note the title of the final chapter, 'Prolégomènes à une étude de Philon'.

[2] Nikiprowetzky (1977) 12–49.

[3] The ending -ων indicates that it was originally a name derived from the adjective (used as a noun) φίλος, i.e. 'dear', in Dutch 'lieverd'; cf. Kühner–Blass (1890–1904) 1.1.476, 1,2.281, and compare 'Αγάθων (from ἀγαθός, = 'goodie'), Τρύφων (from τρυφή, = 'sweetie' or

world.[4] In Egypt the name occurs at least 80 times in papyri, and indeed 9 times in the Zeno archive alone.[5] It is one of the Greek names most frequently found among Jews.[6] In Rome too it occurs on numerous inscriptions.[7] It is hardly surprising, therefore, that the name was carried by a large number of men of some fame or prominence in antiquity. Pauly-Wissowa's *Realencyclopädie* lists no less than 66 Philos.[8] Of these about 15 (other than 'our' Philo) achieved prominence in art, literature or philosophy, as indicated in the following list:

GREEK

Philo of Athens, sceptic philosopher (4th c. BC), = RE (37)
Philo of Megara, dialectical philosopher (4th c. BC), = RE (39)
Philo of Eleusis, architect (4th c. BC), = RE (56)
Philo of Herakleia, paradoxographer (3rd c. BC), = RE (42)
Philo of Byzantium, engineer (3rd–2nd c. BC), = RE (48), various writings extant
Philo of Larissa, Academic philosopher (1st c. BC), = RE (40), extensively reported in Cicero
Philo of Tarsus, doctor/pharmacologist (1st c. AD), = RE (47) fragments extant
Philo of Gadara, mathematician (early 2nd c. AD), = RE (50)
Philo of Byzantium, paradoxographer (4th–6th c. AD), RE (49), work on seven wonders of the world extant

---

'softy'), and indeed Πλάτων (from πλατύς, = 'broad one'), Σίμων ('flat-nosed one'). Another possibility, to which my colleague G. Mussies drew my attention is that it is a hypocoristic (shortened form) of a longer name such as Φιλοδῆμος etc.

4 Cf. the long list at Pape-Benseler (1911) 1630–31 and now the much longer list in Fraser-Matthews (1987) 472–473 (315 exx. covering only a small part of the Greek world).

5 In the papyri, cf. Preisigke (1922) 465 (at least 30 exx.), Foraboschi (1967) 2.1.322 (at least 50 exx.); for the Zeno archive see Pestman *et al.* (1981) 436–7.

6 Cf. Royse (1991) 11 n. 49, who refers to CIJ 1.xix and its indices. See further Mussies' analysis of Jewish personal names, (1994) 243ff., where Philo would fall in category c4 (Jewish Greek names with no Hebrew equivalent). In a private communication Mussies suggests to me that Philo's name might have had its origin in a theophoric name such as Theophilos or Philotheos. In Egypt, however, surprisingly few Jewish inscriptions and papyri have been found containing the name Philo; cf. CPJ 3.195, Horbury–Noy (1992) 2–3 (but many more indexed on p. 331 for Cyrenaica).

7 Solin (1982) 2.740–742, 63 exx., largely based on the Corpus Inscriptionum Latinorum.

8 See RE XIX 2 (1938) 2526 – XX (1941) 60, with additions at Supplbd. VIII (1956) 469, X (1965) 534. Shorter list at *Kleine Pauly* (Munich 1975) 4.770–777 (by various authors). See also the impressive list in Fabricius (1795) 4.750–754, 46 in all, but with various inaccuracies, including a Philo Pythagoreus from Clement (who is of course a double for 'our' Philo). It may be suspected that the name declined in popularity in later antiquity: in the last two volumes of *PLRE* (Jones–Morris–Martindale), covering the years 395–641, only one Philo occurs.

PHOENICIAN

Herennius Philo of Byblos, historian (1st–2nd c. AD), excerpts extant (in RE see under Herennios (2), but often just called Philo)

JEWISH

Philo the Epic poet (2nd c. BC), = RE (46), fragments extant
Philo the Elder, historian (2nd–1st c. BC), = RE (46)

CHRISTIAN

Philo, bishop of Carpasia (4th c. AD), = RE (29), excerpts extant
Philo the Presbyter (5th c. ad), = RE (31), translator of the Latin Canons of Nicaea
Philo the historiographer (5th–6th c. AD?), = RE (30), fragments extant.

Nearly all these men will have left behind writings which survived for a longer or a shorter time. In practice 'our' Philo was most likely to have been confused with either the Jewish or the Christian Philos, but confusion with other Philos was also easily possible. This question of confusion of names has been touched on by James Royse in his splendid monograph on spurious Philonic texts.[9] He points out that Eusebius was aware of the possibility of confusion when at *Praep. Evang.* 1.9.20 he introduces Philo of Byblos and explicitly warns his reader that he was not ὁ Ἑβραῖος. Clement of Alexandria most likely confuses Philo with the older Jewish historian with the same name when he states at *Str.* 1.141.3 that 'Philo himself also recorded the kings of the Jews, but differently than Demetrius'. The phrase Φίλων καὶ αὐτός suggests that he has the most famous Philo in view, who has indeed already been introduced earlier in the same book (see further below).[10] In modern times there was much confusion between the various Philos, but all such problems seem to have been sorted out. For example, Goodhart and Goodenough in their list of Philonic manuscripts cite 5 mss. 'containing a *Catena on the Song of Songs* in which Philo is cited'. But this work must be attributed to Philo the bishop of Carpasia, as Royse has shown. Finally, while on this subject, we might note that there is yet another, less ancient Philo who can also cause confusion, namely a dialogue-

[9] Royse (1991) 11–12, and esp. n. 49.

[10] If this is correct, it would contradict Royse's assertion in the note just cited that 'only modern scholars have actually assigned texts from another Philo to Philo of Alexandria'. To complicate things further, C-W in their invaluable collection of ancient testimonia at 1.lxxxxvi assert wrongly that Clement had Philo of Byblos in mind.

partner with that name in David Hume's famous *Dialogue concerning Natural Religion* (1779).[11]

The chief interest of our subject lies not in these confusions, but rather elsewhere. The study of the way Philo was referred to can yield important insights into the reception of Philo's writings and thought in the ancient world. Because in the period of antiquity Philo was mentioned only by Christian authors in the extant material at our disposal (with the single exception of Josephus), the results must necessarily be confined to the reception of Philo in the Christian tradition. But it hardly need be said that this tradition was richly varied and underwent many developments in the period of nearly a millenium which we shall be studying. So our subject may well allow us to discover nuances in the way Philo was regarded and received in this period. Moreover this Christian reception remained highly influential until the gradual emancipation of Philonic studies from the stranglehold of orthodox theology in the period from the 17th to the 19th century. I have given an overview of the reception of Philo in the early Christian tradition in a recently published monograph.[12] The subject of how Philo is referred to is raised on a number of occasions in that study, but not treated systematically. So this article should be regarded as a supplement to the material presented there.

Before we commence with the presentation of the evidence at our disposal, it will be worth our while to dwell briefly on a question of methodology. A distinction needs to be made, I believe, between a *title* and a *description*. Titles are what interest us most. By a title I mean an epithet which is added to a name in order to specify and make clear the person to whom the name refers. The reader is supposed to *recognize* or *recall* who is being talked about. A description, on the other hand, has the primary purpose of *introducing* the figure concerned to the reader for the first time, or perhaps of *jolting* a memory which is scarcely expected to recall the name. For this reason a description is generally longer than just a single epithet, drawing attention to a number of defining characteristics. Nevertheless there is a clear connection between the two. Both attempt to typify a person, and thus can show very succinctly and very clearly how he or she is regarded and categorized. Descriptions, because they are somewhat fuller, allow us to fill in the background of the epithets used in titles. In our investigation, therefore, it is necessary to take both titles and descriptions into account.

---

[11] Doubtless suggested by Philo of Larissa. This character is a bother when one searches electronic data-bases.

[12] Runia (1993); see also further below in this volume, pp. 90–110.

The evidence

It is time now to present the evidence. The following list attempts to give all the more important passages in Patristic and related literature in which Philo is given a title or an introductory description. The list is based on a considerably longer list of all references to Philo in Christian literature up to 1000, the date which we have also set for the current investigation.[13] Comparison of the two lists shows that there are a large number of texts in which Philo is not given any kind of title. For example Origen refers to Philo three times, but each time assumes that the reader knows who he is. Didymus the Blind in his commentaries cites Philo's name on six occasions without feeling the need to give him a title. But there are a large number of authors who do provide nomenclature, as will appear in the following list. The list is given in approximate chronological order. Wherever possible I cite the original Greek or Latin text, and add a literal translation in brackets.[14] This list will then be the basis of the discussion of the evidence in the rest of the article.

LIST OF PHILONIC TITLES AND DESCRIPTIONS

JOSEPHUS (37–c. 100)

Antiquitates Iudaicae 18.8.258: Φίλων ὁ προεστὼς τῶν Ἰουδαίων τῆς πρεσβείας, ἀνὴρ τὰ πάντα ἔνδοξος Ἀλεξάνδρου τε τοῦ ἀλαβάρχου ἀδελφὸς ὢν καὶ φιλοσοφίας οὐκ ἄπειρος (Philo, the leader of the embassy of the Jews, a man respected in every way, brother of Alexander the Alabarch, and not unskilled in philosophy).

CLEMENT OF ALEXANDRIA (c. 150–c. 215)

Str. 1.72.4: ὁ Πυθαγόρειος Φίλων (the Pythagorean Philo).

2.100.3: ὁ Πυθαγόρειος Φίλων τὰ Μωυσέως ἐξηγούμενος (the Pythagorean Philo giving exegesis of the works of Moses).

PSEUDO-JUSTIN *Cohortatio ad Gentiles* (between 220 and 300)

§9.2: οἱ σοφώτατοι Φίλων τε καὶ Ἰώσηπος, οἱ τὰ κατὰ Ἰουδαίους ἱστορήσαντες (the most wise Philo and Josephus, who have recounted the history of the Jews).

cf. §13.4: παρ' αὐτῶν τῶν περὶ τούτων ἱστορησάντων σοφῶν καὶ δοκίμων ἀνδρῶν, Φίλωνός τε καὶ Ἰωσήπου (from the wise and reputable men themselves who have recorded these matters, Philo and Josephus).

---

[13] See Runia (1993) 348–356, and further below in this volume, pp. 111–122.

[14] For further details on the editions used etc. see below pp. 111–122.

ANATOLIUS of Alexandria, bishop of Laodicaea (died c. 280)
cited at Eusebius *HE* 7.32.16: Ἰουδαίοις ... τοῖς πάλαι καὶ πρὸ Χρίστου ... ἐκ τῶν ὑπὸ Φίλωνος ... λεγομένων ([this was known] to the Jews who lived long ago and even before Christ, [as you can read] from the writings of Philo).

EUSEBIUS OF CAESAREA (c. 260-339)
Eccl. Hist. 2.4.2: Φίλων ..., ἀνὴρ οὐ μόνον τῶν ἡμετέρων, ἀλλὰ καὶ τῶν ἀπὸ τῆς ἔξωθεν ὁρμωμένων παιδείας ἐπισημότατος. τὸ μὲν οὖν γένος ἀνέκαθεν Ἑβραῖος ἦν, τῶν δ' ἐπ' Ἀλεξανδρείας ἐν τέλει διαφανῶν οὐδενὸς χείρων ... (Philo, a man most distinguished not only among (lit. of) our people but also among (lit. of) those motivated by an outside (secular) education (i.e. pagans). By descent he was a Hebrew from ancient times, inferior to none of the prominent people in authority in Alexandria); cf. 2.5.4 Φίλων ... ἀνὴρ τὰ πάντα ἔνδοξος ... καὶ φιλοσοφίας οὐκ ἄπειρος (Philo, a man distinguished in every respect, and not unskilled in philosophy).
Praep. Evang. 1.9.20 Φίλων ... ὁ Βύβλιος, οὐχ ὁ Ἑβραῖος (Philo of Byblos, not the Hebrew); 7.12.14: Ἑβραῖον ἄνδρα ... Φίλων (a Hebrew man ... Philo); also 7.17.4: ὁ Ἑβραῖος Φίλων (the Hebrew Philo); cf. further 7.20.9, 11.14.10, 11.15.7, 11.23.12.
Praep. Evang. 13.18.12: ὁ τὰ Ἑβραίων πεπαιδευμένος Φίλων (Philo, learned in matters concerning the Hebrews).

EUSEBIUS OF EMESA (c. 300–359)
Frag. in *Catena in Genesim ad* Gen. 2:6: Φίλων ὁ Ἑβραῖος (Philo the Hebrew).

GREGORY OF NYSSA (c. 338–c. 395)
Contra Eunomium 3.5.24: ὁ Ἑβραῖος Φίλων (the Hebrew Philo); same epithet at 3.7.8.

PS. CHRYSOSTOM (387)
In sanctum Pascha sermo 7.2: σοφοὺς Ἑβραίους οἷον Φίλωνα καὶ Ἰώσηπα (Hebrew sages such as Philo and Josephus).

RUFINUS (c. 345– c. 410)
Latin translation of Eusebius' *Eccl. Hist.* (see above); note the following additions to the source: 2.4.2 Filo insignissimus scriptorum (Philo, most distinguished of writers), 2.17.1 a viro disertissimo Filone (by Philo, a most eloquent man).

JEROME (347–420)
Adv. Iov. 2.14: Philo vir doctissimus (Philo, a very learned man).
Comm. in Amos 2.9: Philo vir disertissimus Hebraeorum (Philo the most eloquent of the Hebrews); same description at *Comm. in Hiezech.* 4.10b.
De vir. ill.: 8.4 Philon disertissimus Hebraeorum (Philo the most elo-

quent of the Hebrews); 11.1 Philon Iudaeus, natione Alexandrinus, de genere sacerdotum ... (Philo the Jew, Alexandrian by birth, of priestly descent ...).

Ep. 22.35.8: Philo Platonici sermonis imitator (Philo, imitator of Platonic diction)

Ep. 29.7.1: Iosephus ac Philo, viri doctissimi Iudaeorum (Josephus and Philo, most learned men belonging to the Jewish people).

Ep. 70.3.3: de Philone ... alterum vel Iudaeum Platonem (Philo, a second or Jewish Plato)

Liber Hebr. nom. pref.: Philo vir disertissimus Iudaeorum (Philo the most eloquent of the Jews)

Praef. in libr. Sal.: Iudaei Philonis (of the Jew Philo).

THEODORE OF MOPSUESTIA (c. 350–428)

Treatise against the Allegorists, 14.28 Van Rompay: 'Philon, un juif'[15]

LATIN TRANSLATOR OF PHILO (c. 375–400)

Title of translation of *De vita contemplativa* (cf. C-W 6.xviii): Philonis Iudaei liber de statu Essaeorum, id est Monachorum, qui temporibus Agrippae regis monasteria sibi fectrunt (Philo the Jew's book on the way of life of the Essenes, i.e. monks, who in the times of King Agrippa made monasteries for themselves).

AUGUSTINE (354–430)

Contra Faustum 12.39: Philo quidam, vir liberaliter eruditissimus unus illorum (i.e. Iudaeorum) (a certain Philo, a man of exceedingly great learning, belonging to that group (of Jews [introduced in first line of paragraph])).

ISIDORE OF PELUSIUM (c. 370 – c. 435)

Ep. 2.143: Φίλωνα, καίτοι Ἰουδαῖον (Philo, though a Jew)

Ep. 3.19: Φίλων ὁ θεωρητικώτατος καὶ Ἰώσηπος ὁ ἱστορικώτατος (Philo, highly versed in contemplation, and Josephus, highly versed in history)

Ep. 3.81: Φίλων ... ἄνθρωπος Πλάτωνος ἢ ὁμιλητὴς ἢ ὑφηγητής (Philo, a man who was either disciple or instructor of Plato).

PS.PROCHORUS (fl. 400–450)

Acta Johannis 110.9: ἄνθρωπος Ἰουδαῖος, ὀνόματι Φίλων, ἐπιστάμενος τὸν νόμον κατὰ τὸ γράμμα (a Jewish man named Philo, who knew the Law according to the letter); cf. also 112.4 ὁ Φίλων ὁ ἀκαμπὴς καὶ φιλόνεικος (Philo the inflexible and contentious (sc. interlocutor)).

---

[15] Van Rompay, the translator of this text, informs me that the Syriac probably translates Φίλων, Ἰουδαῖός τις. All discussions of texts preserved in Syriac in this article are based on collaboration with my esteemed colleague, for which I offer him once again my sincerest thanks.

JULIAN OF ECLANUM (386–c. 454)
at Augustine *Contra sec. Jul. resp* 4.123, PL 45.1420: illos Hebraeos, Sirach vel Philonem (those Hebrews, Sirach or Philo).
SALAMINIUS HERMIAS SOZOMEN (c. 400–c. 460)
Eccl. His. 1.12.9: Φίλων ὁ Πυθαγόρειος (Philo the Pythagorean).
CATENA IN GENESIM, CATENA IN EXODUM (c. 450–500)
passim under the headings Φίλωνος, Φίλωνος ἐπισκόπου, Φίλωνος Ἑβραίου (of Philo, of Philo the Bishop, of Philo the Hebrew).
CASSIODORUS (487– c. 580)
Inst. Div. Litt. PL 70.1117B: a Philone doctissimo quodam Iudaeo (by Philo a very learned Jew).
ANONYMOUS ARMENIAN TRANSLATOR OR GLOSSATOR (c. 550?)
Praef. in libr. Philonis De prov. vii: magnae sapientiae vir Philo Israelita fuit (Philo, a man of great learning, was an Israelite).
ISIDORE OF SEVILLE (c. 570 – 636)
Etymologiae 6.2.30: Iudaei Philonis (the Jew Philo).
BARḤADBŠABBA ᶜARBAYA, bishop of Ḥalwan (c. 600)
Cause of the Foundation of the Schools, 375.15: 'Le directeur de cette école et l'exégète fut Philon le Juif'.
ANASTASIUS SINAÏTA (c. 610– c. 700)
Viae dux 13.10.1: ἀπίστου Ἰουδαίου Φίλωνος τοῦ φιλοσόφου (the Jewish unbeliever Philo the philosopher), ὁ μιαρὸς Φίλων (the detestable Philo)
CHRONICON PASCHALE (c. 650)
PG 92.69A: Φίλωνος τοῦ παρ' Ἑβραίοις σοφοῦ (of Philo the sage among the Hebrews).
PS.SOPHRONIUS (c. 700?)
Greek translation of Jerome, *De vir. ill.*: 12 [= Jerome 8], Φίλων ὁ τῶν Ἰουδαίων ἐλλογιμώτατος (Philo, the most eloquent of the Jews); 21 [= Jerome 11] Φίλων Ἰουδαῖος, τεχθεὶς ἐν Ἀλεξανδρείᾳ ... (Philo the Jew, born in Alexandria...).
JOHN OF DAMASCUS (c. 675–c. 750)
Prol. in Sac. Par. PG 95.1040B: ἀπὸ τοῦ Φίλωνος καὶ Ἰωσήπου συνταγμάτων ... Ἑβραῖοι δὲ ἄμφω καὶ λόγιοι ἄνδρες (from the treatises of Philo and Josephus ... both were Hebrews and men of learning).
ARMENIAN TRANSLATOR OF EUSEBIUS' *CHRONICLE*
Chronicle, p. 213: 'Philo from Alexandria, a learned man, was prominent'.
GEORGE SYNCELLUS (died after 810)
Ecloga chronographica 399.6: ὡς Φίλων Ἰούδαιος ἐξ Ἀλεξανδρείας διάγων ἱστορεῖ (as Philo the Jew from Alexandria recounts at some length).

ANONYMOUS Syrian commentator of the works of Gregory of Nazianzus (8th or 9th century)
At the end some quotations are found from other writers, among them two quotations from 'Philo the Hebrew', fol. 98a and 144a in ms. London, Brit. Libr. Add. 17,147.[16]

PHOTIUS, patriarch of Constantinople (c. 820–891)
Bibliotheca cod. 103: Φίλωνος τοῦ Ἰουδαιου (Philo the Jew); cf. 105 Ἀλεξ-ανδρεὺς τὴν πατρίδα.

ANASTASIUS incertus (9th century)
In hexaemeron 7, PG 89.961: Φίλων ὁ φιλόσοφος καὶ τῶν ἀποστόλων ὁμό-χρονος (Philo the philosopher and contemporary of the apostles)

ARETHAS, archbishop of Caesarea (c. 850–c. 940)
Comm. in Apoc. 1, PG 106.504: Φίλωνι τῷ θεωρητικωτάτῳ Ἰουδαίῳ ἀνδρί (Philo the Jewish man most versed in contemplation).

ANONYMOUS list of exegetical authorities (date unknown, no earlier than the 9th century)[17]
Exegesis Psalmorum 29.1: Philo philosophus spiritualis (Philo the spiritual philosopher).

SOUDA (c. 1000)
s.v. Ἀβραάμ: Φίλων, ἐξ Ἑβραίων φιλόσοφος (Philo, a philosopher from the Hebrew people).
s. v. Φίλων: Φίλων Ἰουδαῖος, τεχθεὶς ἐν Ἀλεξανδρείᾳ ... (cf. Sophronius above).

Analysis of the evidence

There are various ways in which this list could be analysed. Each author could be dealt with in turn. But this method would lead to results that were rather fragmented. In my discussion of the evidence I will use a more systematic approach. The nomenclature used for Philo will be presented under nine headings.

(1) Philo a man of learning

If we survey the group of texts as a whole, the first impression is that a large number of them emphasize Philo's great learning. This tendency commences with Josephus, who regards him as 'not unskilled in philosophy', a description which is unclear, and to which we shall return. For

---

16 The work is unedited; information given by Wright (1871) 439b, 440a.

17 List found in some mss. of an East-Syrian Psalm Commentary as well as in one branch of the ms. tradition of the *Gannat Bussāmē* (Garden of Delights), a commentary on the East-Syrian lectionary; see Vandenhoff (1899), Chabot (1906) 491–492, Reinink (1977) 125, n. 74.

Ps.Justin Philo is a sage (σοφός) or most wise (σοφώτατος). The same general epithet returns in two authors dealing with Paschal questions, Ps.Chrysostom and the *Chronicon Paschale*.[18] Eusebius emphasizes the great distinction of both his sacred and his secular learning (παιδεία); the latter aspect is again emphasized on one occasion in the *Praeparatio Evangelica*, a work that gives quotations from no less than nine Philonic treatises.[19] According to the Armenian translator[20] Philo was a man of great wisdom. The greatest emphasis on Philo's learning, however, is found in Jerome, who refers to it on six separate occasions (similar descriptions found in Rufinus and Augustine are very likely dependent on him). Jerome is the first (together with Isidore) to record the proverb 'either Plato philonizes or Philo platonizes', interpreting it as referring to the similarity of both thought and style.[21] Against this background we can understand why sometimes Philo's learning is praised in a general way (note especially *doctissimus*, *eruditissimus*), but on other occasions special emphasis is placed on his eloquence (*disertissimus*, cf. ἐλλογιμώτατος in the translation of Jerome's account in Ps.Sophronius). If Philo is a second or Jewish Plato, and an imitator of Plato's style, then eloquence can hardly be denied him. That Philo was a distinguished (and prolific) writer is noted only by Rufinus, who adds this information to his translation of Eusebius.[22] A final text that emphasizes Philo's learning is found in Johannes Damascenus, who draws extensively on Philo in his *Sacra Parallela*.[23] The Greek epithet λόγιος which Johannes uses probably refers to learning in general rather than just to his eloquence. Other passages among our texts refer to more specific aspects of Philo's learning. These we shall now examine separately under the next three headings.

(2) Philo as historian

One of the reasons that Philo was a valuable source for Christian writers was that he furnished much historical information, not only about early Pentateuchal times, but also concerning the crucial events at the time of and just after Jesus' death. Various writers point out that he was a contemporary of the apostles (e.g. Anastasius incertus in the 9th century). In the descriptions cited above, this aspect is explicitly brought forward by

[18] On the use of Philo in the Easter controversies see further Runia (1993) 231–234.
[19] List at *ibid.* 223.
[20] Or glossator; see further below n. 73.
[21] On this proverb see further Runia (1993) 4, 208, 313–314, 323.
[22] The three biographical accounts in Eusebius, Jerome and the *Souda* indicate this feature at greater length, because in each case a long list of Philo's works is given.
[23] On Philo in the *Florilegia* derived from Johannes see further Royse (1991) 26–27.

only one author, Ps. Justin, whose aim is to convince his pagan readers about the antiquity of the Jewish-Christian tradition. On both occasions he connects Philo with the other great Jewish author who wrote in Greek, Josephus.[24] The connection with Josephus occurs in four other Christian sources: Ps.Chrysostom, Jerome, Isidore, John of Damascus. Of these all but one join them together and describe them as learned. The exception is Isidore, who distinguishes between them, calling Josephus a supreme historian and Philo a supremely speculative thinker. We return to this text under (4).

(3) Philo the philosopher

φιλόσοφος and φιλοσοφία are notoriously ambiguous words. In later antiquity they can refer to Greek philosophy, but just as easily to the Christian faith or to the practice of biblical exegesis.[25] So when Josephus, the first author to mention Philo, says that he was 'not unskilled in philosophy' we may wonder what he is specifically referring to. I suspect that it is to 'Greek' or 'pagan' philosophy. Jewish observers, and perhaps also those outside the Jewish community, will have noted how deep a knowledge of Greek philosophy is presumed by Philo's literary *œuvre*. But there is no way of being sure, since Josephus, not unlike Philo (on whom he probably to some degree depends),[26] regards Greek philosophy as posterior to and dependent on Jewish philosophy or wisdom, which in his view is to be equated with fundamental Jewish religious convictions centred on the Law.[27]

In the case of Clement of Alexandria, the first Christian author to refer to Philo, there can be no doubt whatsoever that the title he uses, Philo the 'Pythagorean' or 'follower of Pythagoras', refers to Greek philosophy. In Clement's day the Pythagoreans were a recognized philosophical 'school' (αἵρεσις), even if in practice there was little to distinguish them from Platonists.[28] Nevertheless it is once again not easy to deter-

---

24 On Josephus' reception in the Christian tradition see now the excellent survey in Schreckenberg (1991) 3–148. There are significant parallels with the process of Philonic reception. But he does not give a systematic analysis of (i) the relation to Philo, or (ii) the specific nomenclature used for Josephus. In the Syrian tradition there is an interesting, if wholly erroneous, connection made between the two by Bar-Hebraeus (13th cent.) in his *Chronography* (p. 49 Wallis Budge): 'And at that time Felix, the Eparch of Egypt, was sent, and he afflicted the Jews for seven years, and because of this ambassadors were sent to Gaius that they might break him, namely Josephus, the wise man, and Philo the Hebrew philosopher, who was from Alexandria.'

25 Cf. Malingrey (1961) 99ff. and *passim*, *PGL* s. vv., Görgemans (1989) 619–620.

26 See esp. *C. Ap.* 1.162ff., 2.168, and further Pilhofer (1990) 193–206.

27 Cf. *TDNT* 9.182–184, Mason (1991) 185f. (with further references).

28 As noted by Whittaker (1987) 115.

mine what Clement means by the epithet.[29] Given the contexts—in the first passage Philo is cited in order to prove the antiquity of 'Jewish philosophy', in the second it is expressly stated that he is 'giving exegesis of the writings of Moses'—it is to my mind not likely that he means that Philo was a member of the Pythagorean school. It is possible that he is alluding to Philo's great knowledge of this area of Greek philosophy, as Eusebius was to do a century later when he introduces Philo in his *Historia Ecclestiastica* and states that he 'showed a special zeal for the study of Plato and Pythagoras'.[30] Another possibility is that there were aspects of Philo's thought and exegetical practice, e.g. his extensive references to numbers and their symbolism in his exegesis, that reminded Clement of Pythagorean philosophers.

Remarkably Clement's epithet returns once more in the extant tradition, namely in the 5th century historian Sozomen's account of the early monastic movement. Where did Sozomen, who was of course heavily indebted to earlier material, get it from? Recently it has been suggested that the above-mentioned passage in Eusebius was his source.[31] I regard this as rather unlikely, since why would he choose the school of one philosopher at the expense of that of the other (which was in fact more famous)? A few pages earlier (1.1.12) Sozomen informs his reader that he wrote a short account of the history of the Church up to the time of Constantine in two books, in which one of his sources was 'Clement' (in addition to Eusebius). He may mean the *Pseudo-Clementina*,[32] but he may also mean Clement of Alexandria,[33] whose lost *Hypotyposeis* contained much quasi-historical material on the apostolic age.[34] If so, then this work of Clement may be his source for the Philonic epithet which he uses.[35]

Another reference to Philo as philosopher is implied in the famous proverb on Philo's Platonism cited by Jerome and Isidore of Pelusium, which has already been discussed under (1) above, especially if the

---

[29] The question remains surprisingly unaddressed in Van den Hoek's excellent monograph on Clement's use of Philo, (1988). I intend to deal with this question in greater detail elsewhere. See further my remarks at (1993) 136, 147, 150.

[30] *HE* 2.4.3: ὅτε μάλιστα τὴν κατὰ Πλάτωνα καὶ Πυθαγόραν ἐζηλωκὼς ἀγωγήν.

[31] In the note by Sabbah in Grillet-Sabbah-Festugière (1983) 166.

[32] As argued at *ibid*. 116.

[33] As concluded by Bidez-Hansen (1960) 458.

[34] On this work, which was sighted as late as 1779, see Duckworth–Osborn (1985), esp. 74–77, where it is noted that Eusebius made use of Clement's material.

[35] And so this may be evidence in favour of the view that Eusebius' story about the origins of the Alexandrian church and the Philonic monks there was derived from Clement, as I suggest at (1993) 7. Sozomen's description of the early monks is, however, taken entirely from Eusebius; cf. *ibid*. 229.

imitation involved is taken to refer to thought as well as (or rather than) style.[36]

In a number of very late documents the epithet 'philosopher' returns.[37] Anastasius the Sinaite, a rabid defender of orthodoxy, uses it in most pejorative fashion, connecting it with the fact that Philo was a Jew and an unbeliever (how much worse can one be!).[38] In the *Souda* Philo is introduced as a 'philosopher from the Hebrew people' in connection with the lemma on Abraham. The implication is that 'philosopher' here has to do with biblical interpretation. There are a number of other texts pointing in the same direction, which we will discuss in more detail under the next category.

(4) Philo the exegete

Only in one text is Philo directly referred to as 'exegete' (though more as a description than as a title), namely in the Syriac writer Barḥadbšabba ᶜArbaya, who regards him as founder of the Alexandrian school of exegesis, and the one whose example led the great Origen astray.[39] Other texts, however, point towards the same aspect of his literary activity. Clement, as we saw, calls Philo a 'Pythagorean', but immediately adds that he gives exegesis of Mosaic scripture. The next relevant text is the letter of Isidore (*Ep.* 3.19) in which he is called ὁ θεωρητικώτατος. What is the contemplation (θεωρία), we may ask, in which Philo is so highly versed? When explaining the epithet Isidore states that Philo 'turns almost the entire Old Testament into allegory', so that there can be no doubt that the epithet refers especially to the practice of allegorical or 'speculative' exegesis.[40] Exactly the same epithet is used five centuries later by Arethas when referring to Philo's praise of the hebdomad (i.e. in *Opif.* 89–127).[41] In the Syriac tradition Philo's name occurs in a long and rather disorganized list of *nomina doctorum patrum orthodoxorum* together with the title *philosophus spiritualis*. Philo appears to be the only

---

[36] Resemblance of thought is explicitly stated by Jerome in *De vir. ill.* 11.7 (and taken over in Ps.Sophronius and the *Souda*) and it strongly implied at *Ep.* 70.3.3. Isidore of Pelusium too implies it at *Ep.* 3.81, as I observe at (1991) 315. Augustine, however, in his only mention of Philo at *C. Faustum* 12.39 emphasizes only the stylistic resemblance, and perhaps implicitly denies the similarity of thought (but he does emphasize Philo's learning).

[37] Note also the 13th cent. text of Bar Hebraeus cited above in n. 24.

[38] At (1993) 210 I note that this is the most negative text on Philo in the entire tradition.

[39] See *ibid.* 269–270. The words 'and exegete', deleted in the Scher's translation, have been reinstated by Van Rompay.

[40] See translation and comments on this text at Runia (1991) 310–312.

[41] Arethas writes ἐν λόγῳ αὐτοῦ τῷ εἰς τὴν κατὰ Μωυσέα φιλοσοφίαν, where we might suspect that the last word is substituted for κοσμοποιΐαν in the title of *Opif.*

non-Christian in the list, but is included as a member of the exegetical tradition[42] The title certainly refers to his exegetical activity. If the author has Philo's allegorizing in mind, it may be equivalent to the Greek φιλόσοφος θεωρητικός. We note, however, that the 9th century Ps.Anastasius speaks in similar terms about the early 1st and 2nd century exegetes who 'spiritually contemplated the Paradise story' (πνευματικῶς τὰ περὶ παραδείσου ἐθεώρησαν), so it is also possible that the term may be equivalent to πνευματικός.[43]

(5) Philo the Hebrew

It is time to turn to a quite different aspect of our theme, the use of titles and descriptions to indicate Philo's descent. With one exception the relevant texts can be divided into two groups, those that describe Philo as 'the Hebrew' (ὁ Ἑβραῖος), and those that describe him as Jewish or 'the Jew' (ὁ Ἰουδαῖος). In our sources the first group begins with Eusebius of Caesarea, the man who did more than anyone else to place Philo on the Christian map. For Eusebius Philo is 'a Hebrew by descent'. Elsewhere too he consistently refers to Philo by this epithet. Other 4th century texts in Eusebius of Emesa, Gregory of Nyssa, Ps.Chrysostom all use the same title. It is used by Jerome too (but less frequently than the other title *Iudaeus* —twice as opposed to five times), and also by the opponent of Augustine, Julian of Eclanum. The author of the *Catena*[44] employs it towards the end of the 5th century, as do four later writers (author of the *Chronicon Paschale*, John of Damascus, an Anonymous Syriac writer, and the *Souda* once). We shall see in the following section, however, that this epithet is used less than that of Philo 'the Jew'.

What do Christian authors mean to say when they call Philo 'the Hebrew'? The relation between the epithets Ἑβραῖος and Ἰουδαῖος is by no means straightforward, and has so far been insufficiently researched.[45] One must be careful not to over-interpret the evidence. The

---

[42] The only other figure in the list earlier than the 4th century is Origen. In passing we note that Philo is described as philosopher in the following Syriac text taken from the *Anonymi auctoris Chronicon ad annum Christi 1234 pertinens* (translation at Chabot (1952) 100): Pilatus autem post tribulationes quae ei acciderunt, seipsum necavit, ut scripsit Philo philosophus. The text is later than our cut-off point, but doubtless contains earlier material (the information is clearly—and mistakenly—taken from Eusebius *HE* 2.7.1).

[43] Text at C-W 1.cix. Johannes Damascenus in the Prologue to his famous *Sacra Parallela* calls Philo and Josephus λόγιοι. The content of this work is primarily theological and philosophical, so presumably Johannes had these aspects of Philo's writings in mind when he wrote this passage.

[44] On this author see below p. 20.

[45] Three studies should be mentioned: Kuhn–Gutbrod (1965), Arazy (1977), Tomson

terms may be used in a neutral fashion, without any particular overtones. It is possible, however, to draw broad lines of division between the two terms. Philo's own usage is revealing in this respect.[46] He uses Ἑβραῖοι as a term to describe the ancient lineage of the Jewish nation going back to the Patriarchs, or he relates it to the use of the Hebrew language (and especially the intepretation of Pentateuchal names). It occurs very frequently in the *Lives* of Abraham, Joseph and Moses. The only instance where he uses it in a post-biblical context is when he speaks of the Hebrews who came from Jerusalem to translate the Books of Moses (*Mos*. 2.31). Here the term probably indicates that they were speakers of Hebrew. Philo would not have described himself as a 'Hebrew'. On the other hand Ἰουδαῖος is Philo's usual way refering to contemporary Jews in their socio-political situation. It occurs no less than 79 times in his two political treatises. In other treatises it is less common, but always with reference (direct or indirect) to the contemporary situation.[47] Revealingly it is *never* used in the Allegorical Commentary, presumably because this work is written for insiders.[48] Philo would have regarded himself as a *Ioudaios*.[49] A similar usage is encountered in Josephus: '*Ioudaioi* is the regular name for post-biblical Jews'.[50] Surprisingly at the outset of his *Jewish War* he describes himself as γένει Ἑβραῖος (a Hebrew by descent).[51] I agree with Tomson against

---

(1986). All three examine three names, Ἰουδαῖοι, Ἰσραήλ, Ἑβραῖος. The first examines primarily Jewish (including Hellenistic–Jewish) and New Testament evidence, as does the third, which moreover attempts to apply sociological criteria to the subject. Only the second takes into account Greco-Roman and Patristic usage, but the analysis given in this unpublished work is rather primitive and parochial. It is remarkable that Feldman (1993) in his compendious work on Jew and Gentile does not touch on this issue at all. A full examination of Patristic usage of the two terms is thus very much a desideratum. On the use of Ἑβραῖος in non-Jewish writers see also Stern (1974–84) 2.160. Lemche's statement (1992) 95 that 'only in the Greco-Roman tradition did Greek *Ebraios* (sic) become the ordinary way of indicating Jews, and thereafter this tradition was taken over by the Christian church and became a general way of designing members of the Jewish people' is in this unnuanced form not correct. According to Kuhn–Gutbrod (1965) 372 it is rare in Greek literature, but this too is somewhat exaggerated. The truth lies somewhere in between.

[46] Cf. Kuhn–Gutbrod (1965) 373–375, Arazy (1977) 1.141–158, Tomson (1986) 136–137. On the related (but for us not relevant) issue of the relation between two terms Ἑβραῖος and Χαλδαῖος see Wong (1992).

[47] Rightly observed by Tomson (1986) 137.

[48] Note the reference to Jews (and Egyptians) practising circumcision at *QG* 3.48, which clearly has a contemporary reference.

[49] Cf. King Agrippa's self-description at *Legat*. 278.

[50] Tomson (1986) 138.

[51] There are doubts about the text here, since the oldest ms. and Eusebius delete these words.

Gutbrod that Josephus here is exploiting the connotations of ancient prestige that the title connotes.[52]

Against this background there can be little doubt that Eusebius' description of Philo as 'the Hebrew' is deliberate. Philo, who is such a valuable source of information on the beginnings of the Church in Alexandria, belongs to those respected and (relatively) ancient members of the Jewish people who lived before the fall of Jerusalem. Arazy accuses Eusebius of a 'double standard' in his use of appellations: Philo is 'a Hebrew by racial descent', while the people whom he represents and whose troubles he recounts are 'Jewish'.[53] Other Jews who are called Ἑβραῖοι are Josephus and Trypho, the dialogue-partner of Justin Martyr. Arazy concludes: '(1) Any time a positive image of the Jews, contemporary or ancient is to be presented, *Hebraios* is the proper appellation. (2) The appellation *Ioudaios* should be used in pointing out the negative character of the Jews, both contemporary and their ancestors.'[54] This statement is no doubt too clear-cut, and may well need to be qualified by further research. But it seems on the right track. It is supported by an analysis of the evidence in Origen by De Lange, who concludes that '*Ioudaios*, in many mouths, was a sneering expression, even perhaps a term of abuse; *Hebraios*, on the other hand, was a liberal's word, leaning over backwards to give no offence'.[55]

The positive connotations of the title Ἑβραῖος are confirmed by our texts. In almost every case the context is non-polemical and, by implication at least, favourable. Gregory of Nyssa sympathizes with Philo because his ideas are filched by the heretical Neo-Arian Eunomius.[56] In the Paschal documents Philo serves as an ancient authority whose testimony carries weight on account of its antiquity, and can be used as ammunition against both Christian (or heretical) opponents and contemporary Jews who follow a different calendar.[57] To be accredited with the possible authorship of one of the Septuagintal writings, as Julian of Eclanum reports, is surely complimentary. The author of the *Catena* and John of Damascus are pleased to be able to make use of Philonic

---

[52] Tomson *ibid.*; cf. Kuhn-Gutbrod (1965) 374, who thinks it refers to the fact that he came from a Palestinian family. Cf. also Arazy (1977) 2.10–11, who is not impressed by Josephus' manœuvre.

[53] Arazy (1977) 2.29.

[54] *Ibid.* 2.30–31.

[55] De Lange (1976) 31. See also his comment at 32: 'Origen has thus prepared the ground for Eusebius' complete repainting of the traditional picture of Jewish history, which finally redefines *Hebraioi*, so that it can stand in contrast to *Ioudaioi*.' It is unfortunate for our theme that Origen never gives Philo a title.

[56] See further Runia (1993) 245.

[57] See further *ibid.* 234.

exegetical material, even if caution is required (as John warns his reader). A final example is more complex. Eusebius of Emesa is pleased to cite Philo the Hebrew in order to defend a non-literal reading of the LXX text. But the preceding passage, which points out that the Hebrew text reads something different than the LXX, is also attributed to 'a Hebrew'.[58] We may suspect a rabbinic exegete or exegetical tradition here,[59] and the epithet probably implies knowledge of the Hebrew language. If Philo is deliberately cited as evidence against Jewish exegesis,[60] then the title, even if it is used on both sides, could still have a positive connotation in his case. Philo as an ancient Hebrew authority is cited in support of a Greek reading that is disputed by a modern exegete who appeals to the authority of the Hebrew text.

(6) Philo the Jew

In our list a larger number of authors call Philo a Jew than a Hebrew. It takes a while, however, before this practice sets in. Josephus and Anatolius of Alexandria (3rd century) do not actually use Ἰουδαῖος as a title, but Philo's name is closely aligned with references to the 'Jews' in the immediate context. Apart from these texts it is not until the end of the 4th century that we see the title Philo the Jew coming into prominence. Jerome uses it very deliberately in his biographical notice of Philo, and it returns on 4 other occasions in his writings. Jerome is not, however, our earliest witness. The reference to Philo as 'a Jew' in Theodore of Mopsuestia antedates his use by about 20 years.[61] We may suspect, however, that Theodore's use of the indefinite article indicates that the epithet is not yet being used as a standard title. It is possible that the Anonymous Latin translator uses the title Philo Judaeus at the beginning of his translation of *Contempl.* at about this time.[62] A little later than Jerome we find

---

58 Text at Petit (1991) 135.

59 Compare the use of Rabbinic material in Origen's exegesis, as sketched in De Lange (1976) 103–132. Kamesar (1993) 150 n.189 speaks of an 'exegetical tradition'.

60 As I argue at Runia (1993) 265.

61 Jerome wrote his *De viris illustribus* in 392–393; cf. Kelly (1975) 174. The mini-treatise 'Against the allegorists' of Theodore is most likely (but not wholly certainly) derived from his *Commentary on the Psalms*; cf. Van Rompay (1982) xlv–xlvii. We know from Theodore's own testimony that this work was his 'debut', written when he was scarcely twenty years of age. Even if allowance is made for some exaggeration, this indicates a date between 370 and 375; see further Vosté (1925) 70–72, Devreesse (1948) 28, Schaüblin (1974) 18–19.

62 The translation is dated to the last quarter of the 4th century by Petit (1977) 1.13. A difficulty is caused by the fact that this title only occurs in the 1527 edition of Sichardus based on the now lost ms. of Lorsch. We cannot be certain that it was not added by the editor himself, although this is unlikely. I would like to thank Mme. Caroline Carlier (Jerusalem) for drawing my attention to this text.

references to Philo the Jew in Isidore of Pelusium and Ps.Prochorus. Thereafter it becomes the most common way of referring to Philo.[63]

Why does Jerome start his biography so demonstratively with the phrase *Philon Iudaeus*? Since most of the early illustrious men whom he describes were of Jewish descent without this being mentioned, the epithet must refer to something else. Most probable, it seems to me, is that it alludes to Philo's religious allegiance. Philo is a Jew who lived during the earliest times of Christianity but remained a Jew. There is, however, not a trace of negative feeling in the use of the title. Jerome is very positive about Philo in this brief report, telling his reader that he places Philo among the ecclesiastical writers because (as Jerome himself believes) he wrote a laudatory account of the early Church in Alexandria. Also, when he calls Philo a 'second or Jewish Plato' the title surely has a positive connotation.

Interpretation of the term *Ioudaios* (or *Iudaeus*) requires more care than the corresponding term *Hebraios* (or *Hebraeus*). As we noted above, it generally refers to contemporary Jews or Jews in the relatively recent past.[64] For Philo and Josephus this means post-exilic Judaism. In Christian terms it means Jews from about the time of Jesus onwards. The word also very often implies a reference to the Jewish religious adherence of the people being described.[65] The reference is by no means necessarily negative, but can easily become such on account of the strong rivalry and frequent antipathy that existed between the two religious groups. Whether *Ioudaios* is used in negative or polemical sense depends entirely on the context. The difference between *Hebraios* and *Ioudaios* in the Christian context may thus be summarized as follows. The use of *Hebraios* may refer to the origins of Christianity in Judaism, but does not imply a contrast between the two religions and their adherents. When *Ioudaios* is used, there is a strong possibility that the author does imply a contrast between Jew and Christian.

If we examine the texts contemporary or later than Jerome in which *Ioudaios* or *Iudaeus* is used, we may conclude that an implicit or explicit contrast with the term *Christianus* is generally present.[66] In Theodore of

---

[63] Examples in Cassiodorus, Isidore of Seville, Barḥadbšabba ᶜArbaya, Anastasius the Sinaite, Ps.Sophronius, Photius, Arethas, the *Souda*.

[64] Cf. Kuhn-Gutbrod (1965) 369–371, Tomson (1986) 136–140 (who emphasizes that it is the name used by Jews in communication with non-Jews, i.e. the outside title in contrast to the inner description Israel). Arazy (1977) *passim* overemphasizes the negative connotations of *Ioudaios*, which leads him to see a more positive development in the 4th cent., when Julian sees the Jews as allies against the Christians.

[65] And so can perhaps even be used of a pagan adherent to Judaism (but who is not a proselyte); cf. Van der Horst (1991) 68–71.

[66] Exceptions are, I think, the two references to Philo as author of the Wisdom of Solo-

Mopsuestia the context is strongly polemical: Origen should not have taken over the method of allegorical exegesis from a Jewish author.[67] In the later Syriac author Barḥadbšabba ᶜArbaya the context is similar, but the tone somewhat less polemical.[68] Isidore of Pelusium in *Ep.* 2.143 praises Philo for reaching some understanding of the doctrine of the trinity 'even though he was a Jew'. Another letter, *Ep.* 3.19, is also interesting. Philo, together with Josephus, is cited in order to refute a Jew (i.e. a contemporary with whom the recipient of the letter has engaged in discussion). Philo and Josephus are described as 'two of your own (i.e. Jewish) writers'.[69] The context in Augustine is overtly, if not aggressively, polemical. In the wholly legendary account in Ps.Prochorus Philo is presented as a typical rabbinical Jew who reads the Law according to the letter and refuses to accept the apostle John's interpretation 'according to the spirit' until he is impressed by a miracle that John performs.[70] The most polemical contexts are to be found in the two late writers Anastasius and Photius, where Ἰουδαῖος has very strong negative overtones indeed.

A final question remains to be answered. Is it significant that towards the end of the 4th century *Ioudaios* starts to replace *Hebraios* as the title most often used for Philo? The answer, to my mind, must be in the affirmative. Through the interventions of Clement, Origen and Eusebius Philo had gained a reasonably comfortable niche within the Christian tradition as a respected Jewish source of historical, exegetical and even theological insight. When this is combined with the legend of Philo Christianus, we may say that he became a Church father *honoris causa*. During the 4th century, however, we observe that the atmosphere changes. It is the time that orthodoxy triumphs over heresy and relations between Jews and Christians deteriorate markedly. The attitude of Ambrose and Augustine towards Philo is ambivalent; that of Theodore of Mopsuestia, as we noted above, is decidedly hostile.[71] It should certainly not be concluded that *Hebraios* is always positive and *Ioudaios* always negative. The use of the terms is much less clear-cut. Often it is fairly neutral. That the increase in the use of *Ioudaios* introduces a new

---

mon in Cassiodorus and Isidore of Seville and the reference to Philo in Arethas, where the term does no more than indicate Philo's ethnic origin.

[67] On this text see further Runia (1993) 264–269.

[68] See further *ibid.* 269–270.

[69] Further comments on these texts in *ibid.* 204–209 and Runia (1991).

[70] As Zahn (1880) liv indicates, one cannot be absolutely certain that the author has our Philo in mind, because the incident is situated in Asia Minor.

[71] See my monograph (1993), but I do not pursue the question systematically beyond 400. On Philo and heresy see also Runia (1992).

more antithetical and 'tougher' (but by no means always uncomplimentary) attitude to Philo seems to me quite clear.

(7) Philo the Israelite

Israel is the 'inner-Jewish' self-designation, which the Christian church successfully appropriated for itself as the 'New Israel'.[72] It is thus surprising to find one text in which Philo is described as an 'Israelite', namely in the introduction to the Armenian translation of Philo's writings. It is not known who the writer of this text is. It is, as far as I can tell, quite possible that it was the translator himself.[73] The author could just have easily used the Armenian equivalent of *Hebraeus*, but not so easily *Iudaeus*.[74] It is thus a puzzle why he uses the term 'Israelite'. Perhaps it is suggested by his account of the double diaspora of the Jewish people, first at the time of the Old Testament, secondly at the time of the New.[75] The term, we might add, also has a respectable New Testament background, being used there six times, twice in well-known statements of the Apostle Paul about his own lineage (Rom. 11:1, 2 Cor. 11:22).

(8) Philo the Bishop

In one group of Christian documents Philo is endowed with the title ὁ ἐπίσκοπος (the Bishop), namely the *Catena in Genesim* and the *Catena in Exodum*, extensive collections of excerpts from scriptural commentators ordered in the sequence of the biblical text. Philo is quoted on numerous occasions in these works, but the extracts are taken from a limited section of his corpus (only *QG* 1.55–4.228, *QE* 2.1–49, and a few excerpts from *Mos.* 1).[76] Until recently it was thought that these *Catenae* were composite documents that grew by accretion. But recently Françoise Petit

---

[72] Cf. esp. Tomson (1986) *passim*.

[73] Text at Aucher (1822) vii–xi. Above the text we read 'Outline of the translator or interpreter which precedes the books of Philo on Providence', but this may be simply the surmisal of Aucher the editor, as my colleague J. J. S. Weitenberg informs me. In this case it is also possible that the piece is of much later date. Terian (1981) 6 simply speaks of an 'anonymous scholion'.

[74] According to Weitenberg the Armenian word *hrēaj* (= Jew) is not easily used as a title, whereas for the word *ebrajecʿi* there is no problem.

[75] The account begins by stating that it is not certain from which tribe Philo came. Cf. Jerome's statement that Philo was *de genere sacerdotum*, which according to Schwartz (1984) is not likely to be legendary. The Armenians seem to have been interested in the fate of the Jewish captives. According to the History of the 8th cent. author Moses Khorenats'i one of the leading Armenian families descended from a Jewish captive at the court of Nebuchadnezzar; cf. Thomson (1978) 30.

[76] See the discussion at Royse (1991) 14–25; at 17 n.12 he notes that C-W cite some quotations from *Mos.* 2 from the *Catenae in Numeros*, but he adds that their sources are of doubtful quality (at *Mos.* 1.220 C-W also cite a quote in the *Catena in Psalmos*).

has argued that the *Catena in Genesim* at least is basically the work of a single anonymous compiler, and she has commenced on an edition of the entire work in which the excerpts scattered over the various mss. are brought back together in an integral text.[77] Certainly the manner in which Philo is cited offers support to her thesis. The method is utterly consistent: the excerpt is preceded by Philo's name in the genitive, without a title, or with the titles Ἑβραίου or ἐπισκόπου. The third option is the most common, followed by the second, while the name only is relatively infrequent.[78] The provenance of the quotation is never given. (This is in clear contrast to the *Florilegia*,[79] where the location is often told, but Philo is never given a title as far as I know.) In the case of Christian bishops the Catenist sometimes also gives a place-name, e.g. Eusebius bishop of Emesa, Dionysius bishop of Alexandria etc.[80] This is never done in Philo's case. It would seem that the title of Philo the bishop is an idiosyncratic *trouvaille* of the unknown author. It indicates respect (as does the epithet Ἑβραῖος), as well as a complete acceptance of the legend of Philo Christianus. To my mind, however, the usage of the two epithets remains puzzling because they appear to cancel each other out. If Philo is a Hebrew, he is no Bishop, and vice versa.[81]

(9) Philo the Alexandrian

Remarkably, given modern usage, the fact that Philo came from Alexandria is virtually never exploited as an epithet or title in our extant sources. Philo's geographical origin is naturally mentioned in the six biographical accounts that we have (Josephus, Eusebius, Jerome, Ps.Sophronius, Photius, the *Souda*).[82] But elsewhere it is only used as a title in two rather late texts, the Armenian translation of Eusebius' *Chronicle* and the chronographic work of George Syncellus. Since both these works make use of the Eusebian chronicle tradition we might

---

77 So far she has reached Gen. 11 in two volumes, Petit (1992–93); her hypothesis on the author is presented at (1992) xiv.

78 A good impression of the complexity of the transmission can be gained by looking at the collection of lemmata from *QG* and *QE* published in Petit (1978). Because the published information is incomplete, I shall give no analysis of the variations in the titles, except to say that the name alone is found mainly in the Leningrad codex.

79 Also collections of excerpts, but not to be confused with the *Catenae*; cf. Royse (1991) 26–58.

80 Cf. Petit (1991–93) nos. 237, 225.

81 Alan Mendelson suggests that Bishop might be used loosely for a eminent religious person, regardless of 'denominational' membership. Compare the way that in the 19th century one spoke of the 'Jewish Church'.

82 Cf. also the anonymous Armenian translator, who relates Philo to the members of the Alexandrian synagogue mentioned in Acts 6:9, and Barḥadbšabba ᶜArbaya, who names Philo as the director of the Alexandrian school.

wonder whether the title stood in the original Eusebian work (which has not been preserved in Greek). The fact that it is missing in Jerome's translation and reworking of the work argues against this possibility. In this context it is interesting to note the practice of the bibliophile Byzantine Patriarch Photius in his *Bibliotheca*. He regularly cites pagan and Christian authors from Alexandria by means of their name and the epithet 'Αλεξανδρεύς. For example, at *cod.* 49 he records that he has read a book of 'the saintly Cyril the Alexandrian', and at *cod.* 106 (straight after the 3 chapters devoted to Philo) he mentions the *Hypotyposeis* of 'the blessed Theognostus of Alexandria the exegete', possibly head of the Alexandrian school in the period after Origen. But in the case of Philo he commences (cod. 103) with the usual formula ἀναγνώσθη Φίλωνος 'Ιουδαίου (were read of Philo the Jew...), and Philo's Alexandrian origin is mentioned only at the end of *cod.* 105, as part of a brief biographical sketch similar to what is found in Jerome and Ps.Sophronius.[83]

Some conclusions

On the basis of the above discussion the following summary of results can be given.
(1) The titles and descriptions bestowed on Philo concentrate for the most part on two features, his learning and his Jewish descent.
(2) A considerable number of authors express their respect for Philo's learning in general terms, particularly when he is associated with Josephus. If the reference is more specific, then it usually insists on Philo's skill in philosophy. On a number of occasions the phrasing or the context of the reference to Philo's learning or philosophical prowess suggests that it is based on his allegorical exegesis of scripture. The most specific references are those that allude to the proverb comparing Philo with Plato and the title 'Philo the Pythagorean' found in Clement (and taken over in Sozomen).
(3) Two epithets are used to describe Philo's Jewish descent. Until the end of the 4th century *Hebraios* is clearly dominant. Thereafter *Ioudaios* begins to take over, even if it never wholly supplants the other title. Jerome appears to have played an important role in this development, particularly in the West. The reference to 'Philo a Jew' in Theodore of Mopsuestia is most likely earlier than Jerome's description of Philo as *Iudaeus* in his *De viris illustribus*. The title *Hebraios* is in all cases a sign of respect. The interpretation of the term *Ioudaios* is more difficult. Implicit in this term is a contrast with Christianity. It can be meant neutrally, or

---

[83] On this biographical material see Schamps (1987) 460–469.

even have a positive connotation. There are also texts in which the context shows that the reference has a distinct polemical edge.
(4) The title Philo the Bishop, which implies full acceptance of the legend of Philo Christianus, is idiosyncratic, and is only found in the *Catenae*.
(5) Philo's Alexandrian origin is rarely mentioned and never used as a title.
(6) The majority of titles and descriptions used for Philo are positive in content and intent. This reflects the generally positive attitude taken towards him in the Christian tradition.

Finally it is appropriate to end our discussion by drawing some conclusions on *why* titles and epithets are used to describe Philo. Earlier I made a distinction between titles and descriptions. Titles are used to specify who is being talked about, descriptions are used to introduce or bring to mind the figure concerned. There can be no doubt that some of the titles we have discussed (especially *sophos*, *philosophos*, *Hebraios*, *Ioudaios*) are used to indicate which Philo is being talked about. But it seems to me on the basis of our evidence that the titles are not used primarily for the purpose of distinguishing Philo from others who carry the same name. Two arguments support this view. Firstly we recall the fact that Philo is very often cited without any kind of label at all.[84] Secondly it is rather unexpected that *Alexandreus* is never used to identify Philo. It would appear that identificatory labels in Philo's case were not really necessary. Even though there were other Philos with whom some of the more learned members of the Christian community were familiar, these were not of a stature that they could easily be confused with 'our' Philo. Philo is given an epithet mainly in order to tell the reader something about him, and, as we have seen, the epithet is often chosen in relation to the context in which it is used. This has made the subject treated in the present article all the more interesting, because it in fact allows a kind of miniature view of the way that Philo was received in the Christian tradition.

The contrast with our modern situation, mentioned at the outset of the article, is interesting. Today Philo is never called 'the Hebrew' anymore because that title in English, when used of persons, is reserved for the period of the Old Testament or Hebrew Bible.[85] Since the Second World War the title Philo Judaeus too has largely gone out of fashion.[86]

---

[84] See above p. 5.
[85] This is different in Italian, where it still occasionally occurs: cf. R-R nos. 6501, 6820.
[86] It was still the preferred title of Goodenough, e.g. in the bibliography that he com-

The reason for this, I suspect, is that a geographical location is regarded as more neutral than an ethnic origin—an important consideration in our century with its baleful (and alas continuing) history of racial discrimination. Thus we see that today Philo is generally called 'the Alexandrian'. The chief purpose of this practice is to distinguish him from the many other Philos in the Greco–Roman world. This modern habit does not have its roots in antiquity, as far as we can tell from our sources. But even today, of course, it is in certain contexts hardly necessary to identify our hero. In the pages of this Annual, for example.[87]

University of Leiden

---

piled with Goodhart (1938). Perhaps if his *Introduction to Philo Judaeus* had first been written in 1962 rather than 1940 he might have chosen the alternative title. It seems that the title Philo the Jew is *never* used anymore (not a single example in R-R). For an example of a very deliberate use of the title 'Philo the Jew' in Modern Hebrew see the remark on Rav Hanazir's *Qol Hanevoua* at Neher (1986) 390 n. 6.

[87] Apart from my colleagues Van Rompay and Weitenberg already mentioned in the notes, I would also like to thank Alan Mendelson (Hamilton, Canada), Gerard Mussies (Utrecht), James Royse (San Francisco), David Satran (Jerusalem), and Daniel Schwartz (Jerusalem) for their helpful comments on various draft versions.

Bibliography

A. Arazy, *The Appellations of the Jews (Ioudaios, Hebraios, Israel) in the Literature from Alexander to Justinian* (diss. New York 1977).

J. B. Aucher, *Philonis Iudaei sermones tres hactenus inediti: I. et II. De Providentia et III. De animalibus* (Venice 1822).

J. Bidez and G. C. Hansen, *Sozomenus Kirchengeschichte*, GCS (Berlin 1960).

J. -B Chabot, 'Note sur l'ouvrage syriaque intitulé 'Le Jardin des Délices'', in C. Bezold (ed.), *Orientalische Studien Theodor Nöldeke zum siebzigsten Geburtstag (2. März 1906) gewidmet* (Giessen 1906) 1.487–496.

—, *Anonymi auctoris Chronicon ad annum Christi 1234 pertinens*, CSCO 109 = Scriptores Syri 56 (Louvain 1952).

R. Devreesse, *Essai sur Théodore de Mopsueste*, Studi e Testi 141 (Vatican City 1948).

C. Duckworth and E. F. Osborn, 'Clement of Alexandria's *Hypotyposeis*: a French Eightheenth-century Sighting', *JThS* 36 (1985) 67–83.

J. A. Fabricius, *Bibliotheca Graeca* (Hamburg 1705–28, 1795[4]).

L. H. Feldman, *Jew and Gentile in the Ancient World* (Princeton 1993).

D. Forabaschi, *Onomasticon alterum papyrorum: Supplement al Namenbuch di F. Preisigke*, 2 vols. in 3 (Milan–Varese 1967).

P. M. Fraser, and E. Matthews, *A Lexicon of Greek Personal Names, vol. 1 The Aegean Islands, Cyprus, Cyrenaica* (Oxford 1987).

H. Görgemans, 'Art. 'Philosophie' IIA, Griechische Patristik', *Historische Wörterbuch der Philosophie* 7 (Munich 1989) 616–623.

E. R. Goodenough, *An Introduction to Philo Judaeus* (New Haven 1940, Oxford–New York 1962[2]).

H. L. Goodhart and E. R. Goodenough, 'A General Bibliography of Philo Judaeus', in E. R. Goodenough, *The Politics of Philo Judaeus: Practice and Theory* (New Haven 1938; repr. Hildesheim 1967) 125-321.

B. Grillet, G. Sabbah and A.-J Festugière, *Sozomène Histoire Ecclésiastique*, SC 308 (Paris 1983).

A. van den Hoek, *Clement of Alexandria and his Use of Philo in the Stromateis: an Early Christian Reshaping of a Jewish Model*, VChr.S 3 (Leiden 1988).

W. Horbury and D. Noy, *Jewish Inscriptions of Graeco-Roman Egypt* (Cambridge 1992).

P. W. van der Horst, *Ancient Jewish Epitaphs*, Contributions to Biblical Exegesis and Theology 2 (Kampen 1991).

A. M. Jones, J. R. Martindale, and J. Morris, *The Prosopography of the Later Roman Empire, vol. 1 A.D. 260–395, vol. 2 A.D. 395–527, vol. 3 A.D. 527–641*, 3 vols. in 4 (last two volumes edited by Martindale only) (Cambridge 1971–92).

A. Kamesar, *Jerome, Greek Scholarship, and the Hebrew Bible*, Oxford Classical Monographs (Oxford 1993).

J. N. D. Kelly, *Jerome: his Life, Writings, and Controversies* (London 1975).

K. G. Kuhn and W. Gutbrod, 'Art. Ἰσραήλ κτλ', *TDNT* 359–391.

R. Kühner and F. Blass, *Ausführliche Grammatik der geiechischen Sprache*, 2 volumes in 4 (Hannover 1890–1904[3]).

N. de Lange, *Origen and the Jews: Studies in Jewish-Christian Relations in Third-*

Century Palestine, University of Cambridge Oriental Publications 25 (Camridge 1976).

N. P. LEMCHE, 'Art. 'Hebrew'', *ABD* 4 (1992) 95.

A M. MALINGREY, *'Philosophia': étude d'un groupe de mots dans la littérature grecque des Présocratiques au IVe siècle après J.-C.* (Paris 1961).

S. N. MASON, *Flavius Josephus on the Pharisees: a Composition-critical Study*, SPB 39 (Leiden 1991).

G. MUSSIES, 'Jewish Personal Names in some Non-Literary Sources', in J. W. VAN HENTEN and P. W. VAN DER HORST (edd.), *Studies in Early Jewish Epigraphy*, Arbeiten zur Geschichte des antiken Judentums und des Urchristentums 21 (Leiden 1994) 242–276.

A. NEHER, 'Les références à Philon d'Alexandrie dans l'œuvre du Rav Hanazir, disciple du Rav Kook *(Qol Hanevoua*, 1970)', in A. CAQUOT, M. HADAS-LEBEL and J. RIAUD (edd.), *Hellenica et Judaica: hommage à Valentin Nikiprowetzy* (Leuven 1986) 385-390.

V. NIKIPROWETZKY, *Le commentaire de l'Écriture chez Philon d'Alexandrie: son caractère et sa portée; observations philologiques*, ALGHJ 11 (Leiden 1977).

W. PAPE and G. BENSELER, *Wörterbuch der griechischen Eigennamen* (Graz 1959, = reprint of 1911³).

P. W. PESTMAN *et al.*, *A Guide to the Zenon Papyri (P.L. Bat. 21)*, 2 vols., Papyrologia Lugduno-Batava 21 (Leiden 1981).

F. PETIT, *L'ancienne version latine des Questions sur la Genèse de Philon d'Alexandrie*, 2 vols., Texte und Untersuchungen 113–14 (Berlin 1973)

—, *Quaestiones in Genesim et in Exodum: fragmenta graeca*, PAPM 33 (Paris 1978).

—, *La Chaîne sur la Genèse: Édition intégrale*, 2 vols. (so far), Traditio Exegetica Graeca 1–2 (Louvain 1991–93).

P. PILHOFER, *Presbyteron kreitton: Der Alterbeweis der jüdischen und christlichen Apologeten und seine Vorgeschichte*, WUNT 2.39 (Tübingen 1990).

F. PREISIGKE, *Namenbuch* (Heidelberg 1922).

G. J. REININK, 'Die Textüberlieferung der Gannat Bussame', *Le Muséon* 90 (1977) 103–175.

L. VAN ROMPAY, *Théodore de Mopsueste: Fragments syriaques du Commentaire des Psaumes (Psaume 118 et Psaumes 138–148)*, CSCO 436 Scriptores Syri 190 (Louvain 1982).

J. R. ROYSE, *The Spurious Texts of Philo of Alexandria: a Study of Textual Transmission and Corruption with Indexes to the Major Collections of Greek Fragments*, ALGHJ 22 (Leiden 1991).

D. T. RUNIA, 'Philo of Alexandria in Five Letters of Isidore of Pelusium', in *idem*, D. M. HAY and D. WINSTON (edd.), *Heirs of the Septuagint. Philo, Hellenistic Judaism and Early Christianity: Festschrift for Earle Hilgert*, BJS 230 [= *SPhA* 3 (1991)] (Atlanta 1991) 295–319.

—, 'A Note on Philo and Christian Heresy', *SPhA* 4 (1992) 65–74.

—, *Philo in Early Christian Literature: a Survey*, CRINT III 3 (Assen–Minneapolis 1993).

J. SCHAMPS, *Photios historien des lettres: la Bibliothèque et ses notices biographiques*, Bibliothèque de la Faculté de Philosophie et Lettres de l'Université de Liège 248 (Paris 1987).

C. SCHAÜBLIN, *Untersuchungen zu Methode und Herkunft der antiochenischen Exegese*, Theophaneia 23 (Köln–Bonn 1974).
H. SCHRECKENBERG, 'Josephus in Early Christian Literature and Medieval Christian Art, in *idem* and K. SCHUBERT, *Jewish Historiography and Iconography in Early and Medieval Christianity*, CRINT III 1 (Assen–Minneapolis 1992) 1–138.
D. R. SCHWARTZ, 'Philo's Priestly Descent', in F. E. GREENSPAHN, E. HILGERT and B. L. MACK (edd.), *Nourished with Peace: Studies in Hellenistic Judaism in Memory of Samuel Sandmel*, Scholars Press Homage Series 9 (Chico, California 1984) 155-171.
H. SOLIN, *Die griechischen Personennamen in Rom: ein Namenbuch*, 3 vols. (Berlin–New York 1982).
M. STERN, *Greek and Latin Authors on Jews and Judaism*, 3 vols. (Jerusalem 1974-84).
A. TERIAN, *Philonis Alexandrini de Animalibus: the Armenian Text with an Introduction, Translation and Commentary*, Studies in Hellenistic Judaism: Supplements to Studia Philonica 1 (Chico, California 1981).
R. W. THOMSON, *Moses Khorenats'i History of the Armenians* (Cambridge Mass.–London 1978).
P. TOMSON, 'The Names Israel and Jew in Ancient Judaism and in the New Testament', *Bijdragen* 47 (1986) 120–140, 266–289.
B. VANDENHOFF, *Exegesis Psalmorum, imprimis Messianicorum apud Syrios Nestorianos e codice usque adhuc inedito illustrate* (Rheine 1899).
J. M. VOSTÉ, 'La chronologie de l'activité littéraire de Théodore de Mopsueste', *Revue Biblique* 34 (1925) 54–81.
E. A. WALLIS BUDGE, *The Chronography of Gregory Abû 'l Faraj, the Son of Aaron, The Hebrew Physician, Commonly Known as Bar Hebraeus, being the First Part of his Political History of the World* (Oxford 1932).
J. WHITTAKER, 'Platonic Philosophy in the Early Centuries of the Empire', *ANRW* II 36.1 (Berlin-New York 1987) 81-123.
C. K. WONG, 'Philo's Use of Chaldaioi', *SPhA* 4 (1992) 1–14.
W. WRIGHT, *Catalogue of Syriac Manuscripts in the British Museum, acquired since the Year 1838, Part II* (London 1871).
T. ZAHN, *Acta Johannis* (Erlangen 1880).

SAMARITANS AND HELLENISM

PIETER W. VAN DER HORST

From Alexander the Great's conquest of the Middle East in 332 BCE onwards it was not only the Jewish but also the Samaritan community in the land of Israel that came more and more within the Greek sphere of influence. Most regrettably, however, we must add immediately that we know very little of Samaritan Hellenism. Some passages in 2 Maccabees (6:2) and in Josephus (*AJ* 12.257–264) would seem to indicate that Samaritans, like the radical Judaean Hellenists in Jerusalem, requested the Seleucid king Antiochus IV Epiphanes in 167 BCE to hellenize their cult and change their sanctuary for the Lord on Mt. Garizim into a temple of Zeus Olympios or Xenios. But the translation of the passage in 2 Macc. is highly uncertain,[1] and the Josephan passage may well imply that it was only a small minority of the Samaritans (or even a group of non-Samaritan Sidonian colonists in Samaria) who made this request.[2] This second point has to do with the fact that it is unwarranted to translate the Greek term *Samaritai* always with 'Samaritans', a point that I will return to later. Be that as it may, whether or not it were Samaritans who asked for a hellenization of their cult, we can nonetheless clearly observe that Hellenistic culture began to exert its influence on both 'liberal' and 'orthodox' Samaritans—I use this anachronistic terminology for the sake of convenience—as it did on all other Jews in Hellenistic Palestine. However scanty the remains of Samaritan Hellenistic literature may be, they clearly demonstrate that Samaritans indeed adopted the Greek language and even Greek literary forms to voice their ideas.

This literature, however, shows two opposing tendencies, a syncretist approach and a strict approach to Scripture. On the one hand we have a fragment of an anonymous Samaritan historian, who is commonly called Ps.Eupolemus because the fragment has been wrongly ascribed in the process of transmission to the Jewish author Eupolemus. It probably dates to the second cent. BCE.[3] (Perhaps we have two fragments, but the small second fragment may well derive from another author; it has

---

[1] J. A. Goldstein, *II Maccabees*, Anchor Bible 41A (Garden City 1983) 523–539 (cf. 273); R. Doran, '2 Maccabees 6:2 and the Samaritan Question', *HTR* 76 (1983) 481–485.

[2] R. Egger, *Josephus Flavius und die Samaritaner*, NTOA 4 (Fribourg–Göttingen 1986) 260–283.

[3] Edition, translation and commentary are now most easily available in C. R. Holladay, *Fragments from Hellenistic Jewish Authors* I (Atlanta 1983) 157–188.

The Studia Philonica Annual **6 (1994) 28–36**

been handed down as an *adespoton*).[4] The larger first fragment displays a marked religious openness in the way it incorporates Greek and Babylonian mythological figures into the biblical genealogy of Gen 10. The Greek god Kronos is identified with the Babylonian deity Bel and receives a place in this genealogy as the father of Canaan. (In the dubious second fragment Bel is called on the one hand the one who escaped the great flood, and on the other the one who built the tower of Babel, which might even imply the equation of Bel with Noah and of Bel with Nimrod, and hence perhaps even of Noah with Nimrod (!), who is often called the builder of the tower of Babel in Jewish haggada,[5] *if*, that is, the fragment derives from a Jewish author—or a Samaritan one for that matter—which remains doubtful.) It is noteworthy that by means of this device the author simply makes these pagan gods into human beings, a kind of demythologization that is so strongly reminiscent of the theories of the Hellenistic author Euhemerus that the conclusion can hardly be avoided that this way of dealing with these gods has been inspired by knowledge of euhemeristic ideas. (Euhemerus of Messene, who worked early in the 3rd century BCE, earned his fame by his anthropological theory of the gods, as put forward in his *Hiera Anagraphe* (*Sacred Record*), to the effect that the gods of popular worship had originally been great kings and generals to whom mankind had shown their gratitude for their amazing and helpful deeds by worshipping them as gods; this theory enjoyed some popularity not only in critical Greek and Roman circles but also among some Jewish and Christian authors in antiquity.[6]) In a strongly demythologizing and euhemeristic way the author of this passage claims that the chief deity of the Babylonian and Greek pantheon was originally nothing but a mortal being. It should be added, however, that there is an important point of difference between the way this author uses Euhemerism and the way it is found in other Jewish (and Christian) authors: whereas the latter mostly use the theory as a means of criticizing or even ridiculizing pagan religious traditions, our Samaritan author uses it to incorporate elements from these pagan traditions into his own biblical world-view (comparable to *Orac. Sib.* 3.105-161).

In the same fragment of Ps.Eupolemus we further find that Enoch is

---

[4] See R. Doran, 'The Jewish Hellenistic Historians Before Josephus', *ANRW* II 20.1 (Berlin–New York 1987) 246–297, esp. 270–1.

[5] P. W. van der Horst, 'Nimrod After the Bible', in *idem*, *Essays on the Jewish World of Early Christianity*, NTOA 14 (Fribourg 1990) 220–232.

[6] On Euhemerus see the exhaustive bibliography in the latest critical edition of his fragments by M. Winiarczyk, *Euhemeri Messenii reliquiae* (Stuttgart–Leipzig 1991) XVIII–XXXVI.

identical to the Greek Atlas. According to this author, Enoch taught Abraham astrology—Enoch being the inventor of this science as Atlas was among the Greeks—and the patriarch passed on this sacred knowledge to the Phoenicians and Egyptians! Confusingly enough, elsewhere in the same fragment Abraham himself is also said to have been the inventor of astrology. Anyhow, we see here a markedly 'syncretistic' way of interpreting Scripture, in which the typically hellenistic motif of the great prestige of the 'first inventor' (πρῶτος εὑρέτης)[7] plays such an important role that all the biblical and post-biblical warnings against astrology could not prevent the author from attributing the discovery of what was regarded as one of the most significant accomplishments of mankind to the great culture-hero Abraham (or to Enoch by identifying him with Atlas).[8]

So far nothing specifically Samaritan has been mentioned. In the same fragment, however, we also find the striking anachronism that Abraham was received by Melchizedek (probably) in the temple of the Most High on Mt. Garizim. To be sure, Genesis 12:7 states that, when Abraham entered the land of Canaan, he came to 'the place at Shechem', and Genesis 14:18 tells about a meeting between Abraham and Melchizedek, Priest of the Most High in Salem, but in a fascinating haggadic turn Ps.Eupolemus combines the two stories and embellishes them by making Melchizedek receive the patriarch in the temple of the Most High on Mt. Garizim, presumably also because the LXX has Salem located in Samaria (Gen. 33:18). This is obviously an attempt to legitimize the Samaritan cult on that mountain over against that in Jerusalem by forging a positive link between the ancestor of the people of Israel and the main site of the Samaritan cult (see the quotations in Eusebius, *Praep. Evang.* 9.17.1-9).[9]

The openness towards pagan culture which this author demonstrates, even to the point of claiming the prestigious 'science' of astrology to be the invention of the 'Samaritan patriarch' Abraham (or of his remote ancestor Enoch), demonstrates in a very striking way that this anonymous Samaritan had no fear of Hellenistic culture: 'it must simply be

---

[7] See K. Thraede, Art. "Erfinder II (geistesgeschichtlich)', *RAC* 5 (1962) 1191–1278.

[8] On Jews and astrology see J. H. Charlesworth, 'Jewish Astrology in the Talmud, the Pseudepigrapha, the Dead Sea Scrolls, and Early Palestinian Synagogues', *HThR* 70 (1977) 183–200; *idem*, 'Jewish Interest in Astrology during the Hellenistic and Roman Period', in *ANTW* II 20.1 (Berlin–New York 1987) 926–950.

[9] With the commentary by Holladay *Fragments* I (see note 3) 178–187; but see also the comments by H. G. Kippenberg, *Garizim und Synagoge* (Berlin 1971) 74–85 and 148–150, and by B.-Z. Wacholder, 'Pseudo-Eupolemos' Two Greek Fragments on the Life of Abraham', *HUCA* 34 (1963) 83–113.

assimilated into existing structures'.[10] Or, as the most recent editor of the fragments rightly remarked, because the fragments from Ps.Eupolemus 'reflect an outlook which both knows and values pagan mythological traditions, it may be necessary to modify the common view of Samaritans as a sect immune to outside influences'.[11] Tiny though this fragment (or both fragments) may be, it shows (or they show) us the midrashic traditions of a group of Samaritans, who welcomed Greek culture and tried to work out a synthesis between their own traditions and the dominant Hellenistic civilization.

By way of contrast we have the fragments of the epic poet Theodotus (also probably from the second century BCE)[12]. These fragments reveal a much more strictly biblical outlook than in the case of Ps.Eupolemus. In his poem on the history of Shechem (written in Homeric style and language, which in itself is an indication of a more than superficial knowledge of Greek culture!) this author glorifies the murder of the Shechemites by Simeon and Levi (Gen 34). He presents the murder as carried out on God's command, a non-biblical motif not unknown in Jewish haggadic elaborations of this biblical chapter.[13] The author has Simeon convince his brother Levi that killing the Shechemites is justified by citing an oracle: 'For well have I heard a word from God, for he once said that he would give to Abraham's sons ten nations', a promise derived from Gen. 15:18-21 and interpreted as if 'give to Abraham's sons' meant 'have them killed by Abraham's sons'. He also places a heavy emphasis on the importance of an absolute prohibition of mixed marriages with uncircumcised gentiles. Jacob says to the leader of the Shechemites concerning the necessity of their being circumcised: 'For indeed this very thing is not allowed to Hebrews, to bring home sons-in-law and daughters-in-law from another place, but only one who boasts of being of the same nation... That one [God] once, when he led the noble Abraham out of his fatherland, called himself from heaven the man with all his house to strip off the flesh from the foreskin, and thus he accomplished it; and it remains unchanged since God himself uttered it' (quoted in Eusebius, *Praep. Evang.* 9.22.6-7).

---

[10] G. E. Sterling, *Historiography and Self-Definition: Josephos, Luke-Acts and Apologetic Historiography* NTSup 64 (Leiden 1992) 206.

[11] Holladay *Fragments* I (see note 3) 160.

[12] Available in C. R. Holladay, *Fragments from Hellenistic Jewish Authors* II (Atlanta 1989) 51–204.

[13] See the references in P. W. van der Horst, *Joods-hellenistische poëzie* (Kampen 1987) 58–67; *idem*, 'The Interpretation of the Bible by the Minor Hellenistic Jewish Authors', in M. J. Mulder (ed.), *Mikra. Text, Translation, Reading and Interpretation of the Hebrew Bible in Ancient Judaism and Early Christianity*, CRINT 2.1 (Assen–Philadelphia 1988) 519–546, reprinted in his *Essays* (see note 5) 187–219, esp. 194–196.

Theodotus' poem has often been regarded as an anti-Samaritan work, for instance by John Collins.[14] It is said to have been composed in order to justify the destruction of the temple on Mt. Garizim by John Hyrcanus in about 110 BCE (recent archaeological discoveries seem to have overturned the traditional dating of this event in 129/128 BCE[15]). I must confess that I find this a highly improbable interpretation. I would rather suggest that a poem from the second century BCE on the history of Shechem of all places, which is even called by the author 'a holy city' (fr. 1 in Eusebius, *PE* 9.22,1),[16] can only derive from a Samaritan author; it is unthinkable that a non-Samaritan, Jewish author would sing the praise of a city that was the cultic centre of the rival sect of the Samaritans. And this is exactly what he does in the very first fragment of this poem.[17] In addition there is such a strong emphasis on the fact that the opponents of Jacob's son are uncircumcised, where all male Samaritans are circumcised—and every Jew knew that!—that it is utterly improbable that we have here a writing by a Jew directed against the Samaritans. Moreover, the Samaritans of Theodotus' time certainly did not claim to be descendants of the pre-Israelite pagan Shechemites, but of the Israelites (and hence also of the sons of Jacob) who had been left behind in the land at the time of the deportation of the Northern Kingdom (722 BCE) and the Assyrian exile. The contents of the poem are from beginning to end most easily to be explained on the assumption that the author was a Samaritan. Therefore the poem should most probably be read as a piece of Samaritan propaganda literature in which the author presents the remote ancestors of the Samaritans as zealous, law-abiding, anti-pagan Israelites[18]. Ps.Eupolemus and Theodotus thus give us glimpses of the diversity of the haggada and the multiformity of the religion of the Samaritans in the Hellenistic period. Unfortunately, what we can learn from them is not much, but it *is* enough to demonstrate that in the

---

[14] J. J. Collins, 'The Epic of Theodotus and the Hellenism of the Hasmoneans', *HThR* 73 (1980) 91–104.

[15] See R. Pummer, 'Einführung in den Stand der Samaritanerforschung', in F. Dexinger & R. Pummer (Hrsgg.), *Die Samaritaner* (Darmstadt 1992) 59.

[16] Although I am aware of the possibility that ἱερὸν ἄστυ here is no more than a Homeric 'Floskel' (cf. *Od.* 1.2 Τροίης ἱερὸν πτολίεθρον), I am convinced that for our author it has a full religious sense.

[17] Holladay, *Fragments* II (see note 12) 106–9 (= Eusebius, *PE* 9.22.1). Even though Alexander Polyhistor (*ibid.*) says that the quotes are from Theodotus' work περ ὶ Ἰουδαίων, this need not be taken as the title of the work (Holloday, *ibid.* 55–6). Whatever the exact title may have been, what matters is that the poem displays an unusually great interest in Shechem, and that in a very positive sense.

[18] See J. Freudenthal, *Alexander Polyhistor und die von ihm erhaltenen Reste jüdäischer und samaritanischer Geschichtswerke*, Hellenistische Studien 1–2 (Breslau 1875) 82–103; also Van der Horst in the publications mentioned above in note 13.

Hellenistic period there were already clearly diverging movements in Samaritanism, and that these differences were related to the extent of the influence of Hellenistic culture.[19]

From the post-Hellenistic period no Samaritan writings in Greek have been preserved, but the extant fragments of the *Samareitikon*, the Samaritan Bible in Greek, create the impression that, at least in the diaspora, the Samaritans had to use a Greek translation of their Pentateuch because they, like other Jews, could no longer understand the biblical text in its original language.[20] Recent discoveries of Samaritan inscriptions in Greek in various parts of the Hellenistic and Roman world, inscriptions in which biblical passages are quoted in Greek, corroborate this impression.

This leads us to our second set of evidence, namely the Samaritan inscriptions from the diaspora. Although this material is of a non-literary nature, it does furnish important evidence for the study of hellenization among the Samaritans in late antiquity. Moreover it also affords us insight into the question to what extent a Samaritan diaspora existed in the Hellenistic world, *i.e.* in an environment in which this community was exposed to Greek culture, even more than in their homeland. A word of caution, however, is in order at this point. Even though there is a growing awareness among scholars that the Greek terms Σαμαρίτης and Σαμαρεύς and the Latin term *Samaritanus* do not necessarily always mean 'Samaritan', it is by no means yet common knowledge. Too many inscriptions have been claimed, also in the recent past, as evidence of a Hellenistic Samaritan diaspora without sufficient justification, as I have tried to demonstrate elsewhere.[21] I therefore state once again clearly and emphatically that strict methodology requires that we translate these terms by 'Samaritan' *only if* we have other indicators, apart from that term itself, to the effect that we have to do with a member of the Samaritan religious community. The reason for this is that the words concerned can also denote a 'Samarian', which is the recently coined term for an inhabitant of Samaria who is not a member of that religious community. This is an important distinction that one should never ignore. Unfortunately ancient authors or scribes are only on rare occasions aware of this problem of terminological ambiguity: a notable exception is the late papyrus *CPJ* 513, a divorce deed from 586 CE,

[19] I leave Thallus out of account here because I do not regard him as a Samaritan author.
[20] S. Noja, 'The Samareitikon', in A. D. Crown (ed.), *The Samaritans* (Tübingen 1989) 408–412; but see the reservations expressed by E. Tov, 'Die griechischen Bibelübersetzungen, in *ANRW* II 20.1 (Berlin–New York 1987) 185–186.
[21] See P. W. van der Horst, 'The Samaritan Diaspora in Antiquity', in *idem*, *Essays ...* (see note 5) 136–147.

where the scribe unambiguously states that the two people concerned were Σαμαρῖται τὴν θρησκείαν, 'Samaritans by faith', and so clearly gives a quite exceptional clarification of the ambiguous term *Samaritai*. This is not the place to present a list of indubitable instances of epigraphic Samaritans, but let us quote some illustrative examples with the question of Hellenization in mind.

In 1980 two Samaritan inscriptions in Greek were found on the small but significant Greek island of Delos.[22] Both inscriptions, dating from the third to second and from the second to first century BCE respectively, do not speak about Samaritans explicitly, but they do speak about 'the Israelites on Delos who pay their first offerings to the sanctuary (of) Argarizin'. The mention of *Argarizin* (the Greek transcription of Samaritan *har-Garizim* = Mt. Gerizim) leaves no room for doubt[23]. The self-identification as Israelites is also suggestive. Do they wish to distinguish themselves from those called *Ioudaioi*, who had their own synagogue nearby on Delos? These Delian Samaritans honour a certain Sarapion of Cnossos (on Crete) and Menippus of Heraclea (which Heraclea is unknown) for their benefactions towards the community, possibly the building of a synagogue. One of the interesting things about these inscriptions is not only that they are witnesses to a very early presence of a Greek speaking community of Samaritans on Delos, but also that they make it very probable that as early as the second century BCE Samaritans, who were most probably Greek speaking, lived in Crete (on account of the mention of Sarapion of Cnossos; I am aware that another interpretation of the evidence is possible). Further it has to be noted that these Samaritans had already adopted in this relatively early period the typically Greek custom of honouring benefactors of the community with golden crowns or wreaths and immortalizing this honorific decree by inscribing it upon a stone set up in public, which is also a clear sign of Hellenization in this religious community. 'The steles themselves, the form and language of the inscriptions, and the honors paid to benefactors all follow the most proper and common Greek style.'[24]

Another rather spectacular recent discovery is an inscription from a Samaritan synagogue in Thessalonica from the fourth, possibly the fifth

---

22 Ph. Bruneau, ''Les Israélites de Délos' et la juiverie délienne', *Bulletin de correspondence hellénique* 106 (1982) 465–504.

23 See, however, the cautionary words by R. Pummer, 'ARGARIZIN: a Criterion for Samaritan Provenance?', *JSJ* 18 (1987) 18–25.

24 A. T. Kraabel, 'Synagoga Caeca: Systematic Distortion in Gentile Interpretations of Evidence for Judaism in the Early Christian Period', in J. Neusner & E. S. Frerichs (eds.), *"To See Ourselves as Others See Us". Christians, Jews, "Others" in Late Antiquity* (Chico California 1985) 222.

century CE.[25] In this inscription of 20 lines one finds first a *berakhah* in Samaritan Hebrew (*barukh 'elohenu le'olam*), no doubt because it was a liturgical text; then in Greek the priestly blessing from Numbers 6:22–27, with a dozen or so deviations from the Septuagint that probably derive from a Samaritan revision of the Septuagint (not necessarily the *Samareitikon*), then another *berakhah* in Samaritan Hebrew (*barukh shemo le'olam*), and finally a Greek dedication to Siricius from Neapolis (Nablus), most probably the rhetorician Siricius who was a teacher of rhetoric in Athens in the fourth century.[26] Although it cannot be determined with absolute certainty from this dedication whether this rhetorician was really a Samaritan, it is at the very least possible. *If* he was, we have to consider the implications of a Samaritan being a sophist who taught rhetoric in Athens for our understanding of the extent of Hellenization among certain segments of the Samaritan community in late antiquity. In this connection it is worthwile to remember that Procopius writes in his *Anecdota* (27.26–31) that in the reign of the emperor Justinian (527–565) there was in Constantinople a senator of high repute, Faustinus, who had become Christian in name but had in fact remained a Samaritan (a kind of Marrano Samaritano *avant la date*!). This senator was accused before Justinian of hostility towards Christians and condemned to exile, but he was able to bribe Justinian so that the verdict was not carried out. This passage has given rise to the suspicion, rightly I suppose, that in the early Byzantine period there must have been more crypto-Samaritans in government service, which implies a thorough knowledge of things Greek among Samaritans. And finally, Damascius tells us in his *Vita Isidori* (fr. 141–144, p. 196 ed. Zintzen) that Proclus' successor as head of the Platonic Academy in Athens, Marinus, was originally a Samaritan, who, under the influence of Greek philosophy, had become an apostate and adopted paganism. This Marinus wrote, among other things, commentaries on Plato's *Philebus* and *Parmenides,* an introduction to Euclides' *Data*, and a *Vita Procli* (the latter two works still extant).[27]. A stronger and more striking example of the influence of Hellenistic culture on Samaritan intellectuals could hardly be given.

But it is not only synagogue inscriptions in the diaspora that make

---

[25] B. Lifshitz & J. Schiby, 'Une synagogue samaritaine à Thessalonique', *RB* 75 (1968) 368–378.

[26] On him see W. von Christ, W. Schmid and O. Stählin, *Geschichte der griechischen Litteratur* II 2 (München 1924) 947, 1102.

[27] See J. R. Masullo, *Marino di Neapoli: Vita di Proclo* (Napoli 1985) and M. Stern, *Greek and Latin Authors on Jews and Judaism* II (Jerusalem 1980) 673–675. I have not seen M. Luz, 'Marinus: An Eretz-Israel Neoplatonist at Athens', in: A. Kasher *et al.* (edd.), *Greece and Rome in Eretz Israel* (Jerusalem 1990) 92–104.

clear that many Samaritans spoke and read Greek. In Ramat Aviv, to the north of Tel Aviv, an excavation of an ancient Samaritan synagogue has yielded three inscriptions: one of them in Samaritan Aramaic, two of them in Greek, the only complete one reading 'Blessing and peace be upon Israel and upon this place, Amen'. And also in another Samaritan synagogue in ancient Palestine, in Beth She'an-Skythopolis, three of the four inscriptions found there are in Greek, and only one in Samaritan Aramaic.[28] And, most remarkably, recent excavations of Samaritan synagogues in the area of ancient Samaria itself, all of them dating from the 4th to 6th cent. CE, have yielded only Greek synagogue inscriptions.[29] The geographical spread of the inscriptions from both the diaspora and the land of Israel, almost all of them in Greek, indicates that Samaritans lived all over the ancient world, from Rome to Persia. It is far from improbable that the majority of them, just like the other Jews, lived in the diaspora and that only a minority lived in the old Samaritan area.

All this would imply that we have to envisage a situation in which the majority of the Samaritans understood and even spoke Greek. This would make it exactly parallel to the Jewish situation in the later Roman Empire, where there was a Hebrew-speaking minority in the land of Israel, and a Greek speaking majority in the diaspora, as well as a large number of Greek-speakers in the homeland itself. We have seen fragments of the Greek writings of at least two Samaritan authors (and there certainly were more), we have seen quite a number of Greek inscriptions both in and outside the homeland, we have seen Samaritan communities adopting Hellenistic modes of honouring benefactors, we have seen a Samaritan Platonist philosopher and perhaps a teacher of rhetoric, and finally also a Samaritan as a high official at the Byzantine court (and here too there were certainly more). This is a fascinating picture, which makes us want to know more. It is highly regrettable that almost all the relevant evidence on Samaritan Hellenism (or Hellenistic Samaritanism) has been lost. But recent finds give us hope that new discoveries in the future will gradually enlarge our knowledge of this aspect of Samaritan thought and culture, both inside and outside of the Samaritan area.[30]

Utrecht University

---

[28] See G. Reeg, *Die antiken Synagogen in Israel, II: Die samaritanischen Synagogen* (Wiesbaden 1977) 572–3, 631.

[29] I. Magen, 'Samaritan Synagogues', *Qadmoniot* 25 (1992) 66–90 (Hebrew).

[30] This article is a much expanded version of my short contribution on Hellenism in A Companion to Samaritan Studies, edd. A. D. Crown, R. Pummer and A. Tal (Tübingen 1993) 117–118.

JEWISH TRADITIONS ON ALEXANDER THE GREAT

RICHARD STONEMAN

I

Alexander the Great's conquest of the Levant was accompanied by violence, terror and massive destruction. The siege of Tyre lasted seven months (January to August 332) and was concluded by the slaughter of six thousand of the defenders, followed by the crucifixion of a further two thousand Tyrian prisoners.[1] Gaza fell more swiftly, but the captain of the defenders, Betis, was punished on his capture with the fate that Hector had suffered at the hands of Achilles: thongs were passed through his ankles, and he was dragged to his death behind Alexander's chariot.[2] The region was apparently subdued, and Alexander continued to Egypt; but early in 331 a revolt by the Samaritans, who burnt their Macedonian satrap Andromachus alive, necessitated further action. The leaders of the revolt were executed. A recent find of documents in a cave at Wadi Daliya was surrounded by the bones of 205 refugees from Alexander's vengeance who had been shut up in the cave and smoked to death. It has been suggested that the prophecy of the destruction of the 'city of chaos' in Isaiah 24–27 (the date of which cannot be determined objectively) may be a reflection of this destruction in Samaria.[3]

A few Jewish writings of antiquity refer to these contributions of Alexander to the sum of human misery. The First Book of Maccabees begins (1:1):[4]

> Alexander of Macedon, the son of Philip, marched from the land of Kittim, defeated Darius, king of Persia and Media, and seized his throne, being already king of Greece. In the course of many campaigns he captured fortified towns, slaughtered kings, traversed the earth to its remotest bounds, and plundered innumerable nations. When at last the world lay quiet under his rule, his pride knew no limits.

Apart from the allusion to Alexander's pride, this passage (composed about 103 BCE) is remarkably restrained in its characterisation of the

---

1 Q. Curtius Rufus (ed. E. Hedicke, Bibl. Teubneriana, Leipzig 1908) 4.4.16–17.

2 Curt. 4.6.29.

3 M. Hengel, *Jews, Greeks and Barbarians* (London 1980) 3f. with n. 27.

4 The translation is that of the New English Bible.

violence of the great conqueror. Less equivocal by far is 1 Enoch 90 which involves a vision of 'all the birds of heaven—eagles, vultures, kites and ravens' coming to eat a flock of sheep, 'to dig out their eyes, and to eat their flesh.' Our text of 1 Enoch is an Ethiopic one. The original language is disputed, but the choice is between Hebrew and Aramaic, either of which would imply a Palestinian origin rather than diaspora origin for the text.[5] Later in date is a passage of the third book of the *Sibylline Oracles*, probably composed in the reign of the Emperor Nero (3.381–92):[6]

> But Macedonia will bring forth a great affliction for Asia, and a very great grief for Europe will spring up from the race of Cronos, the progeny of bastards and slaves. She will conquer even the fortified city of Babylon. Having been called mistress of every land which the sun beholds, she will perish by evil fate, leaving a name among her much-wandering posterity. Also at a certain time there will come to the prosperous land of Asia a faithless man clad with a purple cloak on his shoulders, savage, stranger to justice, fiery.[7] For a thunderbolt beforehand raised him up, a man. But all Asia will bear an evil yoke, and the earth, deluged, will imbibe much gore.

Even more explicit is a short passage of Book 4 of the *Sibylline Oracles* (4.88–94):[8]

> αὐτὰρ ἐπεὶ σκήπτροισι Μακηδόνες αὐχήσουσιν,
> ἔσται καὶ Θήβησι κακὴ μετόπισθεν ἅλωσις,
> Κᾶρες δ' οἰκήσουσι Τύρον, Τύριοι δ' ἀπολοῦνται.
> καὶ Σάμον ἄμμος ἅπασαν ὑπ' ἠιόνεσσι καλύψει
> Δῆλος δ' οὐκέτι δῆλος, ἄδηλα δὲ πάντα τὰ Δήλου ...
>
> But when the Macedonians boast of sceptres, thereafter there will also be dire capture for Thebes. The Carians will inhabit Tyre, and the Tyrians will perish. Sand will cover all Samos under beaches. Delos will no longer be visible, and all the affairs of Delos will be inconspicuous. Babylon, great in appearance but insignificant in battle, will stand, built on useless hopes.

It is not impossible that whoever wrote Isaiah 23, the prophecy of the destruction of Tyre, had Alexander's campaign in mind, though the passage nominally refers to an attack by the Babylonians also referred to by Ezekiel 26–28.[9]

Here then is a body of evidence for a very negative opinion of

---

[5] Cf. E. Isaac's Introduction to his translation in J. H. Charlesworth, *The Old Testament Pseudepigrapha I* (London 1983) 5.

[6] *Sib* 3.381–92, translated by J. J. Collins in Charlesworth, *op. cit.* (n. 5) vol I. 370. See D. S. Potter, *Prophecy and History in the Crisis of the Roman Empire: A historical commentary on the thirteenth Sibylline Oracle* (Oxford 1990) 97.

[7] The man with a purple cloak may, like the 'affliction' of the previous sentences, be Alexander. Or it may refer to the great persecutor of Jews, Antiochus IV Epiphanes.

[8] Also of imperial date: Potter (*op.cit.*, n. 6) 98.

[9] It is curious that a footnote in the Jerusalem Bible on the latter passage remarks:'The radical destruction prophesied here was only accomplished later, by Alexander the Great.' Further reference to the siege of Tyre at Zechariah 9:1–8.

Alexander held by Jewish writers. Yet these passages are far from typical of the Jewish tradition as a whole. And it is striking that even these statements date from the end of the second century BCE at earliest, and are written in response to contemporary hostility to the Jews which began in Egypt in the reign of Ptolemy IX. In the Jewish tradition as it has been handed down from Hellenistic times even to the present, Alexander is a hero, a favourer of the Jews and a folk-hero to whom many anecdotes and wise sayings are attached in the same way that they are to Solomon and other Jewish heroes.

The rest of this paper will attempt to define the context of the change from villain to hero, and then to trace the fortunes of the folk-hero Alexander in Jewish lore and literature.

The most important document exhibiting a favourable Jewish attitude to Alexander is the account in Josephus' *Antiquities of the Jews* of Alexander's supposed visit to Jerusalem, a text which has been often discussed.[10] In fact there is rather little reason to suppose that Alexander ever visited Judaea in person; apart from the Josephus narrative, the only evidence is a passage in Pliny (*NH* 12.55.117) which simply remarks on the way of tapping the balsam trees of Judaea 'when Alexander the Great was campaigning in that country.'

The narrative in Josephus falls into three parts, of which the first and third are in fact inconsistent with one another.

1. (*AJ* 11.321–325) The Samaritans under the leadership of Sanballat (Greek Sanaballetes) approach Alexander as he is beginning the siege of Tyre, and offer him their support. In exchange for this support Alexander allows the Samaritans to build a temple of their own, independent of that in Jerusalem. Sanballat points out that this course of action will split the Jews and thus weaken their resistance to Alexander.

2. (*AJ* 11.326–339) The high priest Yaddua (Greek Jaddus), who had defied Alexander and vowed resistance (317–19), is in a panic at the approach of Alexander to Jerusalem. God tells him in a dream to go out, accompanied by the priests, all dressed in their priestly robes, to meet the conqueror on Mount Scopus (where Titus marshalled his forces for his final onslaught on the city, and where the Hebrew University now

[10] R. Marcus, appendix C to the Josephus LCL 6.512–532, 'Alexander the Great and the Jews'; A. Momigliano, 'Flavius Josephus and Alexander's Visit to Jerusalem,' *Athenaeum* n.s. 57 (1979) 442–8, and in *Settimo Contributo all storia degli studi classici e del mondo antico* (Rome 1984), 319–29; Italian translation, 'Flavio Giuseppe e la visita di Alessandro a Gerusalemme' in *Pagine Ebraiche* (Turin 1987) 85–93; S. J. D. Cohen, 'Alexander the Great and Jaddus the High Priest according to Josephus,' *AJS Review* 7–8 (1982–83) 41–68; L. L. Grabbe, 'Josephus and the Reconstruction of the Judaean Restoration,' *JBL* 106 (1987) 231–46.

stands). Alexander, for his part, has been warned in a dream he had at Dium in Macedonia to make obeisance to the God whose representative he would meet clad in such robes. He therefore kneels before Yaddua and sacrifices in the temple. The priests then show Alexander the Book of Daniel, with its prophecy of the Greek conquest of Persia (8.5–8, 21–22).[11]

3. (*AJ* 11.340–45) The Samaritans of Shechem, seeing the favour accorded by Alexander to the Jews, decided to profess themselves Jews. But Alexander sent their representatives away pending inquiries into whether Samaritans should really be regarded as Jews, and had many of the soldiers of Sanballat accompany him to Egypt where they were established as a garrison in the Thebaid.

The first of these episodes, as Momigliano has pointed out, has a pro-Samaritan tendency, while the third is broadly anti-Samaritan. The second belongs to a tradition reflecting mainstream Judaism. If Alexander had already favoured the Samaritans as in the first episode, he cannot in logic have been unsure of their credentials as in the third. In fact there are good reasons for denying historicity to all three episodes.

In the first place Sanballat is otherwise known as governor of Samaria in the time of Nehemiah, c. 407 BCE. It is possible that there might have been a second governor of the same name, and in fact another Sanballat is named in one of the papyri from the Wadi Daliyeh;[12] but it is more likely that Josephus or his source has imported the rather similar story involving Jehoiada from Nehemiah 13:28.

In the second place it is well-known that the Book of Daniel shown to Alexander was composed about 165 BCE, nearly two hundred years after Alexander passed through the Levant.[13] The prophecy in chapter 8 is certainly intended to refer to Alexander, the 'he-goat from the west, encroaching over the entire surface of the world though never touching the ground, and between its eyes the goat had one majestic horn,' which destroys the two-horned ram representing the empire of Darius. The prophecy continues with the division of Alexander's empire and the iniquities of Antiochus Epiphanes who 'abolished the perpetual sacrifice and overthrew the foundations of the sanctuary.'

The third episode is likewise in conflict with the course of events as reported in other sources, notably Quintus Curtius (4.8.9): after the revolt of the Samaritans against their satrap, Samaria was crushed and

---

[11] There are accounts of this visit also in George the Monk, *Chronicle* 1.19 (ed. C. de Boor (1904) 1.24–39), and in the Armenian translation of Eusebius 2.223.

[12] F. L. Cross, *HThR* 59 (1966) 201–11.

[13] For the latest discussion of the date of Daniel see now W. S. Towner in *The Oxford Companion to the Bible*, edd. B. M. Metzger and M. D. Coogan (Oxford 1994) s.v.

turned into a Macedonian colony. It was this event that precipitated the schism of the Samaritans and the Jerusalem community of Jews and the building of the temple on Mt Gerizim.[14] In fact the transfer of Samaritan soldiers to Egypt is an act of Ptolemy I, reported by Josephus *AJ* 12.8

Another version of Alexander's dealings with the Samaritans needs to be noted here. It comes from an early rabbinic (i.e. 1st to 2nd century CE)[15] source, *Megillath Ta'anith*, and lists as one of the days when fasting is forbidden the 21st Kislev, when the Samaritans asked Alexander for permission to build a schismatic temple on Mt. Moriah. However, the meeting of Alexander with the Jewish priests, here led by the High Priest Simon the Just (actually High Priest c. 200 BCE) instead of Yaddua, results in Alexander handing over the Samaritans to Jewish justice. The Samaritans are then dragged behind horses and Mt. Gerizim ploughed over. Again, this last is an act of the last years of the reign of John Hyrcanus, the Hellenizing Jewish king, c. 110 BCE;[16] but it is clear that Alexander would not have given permission to build an independent temple to a people who had just conducted a revolt against Macedonian rule.[17]

Different again is the account in the gamma-recension of the *Alexander Romance* (2.24),[18] where the Jews, at first alarmed at the suicidal bravery of the Macedonian troops, send out the robed procession of priests; Alexander is frightened by them, then pays respect to their god and accepts tribute from them.

It may be mentioned in passing that Yosippon, the tenth century account of Jewish history which incorporates some material from Josephus,[19] uses only the first and second episodes from this story and reverses their order (2.6–8): Alexander meets the High Priest, who this time is Ananias, and having been warned in a dream the previous night

---

14 Cf. M. Hengel, *Judaism and Hellenism* (London 1974) 13. Archaeology confirms that a temple was built on Gerizim in the latter part of the fourth century: L. L. Grabbe, *op. cit.* (n. 10) 241.

15 *SHJP* 1.114.

16 Josephus *AJ* 13.281, *BJ* 1.65.

17 L. L. Grabbe, *op. cit.* (n. 10).

18 The *Alexander Romance* probably goes back to a third or second century BCE Alexandrian original. The earliest recension (alpha), represented by the single MS A, was expanded in the beta-recension of between 300 and 550 CE. The further expanded gamma-recension is probably of the eighth century and exhibits heavy Jewish and Christian influence. For a brief introduction to the textual history see R. Stoneman, *The Greek Alexander Romance* (Harmondsworth 1991) 28–32, where further references are given.

19 The first bilingual edition is Josephus Hebraicus, *Libri VI Hebraice et Latine*, ed. J. F. Breithaupt (1710). The standard modern edition is that of D. Flusser, *Sefer Yosippon* (Jerusalem 1978–80); see also D. Flusser, 'Josippon—a medieval Hebrew version of Jospehus,' in L. H. Feldman and G. Hata (ed.), *Josephus, Judaism and Christianity* (Leiden 1987) 386–397.

makes obeisance to him. He then proposes the erection of a statue of himself in the Holy of Holies. Ananias tactfully points out that this is against the Law and suggests that a better use of the necessary money would be the giving of alms. Alexander then asks to consult the Urim and Thummim:[20] Ananias replies that these are now hidden, but instead prays to God and gives Alexander the advice to continue his expedition. Some time now elapses before Alexander encounters Sanballat in his travels and gives permission for the construction of the Gerizim temple, on condition that Sanballat avoids giving offence to Ananias: thus the prophecy of Deut. 27.12 is fulfilled.

Given that none of these accounts can make any claim to historical truth, the question that arises is when and why they were invented.[21] Various answers have been given. Willrich supposed that the story reflected the circumstances of M. Agrippa's visit to Jerusalem in 52 CE. Büchler, followed by R. Marcus, argued that the whole complex reflects the guarantee of freedom to practise their religion granted to the Jews by Julius Caesar. S. J. D Cohen[22] argues from the absence of the story from Josephus' *Against Apion* that the story is not of Alexandrian origin and therefore must have arisen in Palestine in the early Hellenistic period—a rather risky *argumentum ex silentio*, which in any case does not give any obvious reason for the invention of the legend. More persuasive, in my view, is the answer of Momigliano.[23] Josephus (*AJ* 13.74–79) refers to a very similar dispute between the Jews of Alexandria and the Samaritans of Mt. Gerizim about the relative status of the two temples, in Jerusalem and on Mt. Gerizim, which took place in the reign of Ptolemy VI Philometor (180–45 BCE). He associates the disputes with the arguments over the legitimacy of the Temple founded at Leontopolis by Jews who had left Palestine under the leadership of one of the Oniads. Jews and Samaritans in Egypt had been quarrelling since the reign of Ptolemy I about the relative legitimacy of their ways of life, as is stated by Josephus *AJ* 12.10, and the arrival of Jews of the Palestinian tradition who nevertheless wanted to set up an alternative temple would have intensified the conflict between the groups. In addition, the giving of the Jews authority over Samaria, referred to in the *Megillath Ta'anith* passage, echoes Josephus' claim in *c. Ap.* 2.42 ff, that Alexander gave Samaria to the Jews. In fact this gift was made by Demetrius in 145 BCE (1 Macc. 11:34).

Another argument that suggests an Alexandrian origin of these tales,

---

[20] The operation of these oracular stones is described by Josephus *AJ* 3.214–18.

[21] There is a full discussion of answers given before 1979 in Marcus, *op. cit.* (n. 10). See further the works cited in n. 10.

[22] S. J. D. Cohen, *op. cit.* (n. 10).

[23] Momigliano, *op. cit.* (n. 10).

based on quite different premises, is given by G. Delling.[24] He demonstrates that the phraseology of Alexander's confession of faith in the God of the Jews is couched in language closely paralleled in Hellenistic Alexandria and in particular in the works of Philo.

If our analysis of the creation of this complex of stories is correct, it provides a context also for some other pieces of Jewish lore and history concerning Alexander. First, according to Josephus *c. Ap.* 2.33ff it was Alexander who gave the Jews civic rights in Alexandria. In fact it is certain that their position was only established formally under Ptolemy I (Josephus *AJ* 12.8), though it may well be that Alexander designated one area in Alexandria for the Jews to inhabit.[25] The importance of the founding of Alexandria in Jewish consciousness is emphasized by David Runia,[26] who suggests that the foundation of this city was the model for the description of the creation of the world in Philo's *De opificio mundi*. Secondly, a story found in three places in rabbinic literature[27] describes a dispute carried on before Alexander between the Jews on the one hand and the Ishmaelites, Canaanites and Egyptians on the other. The first two gentile groups claim the right to the land of Palestine, while the third claims compensation for the silver and gold taken by the Jews when they left Egypt. In each case Alexander decides in favour of the Jews by quoting Scripture. The argument raised in the case of the Egyptians, that the Jews are entitled to the wealth as payment for their time of slavery in Egypt, is paralleled in Philo *De vita Moysis* 1.140–142. This gives a *terminus ante quem* for the development of at least this part of the tradition. The emphasis on the relations of the Jews with the Egyptians, and Alexander's part in regulating these, could well belong to a context in which the Hellenistic Jews were concerned about their position in contemporary Egypt. (It is worth noting that Philo shows a certain ambivalence towards Alexander. Though, as we just observed, his attitude is generally a positive one, in line with that of Alexandrian Jewry generally, he does, for example at *Cher.* 56–64, use Alexander as a

---

[24] G. Delling, 'Alexander der Grosse als Bekenner des jüdischen Gottesglaubens,' *JSJ* 12 (1981) 1–51.

[25] H. I. Bell, *Cults and Creeds in Graeco-Roman Egypt* (New York 1953) 37; P. M. Fraser, *Ptolemaic Alexandria* (Oxford 1972) 1.55 doubts whether Alexander made any provision for Jews in the city and regards this as the achievement of Ptolemy Philometor; cf. also *ibid.* 53, 84, 284–5.

[26] D. T. Runia, 'Polis and Megalopolis: Philo and the founding of Alexandria,' *Mnem* 42 (1989) 398–412, reprinted in *Exegesis and Philosophy; Studies on Philo of Alexandria* (Aldershot 1990).

[27] I. J. Kazis, *The Gests of Alexander of Macedon* (Cambridge Mass. 1962), 11f. gives full details.

negative moral example:[28] his pride in his conquest of both Europe and Asia is an example of ἄλογον φρόνημα, of a mind puffed up with its own self-importance. This passage reflects a characteristic attitude of the classical philosophical tradition (both Cynic and Stoic) in which Alexander is regularly an example of τῦφος, puffed-up pride.[29])

I envisage the diaspora community in Egypt which had emigrated from Palestine setting about legitimizing its position under the Ptolemies in quite a systematic way, with the creation of stories and traditions that linked their own fate to that of the founder of the city, Alexander the Great. Whatever Alexander might have done to the people of Palestine in his time, it was now a question of what he, and the legitimizing authority he represented, could be made to do for the Jews of Egypt. The fact that the prophecy in Daniel, of Palestinian origin, was anti-Macedonian was incidental to the main purpose of the legend which was favourable to Alexander.

A legend which has not been previously noted in this connection is that according to which Alexander brought the Throne of Solomon to Egypt.[30] When it had previously belonged to Nebuchadnezzar, the king had attempted to ascend it; but one of the golden lion's paws that formed its supports stretched out and broke his leg. Alexander wisely avoided trying to sit on the throne, though a succeeding Pharaoh Shishak did and was likewise lamed. In the reign of Antiochus Epiphanes the leg of the throne was broken; and according to Esther Rab. 1.2,12 the fragments could still be seen at Rome in the second century CE. The chronology alone reveals this legend as nonsense; yet why should a legend arise in which Alexander brings an important legitimating Jewish relic to Egypt, except in this same context of Jewish self-legitimation in that land?

The legend may usefully be set alongside another concerning Alexander and Solomon,[31] which states that when Alexander conquered Jerusalem, he found there Solomon's books of wisdom. He gave them to his teacher Aristotle who translated them into Greek and then destroyed the originals; thus all the wisdom of the west is really derived from that of Solomon, but Aristotle passed it off as Greek. Now this is a

---

28 D. T. Runia, *op. cit.* (n. 26).

29 See in general W. Hoffmann, *Das literarische Porträt Alexanders des Grossen* (Leipzig 1907). The topics of Alexander's τρυφή and τῦφος are first introduced by Timaeus, and are incorporated in the later rhetorical topos of the Fortune of Alexander. See in brief R. Stoneman, *Legends of Alexander the Great* (London 1994), introduction.

30 2 Targum Esther 1.4; L. Ginzberg, *Legends of the Jews* (Philadelphia 1928–39) 6.452–3.

31 Ginzberg *ibid.* 282–3, quoting the sources. Cf. J. ben-Gorion, *Der Born Judas* (Leipzig, n.d.) 3.210.

story which puts Alexander in a hostile light as a thief and a destroyer, yet at the same time firmly locates him in the development of Jewish civilization. It again testifies to the importance attached by the Jews to the figure of Alexander, which I would attribute not to his actual historical impact on Jerusalem and Judaea, but to his centrality later as a culture-hero in the Alexandria of the Jewish diaspora.

Another small piece of evidence emphasising the association of Alexander and the Jews which belongs to the mid-second century is the series of stories in Ps.-Hecataeus (preserved for us in Josephus *c. Ap.* 1.183ff).[32] They include one about the refusal of the Jews to join in the reconstruction of the temple of Bel at Babylon by Alexander, and one about a skilled Jewish archer in Alexander's army (201ff.).[33] Whoever Ps.-Hecataeus was, he was writing at a time when it was important for the Jews to establish their place in the Hellenistic world and to associate themselves with its originator, Alexander. Religious scruple, however, demanded that their part should be consistent with the Law. Participation in the rebuilding of heathen sanctuaries would, therefore, have been going too far.

II

The first part of this paper has endeavoured to describe a date and context for the emergence of a favourable Jewish view of Alexander despite the historical misfortunes inflicted on the Levant by his conquests, and has located it in Hellenistic Egypt, while most of the material emphasising his savagery is of Palestinian origin. It has employed some legendary material as well as historical analysis to establish a plausible solution. In the second part of the paper I shall change my focus in order to trace, and as far as possible date, the further development of the Jewish legendary tradition about Alexander; this will demonstrate the continuing favourable attitude to Alexander in later Jewish tradition. I shall draw material from three main sources. First, miscellaneous reports in the rabbinic tradition. Secondly, the gamma-recension of the Alexander Romance, which is generally recognised to contain extensive Jewish and Christian material. Thirdly, the several Alexander Romances written in Hebrew, which are in some

---

[32] Jacoby FGrH 264; C. R. Holladay, *Fragments of Hellenistic Jewish Authors* I (Historians) (Chico California 1983) 277–335.

[33] This anecdote reappears in the Chronicle of George the Monk, a narrative heavily coloured (as are many of the medieval Greek Alexander Romances) by Jewish tradition. There is a translation of the relevant passages of George in R. Stoneman, *Legends of Alexander the Great* (London 1994).

cases close to the Greek Alexander Romance, in others less so.[34] I shall begin with stories relating to Alexander's activities in Alexandria.

In Ps.-Callisthenes (1.32, all recensions) a story is told that when the gate of Alexandria was built a large number of snakes emerged, which came to be regarded as guardian spirits of the houses in which they took refuge. This story about snakes is embellished in the third century CE *Lives of the Prophets* by Ps. Epiphanius,[35] which states that the dangerous character of the snakes (and of the river-snakes 'which the Greeks call crocodiles') was neutralised by the prayers of the prophet Jeremiah. The second recension of Ps. Epiphanius tells us:[36]

> We hear from the old men descended from Antigonus and Ptolemy that Alexander the ruler of the Macedonians stood by the tomb of the prophet [Jeremiah] and recognised his rites, and transferred his remains to Alexandria, erecting a circle around them, and thus the race of snakes was banished from that country, and likewise from the river; and he threw in the snakes called *argolaoi*, that is, snake-fighters, which he brought from Argos in the Peloponnese, which is why they are called *argolaoi*, meaning 'clever ones of Argos'; and they have a very sweet and well-omened utterance.

This passage may be considered in conjunction with another from the gamma-recension of Ps. Callisthenes (2.28), which describes how Alexander ascended a high tower in Alexandria and delivered a sermon proclaiming the One God of the Jews, and prayed to him for help in his undertakings. Both passages clearly connect Alexander's activities in Alexandria with his adoption of the Jewish religion and thus, by implication, his favour towards the Jews. The legends are designed as a counterweight to the established version of the earlier versions of Ps.-Callisthenes in which Alexander is credited with establishing the cult of Sarapis in Alexandria, which in fact was the doing of Ptolemy I.[37]

---

[34] An indispensable guide is W. J. van Bekkum, 'Alexander the Great in Medieval Hebrew literature,' *Journal of the Warburg and Courtauld Institutes* 49 (1986) 218–226. See also W. J. van Bekkum, *A Hebrew Alexander Romance according to MS London, Jews' College, no. 145* (Louvain 1992). On Ps. Callisthenes see H. van Thiel, *Leben und Taten Alexanders von Makedonien nach der Handschrift L* (Darmstadt 1983). The gamma-recension is edited by U. Lauenstein, vol. I (Meisenheim am Glan 1962), (vol. II) H. Engelmann (Meisenheim am Glan 1963), (vol. III) F. Parthe (Meisenheim am Glan 1969).

[35] *Prophetarum vitae fabulosae,* ed. Th. Schermann (1907) 9.12.

[36] *Ibid.* 61.11ff = 44.16 (a text attributed to Dorotheus, who fl. 303 CE, was exiled under Diocletian and martyred at the age of 107).

[37] Similarly in the Liegnitz *Historia Alexandri Magni* (A. Hilka, 'Studien zur Alexandersage', *Romanische Forschungen* 29 (1911) 1–71), Alexander is credited with building the Pharos (actually built by Ptolemy), complete with magic mirrors of emerald and supported by four glass crabs. The tale is found first in Mas'udi: see H. Thiersch, *Pharos, Antike, Occident und Islam* (Leipzig – Berlin 1909) 40ff; Minoo S. Southgate, *Iskandarnamah: A Persian Medieval Alexander-Romance* (New York 1978) 194–5; K. Brodersen, 'The Fragile Foundations of a Wonder of the World', *Omnibus* 25 (January

The two passages were used by Friedrich Pfister[38] to argue that major elements of the gamma recension were the product of Jewish invention in Alexandria. In his introduction to the reprinted version of this article in Pfister's *Kleine Schriften*, Merkelbach points out that the discovery, subsequent to Pfister's original article, of the epsilon-recension which must be dated not earlier than 700 CE and which influenced the gamma-recension, invalidates the suggestion that there was a Hellenistic Jewish *Alexander Romance* which formed the basis for the gamma-recension; he avers that gamma must in fact be of Christian origin. Now it is certain that gamma also contains a good deal of Christian material; but that does not invalidate the point that these two stories are likely to have originated in Hellenistic Jewish circles, and it appears to me that they fit neatly in the same context as the other traditions discussed so far.[39]

Curiously, the prophet Jeremiah plays an even more prominent role in more than one of the medieval (perhaps thirteenth century) Greek versions of the *Alexander Romance*.[40] In these, Jeremiah warns the people of Jerusalem that Alexander is coming and states that he has learnt from a dream-vision of the prophet Daniel that Alexander will free the Jews from Persian rule. Shortly thereafter Alexander sees a dream-vision of Jeremiah welcoming him to Jerusalem. When Alexander reaches Jerusalem, Jeremiah takes him on a visit to the Temple and prophesies his complete conquest of Darius and his visit to the islands of the blessed. (He also shows him some important relics such as the sword of 'Goliath the Hellene,' an expression which implicitly identifies the *Rhomaioi*, or Christian Greeks, as continuous with the Jews, and opposed to the pagan Greeks who are identified with the Philistines.)

The prominence of such tales of Jewish interest in medieval Greek writers, both the authors of these romances and George the Monk, suggests a significant Jewish influence on Byzantine Greek writing about Alexander, resulting from a view of Byzantine Christianity as in some sense a development of Jewish tradition. It may be, though it cannot be

---

1993) 5–7, and 'Ein Weltwunder auf gläsernen Füssen', *Antike Welt* 24 (1993) 207–211.

[38] F. Pfister, 'Eine Gründungsgeschichte Alexandrias' *Sb. Heidelberg* 1914, Abh. 11 = *Kleine Schriften zum Alexanderroman* (Meisenheim am Glan 1975) 80–103; cf. also F. Pfister, *Alexander der Grosse in den Offenbarungen der Griechen, Juden, Mohammedaner und Christen* (Berlin 1956).

[39] Delling (*op. cit.* (n. 24), note 2) also remarks that Merkelbach's conclusion that Pfister's argument is invalidated by the discovery of epsilon is far too sweeping, and that Pfister in any case did not argue for Jewish 'composition' of gamma.

[40] K. Mitsakis, *Der Byzantinische Alexanderroman nach dem Codex Vindob. Theol. Gr. 244* (Munich 1967) esp. 64 ff.; A. Lolos, *Ps.-Kallisthenes; Zwei mittelgriechische Prosa-Fassungen des Alexanderromans* I (Meisenheim am Glan 1983), esp. §§ 51–59.

demonstrated, that these medieval traditions preserve a substrate of Jewish legend as early as anything in the pre-sixth century texts—legendary material which somehow did not make it into the western traditions and is forgotten even in the Hebrew sources.

The next legend to which we can give a *terminus ante quem* for its establishment is the Parable of the Eye. This is found in the medieval Latin *Iter Alexandri ad Paradisum*[41] (not known earlier than the twelfth century), and tells how Alexander, having sailed up the Ganges towards Paradise, reaches a walled city from which an old man emerges and gives him a stone resembling an eye. The curious property of this stone is that, when weighed in a balance with any amount of gold, it still draws the balance down; but if sprinkled with a little dust, even a feather can outweigh it. The mystery is explained by two old men who state that the stone is the eye of man, which can never be satiated by gold however much it acquires; but as soon as it is covered in the dust of death, it is as nothing.

Now this legend is also found in the Babylonian Talmud (*Tamid* 32b) where the two advisers are stated to be Jews. Its appearance in this work establishes that it was current before 500 CE. It is probably connected with one of the sayings of Ahikar, 'the eye of man is a fountain, and is never satisfied until it is filled with dust,'[42] and may possibly be echoed also in the Qur'an (Sura 102), 'the emulous desire of multiplying riches occupieth you, until you enter the grave.'[43] From the Talmud it entered the Jewish romance tradition about Alexander (see further below).

The next Talmudic passage to be considered is Alexander's encounter with the Elders of the South (*Tamid* 31b–32a), which is closely modelled on the encounter with the Brahmans in Ps.-Callisthenes[44] and includes the question-and-answer session but not the demand by the Brahmans that Alexander give them immortality. The Jewish character of the sages

---

[41] The text of the *Iter Alexandri ad Paradisum* is edited by A. Hilka in L. P. G. Peckham and M. S. La Du, *La Prise de Defur* (Princeton 1935); there is an English translation in Stoneman, *Legends of Alexander the Great* (London 1994), and a Dutch translation by P. W. van der Horst in *Studies over het jodendom in de oudheid* (Kampen 1993) 96–107: in his discussion van der Horst suggests that the Latin text was translated from a Hebrew original. The story becomes prominent in Middle English literature: M. Lascelles, 'Alexander and the Earthly Paradise in Medieval English Writings,' *Medium Aevum* 5 (1936) 31–47, 79–104, 173–88.

[42] Cf. Prov. 27:20.

[43] This is proposed by F. Conybeare, J. R. Harris and A. S. Lewis, *The Story of Ahikar* (Oxford 1913) lxxxii; cf R. Stoneman, 'Oriental Motifs in the Alexander Romance' (forthcoming in *Antichthon* 26 (1992)) n. 45.

[44] *Alexander Romance* (ed. H. van Thiel) III.5–6. On the Hebrew version see Kazis, *op. cit.* (n. 27) 13–14. On the Greek versions see R. Stoneman, 'Who are the Brahmans?' (forthcoming in *CQ* 1994) and 'Naked Philosophers,' (forthcoming in *JHS* 1995).

is probably a reflection of the belief of some Hellenistic Greek writers that the Jews were in some way descendants of the Indian philosophers: this view is reported by Josephus (*c. Ap.* 1.176–181) and attributed to Clearchus of Soli.[45]

Alexander's encounter with the Brahmans also lies behind another Jewish legend, which we know from a work variously known as *The History of the Rechabites*[46] or *The Story of Zosimus*,[47] in which the Christian saint Zosimus visits the land of the Blessed, stated to be the sons of Jonadab, son of Rechab (8.3). They share with the Brahmans their nakedness, their fruit diet, their habit of engaging in intercourse with their wives twice only (with each occasion resulting in the birth of one child), their wisdom, their freedom from sickness and other saintly traits. The origin of this part of the text has been the subject of controversy. J. H. Charlesworth in his translation identified it as the oldest element of the text, originating in the Palestinian Judaism of the first century CE, and argued that the text was later worked over to become a Christian work. Recently Christopher Knights[48] argues the reverse, that this is one of the latest elements of the text, not to be dated before 200 CE, and is a later insertion into a story of Christian origin. The Jewish origin of this form of the story is not in doubt, but it borrows heavily from the tradition about the Gymnosophists who were already established as a philosophical example in Cynic writings.[49] The adaptation of the Brahman story to the sons of Yonadab may have been made at any date, but it does not represent a truly independent Jewish Alexander-tradition. A visit to the sons of Jonadab is made part of the story of Alexander in Yosippon (2.16.10 ff), though without any of the detail of their way of life. In Yosippon it occupies a position immediately before the admonition of the birds to Alexander to go no further, which follows a little after the Brahman episode in the gamma-recension, though it occurs before the Brahman episode in the other recensions: thus it is clear that Yosippon is drawing on—and heavily abbreviating—the judaizing gamma-recension.

Alexander's relations with the women he encounters are the subject

---

45 I. Levi, *REJ* 26 (1881) 293–300; L. Wallach, 'Alexander the Great and the Indian Gymnosophists in Jewish Tradition,' *PAAJR* 11 (1941) 47–83. The notion may go back to Megasthenes: cf. Clement *Str.* 1.15, probably deriving from Megasthenes.

46 Charlesworth, *op. cit.* (n. 4) 2.443–61.

47 Tr. from the Greek by W. A. Craigie, *Ante-Nicene Fathers* 10.219–224.

48 C. Knights, ''The Story of Zosimus' or 'The History of the Rechabites'?' (forthcoming in *JSJ*).

49 See R. Stoneman, 'Who are the Brahmans?' (*Classical Quarterly* 1994, forthcoming); C. Muckensturm, 'Les gymnosophistes etaient-ils des cyniques modeles?', in M. O. Goulet-Cazé and R. Goulet (eds.), *Le Cynisme ancien et ses prolongements* (Paris 1993) 225–239.

of two aberrant versions in Jewish tradition. First, in the latest of the Jewish Alexander-romances, *The Book of the Gests of Alexander of Macedon* (Sefer Toledoth Alexandros ha-Mokdoni),[50] to be dated 1340–56 CE, he is represented as having sexual relations with Candace the queen of Meroe. In Ps.-Callisthenes it is quite striking that he does not do this, as the novella-form of the whole episode leads us to suppose that he will; furthermore, its close parallel, an Arab legend about Zenobia, does involve a courtship between Zenobia and the Arab chief Jadhima.[51] There is one earlier witness to this turn of events, in the chronicle of the ninth-century George the Monk (George the Sinner),[52] whose account of Alexander concentrates on just three episodes of the Alexander story: the visit to Jerusalem (which reads like a fashion show report), the encounter with the Brahmans, and the dalliance with Candace. It is possible that this story about Alexander and Candace is the result of confusion of Alexander's dalliance with the Amazon queen Thalestris reported in Quintus Curtius and other vulgate sources; but it seems to me likely, since the other two episodes he covers are those of particular interest to Jewish writers, that in this part of his work George is drawing on an unidentified Jewish source.

Secondly, Alexander's encounter with the Amazons takes an unusual form in rabbinic tradition.[53] He asks the women, who live in the city of Carthage, for bread, and they bring him bread made of gold on a table of gold. When he expostulates, they ask him, 'Did you have no bread at home that you had to journey here for it?' The point is the frequently made one of the futility of Alexander's insatiable journeying and conquests.

A similar encounter is that between Alexander and King Kazia,[54] in which again the King offers Alexander various foods made of gold. The episode contains additional material, in which Kazia asks Alexander to solve a dispute between two men one of whom has sold the other a dunghill in which treasure has subsequently been found. The vendor claims that he sold the dunghill but not the treasure. Alexander's solution is that the two men should arrange a marriage between the son of the one and the daughter of the other, so that both treasure and dunghill are kept in the family. There are many such examples of Alexander's Solomonic wisdom in the Talmudic and later legends. The

---

[50] Kazis, *op. cit.* (n. 27).

[51] Tabari 760, in M. Perlmann *The History of al-Tabari* IV (Albany 1987) 141–2; see R. Stoneman, *Palmyra and its Empire: Zenobia's Revolt against Rome* (Ann Arbor 1992) 156–7.

[52] George the Monk, *Chronicle* 1. 19.

[53] Kazis, *op. cit.* 16 with note 56.

[54] Kazis, *op. cit.* 20–22, with references.

source of this one, Leviticus Rabbah, is to be dated between the fifth and seventh centuries CE.[55]

The next legend to which we can assign a *terminus ante quem* is that of Alexander's constructing the Iron Gate to keep out the unclean nations, Gog and Magog. Gog and Magog first appear in the tenth chapter of Genesis, and are mentioned by Ezekiel (38.1–3). In Revelation (20:7–8) they are characterised as the nations dedicated to Satan. Their background is thus fully Jewish. In the gamma-recension of the Alexander Romance Alexander constructs gates at the mountains known as the Breasts of the North to enclose them, or keep them out of the civilised world. This passage is dependent on the *Apocalypse* of Ps.-Methodius, which must belong to the sixth or seventh century CE, though the real Methodius died in 311.[56] The legend should be regarded, then, like much in the gamma-recension, as Christian reworking based on a knowledge of Jewish traditions.[57] Jewish admiration of Alexander has made him the agent of this defence against the enemies of the Jews. (The later identification of the unclean nations with the Ten Tribes of Israel, whose expulsion by Shalmaneser II is referred to in IV Ezra, belongs to a further Christianisation which makes the Antichrist and the Ten Tribes comrades-in-arms who will break through the gate and descend on the world at the end of time).[58]

A handful of other Jewish traditions about Alexander, not related to those of the Romances, are found in various rabbinic sources. They include Alexander's interview with the pirate,[59] deriving from Stoic tradition on Alexander;[60] Alexander's gift of a city to a poor man, likewise deriving from the philosophical tradition;[61] and a tradition that Alexander visited Palmyra.[62] The first two of these at least are interesting as indicating a direct (if scarcely extensive) influence of Greek philosophy on rabbinic teaching.

A final aspect of the Jewish traditions on Alexander, which I shall not consider in detail, is the existence of five narratives about Alexander in

---

55 *SHJP* 94.

56 A. Lolos, *Die Apokalypse des Ps.-Methodios* (Meisenheim am Glan 1978).

57 See also Tabari 518–25. A. R. Anderson, *Alexander's Gate, Gog and Magog, and the Enclosed Nations* (Cambridge Mass. 1932); F. Pfister, 'Eine Gründungsgeschichte Alexandrias' (see n. 26 above).

58 A. Graf, 'La leggenda di Gog e Magog', in *Roma nella memoria e nelle immaginazioni del medio evo* (Turin 1883) 2.507–563.

59 Tsemmah Tsadiq: J. ben-Gorion, *Der Born Judas* 3.186.

60 Cic. *Rep* 3.14,24.

61 J. ben-Gorion, *ibid.*

62 *Ibid.* 274.

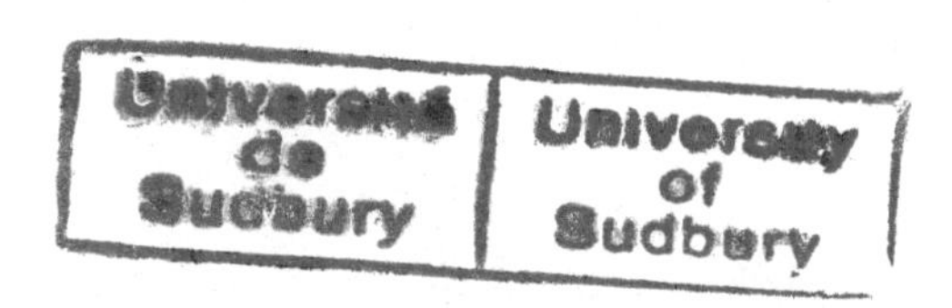

Hebrew which we might collectively refer to as the Hebrew Alexander Romances. These differ widely from one another, and are not directly relevant to my argument about the origin of Jewish traditions on Alexander, though their very existence is striking testimony of the continuing force of Alexander as a symbol in Jewish thought.[63] The most interesting from our point of view is probably the oldest: it is conveniently referred to as *Alexandros ha-Mokdoni*, 'Alexander the Macedonian.'[64] It is unfortunately undatable, though Gaster in his edition is inclined to place it in the ninth century.

A brief summary of its salient features will indicate how far it diverges from the Greek Romance. It begins with an account of Alexander's conception by Galopatria (i.e. Cleopatra, replacing Olympias); the father is not Nectanebo but Bildad. An important character throughout is Alexander's scribe Menahem. It includes a plot of Alexander's brothers against him (like Joseph). He visits Jerusalem, and also a palace with walls of green, red and blue glass. It contains the rabbinic tale of Alexander's decision concerning the man who sold a dunghill. He visits the kingdom of the women in Carthage. The episode of the water of life is distinguished by the fact that it is birds, not fish, which are revivified by the water; the episode leads to Alexander's visit to Paradise and the parable of the Eye. The flight and the diving bell are included, with the unusual conclusion that Alexander is cast up again before he expires because the sea will not tolerate corpses. He rides a lion. He visits the Dogheads and hears the story of the dog who is made king. He visits the land of the Blessed (the sons of Yonadab). His army collect manna on a mountain.

All in all, this account seems to be a wild card, impossible to place in any tradition. It contains elements from Ps. Callisthenes (the beta-recension), along with stories deriving from the Old Testament or from rabbinic teaching, and other elements which have no known affinities.

---

63 The five romances are (i) *Alexandros ha-Mokdoni*: M. Gaster, 'An Old Hebrew Romance of Alexander,' *JRAS* (1897) 486–549 = *Studies and Texts* II (1925–8) 814–79; (ii) *Ma'aseh Alexander*: D. Flusser, 'Ma'aseh Alexandros Lefi Ketab-Yad Parma,' *Tarbiz* 26.2 (Dec. 1956), 166; (iii) the sections of Yosippon devoted to Alexander: see n. 19 above; (iv) *Sefer Toledoth Alexandros*, found in two MSS in Paris and London: the Paris MS is edited by I. Levi, *Sefer Toledoth Alexandros* in *Sammelband kleiner Beiträge aus HSS* (Berlin) II 1886 = *Le Roman d'Alexandre* (Paris 1887), and the London MS by W. J. van Bekkum, *A Hebrew Alexander Romance according to MS London, Jews' College, no. 145* (Louvain 1992); (v) *Sefer Toledoth Alexandros ha-Mokdoni*, composed by Immanuel ben Jacob Bonfils (active 1340–1356 CE): edited by I. J. Kazis, *The Book of the Gests of Alexander of Macedon* (Cambridge Mass. 1962).

64 Gaster, *op. cit.* (n. 63).

This work concludes our survey of the Jewish texts relating to Alexander. Can any conclusions be drawn?

The first part of the study showed that a favourable Jewish tradition about Alexander was established in Ptolemaic Alexandria and overlaid the hostile traditions of some early Palestinian writings to the point of obliterating them. The inclusion of several legends in rabbinic teaching which were drawn directly from the Greek philosophic tradition indicates influence of Greek on Jewish thinking in this crucial period, though such influence has sometimes been denied or minimised.[65] A reverse traffic was also clear at several points, where Alexander acquired traits appropriate to great Jewish heroes like Moses (manna), Solomon (wise judgment) or Joseph (the plot by the brothers). The appearance of angels at various points in the stories (e.g. Alexander's dream of the High Priest) also adds a Jewish colour even to the Greek stories.[66] The incorporation of such works in the Arabic tradition as the *Sayings of the Philosophers* and the *Secret of Secrets* colours the medieval picture of Alexander, making him a model of kingship—very much the Islamic view—but the pre-Islamic Jewish sources offer a more complex picture. Here he is still Alexander the adventurer; but with God on his side he has lost the vicious characteristics that make him so ambiguous in the Greek tradition. The dominant impression is of a hero clever at solving problems and reconciling disputes, a protector of civilisation (Gog and Magog) and an enthusiast for knowledge. All in all, a Solomonic hero. Perhaps the legend that all the wisdom of the Greeks was drawn from the books of Solomon which Aristotle destroyed should not be interpreted as a hostile account, but as conveying the idea that Alexander had inherited the Jewish tradition. As the Jews began to disperse around the world and mingle with the Greeks and other gentiles, the Hellenic Alexander was of comfort as an indicator that Jewish tradition could be kept intact even in a gentile framework. The Hellenic vessel bore the Jewish draught. Thus Alexander became one of the continuing bearers of meaning for Jewish civilisation.

London

---

[65] E.g. L. H. Feldman, *Jew and Gentile in the Ancient World* (Princeton 1993).

[66] On dream oracles see D. Aune, *Prophecy in Early Christianity and the Ancient Mediterranean World* (Grand Rapids 1983) 143–144.

CHARISMATIC EXEGESIS: PHILO AND PAUL COMPARED[1]

SZE-KAR WAN

Ever since the discovery of *pesher* commentaries among the Dead Sea Scrolls, 'charismatic exegesis' has become a standard category in Biblical studies. Characteristic of the *pesharim* is a claim to inspired exegesis of the biblical text.[2] One oft-quoted passage in the Habukkuk Commentary maintains that though God had spoken through Habukkuk, the real meaning was revealed in the end time only to the Teacher of Righteousness, 'to whom God made known all the mysteries of the words of his servants the prophets.'[3] Since in this case the interpreter is granted a higher, more privileged status than even Habakkuk himself, there can be little doubt that the exegesis of the prophecy must have taken on a revelatory character similar to prophetic utterance.[4] The Essenes were not unique in this regard. The Zealots, according to Josephus, were moved to revolt by a messianic text, unidentified except as an 'ambiguous oracle found in the holy Scriptures,' which many 'wise men' mistook to be foretelling the ascendancy of one of their own to universal rulership.[5]

[1] I wish to thank David Satran, Irene Eber, Marinus de Jonge, David Runia, David Hay, Christian Høgel, as well as members of the SBL Mediator Figure Group, in particular Larry Hurtado and Alan Segal, for their willingness to read successive drafts of this paper and offer their valuable criticisms.

[2] See Horgan, *Pesharim*, for texts and translations of all the *pesharim*. See the classic study by Ellinger, *Habakuk-Kommentar*, *passim*. Ellis, *Paul's Use of the Old Testament*, 139–41, also suggests that the interspersing of text and commentary is a consistent characteristic of *pesher* commentary.

[3] 1QHab 7.1–5 on Hab 2:2b (tr. Horgan).

[4] This is possibly indicated by 1QHab 2.8–9, 'the priest into [whose heart] God put [understand]ing to interpret all the words of his servants the prophets' (tr. Horgan), though it remains unclear whether 'priest' here is to be identified with the Teacher of Righteousness. The lacunae in the crucial places also make it difficult to be certain.

[5] *BJ*. 6.312–13: ἦν χρησμὸς ἀμφίβολος ὁμοίως ἐν τοῖς εὑρημένος γράμμασιν, ... τοῦθ' οἱ μὲν ὡς οἰκεῖον ἐξέλαβον καὶ πολλοὶ τῶν σοφῶν ἐπλανήθησαν περὶ τὴν κρίσιν.... See discussion of this passage in Aune, *Prophecy*, 140–42; Hengel, *Zeloten*, 243–46. There is also endless discussion, largely speculative, on the identity of the text alluded to by Josephus; see, e.g., Hengel, *Zeloten*, 244–46; Aune, *Prophecy*, 140–41; Blenkinsopp, 'Oracle of Judah,' *passim*. It is of course possible that Josephus's report here is influenced by his own views of prophecy and interpretation (see below), but unlikely. The same *casus belli* is similarly reported by Tacitus, *Hist*. 5.13, and Suetonius, *Vesp*. 4.5. The Roman authors were most likely not dependent on Josephus; see Lindner, *Die Geschichtsauffassung des Flavius Josephus*, 72; and Thackeray, *Josephus*, 37–38, who argues for a common source.

***The Studia Philonica Annual* 6 (1994) 54–82**

Josephus mentioned this in order to emphasize his non-eschatological understanding of the oracle, as is clear from his ensuing application of the oracle to Vespasian.[6] But this should not obscure his report that charismatic exegetes or 'wise men' were at least partly responsible for the establishment of the Zealots' position.[7] Josephus himself related to his readers his own ability as an inspired interpreter of biblical oracles and dreams.[8] Though he never applied the title 'prophet' to himself, he nevertheless compared himself to Jeremiah in judgment of Jerusalem (*BJ* 5.591–93) and could recount incidents of inspired (ἔνθους) understanding of the biblical prophecies.[9]

As a result of these and similar observations, David Aune has attempted to define charismatic exegesis as *inspired eschatological commentary*. Such exegesis presupposes that 'the sacred text contains hidden or symbolic meanings which can only be revealed by an interpreter gifted with divine insight' and that 'the true meaning of the text concerns eschatological prophecies which the interpreter believes are being fulfilled in his own day.'[10] Aune's definition denotes three factors contributing to the rise of charismatic exegesis: (1) a belief that prophecy did not cease after the prophets of old; (2) a reliance on a written sacred text; (3) and an expectation of the end time. But to limit charismatic exegesis to eschatological writers is to foreclose the category prematurely; it does not do justice to the intricate connection between mysticism, broadly conceived, and scriptural interpretation, as Gershom Scholem has long ago indicated.[11] It does not explain, for example, why a non-eschatological and non-messianic writer like Philo nevertheless did claim some type of divine inspiration in his commentaries, or conversely why Paul, whose apocalyptic and mystical propensities have

---

[6] So De Jonge, 'Josephus,' 205–19, following Blenkinsopp, 'Oracle of Judah,' *passim*.

[7] See Hengel, *Zeloten*, 243: Since the underlying biblical text was not immediately comprehensible without the σοφοί, these latter must have been charismatic interpreters.

[8] *BJ* 3.352: [Josephus, speaking in the third person] ἦν δὲ καὶ περὶ κρίσεις ὀνείρων ἱκανὸς συμβαλεῖν τὰ ἀμφιβόλως ὑπὸ τοῦ θείου λεγόμενα... That τὰ ἀμφιβόλως ὑπὸ τοῦ θείου λεγόμενα must refer to biblical prophecies is clear when he immediately claimed to possess priestly acquaintance of biblical matters: ἱερῶν βίβλων οὐκ ἠγνόει τὰς προφητείας.

[9] *BJ* 3.353. For a study of Josephus's self-understanding as prophet, see Feldman, 'Prophecy, Josephus, mysticism,' 438, 441.

[10] Aune, *Prophecy*, 339; cf. his general discussion on Jewish charismatic exegesis (pp. 139–44) and on early Christian charismatic exegesis (339–46).

[11] Scholem, *Kabbalah and its Symbolism*, 5–31. This is not the place to discuss the complex relationship between apocalypticism and mysticism. Suffice to say that recent scholarship has begun to question the time-honored, but misleading in my view, distinction between these two genera, which presuppose the same type of experience. See, e.g., Segal, *Paul the Convert*, 34–58.

long been noted, seldom if at all appealed to inspired exegesis.[12] To the end of broadening the prevailing meaning of charismatic exegesis, therefore, I will examine several passages from Philo and Paul relevant to this issue. The specific question I wish to pose is how scripture functions in their *personal* ecstatic experiences if at all and *vice versa*. Their general views on the relationship between exegesis and mysticism are obviously important, but my primary concern here is whether and, if so, in what manner their ecstatic experiences have affected their treatment of the biblical text.[13]

Charismatic Exegesis in Philo

There are four passages in the extant corpus in which Philo speaks of his own experience: *Migr.* 34–35; *Spec.* 3.1–6; *Somn.* 2.250–54; *Cher.* 27–28. It remains to be established, however, whether these depict authentic experiences of ecstasy and, if they do, whether they are connected to scriptural exegesis.

De migratione Abrahami 34–35

While engaging in a long discourse on the soul's journey from the world of senses to the world of Logos and Wisdom, Philo makes a distinction between the inferior products of a mind travailing on its

---

[12] Paul's charismatic exegesis has been rigorously defended by Ellis, *Prophecy and Hermeneutic*, 152ff. But see the rebuttal, decisively I think, by Aune, *Prophecy*, 342–45. Aune nevertheless concedes that the citation of Isa 59:20–21; 27:9 as μυστήριον in Rom 11:26b–27 might have been an oracular inflation in the manner of charismatic exegesis (252); see also Ellis, *Prophecy and Hermeneutic*, 139–41.

[13] It should be noted that the subject of this paper is ecstasy and not mysticism, even though both categories presuppose some kind of consciousness alteration in Philo. Mysticism, according to Dodds, entails the subject's raising himself or herself above the body to meet the deity and is the 'belief in the possibility of an intimate and direct union of the human spirit with the fundamental principle of being, a union which constitutes at once a *mode of existence* and a *mode of knowledge* different from and superior to normal existence and knowledge. Ecstasy or 'trance-mediumship' has to do with the spirit's descending into a human body, vacating the resident human mind or soul. (Cf. Dodds, *Age of Anxiety*, 69–70, 72; emphasis supplied.) Dodds's view of ecstasy and rationality as mutually exclusive implies a decided passivity of the mind. Dodds, *Age of Anxiety*, 54 and n. 2, following ancient writers, has suggested that there are two types of psychological dissociation: 'one in which the subject's normal consciousness persists side by side with the intrusive personality, and on the other hand a deeper trance in which the normal self is completely suppressed, so that it retains no memory of what was said or done. In the former case the subject may simply report what the intrusive voice is saying; in the latter the voice speaks in the first person through the subject's lips, as 'Apollo' professes to do at Delphi or Claros.' See also Dodds, *Greeks and the Irrational*, 297. A more nuanced and balanced view has been advanced by Aune; see n. 19 below.

own (such are 'poor abortions, things untimely born') and the superior results that come from God ('birth perfect, complete and peerless;' §33). At this point, Philo makes an autobiographical aside (*Migr*. 34–35):[14]

> I am not ashamed to describe in detail my experience which I know from having experienced it numerous times. Sometimes, planning to approach the *usual writing of philosophical teachings* and knowing exactly what must be composed, I found my mind barren and sterile and ended without accomplishment, chiding my mind for its self-conceit and being astounded by the power of the Being, on account of whom the wombs of my soul are both opened and closed. At other times, approaching it empty, I suddenly became full when thoughts are showered and sown invisibly from above, so that I was *seized in Corybantic frenzy by divine inspiration* and was ignorant of every thing, place, people around me, words spoken, words written. For I obtained expression, thought, enjoyment of light, a keenest vision, a pellucid distinction of such things as if they were displayed in visible forms.

E. R. Dodds has suggested that much of the language here reflects but a 'quasi-mystical experience,' similar to inspiration common to writers 'when ideas flow unbidden to his pen.'[15] But 'Corybantic frenzy by divine inspiration' (ὡς ὑπὸ κατοχῆς ἐνθέου κορυβαντιᾶν) clearly recalls *Her*. 264–65, where Philo characterizes ecstasy (ἔκστασις), along with 'inspired possession and prophetic madness' (ἡ ἔνθεος ἐπιπίπτει κατοκωχή τε καὶ μανία), as the consequence of the dimming of the mind: 'The mind in us is displaced from its house at the entry of the divine spirit and reoccupies it only at its departure. For the mortal may not cohabit with the immortal.' Ecstasy is not always posed as the opposite of the mind, however, as if the two were mutually exclusive; more often than not the mind is an active participant in contemplation of the divine when it comes under the sway of the spirit. The mind, for example in *Plant*. 39, is said to delight in the Lord when it is caught up in frenzy (ὑπὸ θείας κατοχῆς). In an interpretation of the creation of man in Gen 1:26, made famous by its literary parallelism to Plato's *Phaedrus* myth, the soul on 'soaring wings'[16] is seized by 'a sober intoxication just as the Corybants in divine possession' (μέθῃ νηφαλίῳ κατασχεθεὶς ὥσπερ οἱ κορυβαντιῶντες ἐνθουσιᾷ) and contemplates the archetypal paradigms (*Opif*. 70–71).[17] The Therapeutae and Flaccus, likewise, are said to have

---

[14] I am responsible for all the translations unless noted otherwise.

[15] Dodds, *Age of Anxiety*, 71 n. 5.

[16] Πτηνὸς ἀρθείς. The soul is compared to 'winged carriage' (ὑπόπτερον ζεῦγος; *Phdr*. 246A); to Zeus's own chariot (πτηνὸν ἅρμα; 246E); and to 'the chariots of the gods' (τὰ θεῶν ὀχήματα; 247B).

[17] See *Phdr*. 249C, where the philosopher's soul is said to mount up wings and, being ever initiated into the perfect mystery (τελέους ἀεὶ τελετὰς τελούμενος), beholds God as being truly divine (θεὸς ὢν θεῖός ἐστιν).

experienced Corybantic frenzy.[18] Whether the mind is passive under divine influence or remains active in cooperation with it, ἔκστασις connotes a distinction between two states of consciousness.[19]

The language in *Migr.* 34–35 is also reminiscent of Philo's depiction of prophetic enthusiasm. In *Conf.* 59, for example, Philo claims that the biblical text of Exod 19:8 has been spoken under divine inspiration (ὑπὸ κατοκωχῆς ἐνθέου). The giving of the decalogue is achieved by the hearing of a mind under inspiration (ἡ τῆς ἐνθέου διανοίας) meeting the spoken words (*Decal.* 32–35), thus giving further indication that in Philo the mind sometimes remains active under inspiration.[20] The special laws are likewise given through Moses the most perfect prophet when he is filled with the divine spirit (ἀναπλήσας ἐνθέου πνεύματος; *Decal.* 175).[21] A most telling passage is *Somn.* 2.1–2, in which a soul in sleep and detached from the encumbering effects of the body can come under Corybantic frenzy and divine enthusiasm and obtain prescient power to predict the future (ἡ ψυχὴ... κορυβαντιᾷ καὶ ἐνθουσιῶσα δυνάμει προγνωστικῇ τὰ μέλλοντα θεσπίζῃ).[22] In none of these texts does Philo use the Corybantic and enthusiastic language merely to convey a weak sense of literary inspiration. On the contrary, his description of inspiration in *Migr.* 34–35 rather conforms to his general view of ecstasy and prophecy.

It is possible that 'usual writing of philosophical teachings' (κατὰ τὴν συνήθη τῶν κατὰ φιλοσοφίαν δογμάτων γραφήν) is a reference to commentary writing,[23] in which case this would be a prime candidate for charismatic exegesis. But context and substance suggest that the phrase probably refers only generally to literary composition. The overall intent

---

[18] *Contempl.* 11–12: The Therapeutae are compared to the Bacchanals and Corybants (καθάπερ οἱ βακχευόμενοι καὶ κορυβαντιῶντες); *Flacc.* 169: Flaccus is said to become 'possessed in Corybantic frenzy' (ὥσπερ οἱ κορυβαντιῶτες ἔνθους γενόμενος) and as a result regrets his evil deeds against the Jews.

[19] David Aune distinguishes between two forms of altered conscious states, 'possession trance' and 'vision trance.' The former renders the possessed medium a passive conduit for the divining spirit. The latter involves 'visions, hallucinations, adventures, or experiences of the soul during temporary absences from the body' but leaves the medium in full command of his or her faculties; cf. Aune, *Prophecy*, 19–20.

[20] Winston, 'Two Types of Mosaic Prophecy,' *passim*, has argued on the basis of this passage that one should distinguish between two types of prophecy in Philo, the 'ecstatic' and the 'hermeneutical.'

[21] See *Migr.* 84; *Mos.* 1.175, 201 for uses of ἔνθους in the context of the prophecy of Moses; *Mos.* 1.277, 286: prophecy of Balaam; *Spec.* 4.48–52: false prophets; *QG* 3.9: prophecy in general.

[22] Cf. also *Deus* 138–39; *Prob.* 80.

[23] So D. T. Runia suggested in the first edition of his *Philo and Plato's* Timaeus (Amsterdam 1983) 547 n. 8. This view was later abandoned in the second edition of the work. See also Hay, 'Philo as Exegete,' 46–47, who though less sure, suggests something similar.

of the passage is a sharp distinction between what Philo as a writer could obtain by his own means, presumably meaning the exercise of rational tools, and what he could learn as a result of direct revelation from God. Such a distinction between human and divine initiatives is not limited to literary activities; elsewhere Philo depicts the same scene but in the wider context of contemplation. Commenting on the Israelite experience of being bitten by snakes and scorpions and plagued by thirst in the desert (Deut 8:15–16), Philo notes that he himself is frequently afflicted in similar fashion, though only allegorically (*Leg*. 2.85):

> For I myself many times, leaving behind kinsfolk, friends, homeland and going into the wilderness to consider *something worthy of contemplation* (τι τῶν θέας ἀξίων), I would gain nothing. Instead, my mind, scattered and bitten[24] by passion, would withdraw to diametrically opposite matters. Sometimes, however, even in a full crowd I achieve quietude of mind, after God has dispersed the psychic crowd, all the while teaching me that it is not differences in location but God, energizing and leading the carriage of the soul[25] to wherever he chooses, that effects the superior and the inferior.

Crystallized in this passage is Philo's general principle that ecstasy as experienced by human beings remains a divine prerogative, a point which Philo elsewhere illustrates with the figure of Hannah, the 'divine grace' that makes the vision of God possible.[26] Seen in this larger context, the experience depicted in *Migr*. 34–35 does not represent a radical departure either in technique or in its phenomenological details; philosophical rumination, which includes but is not limited to biblical exegesis, is simply 'something worthy of contemplation.'

De specialibus legibus 3.1–6

In an extended passage Philo laments the lost opportunity of philosophical studies owing to the exigencies of the mundane, without specifying what the obstacles might have been:[27]

> §1 There was a time when I devoted myself to philosophy and the contemplation of the universe and its contents, when I enjoyed the beauty, extreme loveliness, and true felicity of its [all-encompassing] Mind, when I consorted constantly with divine principles and doctrines, wherein I rejoiced with a joy that knew no surfeit or satiety. I entertained no mean or lowly thought nor did I go crawling after fame, riches, or

---

[24] The use of σκοπίζειν, δάκνειν, and ἔρημος here is obviously triggered by Deut 8:15–16, where all three terms are used. Note the use of σκεδάννυμι in the following sentence.

[25] For similarities with Plato's *Phaedrus* myth see n. 17 above.

[26] For the etymological interpretation, capitalizing on the Hebrew meaning of 'Hannah,' see *Ebr*. 145–46 and Lewy, *Sobria Ebrietas*, 3–8, 40–41.

[27] I have decided to use the beautiful, almost lyrical translation by Winston, *Philo*, 75–76, even though here and there I might have taken issue with it.

bodily delights, but seemed always to be borne upward into the heights to the accompaniment of some soul-possessing inspiration and to revolve with the sun and moon, and the whole heaven and universe. §2 It was then, ah then, that I crouched down from above the ethereal heights, and straining the mind's eye, as if from some heavenly lookout, beheld the innumerable[28] spectacles of all things that are on earth and accounted myself happy in that I had escaped by main force the grievous calamities of mortal life.

§3 But here there lay in wait for me the worst of evils, envy, hater of the good, which suddenly assailed me and ceased not to drag me violently downward till it had hurled me into the vast sea of civil cares, in which I am tossed about, unable even to rise to the surface. §4 Yet in spite of my groans I endure, thanks to my longing for culture, rooted in my soul from my earliest youth, which ever has pity and compassion for me, rouses me, and raises me up. It is on its account that I sometimes raise my head and with the soul's eyes—dimly indeed, for the mist of strange affairs has obscured their acuity of vision—I yet look around at the things about me as best I can, in my yearning to draw in a breath of life pure and unmixed with evil. §5 And if unexpectedly I obtain a brief spell of fair weather and a calm from civil tumult, with wings I float on the waves and virtually traverse the air, wafted by the breezes of knowledge that often persuade me to come and spend my days with her, and slip away as it were from harsh masters, not only men but also affairs, which pour in on me like a torrent from various sides.

§6 Yet it is fitting to render thanks to God even for this, that though overwhelmed by the surf I am not swallowed up in the deep, but can also open the soul's eye, which in my despair of every good hope I thought had become incapacitated, and am illuminated by the light of wisdom, and am not for the whole of my life delivered into darkness. Here I am, then, daring not only to read the sacred oracles of Moses (τοῖς ἱεροῖς Μωυσέως ἑρμηνεύμασιν),[29] but also in my fondness for knowledge to peer into each of them and unfold and bring to light what is unknown to the multitude.

In what has been described as 'Paradise Lost,'[30] Philo makes a distinction between *vita activa,* which he evidently despises, and *vita contemplativa*, into which he can now enter only occasionally.[31] How such inspiration is engendered, Philo does not elaborate, except for an obscured reference to the reading of the Mosaic Law towards to the end of the passage, a reference that serves as a transition to the rest of the treatise. Alan Segal recently commented:[32]

---

28 Literally 'unspeakable' (ἀμύθητος), though Philo elsewhere seems to use the word with the meaning 'numerous,' 'unspeakably many;' cf. *Opif.* 43; *Leg.* 1.61.

29 Winston has 'the sacred interpretations of Moses.'

30 The phrase is Winston's; cf. Winston, *Philo*, 75. See also Lewy, *Philo*, 38 n. 1.

31 E. R. Goodenough has attempted to tie this passage to Philo's own political career; see Goodenough, 'Philo and Public Life,' 77–79; Goodenough, *Politics of Philo*, 66–69; Goodenough, *Introduction to Philo*, 5–7. See, however, critique by F. H. Colson, PLCL 7.631–32.

32 Segal, 'Heavenly Ascent,' 1356; emphasis supplied. Cf. also Nikiprowetzky, *Le commentaire*, 106, who thought Philo merely borrowed Platonic categories for his interpretation of the Mosaic Law.

> These personal observations begin without reference to particular scripture. They imply that in his youth, ... he had time for pure meditations and thus his soul would soar in the universe... Though he sadly reports his present inability to continue such scholarly, rhapsodic ascents into mystical thought, at the end of the passage Philo maintains that he can still ascend through his mind's meditations of divine scripture. Thus, for Philo, the activity of the mind, *under the guidance of scripture,* leads to ascent to the divine.

The suggestion that exegesis may lead to ascent is perhaps an overstatement. The sequence of thought in *Spec.* 3.1–6 goes from a heavenly ascent regularly experienced to a curtailed vision, occasioned by 'a brief spell of fair weather and a calm from civil tumult' that comes 'unexpectedly' (ἐξ ἀπροσδοκήτου[33]). If anything, it is his 'my *longing for culture*, rooted in my soul from my earliest youth' (ὁ ἐκ πρώτης ἡλικίας ἐνιδρυμένος τῇ ψυχῇ παιδείας ἵμερος), that keeps alive his hope for ecstasy. Now παιδεία could perhaps include scriptural studies but need not do so exclusively.[34] On the contrary, it is the realization that such heavenly journey is still possible that gives him the courage to delve into the inner intricacies of scripture. Though there is an undeniable connection between ecstasy and exegesis, the latter is presented here as a result rather than a precondition. If *Migr.* 34–35 and *Leg.* 2.85–86 are any indication, the sharp distinction between divine initiative and human effort speaks against any attempt to engender such ecstatic experiences, even by means of scriptural studies. These ecstatic experiences, moreover, do not lead to specific exegesis.[35]

In spite of the hazy relationship between ecstasy and exegesis, the ecstatic experience described in these passages seem trustworthy enough. David Hay raises doubts about the veracity of these accounts, suggesting instead that the conventional usage of such terms as 'Corybantic' and 'Bacchic' (cf. *Opif.* 71; *Ebr.* 146; *Her.* 69; *Somn.* 2.1) might have stemmed from Plato (e.g., *Symp.* 215E).[36] But otherworldly visions or journeys, or their articulations, could and perhaps must conform to some con-

---

[33] The expression is used with suggestion of divine intervention in *Ebr.* 111 (God *suddenly* delivering Moses and the Israelites at the Red Sea; Exod 14:7); *Her.* 249 (Abraham's ecstasy in Gen 15:12 coming *suddenly* upon him); *Somn.* 1.71 (Logos appearing *suddenly* to the soul without warning); 2.145 (Evil *suddenly* seizing the soul); *Mos.* 1.170 (= *Ebr.* 111), 257 (God *suddenly* and unexpectedly providing Moses blessings); *Spec.* 2.219 (divine blessings which come *suddenly* and unexpectedly). Cf. also general usages of the expression in *Somn.* 2.268; *Ios.* 211, 214; *Mos.* 1.136; 2.203; *Praem.* 165; *Legat.* 184, 197, 342.

[34] For a study of Philo's view of secular education and παιδεία, see Mendelson, *Secular Education, passim.*

[35] See also *Cher.* 48; *Her.* 30; 69–70; 264–65; *Opif.* 70–71.

[36] Hay, 'Psychology of Faith,' 905 n. 115. One might also add *Phdr.* 246A–257A. Essentially the same point was made by M. Pohlenz in the context of discussing *Cher.* 27; see n. 44 below.

ventional genres of literary expression, behind which possibly 'lies a tradition of active, living ecstatic experience.'[37] Similarity by itself is no proof against authenticity; the criterion of dissimilarity cannot be used to test the authenticity of ecstatic and mystical experiences.

De somniis 2.250–54

In *Somn.* 2.250–54, Philo allegorizes the 'city of God' of Ps 46:4 (LXX 45:5) as 'vision of peace,' an etymological interpretation of Jerusalem. Such a true city, cannot be material and can only be the soul or mind, which alone is worthy to be the house of God (2.250–51):

> The city of God is called 'Jerusalem' by the Hebrews, whose name, translated, means 'vision of peace.' Seek not, therefore, the city of the Being in regions of earth—for it is not constructed with wood and stone—but in a soul that is peaceful, keen-sighted, and that cultivates as a goal the contemplative and peaceable life. Who could find a grander and holier house in all that belong to God than a mind that loves contemplation, strives to see all, and never even dreams of desiring strife or confusion?

At this point Philo relates his experience with the spirit (2.252–54):

> Once again, the invisible Spirit, accustomed to be an unseen acquaintance, speaks (ὑπηχεῖν) to me, 'You there—you seem to be ignorant of a great and much fought-for matter, the very thing that I will reveal to you without reservation, for I have instructed you many other opportune lessons. Know then, my friend, that God alone is the most truthful and veritable peace, whereas every generated and corruptible being is an unremitting war. For God is free, but existence is contingent. Whoever, then, is strong enough to forswear war, contingency, generation, and corruption and to flee towards ungeneration, towards uncorruption, towards the free, towards peace, may justifiably be called the residence and city of God. It makes no difference to you, therefore, to call the same underlying reality either 'vision of peace' or 'vision of God,' since among the many-named powers of the Being, peace is not only a member of a company but also a leader'.

Here as in *Migr.* 45–46 (and *Cher.* 27–28 below), Philo claims inspiration to be a regular occurrence. The invisible spirit is called the 'unseen acquaintance' of the mind who has instructed Philo 'many other opportune lessons.' But note the order of presentation: first, the etymology is given; then and only then does Philo report his experience with the spirit. The invisible spirit speaks *after* the etymological identification and does claim to disclose the fundamental exegetical insight of the

[37] Stone, 'Apocalyptic—Vision or Hallucination,' 419–28. As Eliade, *Shamanism*, 13–14, 81–85, 259–87, has shown, even shamans, adepts of the techniques of ecstasy, must first learn their native, ancestral mythologies and cosmologies before they could practice their arts. Katz, 'Language, Epistemology, and Mysticism,' 22–74, makes essentially the same point from a philosophical point of view.

passage. The allegory presented here is therefore not 'spiritual exegesis,' as R. Meyer alleged.[38] What the spirit discloses is the character of God and his relationship to the divine powers. The substance of the spirit's revelation is twofold. First, it teaches the distinction between God's self-determined freedom and the dependent contingency of existence; the former encompasses peace, the latter war. One must flee war and embrace peace. Second, God is further differentiated from his powers, which have many names. Peace is then identified as one of the powers and in fact their leader. This cryptic description of God and his powers will become clearer when we consider *Cher.* 27–28.

The term ὑπηχεῖν is Philo's usual term for inspiration but not a technical term for Mosaic prophecy.[39] Philo is not here or anywhere modeling himself after Moses, as if he were promulgating new prophecies.[40] Philo does not appear to use the same terms to describe his ecstatic experience and the inspiration of Moses and he never calls himself 'prophet,' reserving it strictly for Moses.[41] Moses the prophet was also an interpreter or transmitter (ἑρμηνεύς) of God's oracles, though under inspiration Moses could prophesy through questions to God or by himself (*Mos.* 2.188–91). These functions Philo never arrogates to himself. The same reservation can be observed in Josephus, the Essenes, the Zealots, and the later rabbis; a notable exception are the early Christians, who applied the title prophet to themselves rather liberally.

De cherubim 27–28

In a detailed, lemma-by-lemma exegesis of Gen 3:24, Philo considers the identities of the two cherubim stationed outside Paradise after the expulsion of Adam and Eve and the turning sword of flame (*Cher.* 21–30). Philo first presents a cosomological interpretation, comparing the two cherubim to the outer and inner spheres of the fixed stars (§§21–25), and then a second interpretation, comparing the two cherubim to the earth's two hemispheres and the flaming sword to the sun (§§25–26). At this point, Philo proposes a third, superior option, according to which the two cherubim are the two powers of God and the flaming and turning sword represents Logos. Unlike the first two interpretations, however, this third position is reached under inspiration (*Cher.* 27–28):

---

38 Meyer, 'Προφήτης,' 823.

39 So Nikiprowetzky, *Le commentaire*, 37 n. 158, *contra* Bieder, 'Πνεῦμα, κτλ,' 374–75.

40 This is the basic conclusion of Hay, 'Philo as Exegete,' 47 and n. 16, against Hecht, 'Scripture and Commentary in Philo,' 164.

41 David Runia has alerted me to *Anim.* 7, where Philo calls himself an 'interpreter,' sharply distinguishing it from 'teacher.' 'Interpreters present through accurate recall the things heard from others,' while 'teachers impart their own knowledge' (tr. Terian).

> Then I heard an even more worthy explication in my soul which is accustomed to be frequently possessed by God and to divine what it does not know. This I will recollect from memory if I can. It said to me, 'God is indeed one, but his highest and foremost powers are two, Goodness and Authority: it is through Goodness that he begot all and through Authority that he rules the begotten. And there is a third gathering both and standing between them, namely Logos: for it is through Logos that God is both sovereign and good. The Cherubim, therefore, are symbols of these two powers, Sovereignty and Goodness, while the flaming sword is the symbol of Logos. For exceedingly swift[42] and fiery is Logos—and even more so is that of the Cause—because this is that which preceded and outstripped all, was conceived before all, and was manifested above all'.

There have been doubts about the authenticity of the experience related here. V. Nikiprowetzky has argued that what Philo calls inspiration here is none other than 'intuition intellectuelle,' not 'révélation extatique ou gnostique,' and that this passage represents a reflection of the identities of the two powers, even though Philo himself might have been experienced it as mystical.[43] More than fifty years ago Max Pohlenz expressed similar reservations, noting that the allegedly inspired interpretation looked suspiciously like his more refined and elaborate allegories elsewhere.[44] What Pohlenz had in mind principally was *Fug.* 95,[45] but one could also mention *Mos.* 2.99; *QG* 1.57; 2.51; 4.2; *QE* 2.62, none of which appeals to any ecstatic experience. *QG* 1.57 is especially troublesome, since it deals with the very same identities of the cherubim and flaming sword of Gen 3:24. But the existence of two divine powers in a monotheistic environment was a known problem in early Hellenistic and Rabbinic Judaism;[46] what is said above with regard to the authenticity of the experience in *Migr.* 34–35 and *Spec.* 3.1–6 is therefore applicable here as well. That Philo's report conforms remarkably well to

---

[42] This is a literal translation of ὀξυκινητότατον. The adjective is elsewhere used in *Leg.* 60; *Sacr.* 65, 66; *Post.* 19; *Agr.* 106; *Fug.* 158; *Mut.* 178; *Somn.* 2.67.

[43] Nikiprowetzky, *Le commentaire*, 36–37 n. 158; I owe this reference to Runia.

[44] Pohlenz, 'Philon,' 409–87; esp. 474. Pohlenz also observed that Philo does not use the term 'ecstasy' in *Cher.* 27, a fact that can be explained by his tendency to use ἔστασις with negative connotations; *ibid.* and 472–73. The same view is expressed by Völker, *Philo*, 288–89; and Bréhier, *Philon*, 197; but Bréhier was nevertheless willing to grant the authenticity of Philo's ecstatic experiences. See the critique of Pohlenz and Völker by Sowers, *Hermeneutics*, 42 n. 25. For discussion of the use of ἔστασις in Hellenic and Graeco-Roman times, see Dodds, *Greeks and the Irrational*, 77, 94–95 n. 84; and Dodds, *Age of Anxiety*, 71–72.

[45] See Pohlenz, 'Philon,' 441–44.

[46] See the comprehensive study of the topic by Segal, *Two Powers in Heaven*, 159–81, for a comparison of these two powers to Rabbinic traditions. Cf. also Hurtado, *One God, One Lord*, 146 n. 12; Barker, *Great Angel*, 114–33. For a general discussion of the two divine powers Goodness and Sovereignty in Philo, see Wolfson, *Philo*, 1.217–226; Pohlenz, 'Philon,' 441. For a discussion of how *Cher.* 27–28 reflects Philo's adoption of the Platonic theme of divine powers into his own thoughts, see Runia, *Philo and* Timaeus, 113, 134 .

his discussion of the divine powers and Logos elsewhere is precisely what one would expect and is no proof against the authenticity of Philo's experience.

More recently David Hay, without explicitly discounting the possibility of an authentic experience, nevertheless argued that ecstasy is subordinate to reasoned exegesis and that even here Philo's mode of exegesis is primarily a rationalistic and not an ecstatic one.[47] According to Hay, Philo fails in *Cher.* 27 to provide a 'phenomenological description of what it was like to hear the inner voice' and, in spite of the claim of inspiration, he seems to feel obligated to adduce exegetical arguments in support of his preferred interpretation.[48] If I understand Hay correctly, a surer sign of authentic ecstatic exegesis would have been a fuller description of the ecstatic experience accompanied by dogmatic assertion without elaboration. G. Scholem long ago showed that Jewish mysticism was distinguished from its Greek and Graeco-Roman counterparts precisely in its lack of detailed, blow-by-blow description of the experience itself. Jewish mystics tended to be much less descriptive and verbose about the experience itself and much more concerned with the result of that experience. In this regard Philo was not unlike his fellow Jewish mystics.[49]

These doubts notwithstanding, there is good reason to take Philo's statement at face value. In all these objections, a questionable dichotomy between ecstatic experience and exegesis seems to be operating. It has been assumed but never shown why *Cher.* 27–28 cannot be describing a first-hand ecstatic experience *and at the same time* solving an exegetical issue. If one is willing to entertain the possible coexistence of exegesis

---

[47] Hay, 'Philo as Exegete,' 40–52.

[48] Hay, 'Philo as Exegete,' 44 and n. 8. His general assessment of Philo's inspired experience is equally negative: citing *QG* 4.140 and Runia, *Philo and* Timaeus, 539–42, in support, he writes, 'Although Philo felt carried 'beyond himself' in his experiences of inspiration, he very often presents his biblical interpretations along with reasoning designed to substantiate them. He does not typically invite, let alone demand, that readers accept his views simply because they are his. True religion is not wholly within the grasp of human reason, but Philo's faith typically seeks rational understanding insofar as that is possible. Perhaps he did not claim definitive exegetical results because for him biblical exegesis was an ongoing process in which no mortal arrived at total comprehension' (49 and n. 23).

[49] Cf. Scholem, *Major Trends in Jewish Mysticism*, 15–16. This objection, similar to the one discussed above, is fundamental to any acceptance or rejection of any ecstatic or mystical experience. Such an experience is by definition otherworldly and is supra-rational. It is an experience beyond the limits of linguisticality; to describe it in ordinary human language is therefore a compromise at best and at worst a caricature. The rise of such otherworldly literary genera as apocalyptic or mystical literature is on one level the development of a language or syntax to convey such otherworldly experiences.

and ecstatic experience in Philo, then his introduction reads remarkably like an autobiographical description of an oft-experienced seizure by the divine (*Cher.* 27):[50]

> ἤκουσα δέ ποτε καὶ σπουδαιοτέρου λόγου παρὰ ψυχῆς ἐμῆς εἰωθυίας τὰ πολλὰ θεοληπτεῖσθαι καὶ περὶ ὧν οὐκ οἶδε μαντεύεσθαι· ὅν, ἐὰν δύνωμαι, ἀπομνημονεύσας ἐρῶ.

This statement, composed entirely in the first person, contains a number of words that look at first like technical terms of prophecy and divination but at closer examination turn out to be common, descriptive terms outlining an ecstatic experience that both Philo and his readers can easily share. θεοληπτεῖσθαι is a *hapax legomenon* in the extant Philonic corpus, but its basic meaning 'to be seized by the divine' is clear enough.[51] The adjective θεόληπτος is used in *Aet.* 76, probably connoting divine inspiration, but gives no indication that it is used in the technical sense of divination or prophecy.[52] μαντεύεσθαι was a standard term for divination and seemed predominantly used as such by classical writers.[53] In the extant corpus of Philo, however, none of the five uses of the terms outside the present passage (*Leg.* 3.227; *Conf.* 118; *Ios.* 106, 182; *Spec.* 3.18) has any connection to divination, prophecy, or oracle. All five have to do with a human subject trying to predict or anticipate the future with some type of premonition. Sometimes the premonition is validated,[54] sometimes it is proven wrong,[55] but in none of the passage

---

[50] So the judgment of Winston, *Philo*, 34, with whom Runia disagrees. Cf. also Sowers, *Hermeneutics*, 41.

[51] Liddell and Scott (*s.v.*) list *Cher.* 27 as the only occurrence for θεοληπτεῖσθαι.

[52] The passage in fact points in the opposite direction. Philo reports the Boethus of Sidon and Panaetius to have abandoned the Stoics doctrines of conflagrations and regenerations and adopted the more *religious teaching* (ὁσιώτερον δόγμα) of the world's indestructibility *under divine inspiration* (ἅτε θεόληπτοι). Without further elaboration, it would appear that the abandonment could have resulted from rational argument as much as from 'inspiration.' The term could therefore refer to some type of religious conversion in general, though the specific notion of divine inspiration cannot be discounted *a priori*.

[53] Liddell-Scott, *s.v.:* μαντεύεσθαι is obviously related to two older classical terms of divination and frenzy: μαίνεσθαι ('to be mad [of Bacchic frenzy],' 'to be driven mad [by the gods]') and μάντις ('diviner,' 'seer,' 'prophet'); see discussion of these two terms in Dodds, *Greeks and the Irrational*, 70 and 87 n. 37. Plato, as is well-known, in *Phaedrus* 244B–262D distinguishes four types of 'frenzy' or 'inspiration' (μανία): the Apollonian frenzy of divination, the Dionysian frenzy of purity, the poetic frenzy of the Muses, and the philosophical Eros. See discussion of Platonic frenzy in Dodds, *Greeks and the Irrational*, *passim* but esp. 64–65; and Linford, 'Corybantic Rites in Plato,' 163–72.

[54] Cf. *Conf.* 118: the arrogant builders of Babel unwittingly *foretell* their destruction and dispersal; *Ios.* 106: impressed by Joseph's show of wisdom, the Pharaoh *has an inkling* that his dream would be deciphered by Joseph; and *Ios.* 182: father Jacob *senses* calamities befalling his sons.

[55] Cf. *Leg.* 3.277: farmers bitterly disappointed in spite of what they *have expected* to harvest; *Spec.* 3.18: fratricidal kings *anticipate* their siblings' revolt and murder their own

is the word used in connection with the kind of technical divination as only a priest or prophet would attempt.[56] Given this general usage of Philo's, the weaker meaning of 'find out,' 'surmise,' or 'anticipate' would also be a part of the intended meaning in *Cher.* 27–28.

Accordingly, the statement that his soul can 'divine (in the non-technical sense) what it does not know' (περὶ ὧν οὐκ οἶδε μαντεύεσθαι) posits an epistemological gap between ecstatic knowledge and knowledge based on human linguisticality. Such a dichotomy between reasoned knowledge and revelation is reflected in Philo's depiction of Mosaic prophecy: it is through the providence of God that Moses discovered 'what by reasoning he could not grasp, for prophecy attains where the mind fails' (*Mos.* 2.6). But unlike Mosaic prophecy, the kind of inspiration described in *Cher.* 27–28 is not limited to the prophets but is available to every soul; it represents only a heightened form of ordinary knowledge. In other words, Philo in this passage is not assuming the role of an authoritative prophet who by dint of privileged insights or technical skills could uncover the meaning of a text otherwise inaccessible to others. Rather, Philo uses terms that ordinary readers could have used and thereby implies that his experience is equally accessible to all.

The clear distinction between conditions *prior to* divine inspiration and conditions *after* points to two different altered states of consciousness. Philo insists that he could only *attempt to remember* what he has learned (ὅν [*sc.* 'the higher thought'] ἐὰν δύνωμαι, ἀπομνημονεύσας ἐρῶ). It is possible, perhaps even necessary, to communicate what is learned under inspiration after the event, albeit with difficulties. Two of the three uses of the verb ἀπομνημονεύειν elsewhere carry the sense of remembrance in the aftermath of an altered state of consciousness and it connotes the same here. In *Ebr.* 173, while discussing the mind's reception of impressions that originate from external objects, Philo speaks of the profusion of colors emanating from the dove's neck causing the mind 'not to remember' temporarily the names of different colors (ὧν οὐδὲ τὰς κλήσεις ῥᾴδιον ἀπομνημονεῦσαι). In *Spec.* 1.98–99 Philo contrasts the ability 'to remember' things past to the state of forgetfulness (λήθη) that is the result of drunkenness. This latter contrast recalls Philo's famous phrase 'sober drunkenness' (μέθη νηφάλιος) whose oxymoronic strength is derived from the sharp contrast between drunkenness induced by wine and frenzy produced by the indwelling spirit.[57]

---

brothers.

[56] For Philo's view on prophecy, esp. the Mosaic prophecy, see Wolfson, *Philo*, 2.3–72.

[57] The other usage of the verb in *Flacc.* 146 is general; see also Plato, *Phdr.* 228A. For the

Ecstatic experience can be expressed and its articulation may conform to a prior, acceptable doctrine of God, since Philo does manage to present a coherent picture of the two divine powers and Logos immediately after *Cher.* 27–28. His statement, 'God is indeed one, but his highest and foremost powers are two, Goodness and Authority,' is intended not as a justification for his exegesis,[58] but as a further description of his vision. It is indeed by means of Logos that God is both sovereign and good. But once Logos is recognized and the new understanding grasped, the differentiation between the two powers melts away, the divine powers dissolve into each other, and the mind is left with a vision of God who appears *at once* royal and beneficent (*Cher.* 29):

> Receive, O my mind, the unadulterated impression of each of the cherubim, so that having been instructed clearly regarding the Sovereign and Goodness of the Cause you may reap the fruits[59] of a happy lot. For you will know immediately the union and commingling of the unmixed powers: God is good when Sovereignty is revealed and God is sovereign when Goodness is revealed.

Logos seems to have disappeared in this passage. Or has it? Logos plays the mediating role between the two powers ('for it is through Logos that God is both sovereign and good;' *Cher.* 27); once that role is fulfilled, there is no longer any need to refer to Logos explicitly.[60] It is by means of appreciating the centrality of Logos that the soul integrates the vision of the multiple powers and sees the kingly manifestation through the beneficent and the beneficent manifestation through the kingly. The vision has not revealed what is beyond the powers; what the soul sees in this context is not so much God as Logos.[61] When Logos does reappear in the subsequent interpretation of Abraham, it becomes the tool which Abraham 'the wise' used 'to divide and to burn away the mortal from himself, that he might fly high up to God with his mind stripped naked' (*Cher.* 31).[62]

---

phrase 'sober drunkenness,' see esp. *Ebr.* 145–46; *Fug.* 166; *Leg.* 1.82–83; *Prob.* 12–13; *Leg.* 3.82; *Opif.* 70; *Fug.* 31; *Mos.* 1.187; *Contempl.* 89; and detailed discussion of these passages by Lewy, *Sobria Ebrietas*, *passim* but esp. 3–41.

[58] *Pace* Hay, 'Philo as Exegete,' 44 and n. 8.

[59] The literal seems to be the best translation of καρποῦσθαι, though in *Spec.* 3.1 I have rendered it 'enjoy.'

[60] Another way to conceptualize what I call here the 'mediating role' of Logos is to see it as the sum total of all powers; cf. Segal, *Two Powers in Heaven*, 169, 175, 177.

[61] Cf. also *Conf.* 95–96, where Philo goes to great lengths to demonstrate that what Moses saw in Exod 24:10–11 was not God himself but only Logos. What enables Philo to make this distinction is the text of the LXX εἶδον τὸν <u>τόπον</u> οὗ εἱστήκει ὁ θεὸς τοῦ Ἰσραήλ. See the discussion of *Conf.* 95–96 in Segal, *Two Powers in Heaven*, 167–68, and his discussion of τόπος and its relation to the rabbinic interpretation of מקום on pp. 161–62. Cf. *Abr.* 121–22; below.

[62] I.e., Abraham's 'fire and knife' in the sacrifice of Isaac (Gen 22:6) allegorized as a

This reading of *Cher.* 27–29 can be corroborated by the different stages of the soul's ascent to God delineated in *Abr.* 119–22. In the course of allegorizing Abraham's three visitors (Gen 18:2) as multiple manifestations of God (*Abr.* 107–30), Philo writes that only a mind illumined by the light of God could have access to the symbolic significance of the text (*Abr.* 119):[63]

> Spoken words are symbols of things apprehended *by the mind only*. When the soul, as if under the noonday sun of God, is completely bathed in light and, having been utterly filled with noetic light, it becomes unshaded by the outpouring beams all around, it grasps a triple vision of an underlying unity: one as the Being, the other two as shadows beaming forth from it.

The language here is less explicitly ecstatic and the passage does not purport to be autobiographical, but it is no less clear that here as in *Cher.* 27–29 understanding takes place at the point where God meets the mind and grants it a privileged vision. This vision itself, Philo goes on to tell us, discloses an appearance sometimes of *three*, sometimes *one*, depending on the stage of ascent that the mind has achieved (*Abr.* 121–22):

> But as someone standing nearest to the truth[64] would say that the central one is the Father of all..., while the two on either side are the powers most senior and nearest to the Being, the *creative* and the *regal*... Being flanked, then, by each of his two powers, the central being appears to the visionary mind (τῇ ὁρατικῇ διανοίᾳ) as an image sometimes of one and sometimes of three: *of one*—when, purified, it scales the greatest height and, transcending not only the multitude of numbers but also the dyad, that neighbor to the monad, it presses on to the idea which is unmixed and untangled and in need of nothing else whatsoever by itself; *of three*—when, not yet initiated into the great mysteries, it still celebrates but the minor rites and cannot grasp the Being by itself alone apart from all else except through its activities, either creating or ruling .

A discussion of what the 'great mysteries' are would take us too far afield,[65] but it should be clear that the two visions detailed here, the lower and the higher, are identical to the vision complex of *Cher.* 27–28. According to this schema, the mind progresses from an apprehension of God's nature through his multiple manifestations to an apprehension of his unity. In the lower vision, the mind grasps God only by means of his functionalities and potencies, while the higher vision affords the

---

copy of the 'flaming sword.' Segal, *Two Powers in Heaven*, 171, comments on *Migr.* 173: 'There can be no doubt that Philo meant to say that rare men of uncommon abilities can share in God's immutability by being summoned into or guided into His presence by means of the *logos*.'

[63] See also *Her.* 264–65, in which ἔκστασις is said to take place when the 'noon day sun' pours into the whole soul.

[64] ὡς ἄν τις ἐγγύτατα τῆς ἀληθείας ἱστάμενος. Does it reflect mystical experience?

[65] A full discussion of this can be found in Goodenough, *By Light, Light*, 95–120, 235–64.

seer a vision of the true nature of God, which is unitary.[66] Philo's experience, like all mystical experiences, can never be fully authenticated by any historical criterion. On the other hand, if Philo's words are taken seriously without *a priori* biases, they disclose a vision that coheres remarkably well with his view of the soul's mystical ascent. Unless one is ready to argue for either deception or self-delusion, one would have to admit of authenticity.[67]

The result of Philo's experience is the specific exegesis of a text. The second half of Philo's statement in *Cher.* 27–28, which identifies the cherubim as symbols of the two powers, is syntactically dependent on the main verb ἐρῶ and is therefore properly a part of the revelation received by the soul. Unlike the detailed, lemma-by-lemma method of the *pesharim*, the scope of Philo's revelatory exegesis is strictly limited to the identities of the cherubim as the powers of God and the flaming sword as Logos. In this respect Philo's hermeneutical method resembles that of the Zealots, according to which the text is made intelligible first by a single point of identification—obtained through divine inspiration—that equates the oracular text to a messianic figure. This identification then provides coherence and substance for the interpretation of the remainder of the text.[68] In similar fashion, the procedure in *Cher.* 27–28 takes Philo first to an identification between the cherubim and the powers of God, an identification disclosed to him by the spirit. Out of this single point of comparison, the rest of biblical text is then exegeted by its own rule of coherence and its moral lessons are drawn as a consequence.

This type of charismatic exegesis as exemplified in *Cher.* 27–28 is unique among the passages surveyed in this study and is the only such instance in the extant corpus of Philo. But two considerations lead one

---

66 Thus also *Mut.* 15–23, where the phrase ὤφθη κύριος τῷ Ἀβραάμ (Gen 17:1) triggers a long discourse on the meanings of the different divine names. Philo makes a distinction among the three different divine manifestations of 'Lord,' 'God,' and 'Lord God.' To the foolish Pharaoh 'Lord' makes his appearance. To those who are on the way to betterment are applied the words 'I am thy God.' But it is to the perfect, that is to say to *Israel* at the giving of the decalogue (Exod 20:2) and to Jacob when his name is changed to *Israel* (Deut 4:1), does the Existent One appear as 'Lord God;' see the more detailed discussion of this passage in Segal, *Two Powers in Heaven*, 177–78. 'Israel' is, of course, etymologized as 'the visionary nation or kind' (τὸ ὁρατικὸν γένος); for discussion of the range of meanings for 'Israel' in the writings of Philo, see Birnbaum, 'Israel the Nation that Sees God.' See the summary discussion of the different stages of the soul's ascent by Hay, 'Psychology of Faith,' 902–907; and the discussion of the two stages of the mind's understanding in Wolfson, *Philo*, 2.26–27; Goodenough, *By Light, Light*, 95–97.

67 This is the conclusion reached, albeit via a different route, by Winston, 'Was Philo a Mystic?,' 15–41.

68 See Hengel, *Zeloten*, 242–46, and nn. 5–8 above.

to suspect that the practice is probably more common than is explicitly documented. First, in the only two passages in which the contents of the ecstatic experience are disclosed, *Somn.* 2.250–54 and in *Cher.* 27–28, Philo recounts the same vision, namely the powers of God and, through the powers, the unitary Being standing behind them. Second, the close correspondence between the visions of *Abr.* 119–22 and *Cher.* 27–28 raises the distinct possibility that Philo has identified himself with the biblical character of Abraham, whose visionary experience has become Philo's own and *vice versa*.[69] Even though *Abr.* 119–22 does not purport to be autobiographical, the exegesis contained therein may nevertheless be a product of an ecstatic vision.

Ecstatic Experience of Paul: 2 Corinthians 3:1–4:6

The polemical background of 2 Cor 3:1–4.6 can no longer be determined with certainty.[70] The following three points, however, can be demonstrated without depending on any one particular hypothesis. First, this is, among other things, an exegetical debate. Either Paul or his opponents attempted to persuade the Corinthians by means of an exegesis of Exodus 34, in particular vv. 29–35, where Moses returns to the Israelites after his ascension to Mt. Sinai and the reception of the Law from God. This Paul deals with directly in 2 Cor 3:7–18, though the references to stone tablets (3:3) and covenants (3:4–6) are obvious allusions to Exod 34:1, 4, 10–28.

Second, Paul's attitude towards Moses is uncharacteristically positive in 2 Cor 3:7–18. In view of the usual polemics against the law and Moses, it is surprising that this section begins with a statement that the old Mosaic covenant came about in glory. Paul grants that Moses himself so reflected the glory of God as a result of his ascension that the Israelites could not gaze directly into his face (v. 7). Presupposed in Paul's retelling of the Exodus story is most likely a Hellenistic-Jewish tradition according to which an encounter with the divine would result in a transformation of the seer. The same tradition is also reflected in Paul application of it to the believer's own experience in v. 18.[71] Granted, the purpose of v. 7 is polemical, as is clear in the immediately

---

[69] I owe this point to David Runia.

[70] Cf., e.g., Windisch, *2. Kor.*, 23–26; Schulz, 'Decke des Moses,' 1–30; Georgi, *Opponents*; Van Unnik, '"With Unveiled Faces,"' 153–69; Collange, *Enigmes, passim*; Bultmann, *2. Kor.*, 74–112; Theissen, *Psychological Aspects*, 117–75; Murphy-O'Connor, '*Pneumatikoi* and Judaizers,' 42–58; Segal, *Two Powers in Heaven*, 151–56; Belleville, *Reflections of Glory*, 211–16; Newman, *Paul's Glory-Christology*, 229–35.

[71] Cf. Segal, *Paul the Convert*, 60–61 for discussion of 2 Cor 3:7, 18. See further discussion under Point Three below.

following verse; Moses is propped up only to be crushed. If the covenant of Moses, etched in stone, came in glory, Paul argues, how much more (πῶς οὐχι μᾶλλον) glorious will be the covenant of the Spirit (v. 8). In the polemical syntax of Spirit *versus* letter and life *versus* death established in v. 6, Paul's concession to Moses' glory then becomes an absolute contrast between Spirit and death. This contrast Paul makes explicit by identifying the Mosaic covenant as a 'covenant of death' (v. 7a). But the polemical edge here should not detract from Paul's positive evaluation of Moses. The logic of the *a fortiori* argument of vv. 7–8 depends on *both* the assumed superiority of the new covenant of the Spirit *and* the assumed soundness of the Mosaic covenant. Paul must have thought that his interlocutors were convinced of both points before he adopted this type of argument.[72] Moreover, Murphy–O'Connor and others have noted the similarities of Paul's presentation of Moses in 2 Cor 3:7 to the Philonic Moses.[73] In particular, the inability of the Israelites to gaze into Moses' glorious countenance is paralleled only in Philo:[74]

> Ascending at divine commands a mountain—the highest and holiest in the surrounding area—that was inaccessible and pathless, [Moses] is said to have remained for the said period of time, while taking nothing that would provide the need for nourishment. After forty days, it is said, he descended with a far more goodly countenance than before he ascended, so much so that those who saw him were awestruck and astounded and their eyes were unable to withstand for long because beams radiated forth like sunlight.

Whether this position was espoused by Paul's opponents,[75] the *Pneumatikoi* of 1 Corinthians,[76] or the pre–conversion Paul,[77] is not crucial for

---

[72] Collange, *Enigmes*, 75, suggests that Paul's opponents might have been influenced by a kind of Moses-mysticism.

[73] Murphy-O'Connor, '*Pneumatikoi* and Judaizers,' 51. The similarity of 2 Cor 3:1–4:6 to Philonic language has long been observed by scholars. See Murphy-O'Connor's summary of issues on pp. 53–54.

[74] For comparison of Moses to Orpheus and Hermes-Tat, see Goodenough, *By Light, Light*, 6–7; for use of Moses as a 'divine man' category, see Holladay, *Theios Aner*, 103–98; Meeks, *Prophet-King*, 103–107 (on Philo's presentation of Moses) and 137–42 (Josephus).

[75] So Schulz, 'Decke des Moses,' *passim*, who is followed with minor variations by Georgi. Appealing to Philo, *Mos.* 2.69–70, Georgi, *Opponents*, 254–58, argues that the opponents represented Moses as a 'divine man' (θεῖος ἀνήρ), according to whose superhuman strengths followers can themselves realize the divine.

[76] Murphy-O'Connor, '*Pneumatikoi* and Judaizers,' 50. These *Pneumatikoi*, according to Murphy-O'Connor, are to be identified with the Apollo-faction of 1 Cor 1:12 and the 'mature' throughout 1 Corinthians; they were seduced by a group of outsiders, Judaizers, who advocated the strict observance of the Law. 'Paul's intention is to wean [the *Pneumatikoi*] away from the intruders [*sc.* the Judaizers] by offering a critique of the Moses dispensation in terms to which they would be particularly sensitive, while at the same time presenting the Christian dispensation in a light that would appeal to their

my thesis. More important is the observation that Paul was familiar with the mystical Mosaic tradition in Hellenistic Judaism and used it here with some degree of approval.

Third, Paul here makes reference to his own conversion experience and that of his fellow believers (3:16–18; 4:6). It has been generally recognized that 4:6, 'For it is God who said, "Let light shine out of darkness," who has shone in our hearts to give the light of the knowledge of the glory of God in the face of Christ,' contains a reference to Paul's own conversion experience in the manner of Gal 1:16.[78] The consequence of his conversion, as Segal recently argued, is 'his identification of Jesus as the image and Glory of God, as the human figure in heaven, and thereafter as Christ, son, and savior.'[79] In 3:16–18, with the inclusive ἡμεῖς πάντες (v. 18), Paul uses himself as model for direct experience of the Glory of God, which is open to all believers (v. 16–17).[80] The result of the encounter is transformation: ἡμεῖς δὲ πάντες ἀνακεκαλυμμένῳ προσώπῳ τὴν δόξαν κυρίου κατοπτριζόμενοι τὴν αὐτὴν εἰκόνα μεταμορφούμεθα ἀπὸ δόξης εἰς δόξαν καθάπερ ἀπὸ κυρίου πνεύματος (v. 18).[81] There has been a great deal of discussion on the meaning of the rare word κατοπτρίζεσθαι

---

religious sensitivity' (*ibid.*). Murphy-O'Connor takes the preponderance of Philonic language as indication that Paul intends to seduce the *Pneumatikoi* (the Apollo-faction) away from Judaizers from the outside. One, however, can readily appreciate the affinity of Paul's language here to Philonic thought forms without making recourse to Murphy-O'Connor's rather complicated two-opponent hypothesis. See summary of issues in Belleville, *Reflections of Glory*, 31–35.

77 Theissen, *Psychological Aspects*, 137: 'What Paul says in general about the Jews logically include the Jew Paul and is based psychologically on his experience. Paul treats in this text in a generalized manner his own deception by the radiance of Moses. He himself once sought true knowledge of God from Moses. In this he knew himself to be superior to other erring men. He understood himself as a 'light to those who are in darkness' (Rom 2:19) and saw in Moses the 'embodiment of knowledge and truth' (Rom 2:20). But Christ took the place of Moses. In the light of the revelation of Christ, Paul radically reassessed Moses. The veil, once for him an indication of Moses' immediate service of God which surpassed all others, became for him a symbol of deceit and deception. Paul is correcting his own pre-Christian picture of Moses—not that of his foes.' It seems to me difficult to accept Theissen's theory at face value. Paul has never given any indication that his pre-conversion adherence to Judaism was connected to a mystical Moses; cf. Gal 1:13–14; Phil 3:4–6; etc.

78 So, e.g., Bultmann, *2. Kor.*, 111; Kim, *Origin*, 11–13; Segal, *Paul the Convert*, 61. Bultmann's claim that Paul's citation of Gen 1:3 in 2 Cor 4:6 as πρὸς φωτισμὸν τῆς γνώσεως τῆς δόξης and not simply πρὸς φωτισμὸν τῆς δόξης reflects gnostic language is not convincing to me.

79 Segal, *Paul the Convert*, 61.

80 For the inclusive nature of v. 16, see discussion below.

81 Segal, *Paul the Convert*, 60–61, argues for the ecstatic experience of Paul and his fellow-believers on the basis of the transformative language of 3:18 and Paul's identification of 'Glory of God' as Christ (3:18; 4:6)

in the middle or passive. The word, from κάτοπτρον ('mirror'), is a *hapax legomenon* in the New Testament and appears only once in the extant corpus of Philo (*Leg.* 3.101). It means, in the active, 'to look into the mirror;' in the middle, 'to be mirrored' or 'to behold oneself in the mirror;' and in the passive, 'to be mirrored.'[82] Without attempting to solve this long–standing conundrum,[83] I would simply suggest that the accent of v. 18 lies with the phrase, μεταμορφούμεθα ἀπὸ δόξης εἰς δόξαν ('we are transformed from glory to glory').[84] The background of this language is clearly the Hellenistic–Jewish notion that a vision of the divine is reflected in the progressive transformation of the seer.[85] Believers who turn to the Lord the Spirit (vv. 16–17) with an uncovered face will ascend the ladder of glory and be transformed in the process. This is in stark contrast to Moses, whose veil concealed a fading glory (vv. 7, 13). Not only could believers experience the very vision of God that Moses had on Mt. Sinai; they, in fact, could surpass Moses in acquiring the glory that endures. The underlying motive of 2 Cor 3:16–18, like that of Gal 3:2–5, is polemical: over against a position that elevates the status of Moses, Paul seeks to strengthen the apostolic bond between himself and the believers by appealing to the shared common experience of the eschatological Spirit.

Regarding the second and third points above, Paul and Philo could agree for the most part—with one important exception. The mystical interpretation of Moses's ascent can be richly documented in Philo and reference to his own ecstatic experience is also a familiar appeal in Philo.[86] Philo would have been scandalized by the identification of the Glory of God with a historical person, Jesus, but the Philonic Logos that appears to him in his ecstatic vision (e.g., *Cher.* 27–31) is at least a

---

82 See Liddell-Scott, *s.v.* Cf. the usage of the middle in Zeno 1.66; Sextus Empiricus Πυρρώνειοι ὑποτυπώσεις 1.48; Ath. 15.687C.

83 For a summary of issues, see Belleville, *Reflections of Glory*, 278–83; Bultmann, *2. Kor.*, 93–97; Kittel, 'ἔσοπτρον,' 696–97. Segal suggests that the background of the word should perhaps be sought in the use of magical mirrors; Segal, *Paul the Convert*, 323–24 n. 94.

84 Blass, Debrunner, and Funk, *Greek Grammar of the New Testament*, 87: §159 (4), suggest that τὴν αὐτὴν εἰκόνα be taken as a 'loose accusative' of μεταμορφούμεθα, a suggestion that most commentators follow. I have my doubts, however. Elsewhere in the NT, the use of the passive is found in Matt 17:2 (καὶ μετεμορφώθη ἔμπροσθεν αὐτῶν, καὶ ἔλαμψεν τὸ πρόσωπον αὐτοῦ ὡς ὁ ἥλιος, τὰ δὲ ἱμάτια αὐτοῦ ἐγένετο λευκὰ ὡς τὸ φῶς.) and Rom 12:2 (ἀλλὰ μεταμορφοῦσθε τῇ ἀνακαινώσει τοῦ νοός).

85 Cf. Behm, 'μεταμορφόω, κτλ,' 758–59: 'Paul obviously shares formally the ideas of Hellenistic mysticism in respect of transformation by vision, transformation into the seen image of God, and transformation as a process which is progressively worked out for the righteous.' This perhaps should suggest that 'reflect' might be a better translation of the middle κατοπτρίζεσθαι, in spite of the admittedly scanty linguistic evidence.

86 Note, e.g., the language of 'thousand times' (*Migr.* 34), 'ofttimes' (*Cher.* 27).

functional equivalent. There is material but not structural difference between the thoughts of Philo and Paul. For both, ecstatic experience is not limited to an authoritative figure, be it an interpreter of the sacred text or an apostle, but is accessible to all. Behind both is a didactic intention that goes beyond merely describing the vision at hand. In short, both the material (the mystical Moses tradition) and the method of appropriation (primary ecstatic inspiration) were available to Paul and Philo and were used by both. The major difference between them, however, is Paul's claim that the believer's immediate experience is superior to that of Moses. How does Paul make this final leap? Paul accomplishes this by simultaneously focusing on the veil and on the abolition of the old glory by Christ. Both lines of thought converge in the climactic citation of Exod 34:34 in v. 16.

The fading glory on Moses' face is already adumbrated in 3:7–11, where the superiority of the new covenant to the old is set forth in an uncompromising antithetical relationship. Using the Rabbinic method of קל וחומר (*qal wa–homer; πολλῷ μᾶλλον vel sim.*), Paul derives three pairs of contrast between the old and the new covenants:

vv. 7–8:	Ministry of death	Ministry of the Spirit
v. 9:	Ministry of Condemnation	Ministry of Righteousness
v.11:	That which is being abolished	That which remains

These three points Paul assumes to be incontrovertible, since he does not spend time arguing their validity.[87] Paul, in fact, begins the next verse confidently with ἔχοντες οὖν τοιαύτην ἐλπίδα πολλῇ παρρησίᾳ, thus devoting his next effort to drawing out the implications of these contrasts.

With these general premises in place, Paul can now zero in on the abolition of not just the old covenant but specifically of Moses himself. This Paul accomplishes by moving the thought of vv. 12–16 progressively inwards: that is, from the face of Moses (v. 13) to the minds of Jews (v. 14) and finally to their hearts (v. 15). In each of these three steps the veil is the focal point. Moses's face is *veiled* so that its fading glory might be hidden from the gazing eyes of the Israelites (v. 13).[88] The 'same *veil*' is over 'the reading of the old covenant' among the Jewish contemporaries of Paul, a phenomenon Paul equates to hardness of mind (v. 14). And a *veil* still covers the heart when Moses is read (v. 15).

---

87 See also Windisch, *2. Kor.*, 112–13.

88 The motif of deception has been emphasized by Theissen, *Psychological Aspects*, 121. Πρὸς τὸ μὴ ἀτενίσαι τοὺς υἱοὺς Ἰσραὴλ εἰς τὸ τέλος τοῦ καταργουμένου is best taken as a purpose clause.

Just like the triple contrasts of vv. 7–11, corresponding to each instance of veiledness is its abolition:

Moses laid a *veil* over his face (13a)...	in order to hide its *abolition*[89] (13b).
The *veil* remains on the minds (14a).	It is *abolished* in Christ (14b).
The *veil* is laid on the hearts (15).	It is *taken away* by the Lord (16).

Whatever might have been said about the origin of the veil—be it raised by the opponents,[90] a part of the Jewish rites,[91] or Paul's own innovation[92]—it should be clear that Paul consistently interprets the removal of the veil as superior to keeping it on. The veil serves two negative functions in Paul's retelling of the Exodus story:[93] (a) It shields the appearance of Glory on Moses' face from the people (v. 12), so that the Israelites could not witness the fading of Glory (v. 13) and they could not (v. 14), and still cannot (v. 15), come to Moses directly. (b) The veil also keeps one from facing the Lord directly, so that Moses himself had to take off the veil whenever he came into the presence of the Lord. The implied charge against Paul that his gospel is veiled (2 Cor 4:3) could appear at first puzzling. But it is clearly not Paul's self–understanding that his gospel is veiled in any way; it is only veiled to those perishing who have been blinded by the god of this age (4:4; cf. 2:14–17). By contrast, Paul characterizes his basic attitude as one of 'confidence' (v. 4), 'hope' and 'boldness'[94] (v. 12), and not like the deceptive hiddenness of Moses (v. 13).

Paul collapses these two functions of the veil into one in the climactic citation of Exod 34:34 and in the process removes Moses from the scene (3:16). The following synopsis compares the original LXX text to Paul's adaptation:

---

[89] Grammatically τοῦ καταργουμένου can refer either to κάλυμμα or πρόσωπον. Logically, however, it can only refer to the former.

[90] So, e.g., Georgi, *Opponents*, 261.

[91] So, e.g., Segal, *Paul the Convert*, 152–55.

[92] So, e.g., Theissen, *Psychological Aspects*, 137.

[93] I am consciously circumventing the question how Paul's *opponents* understood the meaning of the veil. This issue has been advanced by Georgi, *Opponents*, 261–64, and need not detour the present discussion. The implied charge of the veil of Paul's gospel by the opponents in 4:3 is also extraneous to the present discussion. Whether a certain 'veil' was imposed upon Paul's gospel by Paul himself or by his opponents does not weaken Paul's argument that *he* considered his gospel open to all but those blinded by the 'god of this age' (4:4). The series of contrasts between the veiledness of his opponents' point of view and the open character of his proclamation (3:4, πεποίθησιν δὲ τοιαύτην ἔχομεν; 3:12, πολλῇ παρρησίᾳ; 4:2, τῇ φανερώσει τῆς ἀληθείας συνιστάνοντες) also point to the same concern.

[94] See Marrow, '*Parrhesia*,' 431–46, for discussion of παρρησία.

LXX Exod 34:34	*2 Cor 3:16*
ἡνίκα δ' ἂν εἰσεπορεύετο Μωυσῆς	ἡνίκα δὲ ἐὰν ἐπιστρέψῃ
ἔναντι κυρίου λαλεῖν αὐτῷ,	πρὸς κύριον,
περιῃρεῖτο τὸ κάλυμμα	περιαιρεῖται τὸ κάλυμμα.
ἕως τοῦ ἐκπορεύεσθαι.	

Three immediate effects are evident: (a) By removing references to specific actions of Moses, λαλεῖν αὐτῷ ('to speak with him') and ἕως τοῦ ἐκπορεύεσθαι ('until he went out'), Paul turns the biblical text into a general statement about encountering the Lord. The change from the more general εἰσπορεύεσθαι to the pregnant ἐπιστρέφειν further underlines Paul's concern to shift the focus to Christian conversion or ecstatic experience. (b) It is the believer, not Moses, that turns to the Lord. This Paul accomplishes by removing 'Moses' from the citation. (c) Once Moses is removed, it is then the Lord, not Moses, that removes the veil. Paul turns the main verb from an imperfect (περιῃρεῖτο) into a present (περιαιρεῖται). Without 'Moses,' the subject of the second part of the sentence becomes τὸ κάλυμμα, thus requiring the verb to be a passive rather than a middle. The veil is therefore removed, namely by the 'Lord,' and Paul makes explicit the agent of removal by identifying κύριος with the eschatological Spirit in v. 17. Paul's adaptation of the Exodus story can be visualized in the following three stages of development:

Exod 34:29–33:	Israelites ⇒ veil ⇒ Moses ⇒ veil ⇒ Lord
Exod 34:34:	Moses ⇒ Lord (veil removed)
2 Cor 3:16:	Believers ⇒ Lord (veil removed)

Thus, the veil is identified with Moses and *both* are removed whenever the believer turns to the Lord. What enables Paul to state with confidence that the believers could remove their veil is most likely his own conversion, which he with open face experienced as a direct vision of the risen Christ (cf. 4:6), just like the one which Moses experienced in his encounter with God. What this implies is that the removal of the veil is not a precondition for turning to the Lord, as if by an act of the will one could contemplate the Lord. Instead, the passive construction of v. 16 (the same passive construction is found in v. 15) means that turning to the Lord is constitutive of the veil's removal. Turning to the Lord means removing the veil and removing of the veil means turning to the Lord. The two acts of turning and removing are complementary halves of the same act.

If this reading of v. 16 is correct, then the preceding verses leading up to it, and in particular v. 15, must be interpreted in light of it. As part of the third contrast between veiledness and its abolition in vv. 12–16, v.

15, 'until today whenever Moses is read, a veil is placed upon their heart,' is a structural antithesis of v. 16 and is formally identical to it. Since v. 16 is an adaptation of the biblical text and is therefore determined by it, v. 15 must have been composed with v. 16 in mind. The parallelism between these two verses cannot be accidental:

2 Cor 3:15	*2 Cor 3:16*
ἡνίκα ἂν ἀναγινώσκηται Μωϋσῆς,	ἡνίκα δὲ ἐὰν ἐπιστρέψῃ πρὸς κύριον
κάλυμμα ἐπὶ τὴν καρδίαν αὐτῶν κεῖται.	περιαιρεῖται τὸ κάλυμμα.

If, as established earlier, the 'veil' of v. 16 is short for *veil and Moses* and both must needs be removed, the 'veil' of v. 15 must also have same meaning. But to do so is to run immediately into the paradox of removing the veil and Moses whenever *Moses* is read!

There is no contradiction, however. The 'Moses' removed in v. 16 is of course the believer's identification in terms of the mysticism of Moses. Since the believer can now have direct access to the Lord, according to Paul, Moses or the mystical tradition bound up in him is relativized. The believer has a glory surpassing even that of Moses. By the same token, whenever 'Moses' is read, that is to say whenever the written text of Moses is read, the authority of its author has already lost its absolute binding power. Paul clearly does not deny the authorship of Moses or obviate the importance of reading the Mosaic law. He is, however, proposing that the believer, equipped with a new, direct encounter with the Lord, the eschatological Spirit, is in a better position to understand the profound meaning of the Mosaic text better than Moses himself. This ought not be surprising, since we have already seen in the writings of the Essenes, who claim a privileged understanding of prophecy denied even to the prophet himself. Unless the veil–Moses is removed when one approaches Scripture, the reading of it will take place only within the context of the old covenant. What Paul is arguing in vv. 15–16 is that one must read Scripture in light of one's mystical experience.

Conclusion

In a recent study comparing the allegorical interpretations of Philo and the second-century Gnostic Valentinus, David Dawson makes the point that while Philo is squarely based on the written text of Scripture, Valentinus appeals to his mystical experience as the fundamental locus of authority.[95] Valentinus's claim, 'like any spiritual or mystical claim,

[95] Dawson, *Allegorical Readers*, *passim* but esp. 11–12, 18–19, 166–67, 238–39. The book also includes a study of Clement. [See further the review elsewhere in this volume. EDITOR]

lies beyond the grasp of literary analysis, deep within autobiographical experience, and depends on that personal experience for its final authority.'[96] If so, Philo's alleged basis on written authority and his main concern for allegorical interpretation (or in the words of Dawson, 'reinscripturation of reality') are complicated by his ecstatic experiences.[97] Philo mentions these experiences only occasionally, as we have seen, but when he does they tend to exert some effect on his reading of Scripture. In theory, therefore, if not in practice, these two different forms of appeal, the mystical and the textual, constitute two loci of authority. There is no evidence in Philo's writings that these two loci were in tension with each other, since Philo's visions of the divine powers turn out to be identical to his allegorical discussions of them. That his theory and praxis might have influenced each other does not militate against this observation, since there is a larger pattern of coherence to his overall allegorical interpretation. The case with Paul, however, is drastically different. Like Philo and the Zealots, Paul insists on reading Scripture in light of his own mystic vision of the resurrected Lord. But this position immediately brings him into conflict with his fellow missionaries, who presumably want to read the Mosaic texts in a different, more Jewish manner. The tension between the mystical and textual authorities is thus concretized and enacted by the two polemical factions. In both Philo and Paul, there is a formal adherence to the canonical authority of scripture, but it is constantly threatened to be undermined by their personal experiences.

The conflict between these two types of authority is ultimately resolved by institutional control. The interpretive strategy adopted by the Essenes resolves this tension by formalizing charismatic exegesis. By insisting that every lemma in the prophetic text must be interpreted in light of inspiration, the Teacher of Righteousness maintains a one-to-one correspondence between mystical and textual authorities. Later Pauline communities likewise restrict the reception of spiritual χαρίσματα to only a few (1 Tim 4:14), which have been freely bestowed during Paul's days (1 Corinthians 12–14). Charismatic exegesis at its most complete development merges these two approaches, so that the mystical experience flows out of the reading of the text and textual interpretation reflects one's mysticism.

Jerusalem

---

96 *Ibid.*, 167.

97 Dawson does recognize that while Philo and Valentinus each maintained their own hermeneutical strategies, they are also known to trespass each other's territory. Philo had his ecstatic and mystical experiences from which he drew his inspiration and Valentinus could present his mystical visions as written texts (*ibid.*, 18–19).

Works Consulted

AUNE, David. *Prophecy in Early Christianity and the Ancient Mediterranean World* (Grand Rapids 1983).
BARKER, M. *The Great Angel: A Study of Israel's Second God* (Louisville 1992).
BEHM, J. 'μεταμορφόω, κτλ,' *TDNT* 4 (1942 [1967]) 758–59.
BELLEVILLE, Linda. *Reflections of Glory: Paul's Polemical Use of the Moses–Doxa Tradition in 2 Corinthians 3:1–18*, JSNTS 42 (Sheffield 1991).
BIEDER, W. 'Πνεῦμα, κτλ.' *TDNT* 6 (1959) 374–75.
BIRNBAUM, Ellen. 'Israel the Nation that Sees God' (Ph. D., Columbia University, 1992).
BLASS, F., A. Debrunner, and Robert Funk. *A Greek Grammar of the New Testament and Other Early Christian Literature,* Tr. by R. Funk (Chicago 1961).
BLENKINSOPP, J. 'The Oracle of Judah and the Messianic Entry,' *JBL* 80 (1961) 55–64.
BRÉHIER, Émile. *Les idées philosophiques et religieuses de Philon d'Alexandrie* (Paris 1925).
BULTMANN, Rudolf. *Der zweite Brief an die Korinther*, Kritisch–exegetischer Kommentar über das Neue Testament (Göttingen 1976).
COLLANGE, J.–F. *Enigmes de la deuxième epître de Paul aux Corinthiens: Étude exégètique de 2 Cor. 2.14–7.4*, SNTSMS 18 (Cambridge 1972).
DAWSON, David. *Allegorical Readers and Cultural Revision in Ancient Alexandria* (Berkeley 1992).
DODDS, E. R. *The Greeks and the Irrational* (Berkeley 1951).
—, *Pagan and Christian in an Age of Anxiety* (New York 1965).
ELIADE, Mircea. *Shamanism: Archaic Techniques of Ecstasy,* Tr. by W. R. Trask (London 1964).
ELLINGER, K. *Studien sum Habakuk–Kommentar vom Toten Meer* (Tübingen 1953).
ELLIS, E. Earle. *Paul's Use of the Old Testament* (Grand Rapids 1957).
—, *Prophecy and Hermeneutic in Early Christianity: New Testament Essays* (Tübingen 1978).
FELDMAN, Louis. 'Prophets and Prophecy in Josephus,' *SBLSP* 27 (1988) 424–41.
GEORGI, Dieter. *The Opponents of Paul in Second Corinthians* (Philadelphia 1986).
GOODENOUGH, E. R. 'Philo and Public Life,' *Journal of Egyptian Archeology* 12 (1926) 77–79.
—, *By Light, Light, The Mystic Gospel of Hellenistic Judaism* (New Haven 1935).
—, *The Politics of Philo Judaeus, Practice and Theory: with a General Bibliography of Philo by H. L. Goodhart and E. R. Goodenough* (New Haven 1938).
—, *An Introduction to Philo Judaeus* (New Haven 1963).
HAY, David M. 'The Psychology of Faith in Hellenistic Judaism,' *ANRW* 2.20.2 (1987) 881–925.
—, 'Philo's View of Himself as an Exegete: Inspired, but not Authoritative,' *SPhA* 3 (1991) 40–52.
HECHT, R. 'Scripture and Commentary in Philo,' *SBLSP* 20 (1981) 129–164.
HENGEL, Martin. *Die Zeloten: Untersuchungen zur jüdischen Freiheitsbewegung in der Zeit von Herodes I. bis 70 N. Chr.* (Leiden 1961).
HOLLADAY, Carl. *Theios Aner in Hellenistic–Judaism: A Critique of the Use of this Category in New Testament Christology*, SBLDS 40 (Missoula 1977).

HORGAN, Maurya. *Pesharim: Qumran Interpretations of Biblical Books*. CBQMS 8, (Washington, DC 1979).
HURTADO, Larry. *One God, One Lord: Early Christian Devotion and Ancient Jewish Monotheism* (Philadelphia 1988).
JONGE, M. de. 'Josephus und die Zukunftserwartungen seines Volkes,' *Josephus–Studien* (Göttingen 1974) 205–19.
KATZ, Steven T. 'Language, Epistemology, and Mysticism,' in *idem* (ed.), *Mysticism and Philosophical Analysis* (Oxford 1978) 22–74.
KIM, Seyoon. *The Origin of Paul's Gospel*, WUNT II/4 (Tübingen 1981).
KITTEL, Gerhard. 'ἔσοπτρον, κατοπτρίζομαι.' *TDNT* 2 ([1935] 1964) 696–97.
LEWY, Hans. *Sobria Ebrietas: Untersuchungen zur Geschichte der antiken Mystik* (Gießen 1929).
—, ed. *Philo: Philosophical Writings* (Oxford 1946).
LIETZMANN, Hans von. *An die Korinther I/II*, HNT 9 (Tübingen 1969).
LINDNER, H. *Die Geschichtsauffassung des Flavius Josephus im Bellum Judaicum* (Leiden 1972).
LINFORD, I. M. 'The Corybantic Rites in Plato,' *University of California Publications in Classical Philology* 13 (1946) 163–72.
MARROW, Stanley B. '*Parrhesia* and the New Testament,' *CBQ* 44 (1982) 431–46.
MEEKS, Wayne A. *The Prophet–King: Moses Traditions and the Johannine Christology*, NT.S 14 (Leiden 1967).
MENDELSON, Alan. *Secular Education in Philo of Alexandria*, Monograph of the Hebrew Union College 7 (Cinncinati 1982).
MEYER, Rudolf. 'Προφήτης, κτλ,' *TDNT* 6 (1968) 821–23.
MURPHY–O'CONNOR, Jerome. '*Pneumatikoi* and Judaizers in 2 Cor. 2:14–4:6,' *AusBR* 34 (1986) 42–58.
NEWMAN, Carey C. *Paul's Glory–Christology: Tradition and Rhetoric*, NT.S 69 (Leiden 1992).
NIKIPROWETZKY, V. *Le commentaire de L'Écriture chez Philon d'Alexandrie*, ALGHJ 11 (Leiden 1977).
POHLENZ, Max. 'Philon von Alexandreia.' *Nachrichten von der Akademie der Wissenschaften in Göttingen, Philologisch–Historische Klasse* 5 (1942) 409–487.
RUNIA, D. T. *Philo of Alexandria and the* Timaeus *of Plato*, 2 Vols. (Amsterdam 1983[1]), Philosophia Antiqua 44 (Leiden 1986[2]) (except at n. 23 second edition is cited).
SCHOLEM, Gershom. *Major Trends in Jewish Mysticism* (New York 1941).
—, *Kabbalah and its Symbolism*, Tr. by R. Manheim (New York 1965).
SCHULZ, S. 'Die Decke des Moses: Untersuchungen zu einer vorpaulinischen Überlieferung in II Cor. 3.7–18,' *ZNW* 49 (1958) 1–30.
SEGAL, Alan. *Two Powers in Heaven: Early Rabbinic Reports about Christianity and Gnosticism* (Leiden 1977).
—, 'Heavenly Ascent in Hellenistic Judaism, Early Christianity, and Their Environments,' *ANRW* II.23.2 (1980) 332–94.
—, *Paul the Convert: The Apostolate and Apostasy of Saul the Pharisee* (New Haven 1990).
SOWERS, S. G. *The Hermeneutics of Philo and Hebrews*. Basel Studies of Theology 1 (Richmond 1965).
STONE, Michael E. 'Apocalyptic–Vision or Hallucination,' *Milla wa–Milla* 14

(1974) 47–56.

THACKERAY, H. St. J. *Josephus: The Man and the Historian* (New York 1929).

THEISSEN, Gerd. *Psychological Aspects of Pauline Theology* (Philadelphia 1987).

UNNIK, W. C. Van. '"With Unveiled Faces:" An Exegesis of 2 Cor. 3.12–18,' *NovT* 6 (1963) 153–69.

VÖLKER, Walther. *Fortschritt und Vollendung bei Philo von Alexandreia* (Leipzig 1938).

WINDISCH, H. *Der zweite Korintherbrief* (Göttingen 1924[9]).

WINSTON, David. *Philo of Alexandria: The Contemplative Life, the Giants, and Selections,* (New York 1981).

—, 'Was Philo a Mystic?' in J. Dan and F. Talmadge, eds., *Studies in Jewish Mysticism* (Cambridge MA 1982) 15–41.

—, 'Two Types of Mosaic Prophecy according to Philo,' *SBLSP* 27 (1988) 442–55.

WOLFSON, Harry A. *Philo: Foundations of Religious Philosophy in Judaism, Christianity, and Islam,* 2 Vols. (Cambridge Mass. 1947).

TWO TYPES OF ECSTATIC PROPHECY ACCORDING TO PHILO

JOHN R. LEVISON

On the basis of *Mos.* 2.187–91, David Winston proffers the intriguing suggestion that, according to Philo, Moses experiences two types of prophetic inspiration: ecstatic and hermeneutical (or noetic).[1] Moses' experience of hermeneutical inspiration entails the quickening of his mind, enabling him to understand the rational divine voice which communicates the laws at Sinai. In this instance, Moses' 'inspired mind ... far from being preempted or rendered passive, is rather extraordinarily quickened and sharpened' to engage in 'a mind to mind communication.'[2] In contrast, Moses' experience of ecstatic inspiration enables him to predict the future. In these instances, Moses speaks 'when inspired and possessed and transported out of himself.'[3]

This is not, however, the only important distinction which Winston draws; he also distinguishes between two types of ecstatic prophecy delineated by Philo. The prophets, Abraham, and Balaam experience possession trances in which they become passive, mindless mediums of God's message. In contrast, Moses' ecstasy is a milder form which leads him to receive impressions of the future without a complete displacement of his rational faculties. Winston is aware of the significance of this distinction:[4]

> If the interpretation offered above is correct, it would readily fit the pattern of uniqueness which frames Philo's portrait of Moses, for it is now evident that not only is Moses' legislative [i.e., hermeneutic] prophecy unique, but even his predictive prophecy, a gift he otherwise shares with Noah and the Patriarchs (*Her.* 260–61), is likewise unique in character, since it is not as with the latter, a product of psychic invasion and displacement.

Corroboration of Winston's thesis

Winston promises to provide evidence for this thesis when he writes:

---

[1] 'Two Types of Mosaic Prophecy according to Philo,' *JSP* 2 (1989) 49–67; see also 'Judaism and Hellenism: Hidden Tensions in Philo's Thought,' *SPhA* 2 (1990) 12–17.
[2] 'Two Types,' 54, 55.
[3] 'Two Types,' 49.
[4] 'Two Types,' 54.

***The Studia Philonica Annual* 6 (1994) 83–89**

> Now a close examination of Philo's description of predictive prophecy will, I believe, reveal that while he has adopted the more radical form of Greek ecstatic prophecy as his model with regard to the prophecies of Abraham and Balaam ... this is not the case with the predictive prophecies of Moses.

Despite the promise of this detailed examination, Winston's analysis of Moses' ecstatic inspiration is focused almost entirely upon Graeco-Roman sources, particularly Plutarch, and includes very little of the Philonic corpus. Winston briefly summarizes two visions of Moses (*Mos.* 2.252, 281) and otherwise makes only the negative observation that the predictive prophecies of Moses contain 'no explicit reference to the displacement of the prophet's mind, to his ignorance of his own prophetic words, or to the fact that God prompts the words that he speaks.'[5]

There is, nonetheless, a repository of evidence which can be unearthed to fulfill Winston's promise of 'a close examination of Philo's description of predictive prophecy.' This evidence, which is the focus of our analysis, provides important data to corroborate and also to refine Winston's thesis.

Not surprisingly, this evidence consists of four examples of Moses' ecstatic inspiration in *De vita Moysis* which follow *Mos.* 2.187–91 in order to illustrate what Philo means by ecstatic prophecy or, as he puts it in *Mos.* 2.191, prophecy 'in the strict sense:'[6] crossing the Red Sea (2.246-57); Moses' announcement of the sabbath (2.258–69); the golden calf (2.270–74); and the rebellion of Korah (2.275-87). In these four narratives, Philo adheres to a strict pattern to describe Moses' experiences of ecstatic inspiration. Philo portrays a unified experience which includes: (1) Moses' emotional response to a situation; (2) his experience of possession; and (3) his subsequent oracular utterance.

First, Moses experiences emotional agitation. (a) He saw the panic and consternation of his people at the Red Sea (2.250). (b) He was struck by awe when food was doubled on the sixth day (2.264). (c) He was deeply moved by the blindness of the people which was evident in the golden calf (2.271). (d) His heart burned with indignation at learning of Korah's rebellion (2.280).

Second, these emotional responses to situations become the immediate causes of Moses' inspiration. In each of these four instances, through the use of participles, particles, and prepositions, Philo emphasizes the

---

[5] 'Two Types,' 53–54. Winston (51–52) does provide ample evidence of the first, more radical form of ecstatic prophecy experienced by the prophets, Abraham, and Balaam, both from Graeco-Roman sources and from the Philonic corpus itself, including *Spec.* 4.49, *Her.* 264, and *Mos.* 1.274. This particular form of ecstasy, however, is not in question.

[6] The fifth, 2.288–92, functions as a brief conclusion to the treatise as a whole.

continuity between Moses' response to the situation and his experience of inspiration.

(a) While he watched the panic of his people at the Red Sea, Moses became possessed, being no longer in himself (2.250). The adverbial participle, ὁρῶν, provides the context of and thus a connection to the main verb, θεοφορεῖται, which denotes inspiration: ὁ δὲ προφήτης ὑπ' ἐκπλήξεως ὁρῶν ... οὐκέτ' ὢν ἐν ἑαυτῷ θεοφορεῖται ... ('with consternation the prophet, seeing ... was taken out of himself by divine possession and uttered these inspired words ...'). This syntactical structure, then, reveals the continuity between Moses' response and his experience of inspiration.

(b) Moses, being awestruck by what was proclaimed and seen in the doubling of food, did not so much guess at but was possessed to speak of the sabbath (2.264). Once again, an adverbial participle, καταπλαγεὶς, provides the context of the main verb employed to depict Moses' thought, ἐστοχάσατο, which Philo then interprets as an inspired utterance: ἐφ' οἷς ἀγγελλομένοις ἅμα καὶ ὁρωμένοις καταπλαγεὶς Μωυσῆς οὐκ ἐστοχάσατο μᾶλλον ἢ θεοφορηθεὶς ... ('Moses, when he heard of this and also actually saw it, was awestruck and, guided by what was not so much surmise as God-sent inspiration ...'). As in the first illustration, the inspiration Moses experiences is not radically discontinuous with his human response and perception.

(c) On account of the blindness of the people (evident in the golden calf) which deeply moved him, Moses, no longer remaining the same, was transformed both in outward appearance and mind (2.271–2). In this instance, the prepositional phrase, δι' ἣν αἰτίαν, directly connects, as cause and effect, Moses' own response and his subsequent transformation and inspiration: ἐφ' οἷς Μωυσῆς περιπαθήσας (followed here by a digression on the blindness of people) ... δι' ἣν αἰτίαν οὐκέτι μένων ὁ αὐτὸς ἐξαλλάττεται τό τε εἶδος καὶ τὴν διάνοιαν ... ('At this, Moses was cut to the heart ... He therefore became another man, changed both in outward appearance and mind ...')

(d) While he was still boiling and on fire with justifiable indignation, Moses was transformed by means of possession into a prophet (2.280). In this story, Philo parallels three participles—ζέων, πεπυρωμένος, μεταβαλὼν—to depict the context of Moses' inspired utterance. His inclusion of the temporal particle, ἔτι, before the first two indicates that Moses' inspiration takes place while his emotional agitation persists: ἔτι δὲ ζέων καὶ πεπυρωμένος ... ἐνθουσιᾷ μεταβαλὼν εἰς προφήτην ... ('While his heart was still hot within him ... inspiration came upon him, and, transformed into a prophet ...')

These four stories portray a consistent view of Moses' inspiration. In each, there is an integral relationship between Moses' response to the people and his experience of inspiration. This view persists in the third part of each illustration, where Moses' prior responses, which gave rise to inspiration, lead directly to an inspired comprehensible, persuasive utterance, introduced three times (2.250; 2.264; 2.280) by the verb, θεσπίζειν, and once by φημί (2.272).[7] Philo's use of adverbial participles and verbs, once again, establishes the connection between Moses' experience of inspiration and his utterances. (a) Moses, no longer being in himself, was possessed and spoke (2.250). In this instance, Philo closely parallels inspiration and utterance: ... θεοφορεῖται καὶ θεσπίζει τάδε ... ('... was taken out of himself by divine possession and uttered these inspired words ...'); (b) Being possessed, Moses spoke of the sabbath (2.264). Here an adverbial participle, used to describe inspiration, gives the impetus for Moses' utterance: θεοφορηθεὶς ἐθέσπισε τὴν ἑβδόμην... ('guided by ... God-sent inspiration, made announcement of the sabbath'); (c) Once possessed, he spoke about the golden calf (2.272). The same syntactical structure obtains here: καὶ ἐπιθειάσας φησί ... ('... filled with the spirit, he cried ...'); (d) Under possession, after being transformed into a prophet, Moses also spoke about Korah's rebellion (2.280). Again, an adverbial participle which describes inspiration (in this case, transformation which arises from inspiration), is the context for speech: ἐνθουσιᾷ μεταβαλὼν εἰς προφήτην καὶ θεσπίζει τάδε (... inspiration came upon him, and, transformed into a prophet, he pronounced these words ...')

This pattern, which Philo carefully develops, reveals the integral connection between Moses' emotional state, his experience of inspiration, and his utterance before the people of Israel. Our analysis of this pattern corroborates in three ways Winston's contention that Moses, according to Philo, experiences what Winston calls 'a milder form of ecstatic prophecy'[8] which preserves rather than displaces his human abilities.[9]

First, Philo's description of inspiration in these illustrations in no way implies an intrusion or a displacement of reason. In this respect,

---

[7] On formal features of Philo's descriptions of prophecy, see D. Aune, *Prophecy in Early Christianity and the Ancient Mediterranean World* (Grand Rapids 1983) 147–52.

[8] Winston ('Two Types,' 53) traces this view to Plutarch's *De def. orac.* 431B–38; *De pyth. orac.* 397BC, and Cicero's *De div.* 1.113.

[9] The vocabulary Philo employs within this pattern confirms the presence of an ecstatic experience. First, twice Philo points to a transformation in Moses. In one instance, Moses, under possession, is transformed into a prophet (2.280). In 2.272, the transformation includes outward appearance and mind. Second, twice Philo employs οὐκέτι to signal a tangible change in Moses. At the Red Sea, Moses becomes possessed when he is no longer in himself (2.250), and in response to the golden calf he no longer remains in himself (2.272). Third, the occurrence of words for divine possession in each instance signals the presence of something other than the rational faculties.

this view of inspiration is different from Philo's definitions of prophecy in *Spec.* 1.65, 4.49 and his descriptions of Balaam's prophetic inspiration (*Mos.* 1.277, 283).

Second, Philo consistently draws a direct line, via inspiration, from Moses' natural emotional response to his oracle. Moses' inspired speeches are outgrowths of human abilities, aided by the process of inspiration. This connection confirms what Philo intimates in *Mos.* 2.288-91, that Moses speaks 'out of himself,' just as God delivers the laws 'out of God's self ...'[10] Inspiration does not interrupt the natural process which begins with Moses' emotional response; on the contrary, Moses is not, like Balaam and other prophets, a mindless channel for God, but speaks, like God, out of his own person, with his emotions and mind intact. This is possible because God actually transfers to Moses God's 'own power of foreknowledge' of future events (190).

This unique phenomenon illuminates what Philo means in *Mos.* 2.187–91 when he writes that Moses, 'appears under that divine possession in virtue of which he is chiefly and in the strict sense considered a prophet' (191). As an *interpreter* of the oracles which God gives in God's own person, Moses is a channel through whom God delivers the laws. As a *dialogue partner*, Moses learns incrementally from God by means of question and answer. As a '*prophet in the strict sense*,' Moses actually possesses God's own knowledge.

Third, the physical transformation of Moses is unlike the wild, frenzied transformation of oracular priests and priestesses, such as we find in the accounts of Aeschylus,[11] Sophocles,[12] Virgil,[13] Strabo,[14] Lucan,[15] and Lucian.[16] The purpose of Moses' transformation is to intensify his ability to lead the Israelites through persuasive speeches (2.272; 2.280). A similar instance occurs in *Mos.* 1.57–59, in which Moses' transformation ('he grew inspired and was transfigured into a prophet') enables him to intimidate the Arabs who have usurped the well of seven women, including his future spouse.[17]

---

[10] Translation mine. Greek, ἐκ προσώπου τοῦ θεοῦ and ἐκ προσώπου Μωυσέως (2.188).

[11] *Prometheus Bound* 875–87, in which Io describes the twitching spasm, the madness, the whirl of the eyes, and the tongue babbling.

[12] *Ajax* 284–330, in which Tecmessa describes Ajax's fit.

[13] *Aeneid* 6.77–82, in which the sibyl storms about the cave in an attempt to shake off Apollo; her mouth raves and her heart is wild.

[14] *Geography* 10.466–8, in which he depicts the frenzy and music of the Curetes.

[15] *Pharsalia* 5.173–5, in which the Delphic priestess, invaded by Apollo, scatters the tripods and boils over with fire.

[16] *Alexander* 12, in which Alexander the Great feigns fits of madness and fills his mouth with foam.

[17] The nature of this transformation becomes clearer in comparison with *Virt.* 217–9,

Refinement of Winston's thesis

This analysis of the pattern of Philo's illustrations provides substantial evidence to support Winston's important thesis that Philo distinguishes Moses' milder experience of ecstasy from other, more radical experiences of ecstasy. It also, however, suggests the need for a refinement of this thesis.

First, Winston claims, 'It is essential to note that Philo invokes the notion of ecstatic possession only to explain the ability of the prophet to predict the future ...'[18] It is true that, according to *Mos.* 2.190, God gives foreknowledge to Moses when he acts as a prophet in the strict sense. But the assertion that Moses' ecstatic inspiration has the sole purpose of prediction constitutes an unnecessary restriction of the scope of ecstatic prophecy. The four illustrations of ecstatic inspiration which Philo proffers have as much to do with the situation of the Israelites in Moses' day as with their future. While Moses' utterances at the Red Sea and during the rebellion of Korah predict the imminent future, Moses' announcement of the sabbath and the command to slaughter leaders responsible for the fiasco of the golden calf are speeches about the present. There is no need, therefore, to limit the purpose of Moses' ecstatic inspiration to prediction.

Second, Winston also contends that 'the ecstatic predictive prophecies of Moses may best be characterized as products of 'vision trance' rather than 'possession trance'.'[19] This too is an unnecessary restriction of ecstatic prophecy. The four illustrations which we analyzed do, as Winston observes, contain two visions; but the accounts of the sabbath and the golden calf do not.

Third, Winston is unclear about what exactly happens to Moses' mind when he experiences ecstasy. It is not displaced, as are the minds of Balaam, Abraham, *et al.* Nor, according to Winston, is Moses' mind quickened, as it is when he experiences hermeneutical or noetic prophecy. When Winston cites Plutarch's views, according to which

which contains an extensive account of the transformation of Abraham, the king-sage-prophet. The implicit emphasis upon persuasive ability in Philo's portrait of Moses' transformation is explicit in Philo's portrait of Abraham: 'Thus whenever he was possessed, everything in him changed to something better, eyes, complexion, stature, carriage, movements, voice. For the divine spirit which was breathed upon him from on high made its lodging in his soul, and invested his body with singular beauty, his voice with persuasiveness, and his hearers with understanding.'

[18] 'Two Types,' 56. The evidence he cites, *Mos.* 2.6, 2.187; *Her.* 261, cannot bear the weight of his argument because these texts do not deal directly with prediction but with the need for inspiration to ascertain what is not immediately accessible to the mind.

[19] 'Two Types,' 54.

'the soul succeeds in relaxing the reasoning element ...'[20], he implies that Moses' mind is relaxed. However, an explicit statement of Philo which occurs at the mid-point of his four illustrations of Moses' ecstatic prophecy (*Mos*. 2.265) mitigates this impression. In his account of Moses' announcement of the sabbath, Philo explicitly connects the mind of Moses and the divine spirit: 'For the mind could not have made so straight an aim if there was not also the divine spirit guiding it to the truth itself.'[21] This statement is significant, for it suggests that Moses' ecstatic prophetic inspiration can engage and quicken the mind, leading it to the truth. There may be, then, a closer relationship between hermeneutical prophecy and ecstatic prophecy than Winston has suggested.

Although these dichotomies may be overdrawn, the central dichotomies Winston draws are valid. There is a distinction between hermeneutical and ecstatic prophecy. Moreover, in the brief compass of this article, we have seen that there is ample evidence within the Philonic corpus both to corroborate and to refine Winston's important thesis that Moses' unique experience of ecstatic prophecy differs from the ecstatic experiences of other prophets.

Eberhard-Karls-Universität
Tübingen

---

20 'Two Types,' 53.

21 For a fuller discussion of the relationship between reason and inspiration, see my 'Inspiration and the Divine Spirit in the Writings of Philo Judaeus,' *Journal for the Study of Judaism*, forthcoming.

SPECIAL SECTION

PHILO IN EARLY CHRISTIAN LITERATURE:

Every once in a while, when a significant work on Philo is published, the Philo of Alexandria Seminar of the Society of Biblical Literature devotes a session to it. Such a meeting took place on 21 November 1994 in Washington, D.C. Four scholars were asked to serve on a review panel of David Runia's latest major work, *Philo in Early Christian Literature*, which had just been published a few months before the meeting. After four enthusiastic presentations various members of the Seminar expressed regret about the ephemeral nature of the proceedings. At their suggestion, the editorial board of *SPhA*—the editor's demurral notwithstanding—decided to publish the responses of all four panelists. Each panelist was asked to comment on specific aspects of the book as well as offer a general assessment. The specific assignments were as follows: Abraham Terian was asked to comment on the transmission of the Philonic corpus, Annewies van den Hoek on the early Alexandrian use of Philo, Robert Wilken on later ecclesiastical use of Philo, and David Winston on Philo's *Nachleben* in Judaism. Full details on the book that they commented on are as follows:

> David T. RUNIA, *Philo in Early Christian Literature: A Survey.* Compendia Rerum Iudaicarum ad Novum Testamentum III 3. Van Gorcum–Fortress, Assen–Minneapolis 1993. xv + 418 pages. ISBN 0-8006-2828-4. $35 (or HFl 95).

As the contributions show, David Runia has once again opened up new avenues of thought. In a sense, this collection is a tribute to him and his many contributions to our common interests.

ALAN MENDELSON
McMaster University

Notes on the Transmission of the Philonic Corpus

Abraham Terian

It is a delightful task to comment on such well-researched, well-documented work. Although the volume at hand is a major contribution to Philonic and Patristic studies, one need not be a scholar in either of these fields to appreciate this book, for in the preliminaries Runia provides a basic introduction to the Philonic corpus and the themes it encompasses. There is even a chapter on Philo and the New Testament (pp. 63–86). Subsequent chapters methodically introduce the Patristic sources considered: both Greek (from the Apostolic Fathers through the Cappadocians and beyond, pp. 87–271) and Latin (from Tertullian through Augustine and beyond, pp. 275–332). Throughout, Runia maintains a fine balance between primary and secondary sources as he considers Philo in early Christianity, both in the East (including the Armenian tradition, pp. 5, 27) and in the West. It is not at all surprising that the coverage of the Latin Fathers is nearly a fourth of that devoted to the Greek Fathers among whom the legend of Philo Christianus originated. The book could have had another proof-reading, but this neglect is minuscule compared with the timeliness of the publication. Not since Goodenough have we seen such fascination with Philo as we are witnessing these days, and this volume will definitely add to the mounting interest.

Runia shows how the Philonic corpus might have travelled from Alexandria to Caesarea (thanks to Origen) and from there to Byzantium (thanks to the edition of Euzoius). In Constantinople certain of Philo's works seem to have become (for a short period at least) part of the Byzantine curriculum, and there they were translated into Armenian in the latter part of the 6th century (Clement's remark that his Alexandrian predecessor's works constitute a handy manual for philosophical and theological understanding may have precipitated such use of certain parts of the Philonic corpus). Runia seems to have some reservations regarding H. Lewy's reconstruction of this setting for the production of the interlinear Armenian translation of Philo (p. 27).[1] For my part, I have not found a better explanation for the Armenian corpus when considering it alongside other Armenian translations with similar

[1] *The Pseudo-Philonic De Jona, Part I, The Armenian Text with a Critical Introduction*, Studies and Documents 7 (London 1936) 15–16.

characteristics and colophons suggestive of the time and place of this kind of translation. It is noteworthy that the Armenian translation of Philo precedes the coming of Stephen of Alexandria to Constantinople as head (*oikoumenikos didaskalos*) of the Imperial Academy (ca. 610), following the Christian takeover of the Neoplatonic School in Alexandria. Could the fate of the Greek text of Philo be linked to curricular changes in Constantinople at this time?

Runia does a good job of explaining the dissemination of Philo's works both before and after Eusebius. Obviously, certain of Philo's works were lost prior to Eusebius, and a few others since the fourth century. A brief explanation is given comparing the Eusebian list with the present corpus and the fragments which when combined account for six titles not found in the Caesarean Father. I agree with the conclusion that the line of transmission of which Eusebius is a witness may not have been exclusive. One of the works not accounted for by Eusebius is Book I of *De Providentia*, the Philonic authorship of which has often been questioned as a result of this omission besides obvious textual corruptions throughout. I am glad that Runia accepts the authenticity of this book without raising any of the objections voiced in past scholarship. Book I is apparently alluded to in the opening lines of Book II, where Philo remarks on Alexander's coming 'to go over what is left on Providence'. This seems to indicate, as do the opening lines in some other sequential works, resumption of the subject being discussed.

In his endeavor to show how widespread the legend of Philo Christianus was, Runia invites attention to the positive as well as the negative attitudes regarding Philo in Christian tradition—including the use made of him by Christian apologists in their anti-Judaistic polemics (as was made also of Josephus). A more significant factor in this development is the early Fathers' fascination with Philo's allegory. I agree with the author that Clement of Alexandria could well be the source of the Philo Christianus legend, a legend enhanced by Origen's treatment of both Philo and Clement of Alexandria as forerunners in the exegetical tradition. This, no doubt, helped pave the way for the acceptance of Philo as a 'Church Father *honoris causa*' (to use Runia's term), an acceptance conditioned by the Ante-Nicaean Fathers' awareness that allegorization helps defend the Scriptures from rationalistic attacks.[1] Understandably, the Philo Christianus legend is much stronger among the Greek-speaking Fathers than among the Latin-speaking Fathers. The latter group, ever-mindful of his Jewishness, had a much more guarded attitude toward him.

---

[1] Cf. Theodore of Mopsuesta's *Treatise against the Allegorists* for Post-Nicaean attitudes.

It is to be expected, perhaps, that I should say something about Philo Christianus in the Armenian tradition. As J. B. Aucher observes, the Armenian version of Philo comes with a 'Preface' which seems to have belonged to a manuscript containing *De Providentia*.[1] It begins with brief remarks on Philo's identity and summary statements on the opening sections of *QG* and *QE* as extant in the Armenian version, and concludes with briefer remarks on Philo's education and the dialogues *On Divine Providence* with Alexander. Judging from its syntax, it is clearly a piece of Armenian composition and not a translation from Greek. Runia paraphrases the content of the opening paragraph accurately and notes the fact that there is no study on this piece (p. 5). In the statements on *QE* the anonymous author claims that Philo 'mentions God's Anointed and confesses His divine authority with the Father' while allegorizing the things pertaining to the priestly robe (i.e., in *QE* 2.117–20). This preface, then, is an independent witness to an intermediate Christian attitude regarding Philo. Other legends on Philo Christianus are found in the Armenian scholia, including the one on his conversion at the hand of John the Apostle.[2]

Guided by his stated methodology and Cohn's list of references to Philo in Christian literature (completed by Runia in an 'Appendix', pp. 348–56), the author proceeds admirably through the earliest Christian writings, the early Alexandrian Fathers, and those in the Alexandrian tradition. It seems that the toughest testing of the methodology comes when dealing with the Cappadocian Fathers. However, here too Runia is at his best, especially as he treats Gregory of Nyssa's *De vita Mosis*, for example, where there is so much reliance on Philo and yet the allusions to him are so very few and anonymous (a tendency epitomized in Procopius of Gaza). Moreover, the Cappadocian Fathers manifest overwhelming reliance on Philo in their hexaemera commentaries, especially on the twofold creation of man: the Philonic influence extends far into their mysticism as they proceed to deliberate on the image of God in man's reasoning faculty. One would have expected more on the subject of Philo's influence on Christian mysticism in the chapter on the Cappadocians than Runia has allowed (pp. 255–60). This could have been pursued without having to determine the extent to which Philo was or was not a mystic. Suffice it to say that for the Cappadocians, as for Philo, (1) the sacred text contained deeper meanings than those readily available to readers, and (2) the vision of God—if not also union with

---

1 *Philonis Iudaei sermones tres hactenus inediti: I. et II. De Providentia et III. De animalibus* (Venice 1822).

2 Cf. the *Acta Johannis* of Pseudo-Prochorus.

God—was possible when pursuing the contemplative path. Thus, the chapter on the Cappadocian Fathers would have been the logical place not only to highlight the extent to which Philo figures in early Christian literature—even in instances where there are neither direct quotations from him nor specific references to him—but also to deal with the topic of mysticism which touches quite a few of the main Philonic themes discussed in early Christian literature.[1] In keeping with his methodology, Runia points to secondary sources on Philo's influence on Christian mysticism.[2]

The most telling use of Philo's works by the Fathers is perhaps that made by Ambrose. The affinities between Philo and the Bishop of Milan are so numerous that the pages alloted to the subject (pp. 291–311) could be doubled easily. Again, Runia makes up for this seemingly brief chapter by inviting attention to H. Savon's work.[3] There is, as many agree, a twofold treatment of Philo in Ambrose: (1) outright utilization of his works, and (2) reinterpretation of his allegory in sacramental terms. As for the latter, some go so far as to see substantial sacramental infusion into Philo's biblical interpretation in much of Ambrose. Be that as it may, what is more curious is the Bishop's personal assessment of Philo. Notwithstanding the use made of our exegete, there was a degree of uneasiness with him, a certain ambivalence, a hidden dissatisfaction with him mainly because of his absolute silence about Christ—if not also for the fact that he is an interpreter of the Torah, an apologist for Judaism. Ambrose tries to rectify these concerns by reinterpreting Philo sacramentally. There were other factors contributing to the Post-Nicaean Fathers' somewhat negative attitude toward Philo. These include their generally anti-philosophical (and occasionally anti-allegorical) disposition and their anti-heretical vigilance that made them cautious lest too much reliance on Philo should enhance Christological heresies—since by virtue of his voluminousness Philo could easily have become a quarry for heretical views (e.g., God's Logos or deed being posterior to God himself). The negative sentiments regarding the often unnamed Philo were verbalized not so much by Ambrose as by his foremost admirer, convert, and best-known pupil: Augustine. After Augustine, interest in Philo subsided in the West. Subsequent references to him in Latin authors come from Rufinus' translation of

---

[1] For a list of these themes see pp. 37–43; note especially those listed under 'philosophical themes'.

[2] Note especially A. Louth, *The Origins of the Christian Mystical Tradition: From Plato to Denys* (Oxford 1981).

[3] *Saint Ambroise devant l'exégèse de Philon le Juif,* 2 vols., Études Augustiniennes (Paris 1977).

Eusebius' *Ecclesiastical History* and, as Runia observes, for the most part these are references to the embassy to Gaius headed by Philo.

There a number of wider implications of the book as well. Runia's survey has numerous bearings on Wolfson's hypotheses in *Philo: Foundations of Religious Philosophy in Judaism, Christianity and Islam* (Cambridge 1947). To begin with, Wolfson's glamorous view of Philo as a great philosopher alongside the giants of the classical tradition finds little support in the fact that there is but scant and comparatively late use made of our Alexandrian author in pagan sources. While Wolfson's assessment of Philo's influence on Christianity finds considerable support in Runia, Wolfson's remaining hypotheses, regarding Philo's influence on Judaism and Islam, are indirectly called into question. The relative obscurity of Philo's works in Jewish and Islamic sources is explicable by the fact that his works were never translated into any Semitic language, whether Arabic, Syriac, or Hebrew in the medieval period. Semblances between Philonic and certain Jewish and Islamic thought appear to be coincidental, owing either to rudiments of common traditions—whether Jewish or Hellenistic—or to cross-currents in medieval times, resulting to a certain extent from contacts with Christianity.

It is paradoxical that the staunchest readers of Philo were neither of his intended audiences, whether Jews or pagans, but Christians. I am convinced that Philo wrote primarily—if not exclusively—for Jewish readers lest his coreligionists yield to non-Jewish influences rampant in the Hellenistic world. His seemingly universalistic appeals are intended to rouse his people to guard and cherish their heritage zealously. Should a pagan happen to read him, that might be a bonus that could lead the individual to venerate Moses. It is equally paradoxical that those responsible for preserving Philo could also be deemed responsible for whatever is lost of his works.[1]

In spite of the Fathers' fascination with Philo and their diverse appropriations of his works ever since Clement of Alexandria, his Jewishness remained a dilemma for them and oftentimes they were unable to conceal their anti-Jewish prejudice. However, their reluctance to name the adopted 'Church Father' in numerous utilizations of his works need not always be interpreted negatively, since such practices were common among writers in Late Antiquity and in the early Byzantine period. As a result of Runia's definitive work, the conclusion might be drawn more emphatically than ever before that Philo was much admired for his exegesis and that the Fathers' debt to him is truly immense.

Sterling College

---

[1] Following E. R. Goodenough, *An Introduction to Philo Judaeus* (New Haven 1940).

Philo in the Alexandrian Tradition

Annewies van den Hoek

David Runia deserves congratulations on the very rich, learned, and instructive book that is under discussion. Its primary focus is the connection of Philo and—in a larger context—Judeo-Hellenistic thought with Christianity, but at the same time, the book also covers a vast area of Christian theological traditions both in the East and in the West in their own right. The cut-off point is the first half of the fifth century, but the Appendix provides references to Philo as late as the year 1000. The book offers much new basic research, is clearly organized, and is easy to find one's way through. Its extensive indices, not only of biblical and Philonic passages, but also of names, places and themes make its wealth of information very accessible.

Every author or group of writings discussed in the book is introduced by a short historical essay, followed by a discussion of the current state of research, and supported by an impressive amount of bibliography. Whenever primary research could not be done, an obvious impossibility with a vast subject like this, Runia did succeed in providing the necessary tools for further research. Every chapter, in fact, could become a dissertation on its own, so there is ample opportunity for future generations of students to take up the leads that Runia has set out so masterfully.

So once again, congratulations on the result of this work, which must have been an enormous challenge from many points of view. Merely achieving a relative consistency of treatment must have been difficult since in some areas, like that of the New Testament, much work had been done, while in other areas, such as Cappadocia or Alexandria in its later phase, which include people like Didymus the Blind and Isidorus of Pelusium, little or no research was to be found.

I would like to raise two points having to do with the early Alexandrian tradition, personified in Clement and Origen, the first authors who gave clear and unmistakable evidence of having read Philo. The first touches on a general methodological problem, while the second is more specific.

The methodological problem has to do with the difficulties involved in comparing two authors. The author's discussion of Origen provides a good illustration. He describes six scholars who have dealt in their own ways with the problem of Philo's influence on Origen. These scholars—

The Studia Philonica Annual **6 (1994) 96–99**

H. Wolfson, H. De Lubac, J. Daniélou, R. P. C. Hanson, R. M. Grant and H. Crouzel—are divided into two major camps: one views Origen as a systematic thinker and another thinks of Origen more as a man of the church for whom 'intellectual concerns are secondary and whose thought is centered around a mystical (i.e. religious) understanding of scripture' (p. 169). It is interesting to read that the people in the first camp (Wolfson, Hanson, Grant) who consider Origen a systematic thinker also regard Philo's influence as profound, while the other side (De Lubac and Crouzel) tend to downplay Philo's importance. Daniélou takes in a slighly ambiguous position between the two parties.

In the course of my own efforts to get a grip on Philo's influence on Clement, I have found similar contrasts in the previous literature. The angle from which scholars approached the issues and the presuppositions they had, sometimes unfortunately led them to diametrically opposed conclusions. For example, one scholar would stress the importance of the concept of the Logos and would say that more than anything else Clement was indebted to Philo in his conception of the Logos. On the other hand, the next scholar would say that many analogies could be found in the allegorization of biblical texts, in thinking about virtues, knowledge and wisdom, but that the only area in which there was *no* influence was the realm of the Logos.

Comparing authors is a tricky business, because it is very easy to approach texts with a kind of tunnel vision and then find exactly what was intended to be found. Therefore, a more neutral basis from which to operate is preferable. Of course, presuppositions are always there, but at least it helps when one is aware of them. The most neutral starting point seems to me the texts as they come, the primary evidence. One should find through comparison how parallel passages relate to one another and to their own contexts. Does comparison reveal real dependency or merely the general cultural baggage of the time? The next stage is to see if true borrowings from author A to author B reveal any serious purpose; in other words, to determine whether the borrowings make a difference for the train of thought or are used only for ornamental reasons.

In the course of my own work, it turned out that Philo was rather frequently called in by Clement as a manual for biblical texts, ready at hand and easy to use. This was, of course, not Philo's only role: there were more serious and substantial reasons to lean on him at other times. Now, if I were only interested in the history of thought and had a high opinion of Clement as a philosopher, I would not be happy to hear that he was a heavy user of handy manuals and that he did not even get the manuals straight. I would eagerly skip over to the more lofty passages as a basis for my analysis. Therefore, mapping out all the material with impartiality—both the welcome and the unwelcome—can protect one from oneself.

It is, of course, a great help to impartiality if one has a vast amount of material. In the case of Clement and Ambrose (and presumably, Origen) one has this numerical advantage. The statistical rule is that big numbers tend to be more accurate. Moreover, if one has enough 'bulk' for a solid literary comparison of texts, the bulk probably will also provide plenty of material for the higher level analysis of philosophical and theological concepts. Clement and Origen, different as they may be from one another, are still ideal points of reference since they are relatively close to Philo in time and in environment. The method, sketched above, of literary comparison leading to comparison of ideas, is, of course, valid only if there is a direct dependency. In the case of indirect influence, other methods have to be used. As Runia shows graphically in his conclusions, the direct tradition funneled through Clement, Origen, and Eusebius leads to indirect traditions afterwards. But the methodology for dealing with these indirect traditions has not yet been clearly spelled out.

My second point is about the rarity of Philo's name in both Clement and Origen. Clement mentions Philo four times: once in a discussion of Philo in which he does not quote him and in three major Philonic passages which include long, often verbatim, strings of Philonic wording. He does not, however, name Philo in any other lengthy borrowing nor in four smaller sequences nor in connection with a variety of fragmentary Philonic materials. Origen, in turn, is no more generous with his credit. He refers to Philo by name three times: twice in *Contra Celsum* and once in his *Commentary on Matthew*.[1] In thirteen other instances, most of which have been 'excavated' by Runia, Origen does not mention Philo explicitly, but does refer to a predecessor who is very likely Philo. For the record, Origen never mentions Clement by name, but he also seems to allude to him in similarly vague terms as 'one of our predecessors'.[2]

Scholars have been puzzled by how rarely the name of Philo is cited, particularly by Clement. Eric Osborn has suggested that Clement did not acknowledge his source for fear of losing people who were attracted to the teachings of Marcion.[3] There is little evidence to support such a

---

[1] *C.Cels.* 4.51; 6.21; *Comm. Matt.* 15.3.

[2] See my 'Origen and the Intellectual Heritage of Alexandria: Continuity or Disjunction', in Robert J. Daly (ed.), *Origeniana Quinta* (Leuven 1992) 40–50.

[3] Eric F. Osborn, 'Philo and Clement', *Prudentia* 19 (1987) 35–49.

hypothesis. Clement, after all, does mention quite a number of other Jewish-Hellenistic writers by name: in addition to his occasional references to Philo, he cites Aristobulos, Artapanos, Demetrios, and the poet Ezechiel.

When we look at the relationship between quotations and names in Clement generally (and his work contains literally thousands of quotations), it is true that his favorite sources, Plato and Paul, are very frequently acknowledged—although not always. In other instances, however, the picture is far less clear. Aristobulos is mentioned four times: twice in connection with borrowings and twice as pure name-dropping. Thus, of the six quotations from Aristobulos, only two are acknowledged (we can check this because the same fragments occur in Eusebius' *Praeparatio Evangelica*). Tatian, who may have been one of Clement's teachers before Clement came to Alexandria, is another important point of reference for this issue. As with Philo, we can be sure that Clement used Tatian directly (and he is one of the few authors, as André Méhat has pointed out, where this can be demonstrated).[1] In the twelve borrowings, his name is mentioned only three times. Moreover, in the two extensive passages from Tatian, both in book I of the *Stromateis* (chapters XVI and XXI), no acknowledgement occurs at all. Clement's other teacher, whom we would like to know much better and to whom Clement professes to be greatly indebted, is hardly represented by a quotation of any sort. We merely can guess that Pantaenus, whom Clement names very rarely, may have been responsible for a number of ideas, but nothing definite can be proven.

Origen who is reputedly not a 'namedropper' may, after all, be fairer to his sources. Although he does not always mention Philo by name (only three times), he at least indicates that he is quoting in the other thirteen instances. Another example helps to confirm this: Origen quotes the *Pastor of Hermas* a good sixteen times and all sixteen quotations are acknowledged, while Clement, who refers to this source equally often, only names him half the time.

With these few examples, I am not pretending to give a complete picture of techniques of citation, but I hope they show how it is worth looking at more evidence before speculating too much about motives for citing by name in the late second and early third centuries.

Harvard Divinity School

---

[1] André Méhat, *Kephalaia; recherches sur les matériaux des 'Stromates' de Clément d'Alexandrie et leur utisilation (thèse complémentaire dactylographiée)* (Paris 1966) 223–27.

Philo in the Fourth Century

ROBERT L. WILKEN

Shortly after I came to Notre Dame my colleague Jean Laporte published a book on Philo entitled *La doctrine eucharistique chez Philon d'Alexandrie.*[1] The title struck me as odd. It would have seemed more appropriate had it been, let us say, *La doctrine eucharistique chez Cyril d'Alexandrie* or *La doctrine eucharistique chez Gregoire de Nysse*. For the term 'doctrine eucharistique' seems to suggest a study of Philo's Eucharistic theology, that is, his theology of the sacrament of the Eucharist. Laporte is a clever fellow and he knew that one of the things that makes Philo interesting, not the only thing to be sure, is that Philo can be read as a Church Father.

And that is what this learned and sophisticated book is about. As Runia observes at the beginning: 'By the end of the Patristic period [Philo] had virtually achieved the status of a Church Father' (p. 3). It is not rare that extracts from his works in the Byzantine catenae are headed with the lemma Φίλωνος ἐπισκόπου.

Yet, as commonplace as it is to note that Philo's writings were preserved in Christian tradition but not among the Jews, and to demonstrate the influence of his writings on early Christian thinkers, for example in the magnificent work of H. Savon,[2] no one has tried to tell the whole story. And this Runia has done and done very well. This is a book to be read, marked, and inwardly digested, and to keep ready at hand for future reference. It is a work to which I will turn often. If I have any reservations about the book it is only that Runia chose the arbitrary date of 400 (he knows the date is arbitrary) to end his survey, leaving out not only the major figures of the fifth century, Cyril of Alexandria, Theodoret of Cyrus, and later writers, e.g., Severus of Antioch, Gregory the Great, Maximus, John of Damascus. But it would be picayune and ungracious to criticize Runia on this point after he has given so much. He has anticipated the objection in his final pages when he distinguishes between a direct and indirect tradition: Clement, Origen, and Eusebius being the chief representatives of the direct tradition, while the later figures are part of the indirect tradition.

The book is too rich and nuanced to summarize its argument. Suffice it to say that Runia treats a number of authors in detail—Justin Martyr,

---

1 ThH 16 (Paris 1972).

2 *Saint Ambroise devant l'exégèse de Philon le Juif.*

The Studia Philonica Annual **6 (1994) 100–102**

Theophilus of Antioch, Clement, Origen, Didymus the Blind, Eusebius of Caesarea, Gregory of Nyssa, Ambrose, Jerome, Augustine—and shows not only that they knew Philo (Augustine had read in Latin the opening chapters of Philo's *Quaestiones et Solutiones in Genesim*), but that they were interested in different works (the most popular were *De vita Moysis, Quaestiones in Genesim,* and *De opificio mundi*) and made different things of him: biblical interpreter, philosopher, Jewish apologist, *et al.*

Let me then turn to one matter of interpretation that is central to the study, his account of Philo's influence on early Christian biblical interpretation, a topic on which Runia is provocative, but where the evidence lends itself to another reading of the sources.

Runia discusses in depth an extraordinary passage from the Syriac version of Theodore of Mopsuestia's introduction to his commentary on Psalm 119, a text which sometimes bears the title *Treatise against the Allegorists.*[1] In this text, Theodore attacks Origen's biblical exegesis, specifically his use of allegory, as dependent on Philo. Runia recognizes how singular the text is and makes much of it in his discussion—rightly. But then he uses it as the basis for a comparison between Theodore and other putative 'Antiochene' exegetes, namely John Chrysostom and Theodoret of Cyrus, who show little dependence on Philo. The comparison leads him to the conclusion that 'this differing attitude to Philo is symptomatic of the gulf that separates the hermeneutical theory and practice of the Alexandrian and the Antiochene schools' (p. 269).

The difficulty here is that the notion of an Antiochene and an Alexandrian school of exegesis is a chimera, and it gives a wrong impression of the reception of Philo in the early church to formulate the issues in this way. Chrysostom, supposedly an Antiochene, is as different from Theodore as he is from Cyril of Alexandria. In his interpretation of the statement in Isaiah 2, 'word will go forth from Jerusalem', for example, Chrysostom follows the tradition, whereas Theodore stands alone in refusing a Christological interpretation.

What this means is that 'Antiochene school' really means Theodore, and perhaps Diodore. And 'Alexandrian' really means Origen (and perhaps Didymus), not Alexandria. Athanasius and Cyril are not Origenistic. What we have in the fascinating passage from Theodore cannot be taken as a statement of a longstanding exegetical tradition in early Christianity. It represents Theodore's distinctive outlook, more pointedly his antipathy to Origen. It is Theodore who stands alone, however, not Origen, since most exegetes followed Origen's lead, not Theodore's.

---

[1] L. van Rompay, *Théodore de Mopsueste: Fragments syriaques du Commentaire des Psaumes (Psaume 118 et Psaumes 138–148),* CSCO 435–36 (Louvain 1982).

What is interesting is that by tracing Origen's exegesis to Philo, Theodore charges Origen with Hellenism. That is really the point of the criticism: Origen, via Philo, introduced 'pagan allegory'. Thus Theodore echoes Porphyry's criticism of Origen. On this point most modern scholars have followed Porphyry and Theodore. How one interprets the early history of Christian biblical interpretation, and more generally the relation of Christianity to Hellenism, will turn on this issue. I am more inclined to follow H. de Lubac (and to interpret the Theodore passage differently) who argued in his *Exégèse Médiévale* that Origen's allegory came from Paul, not the Greeks.[1] It is the merit of Runia's book that he is aware of these issues (as his discussion of Wolfson and Harnack shows) and that in discussing Philo in early Christian literature he makes us think about them in a new way. That one might be led to a different interpretation of the evidence on this point is no argument against this fine book.

University of Virginia

---

[1] *Exégèse médievale: les quatre sens de l'Ecriture,* 2 vols. in 4, Theologie 41–42 (Paris 1959–61).

Philo's *Nachleben* in Judaism

DAVID WINSTON

In his remarkably well-informed and masterful synthesis of the literature dealing with Philo's impact on early Christian writings, Runia includes a brief section on how Philo fared in later Jewish tradition. His assessment here, as elsewhere in the book, is lucid and convincing but it invites supplementation.

Runia raises the question of how we are to explain the rabbinic attitude toward Philo. 'Did they 'condemn him to silence', as Weiss has argued? Or should we take the view of Winston that they were simply not interested in the Philonic project?' Runia then suggests that the rabbis may have rejected Philo precisely because his thought had been exploited by prominent Church thinkers such as Clement, Origen, and Eusebius. 'The process of rejection would then run parallel to the rejection of the Septuagint as an acceptable Greek translation of the Bible' (pp. 14–15). This analogy is certainly useful, but it does not, in my opinion, fully explain the total rabbinic silence concerning Philo. The fact is that there was a sufficiently long interval during which Philo could have left his mark on rabbinic thought before his writings began to be extensively employed by Christians towards the end of the second century CE. Although the Septuagint began to fall into disfavor among Jews in the second century CE,[1] having been displaced by Aquila's radical revision of it,[2] we nevertheless find it positively evaluated in *b. Megillah*

[1] The low esteem that later marks the rabbis' attitude to the Septuagint is reflected in *Massekhet Soferim's* first account of its making in 1.7: 'It once happened that five elders wrote the Torah for King Ptolemy in Greek, and that day was as ominous for Israel as the day on which the golden calf was made, since the Torah could not be accurately translated' (trans. Slotki). The dating of *m. Soferim* is uncertain. Stemberger summarizes the most recent views as follows: 'Since the Babylonian Talmud is frequently cited, this tractate in its present form cannot be dated prior to the middle of the eighth century, even if earlier forms must be assumed' (H. L. Strack and G. Stemberger, *Introduction to the Talmud and Midrash* (Edinburgh 1991) 248). Similarly, in the Gaonic addition to *Megillat Ta'anit* we read: 'On the eighth of Tebet the Law was written in Greek in the days of King Ptolemy and darkness came on the world for three days' (cited by Moses Hadas, *Aristeas to Philocrates* (NewYork 1951) 83).

[2] For an excellent discussion of the statement in *y. Megillah* 1.11, 71c, 'Aquila the Proselyte presented his translation of the Torah before R. Eliezer and R. Joshua and they praised him, and said to him, 'Thou art fairer than the children of men' (Ps 95:3)', see Saul Lieberman, *Greek in Jewish Palestine* (New York 1942) 15–28. The continued popularity of Aquila's translation among Jews, even as late as the sixth century, can be

The Studia Philonica Annual **6 (1994) 103–110**

9a, according to which it was a divinely inspired translation, and in *y. Megillah* 1.11, 71d, where the translators are called 'sages'.[1]

With regard to Philo, on the other hand, we lack any positive rabbinic assessment of him whatever, and are confronted instead by stony silence or at best anonymous allusions to some of his ideas. Upon further reflection, it seems to me that the reason for this was largely due to Philo's writing in Greek, and, perhaps more important, his utter reliance on the Septuagint version and lack of recourse to the Hebrew original. The rabbis never mention any of the Hellenistic Jewish writers who wrote in Greek, including even Josephus who had originally composed his account of the Jewish War against the Romans in his 'ancestral language', presumably Aramaic (*BJ* 1.3). They could hardly credit the exegetical work of one who could not read Scripture in the original. Moreover, as I have already indicated elsewhere, the rabbis were essentially uninterested in Philo's philosophical approach, indifferent as they were to all philosophical speculation generally.

In spite of the fact that Philo is never mentioned by name in rabbinic literature, some echoes of his thought are clearly discernible. Runia has correctly pointed out that 'we do have at least one example of how a third century Jew in Palestine had contact with Philo's works, R. Hosha'ia of Caesarea. Numerous scholars have noted the similarity

---

seen from Justinian's Novella 146 from the year 553: 'We therefore decree that wherever there are Jews who so desire, the Holy Scriptures may be read in the synagogues in Greek... The Jewish interpreters shall not be allowed to corrupt the Hebrew text on account of their being the only ones who understand it, relying as they do on the ignorance of the people who do not notice the corruption. Those, however, who read in Greek are to use the Septuagint, the most accurate translation of all, which is to be preferred... But in order that we may not seem to deny the Jews the other versions, we give them permission to use, if they so wish, the translation of Aquila, although the author is of alien race and his translation shows not inconsiderable differences from that of the Septuagint' (translation in Paul Kahle, *The Cairo Geniza* (New York 1959[2]) 315–16).

[1] Cf. *Avot de R. Natan B* 37, p. 94 Schechter, where they are called *zekenim*, 'elders', a title given only to scholars. Their number, however, is there given as five. This number is also found in the extracanonical *Massekhet Soferim* 1.7, although it is lacking in the important Munich MS of the *Babylonian Talmud*, and according to some scholars is the result of a scribal error (*hazekenim*, 'the elders', having been misread as *he zekenim*, 'five elders'). The notion of the divine inspiration of the translators, too, is found in the second account of the making of the translation in *Soferim* 1.8: 'It also happened that King Ptolemy assembled seventy-two elders and placed them in 72 [separate] rooms without telling them the reason for which he had assembled them. He then went to each one of them and said to him, 'Write for me [a translation of] the Torah of Moses your master'. The Omnipresrent [*ha-Makom*] inspired them and the mind of all of them was identical, so that each on his own wrote the [same translation of the] Torah, introducing [the same] thirteen alterations' (Not all are found in the extant versions of the Septuagint) (trans. Slotki).

between the image used by the Rabbi in *Gen. R.* 1.1 and Philo's striking image of the founding of the city in *Opif.* 17–18' (p. 14). Professor Urbach, however, one of the leading Talmudists of this generation, has argued that R. Hosha'ia's homily contains not the slightest reference to the world of Ideas or to the location of the Ideas. In the analogy, 'the architect does not plan the building in his head, but he makes use of rolls and tablets'—a fact that Philo carefully refrained from mentioning, because it contradicted his purpose in adducing the analogy... The Torah in which God looked contains no forms and sketches of temples, gymnasia, markets and harbors, and this Torah is not a concept but the concrete Torah with its precepts and statutes, which are inscribed in letters. Out of those letters and not from numbers, are the utterances with which the Almighty created the world constructed'.[1] Against this, I should like to point out that the first chapter of Genesis does indeed contain a broad outline of the structure of the universe which could be seen by the homilist as the intelligible pattern employed by the divine architect. It is perfectly clear from the passage in *Leg.* 3.97–99, which is generally thought to reproduce material from Aristotle's *De Philosophia* (Ross, fr. 13, *ap.* Cicero *ND* 2.95–96), that the parallel to the entrances, colonnades and all the other buildings of the analogy, are the heavens revolving in a circle and containing all things within them, the earth, streams of water and air in between, livings things, and varieties of plants and crops. As for the rabbi's obliterating the main object of Philo's analogy—which was to show that just as the city prefigured in the architect's mind held no place externally but was stamped within, so too the intelligible world could have no other location than the divine Logos—it is quite clear that what had caught the fancy of R. Hosha'ia in Philo's analogy was the figure of the architect and his use of a plan for the construction of the city he was commisioned to design. Philo's polemic with some Middle Platonists who probably still maintained that the intelligible Forms were independent of the Demiurge and were perhaps located in some sort of ὑπερουράνιος τόπος or supercelestial realm, held no interest for the rabbi and he therefore ignored that aspect of the analogy. Hosha'ia was only anxious to show that the Torah was God's architectural plan, and writing for fellow Palestinian Jews, unlike Philo, he could take it for granted that the Torah was itself a product of the divine mind. Finally, there is no reference in the rabbi's homily to God's employment of the letters of the Torah as his instrument of creation. It is only stated that the Holy One looked into the Torah, as an architect consulting his plans, and created the world.

---

[1] E. E. Urbach, *The Sages: Their Concepts and Beliefs* (Jerusalem 1979) 200.

Another question that scholars have found intriguing is the extent of knowledge about Philo and his writings by both Jews and Arabs in the early Islamic period. Runia provides an excellent summary of what is known about this and cautiously concludes that 'one must suspect that more evidence will have to be unearthed before solid results can be reached'. I will not discuss the puzzle of the identity of the sect of the *Maghārīya* and al-Qirqisānī's reference to the 'Alexandrian' (*al-iskandarani*) who belonged to that sect, since the evidence available to us is too meager to allow any sound conclusions in this matter. I should like, however, briefly to review the evidence for a knowledge of Philo's writings by both Qirqisānī (1st half of the 10th century) and Saadia (882–942). Bruno Chiesa has suggested that the structure of Qirqisānī's *Kitāb al-Anwār Wal-Marāqib* (*The Book of Lights and Watchtowers*), which revolves around the Decalogue, a characteristic of many later Qaraite works (e.g. Yehudah Hadassi's *Eshkol ha-Kofer*, 12th century; Samuel al-Maghribi's *al-Murshid*, *The Guide*, 15th century), was inspired by Philo's treatises *On the Decalogue* and the *Special Laws*. Bernard Revel had already indicated that 'the Karaites share Philo's view that the Decalogue is the text on which the whole law is but a commentary'.[1] Hirschfeld published a fragment discovered in the Cairo Genizah that derives from Qirqisānī's *Book of Lights*, bk. 6, and which cites a passage from the *Muqaddima* or *Prolegomena* of al-Iskandarani, in which the question is raised as to why God revealed the Decalogue and the rest of the Torah in the desert and not in the city. Two answers are given: (1) This was done on account of the idolatrous practices that took place in the cities (cf. *Mekilta, Pisḥa* 1, Lauterbach 1.3: God revealed himself to Moses in 'the land of Egypt', i.e. outside the city, because it was full of abominations and idols). (2) When God desired to present them with the land of Canaan and wealth... This is compared to a man who has a son. He desires to love him and hand over to him all his property. But before doing so he must be educated and taught, and the property is then given to him'.[2] Rabbinic Midrash raises the same question but gives different answers (*Mekilta* on Exod 19:2: 'It was given in a public place, for had it been given in the Land of Israel, the Israelites would have said to the nations of the world, 'You have no share in it'' (translation Lauterbach

---

[1] Bruno Chiesa and Wilfrid Lockwood, *Ya'qūb Al-Qirqisānī On Jewish Sects and Christianity* (Frankfurt am Main 1984) 28, 45, n. 90. Revel notes that 'the famous nineteenth century Karaite Abraham Firkowitsch (in his preface to *Mivhar Yesharim*) indeed asserts that Philo was a Karaite, but, according to him, Jesus too was a Karaite'; see Bernard Revel, *The Karaite Halakah and its relation to Sadducean, Samaritan and Philonian Halakah* (Philadelphia 1913).

[2] Trans. Hirschfeld, *JQR* 17 (1905) 65–66.

2.198). Philo, however, in *Decal.* 2–17 offers answers similar to those found in Qirqisānī (answers 1 and 3; 2 is very similar to 1, while answer 4 is in the name of others). Leopold Cohn suggested that Philo's treatise *On the Decalogue* could be considered a prologue to his *Special Laws*.[1]

I turn now to Saadia. A fragment of his polemical work against the Qaraites, the *Kitāb al-Tamyiz* (*Book of Distinction*), which appears to have dealt especially with calendrical matters, was found in the Cairo Geniza by Hirschfeld. It reads as follows: 'And as for Judah the Alexandrian, he says that just as there are fifty days between the *bikkurim* of barley and the *bikkurim* of wheat, in the same way there are fifty days between the *bikkurim* of wheat and the *bikkurim* of wine, which is ... at the end of the month of Tammuz, and fifty days between the *bikkurim* of wine and those of oil. The offering of oil is on the 20th day of Elul. He [Judah] provides proof of this'. 'This citation', writes Baumgarten, 'is not found in Philo's extant writings, but the sequence of fifty day periods to which it alludes is characteristic of the calendar of the Therapeutae described by Philo, with the reservation that the festive gatherings of the latter were apparently held every seven weeks, while Saadia refers to only three such periods related to the harvest sequence'.[2] The Temple Scroll shows us that the Qumran sect had three first fruit festivals, each to be celebrated after counting fifty days. Baumgarten concludes that it is now possible to view the pentecontad feasts of the Therapeutae as a reflex of the first fruit festivals at Qumran.

Even more intriguing is the fact that Philo's attempt to classify each of the Torah's commands by assigning it to one of the ten commandments (called γένη or κεφάλαια: *Decal.* 19, 154; *Spec.* 1.1), thereby imposing a logical structure on the vast array of biblical laws, finds no parallel either in Tannaitic or Amoraic sources, although it does appear in late Midrashim, beginning with the eleventh century. In *Bereshit Rabbati* (ed. Albeck, Jerusalem 1940, p. 8), which emanated from the circle of R. Moses ha-Darshan of Narbonne, it is stated: 'Corresponding to the Decalogue, which the Blessed Holy One uttered at Sinai, in which the whole of Torah is comprised, the 613 precepts...' As Urbach has noted:[3]

> ... it seems that the idea reached these works from Saadia. In his *'Azharot* (liturgical poems for the 'Feast of Weeks') he declares at the beginning of the first Commandment, 'And His word is like fire, whose sparks are many precepts shining in each Commandment/In his wisdom, which incorporated in the ten Commandments 613

---

[1] See S. Poznanski, 'Philon dans l'ancienne littérature judéo-arabe', *REJ* 50 (1905) 10–31. The reference to *Mekilta, Pisha* 1 is given by Y. Amir, *Die hellenistische Gestalt des Judentums bei Philon von Alexandrien* (Neukirchen-Vluyn 1983) 140.

[2] Joseph Baumgarten, *Studies in Qumran Law* (Leiden 1977) 137–38.

[3] Urbach, *The Sages* 360–62; Amir, *Die hellenistische Gestalt* 137.

> precepts to teach...' Finally it is stated: 'I have laid up in the Ten Commandments the 613 precepts of the Law of thine adherents ... corresponding to the 613 letters from *'anokhi* ['I', the first word of the Decalogue] to *'asher le-re'ekha* ['that is thy neighbor's', its concluding words]'.

Saadia does not base himself on any internal source. Did Saadia derive this from Philo?

No less suggestive is the fact that Philo derives the dietary laws from the tenth commandment, 'not to covet', which he had previously detached from the objects of this coveting, the common denominator of which is that they belong to 'your neighbor'. The forbidden foods can therefore be connected with the tenth commandment, even though they have nothing to do with the categories of 'mine' and 'yours'. Once again it is striking, as Amir has pointed out, that Saadia too connects the dietary rules with the tenth commandment.[1]

Of considerable interest for Philo's fate in the Latin Middle Ages, as Runia points out, is the fact that throughout this period he was considered the author of one of the semi-canonical books of the Bible, the Wisdom of Solomon. It is this fact that explains why Philo is included in a series of Hebrew prophets who are depicted around a crucifixion on a fresco in the Cathedral of Le Puy and in a similar manner in two series of reliquary busts that were formerly part of the high altar of Münster Cathedral. 'He is included because he is regarded as the author of Wisdom, who according to Patristic tradition prophesies the death of Christ (Wis 2:20). The relevant text is written out on a scroll held in front of both busts' (pp. 331–32). It is interesting to note that Philo's authorship of Wisdom is also taken for granted by one Flavius Mithridates, a Jewish convert to Christianity. The son of a learned Sicilian Jew, he was Professor of Theology at Rome and a teacher of Pico della Mirandola, for whom he translated into Latin a number of Kabbalistic treatises. In a sermon on the Passion that he preached before the Pope and Cardinals in the Vatican on Good Friday 1481, he cites evidence to show that what happened to Jesus had been foretold by the prophets and rabbis. The Pharisees are said by him to have produced against Jesus the widely known authority of Philo the Hebrew, and he then proceeds to cite Wis 2:12–20.[2]

---

[1] Amir, *ibid.* 163.

[2] In chap. 11, Mithridates maintains that the chief doctrine of the Pharisees was that the world is ruled by Fate and that it was this that caused their opposition to Jesus, who denied that doctrine. To bolster their position the Pharisees invoked the testimony of Philo. Mithridates cites many Greek sources for the doctrine of Fate and asserts that the Greeks derived much of their knowledge from the Jews. He cites Numenius' famous saying that 'Plato was nothing but Moses speaking Attic Greek', and that according to

I conclude with a few minor points. Runia notes that the Cappadocian father Gregory of Nyssa, 'discussing the notorious *Spoliatio Egyptiorum* carried out by the Israelites affirms that one cannot truly declare that Moses commanded this action, 'even though to some it seems reasonable (κἄν τισι δοκῇ εὔλογον) that the Israelites should have exacted the wages for their work from the Egyptians by this device' (*DVM* 2.113–14). The anonymous reference here surely points to Philo *Mos.* 1.141' (pp. 258–59). It would be more accurate to say, especially in view of the plural reference to 'some', that the anonymous reference points to Hellenistic Jewish writers such as Ezekiel the Tragedian (*Exagogē* 162: ὧν ἔπραξαν μισθὸν ἀποδῶσι βροτοῖς, 'in order to repay those mortals for the work they did'; cf. Jubilees 48:18: 'so that they might plunder the Egyptians in exchange for the servitude which they subjected them to by force'), the author of the Wisdom of Solomon (10:17: μισθὸν κόπων αὐτῶν), and Philo (*Mos.* 1.141–42: ἀναγκαῖον μισθὸν κομιζόμενοι).

Runia further remarks that 'in Gregory's exegesis of the creation of man at *Opif. Hom.* 2.131D he asks exactly the same *quaestio* as Philo poses in *Opif.* 77: 'Why is man created last of all creatures?' For his answer he also draws on material supplied by Philo. God is like a good banqueteer who does not invite his guests until everything is in readiness. The cosmos has been prepared so that man can be spectator of some of its wonders, and a ruler over others. Gregory thus takes over without reservation Philo's anthropocentrism and the theme of the *contemplatio mundi* so frequent in his works' (p. 253). The same question is raised in *Tosefta Sanhedrin* 8.8–9, where the following answers are offered: 'So that the heretics may not claim that God had a partner in creation; so that if he becomes cocky, he can be told, 'a mosquito preceded you in the works of creation'; so that he could enter immediately upon a mizvah; so that he could enter immediately upon a feast. A parable: It is like a king who built a palace and dedicated it, and prepared a feast, and then invited the

---

Clearchus, Aristotle was himself a Jew (Josephus, *C. Ap.* 1.177–81; Eusebius, *PE* 9.5. This misconception, as Wirzubski points out, is found in Abraham b. Shem-Tob Bibago's *Derekh Emunah* 46c, but derives from a non-Jewish source. Marsilio Ficino, in his *De Christiana Religione*, chap. 26, like Bibago (more correctly Bivagch), took Clearchus to be saying that Aristotle was a Jew. Ficino's source is evidently Eusebius, *PE* 9.5–6. His misunderstanding is based on the misleading punctuation of George of Trebizond's defective Latin translation, available in print since 1470. See Flavius Mithridates, *Sermo De Passione Domini*, ed. Chaim Wirszubski (Jerusalem 1963) 72–75, 101–102. Other Jewish writers who repeat various versions of the Aristotle story are Don Isaac Abravanel, Joseph ibn Shem Tov, Abraham Farissol, Gedaliah ibn Yahya, Solomon ibn Verga, and the Lithuanian Talmudist and historian Yehiel Halperin. Azariah de' Rossi, on the other hand, had the good critical sense to reject it. See Lester A. Segal, *Historical Consciousness and Religious Tradition in Azaria de' Rossi's Me'or 'Einayim* (Philadelphia 1989) 50–51.

guests. Similarly Scripture says, 'Wisdom has builded her house', this is the King of the kings of kings who created the world by wisdom; 'She hath hewn out her seven pillars', these are the seven days of creation; 'she hath prepared her meat, she hath mingled her wine, she hath also furnished her table', these are the seas and the rivers and all the other requirements of the world. 'She hath sent forth her maidens and calleth: whoso is thoughtless and lacks understanding let him turn hither', this is Adam and Eve'.[1]

Finally, Runia points out that 'two incidents in Moses' life are given special prominence in Gregory's account. Here the ultimate goals of spiritual perfection becone manifest. When Moses enters into the darkness of the cloud (Exod 20:21) he 'gains access to the invisible and incomprehensible, and there sees God' (*DVM* 2.163). When Moses later again climbs the mountain and asks God to reveal himself (Exod 33:13), the request is both denied and fulfilled: the desire is fulfilled, and yet it never ceases or comes to be sated (2.232)' (p. 260). In this connection, Gregory writes: 'And the bold request that goes up the mountains of desire asks this: to enjoy the Beauty [of God] not in mirrors and reflections, but in face to face' (trans. Malherbe and Ferguson). Philo employs the same image when he describes Moses' desire to behold God directly as follows: 'Would that I did not behold your form as in a mirror (κατοπτρισαίμην) in aught else than in you' (*Leg.* 3.101).

One last point. Runia notes that according to De Lange, 'Origen's extensive use of etymologies had three possible sources: (a) the works of Philo; (b) *onomastica*; (c) contemporary Jewish traditions. Certainly, he argues, a number of Philo's etymologies are taken over by Origen, but these amount to only a small proportion of all the etymologies found in his works. Moreover he sometimes accompanies the Philonic interpretation by an alternative view. In De Lange's view the source of some of these alternatives may well have been the Rabbinic tradition. A difficulty here that he does not consider is the fact that the etymologies require translation from Hebrew to Greek, which would not interest the majority of Rabbis' (pp. 181–82). The fact is that the rabbis did sometimes derive Hebrew names and words from Greek. Moreover, as Eilberg-Schwartz has pointed out, they thought that other languages may preserve earlier meanings of certain Hebrew words.[2]

Graduate Theological Union

---

[1] Cf. *B. Sanhedrin* 38a; *Gen. R.* 8.6, Theodor-Albeck 61; 15.4, T-A 137. Theodor cites Philo, Gregory of Nyssa, and Ambrosius. Cf. also Seneca *Ep.* 90.

[2] See D. Winston, 'Aspects of Philo's Linguistic Theory', *SPhA* 3 (1991) 120, n. 30.

INSTRUMENTA

REFERENCES TO PHILO FROM JOSEPHUS UP TO 1000 AD

DAVID T. RUNIA

From the very first edition of Philo's complete works it has been customary to include a list of ancient witnesses to Philo that can be gathered from the remains of ancient and early medieval literature. The editions of Mangey and Cohn-Wendland both give quite lengthy lists of passages in which reference was made to Philo.[1] The first of these witnesses is the Jewish author Josephus. The remainder are all Christian sources, for, as we all know, it was in the Christian tradition that Philo was preserved and transmitted. Various additional references are also given in the monographs of Siegfried and Conybeare, and there is a rather undigested complilation of relevant material in the bibliography of Goodhart and Goodenough.[2] So far, however, there has never been an attempt to compile a *complete* list of references to Philo in the ancient and medieval sources. In my recent monograph on *Philo in Early Christian Literature* I decided to include such a list in an Appendix.[3] This list contained a number of omissions and errors. So it seemed worthwhile to publish a second, corrected version of the list as an instrument of research for readers of this Annual.

This list contains all those passages in which Philo is referred to by name. In addition references are also given to texts in which Philo is referred to in anonymous terms, in phrases such as 'some say' or 'one of my predecessors said' (these occur rather frequently in Patristic exegesis). Inclusion of these anonymous references is necessary somewhat arbitrary and incomplete. Such references are marked by a dagger (†). Full details on the texts where the reference is found are not given, but these

---

1 References below on p. 112.

2 C. Siegfried, *Philo von Alexandria als Ausleger des alten Testaments* (Jena 1875); F. C. Conybeare, *Philo about the Contemplative Life* (Oxford 1895, repr. New York 1987); H. L. Goodhart and E. R. Goodenough, 'A General Bibliography of Philo Judaeus', in Goodenough, E. R., *The Politics of Philo Judaeus: Practice and Theory* (New Haven 1938; repr. Hildesheim 1967).

3 *Philo in Early Christian Literature: a Survey*, CRINT III 3 (Assen–Minneapolis 1993) 348–356. See further the special section above pp. 90–110.

can be easily found through consultation of various reference works.[4] I have tried in each case to use the most recent edition available. A very brief summary of the contents of the reference is given (it would take up too much space to include the texts entire). The authors included in the list are presented in approximate chronological order. Some attempt has been made to include references to Philo outside the Latin and Greek tradition, notably in works preserved in Syriac and Armenian.[5] Cut-off point is the date 1000 AD. This date is of course quite arbitrary, and there are a considerable number of subsequent references to Philo in Byzantine and Medieval Latin literature. But we have to stop somewhere, and the competence of the compiler is already being stretched to the limit.

Finally I indicate in square brackets behind each reference if it has been included in earlier lists of testimonia. The lists of Mangey and Cohn are still useful because they print the texts involved (though often in outdated versions). The key used to indicate earlier lists is as follows:

T = A. TURNEBUS, *Philonis Iudaei in libros Mosis, de mundi opificio, historicos, de legibus; eiusdem libri singulares* (Paris 1552): Περὶ τοῦ Φίλωνος (pages unnumbered)

V = Vulgate edition (TURNEBUS–HOESCHELIUS–GELENIUS), *Philonis Ioudaei omnia quae extant opera*, published in various forms in 1613, 1640, 1691, 1729: Illustrium et praecellentium scriptorum de Philone testimonia (pages unnumbered).

M = T. MANGEY, *Philonis Judaei opera quae reperiri potuerunt omnia*, 2 vols. (London 1742): Veterum testimonia de Philone Judaeo (xxi–xxix).

C = L. COHN and P. WENDLAND, *Philonis Alexandrini opera quae supersunt*, 6 vols. (Berlin 1896–1915): Testimonia de Philone eiusque scriptis (1.lxxxxv–cxiii, compiled by Cohn).

Since the sources that refer to Philo are widely scattered throughout diverse linguistic and literary traditions, the present list no doubt contains omissions and in due course will have to be supplemented by new discoveries. For the present time, however, it is as complete as I can make it, except in the case of the Armenian tradition.

---

4 Esp. the *TLG Canon* (edd. L. Berkowitz and K. A. Squitier), and for Patristic sources CPG and CPL; see further also in general the study cited in the previous note.

5 The reception of Philo in these traditions has not yet been thoroughly investigated. I have included all the references to Philo in the Syriac tradition which I know, relying here on the assistance of my colleague L. van Rompay. The references to the Armenian tradition are given *exempli gratia*. In both cases the cut-off point of 1000 AD does not make very good sense.

LIST OF REFERENCES

JOSEPHUS (37– c. 100)
Antiquitates Iudaeorum 18.8.257–260, 4.186 Niese: Philo, leader of the Embassy of Alexandrian Jews to the Emperor Gaius [VMC]

CLEMENT OF ALEXANDRIA (c. 150– c. 215)
Stromateis 1.31.1, 20.5 Stählin: etymologies of Hagar and Sarah [M?C]
Str. 1.72.4, 46.17: Philo the Pythagorean gives many proofs that Jewish philosophy is more ancient than Greek philosophy [M?C]
Str. 1.141.3, 87.25: on the kings of Judah (mistaken reference[6]) [MC]
Str. 1.152.2, 95.16: on the education of Moses as reported in the *De vita Moysis* [M?C]
Str. 2.100.3, 168.2: on great natures hitting on the truth [M?C]

CANON MURATORIANUS (c. 160–200)
fol. 2a.7–9, = lines 69–71: Wisdom of Solomon written by Philo (if Tregelles' emendation is accepted)

ORIGEN (c. 185–254)
Contra Celsum 4.51, 314.30 Borret SC[7]: Origen's opponent Celsus must be referring to the allegories of Philo and Aristobulus [MC]
C. Celsum 5.55, 152.18: allegorical exegesis of daughters of men (Gen. 6:2) in terms of souls desirous of bodies†
C. Celsum 6.21, 232.17: Philo composed a book about Jacob's ladder (i.e. *Somn.*) [MC]
C. Celsum 7.20, 60.5: the Law as two-fold, literal and figurative†
Selecta in Genesim 27, PG 12.97C: the six days in creation account for the sake of order (cf. *Opif.* 13, 26–28)†
Sel. in Genesim 44, PG 12.129D: on Pharaoh the φαῦλος who, attached to *genesis*, celebrates his birthday (cf. *Ebr.* 208)† (perhaps paraphrase of *Comm. in Matt.* 10.22)
Homiliae in Exodum 2.2, 74.3ff. Borret SC: on the Jewish midwives, exegesis Ex. 1:17 (cf. *Her.* 128)†
Hom. in Leviticum 8.6, 34.9ff. Borret SC: on the colour of the leper, exegesis Lev. 13:14–15 (cf. *Deus* 125)†
Hom. in Numeros 9.5, 61.8 Baehrens: ethical interpretation of the alive and the dead, exegesis Num. 17:13 (cf. *Her.* 201)†
Hom. in Josua 16.1, 358.1 Jaubert SC: presbyters in scripture determined not by length of years (cf. *Sobr.* 17)†

---

[6] On this mistaken reference see further above p. 3.
[7] Line number on page, not of chapter.

Hom. in Jeremiam 14.5, 74.26 Nautin SC: the wise man complains to Sophia, exegesis Jer. 15:10 (cf. *Conf.* 49)†

Commentarii in Matt. 10.22, 10.30.5 Klostermann-Benz: on Pharaoh the φαῦλος who, attached to *genesis*, celebrates his birthday (cf. *Ebr.* 208)†

Comm. in Matt. 15.3, 10.354.30 : according to Philo it is better to be a eunuch than to rage after sexual intercourse (citation of *Det.* 176) [MC]

Comm. in Matt. 17.17, 10.635.16: on the principles of anthropomorphic language concerning God† [MC]

Comm. in Matt. frag. *ad* 25:31–34, 11.163.16: on the exegesis of Gen. 1:2 (cf. *Opif.* 32ff.)†

Comm. in Joh. 6.42.217, 151.16 Preuschen: on the descent of souls into bodies, exegesis Gen. 6:2†

PSEUDO-JUSTIN *Cohortatio ad Graecos* (between 220 and 300)

§9.2, 34.21 Marcovich: the 'most wise historians' Philo and Josephus on Moses as ancient ruler of the Jews [MC]

§10.1, 36.8: Philo and Josephus on the life of Moses [MC]

§13.4, 41.29: translation of the LXX is no myth, the author has seen the translators' cells himself and is corroborated by Philo and Josephus [MC]

ANATOLIUS of Alexandria, bishop of Laodicaea (died c. 280)

cited at Eusebius *HE* 7.32.16: evidence of Philo on the date of Easter [C]

PETER, bishop of Alexandria (*sedit* 300–311) and his opponent, the Montanist TRICENTIUS

cited at *Chronicon Paschale* PG 92.73B-C, 76B: appeal to ancient Hebrew sages on the Paschal question†

EUSEBIUS of Caesarea (c. 260–339)[8]

Chronicon ad Ol. 203, 213 Karst: Philo of Alexandria, a learned man, was prominent

Chr. ad Ol. 203, 213 Karst, 176.15–18 Helm: Sejanus attempts to destroy the Jewish people, as recorded in Philo's *Legat.*

Chr. ad Ol. 204, 214 Karst, 177.18 – 178.3 Helm: Flaccus descrates the Jewish synagagues at Alexandria, impelling Philo to undertake the embassy [MC]

Chr. ad Ol. 204, 214 Karst 178.17–20 Helm: statues of Gaius placed in synagagues, as Philo and Josephus report

Historia Ecclesiastica preface to book 2, 100.20 Schwartz: this book put together from writings of Clement, Tertullian, Josephus, Philo

[8] I have not included the references to Philo in the summaries preceding the books of *HE* and *PE*, except the significant remark at the end of the summary of *HE* book 2.

HE 2.4.2–6.4 : Philo introduced and then used as a source for events during the reign of Caligula [TVMC]
HE 2.16.2–18.8: Philo as a source for the first Christians in Egypt, as witness in his *De vita contemplativa*; inventory of Philo's writings [TVMC]
HE 6.13.7: Clement refers to Philo in his *Stromateis*
HE 7.32.16: extract from Canons of Anatolius on the date of Easter, referring to the evidence of Philo and other Jewish authors (see also above under Anatolius) [C]
Praeparatio Evangelica 1.9.20 Mras: Eusebius indicates that he means Philo of Byblos, not 'the Hebrew'
PE 7.12.14—13.7: texts from Philo quoted to prove biblical basis for the 'theology of the second cause' [M]
PE 7.17.4–18.3: again Philonic text used to interpret biblical doctrine, this time on the nature of man
PE 7.20.9–21.5: Philo quoted on the subject that matter is not uncreated (ἀγένητος)
PE 8.5.11–7.21: quotes from Philo's *Hypothetica* on the flight from Egypt and the Mosaic constitution [M]
PE 8.10.19–12.20: quote from same work and *Prob.* on the Jewish ascetic way of life exemplified by the Essenes [M]
PE 8.12.21–14.72: extracts from *Opif.* on creation and *Prov.* 2 on providence to illustrate Jewish theology [M]
PE 11.14.10–15.7: repetition of Philonic material on the second cause [M]
PE 11.23.12–24.12: quotes from *Opif.* on the Mosaic (and Platonic) theory of ideas
PE 13.18.12–16: quotes from *Spec.* 1 on the Mosaic injunction not to worship the heavenly bodies
Demonstratio evangelica 8.2.123, 390.5 Heikel: Philo's evidence on Pilate and the episode of the Golden shields (*Legat.* 299) [M]

EUSEBIUS of Emesa (c. 300–359)
Frag. in *Catena in Genesim ad* Gen. 2:6, no. 194 Petit: citation of fragment from *QG* 1.3 on how 'spring' can be understood collectively

DIDYMUS THE BLIND (313–398)
Commentarii in Genesin 118.24, 119.2, 19 Nautin SC: exegesis Gen. 4:1–2, allegorization of Cain and Abel
Comm. in Gen. 139.12: exegesis Gen. 4:18, Philo is invoked as useful source of information for etymologies (cf. *Post.* 66–75)
Comm. in Gen. 147.17: exegesis Gen. 5:3–5, Philo again useful source if one wants a μυστικὸς λόγος for names and numbers
Comm. in Gen. 235.28, 236.8: exegesis Gen. 16, Philo gives a different allegorical interpretation than Paul for Sarah and Hagar

Commentarii in Ecclesiaten 276.19–22 Gronewald: exegesis of Eccl. 9:9a recalls Philo's interpretation of Hagar in Gen. 16
Comm. in Eccl. 300.15 Gronewald: exegesis Eccl. 10:7–8, citing Philo's life of Moses on philosophers as kings (cf. *Mos.* 2.2)
Comm. in Eccl. 356.10–14 Binder-Liesenborghs: exeg. Eccl. 12:5 on the special nature of the almond tree (cf. *Mos.* 2.186)†
Commentarii in Zacchariam 320.6–9 Doutreleau: sword in Zach. 11:17 recalls oracle to Abraham in Gen. 12:1, which is given an allegorical interpretation†

EPIPHANIUS (c. 315–403)
Panarion (*Adv. Haer.*) 1.29.5.1–3 Holl: One may learn more about the Iessaioi from the historical writings of Philo, who visited the early Christians at Lake Mareotis [MC]

BASIL OF CAESAREA (c. 330–379)
Ep. 3.190, 74.23 Deferrari LCL: Philo interprets manna as if drawing on a Jewish tradition [MC]

GREGORY OF NYSSA (c. 338– c. 395)
Contra Eunomium cap. 9.1, 1.16.20 Jaeger[9]: Eunomius' doctrine of God draws on Philo
C. Eun. 3.5.24, 2.168.17: Eunomius glues together a rag-bag of statements, for which Philo supplies some material
C. Eun. 3.7.8–9, 2.217.19–218.3: further explanation of Eunomius' theft from Philo
De vita Mosis 2.113, 67.22 Musurillo: a literal justification of the *spoliatio Egyptiorum* is rejected†
Vita Mos. 2.191, 98.15: some predecessors have regarded the blue of the high priest's tunic as symbolizing the air†
De infantibus praemature abreptis 77.23–78.23 Horner: man created so that the earth would not be bereft of intelligence†

CALCIDIUS (*floruit* 350 (?))
Commentarius Timaei 278, 282.8 Waszink: Philo interprets the heaven and earth in Gen. 1:1 in terms of ideas and compares them with the creation of archetypal man before corporeal man

PS. CHRYSOSTOM (homily dated 387)
In sanctum Pascha sermo 7.2, PG 59.748: the Hebrew sages Philo and Josephus assure us that Easter must take place after the spring equinox [MC]

---

[9] The summary was probably added by a later hand, as noted by Jaeger in his edition.

AMBROSE (339–397)[10]

De Paradiso 2.11, 271.8–272.2 Schenkl: exegesis of Adam and Even in terms of νοῦς and αἴσθησις†

Par. 4.25, 281.19–282.5: exegesis Gen. 2:15, man's double task in Paradise; Philo as a Jew only gives a moral interpretation [MC]

De Cain et Abel 8.32, 367.2 Schenkl: the Word is not God's product (*opus*) (cf. Philo), but is himself producing (*operans*)†

De Noe 13.43–44, 441.8–21 Schenkl: exegesis Gen. 7.4, rain for forty days and nights refers allegorically to man and woman†

Noe 14.47, 445.9–16: exegesis Gen. 7:15, the double divine name†

Noe 15.52, 449.26: our predecessors on the 15 cubits of Gen. 7:20†

Noe 17.63, 459.1–6: exegesis Gen. 8:15, water as the force of the passions†

Noe 26.99, 482.17: on the exegesis of the repetition of 'God' in Gen. 9:6†

De Abrahamo 2.11.83, 634.14 Schenkl: a question raised by the seemingly excessive death sentence in Gen. 17:14†

De fuga saeculi 4.20, 180.12 Schenkl: the etymology of Bethuel†

RUFINUS (c. 345– c. 410)

Historia Ecclesiastica 2.4–6, 2.16–18 Mommsen: Latin translation of Eusebius' work (see above)

JEROME (347–420)

Adversus Iovinianum 2.14, PL 23.317A: Philo has written a book on the Essenes

Chronicle, translation of Eusebius: see above under Eusebius

Commentarius in Amos 2.9 CCL 76.238.314: etymology of Esau as meaning 'oak'

Comm. in Amos 3.6, CCL 76.304.182: on the seven ages of life (cf. *Opif.* 103ff.)

Commentarius in Danielem 1.1.4a, CCL 75A.779.60: Philo thinks the language of Hebrews was Chaldean [MC]

Commentarius in Hiezechielem 4.10b, CCL 75.171.1160: Philo on the hyacinth of the high-priestly robes (cf. also 8.7, 75.362.850)

De viris illustribus 11, 96.5 Ceresa-Gastaldo: brief biographical notice, together with list of writings (Philo also briefly mentioned in §8.4 on the apostle Mark, §13.2 on Apion) [VMC]

Dialogus adversus Pelagianos 3.6.62, CCL 80.106.62: on the seven ages of life

Epistulae 22.35.8, CSEL 54.1.200.7: Philo reports on sober meals of the Essenes at Pentecost [M]

---

[10] The list of anonymous references in Ambrose is necessarily incomplete.

Ep. 29.7.1, CSEL 54.1.241.17: Philo as interpreter of high priestly vestments [M]

Ep. 70.3.3, CSEL 54.1.704.12: Philo, whom critics call the Jewish Plato, cited in discussion of sound usage of pagan learning [M]

Liber interpretationis Hebraicorum nominum, praefatio, CCL 72.1, 59.1–60.3 Philo according to Origen author of a book of Hebrew etymologies (incompletely cited in C-W) [MC]

Prefatio in librum Iob PL 28.1141A: Philo as one of the witnesses to fact that Hebrews composed poetry (cf. *Contempl.* 80) [MC]

Praefatio in libros Salomonis, PL 28.1308A: some consider Philo to be the author of the Wisdom of Solomon [M]

Hebraicae Quaestiones in Genesim 17:15, CCL 72.21: Sarah's name-change by doubling the R is erroneous†[11]

THEODORE OF MOPSUESTIA (c. 350–428)

Treatise against the Allegorists, CSCO.SS 190, p. 14.27–16.5 Van Rompay: Origen goes astray in learning the allegorical method from the Jew Philo

AUGUSTINE (354–430)

Contra Faustum 12.39, CSEL 25.366, PL 42.274: Philo goes astray in his allegorical exegesis of Noah's ark because he does not take Christ into account [MC]

ISIDORE OF PELUSIUM (c. 370– c. 435)

Epistulae 2.143, PG 78.585–589: unlike other Jews Philo was moved by the Truth to gain some idea of the orthodox doctrine of God as one substance and three hypostases [MC]

Ep. 2.270, PG 78.700C: Philo one of the sages who use μήποτε in the sense of ἴσως or ἔσθ' ὅτε [MC]

Ep. 3.19, PG 78.746A–B: the Jewish affirmation that the lawgiver only spoke literally is refuted by Philo who converts nearly the entire Old Testament into allegory [C]

Ep. 3.81, PG 78.788C–D: quotation from Philo proves that there are beneficent passions [MC]

OROSIUS (c. 378– after 418)

Historiae adversus paganos 7.5.6–7, 445.12 Zangemeister: Philo's embassy before Caligula fails

MARUTA OF MAIPHERKAT (*flor.* c. 410)

Canons III, CSCO.SS 192 p. 9 Vööbus: order of monks had different name in Old Covenant, as testified in Letters prepared by Philo for James, brother of the Lord

---

11 Other anonymous criticisms of Philonic etymologies at Siegfried *op. cit.* (n. 2) 396.

PSEUDO-PROCHORUS (*flor.* 400–450)
Acta Johannis 110.6–112.11 Zahn: Philo has an altercation with the Apostle John, but is converted after John heals his wife from leprosy

JULIAN OF ECLANUM (386– c. 454)
at Augustine *Contra secundam Juliani responsionem opus imperfectum* 4.123, PL 45.1420: unless one should think that the Hebrews Sirach or Philo, who are thought to be authors of the Wisdom of Solomon, are Manichees

THEODORET OF CYRRHUS (c. 393– c. 466)
Quaestiones in Exodum 24 PG 80.251A: Philo interprets Pascha as crossings (διαβατήρια) [MC]

SALAMINIUS HERMIAS SOZOMEN (c. 400– c. 460)
Ecclesiastical History 1.12.9–11, 26.4, 18 Bidez-Hansen: Philo describes the beginnings of the monastic movement [MC]
Eccl. Hist. 7.18.7, 328.11 Bidez-Hansen: Anatolius on Philo on the Easter question (taken over from Eusebius *HE* 7.32.16, see above)

CATENA IN GENESIM, *CATENA IN EXODUM* (end 5th century)
Numerous exegetical extracts from Philo under the headings Φίλωνος ἐπισκόπου, Φίλωνος Ἑβραίου, Φίλωνος.[12]

PROCOPIUS OF GAZA (c. 465– c. 529)
Extensive, always anonymously presented exegetical extracts from *QG* and *QE* in *Commentary on the Octateuch*, PG 87†

CASSIODORUS (487– c. 580)
Institutiones divinarum litterarum PL 70.1117B: Jerome right in attributing the Wisdom of Solomon to Philo [M]

JOHANNES LYDUS (490– c. 565)
De mensibus 4.47 103.14–104.1 Wuensch: Philo in his *Life of Moses* writes of his Chaldean origin and the fact that his books were written in Hebrew

ANONYMOUS ARMENIAN TRANSLATOR OF PHILO'S WRITINGS (c. 550)
Praefatio in libris Philonis De providentia, p. vii–xi Aucher: lengthy notice on Philo's life and description of translated works [C]

ISIDORE OF SEVILLE (c. 570– 636)
Etymologiae 6.2.30: Philo and the Wisdom of Solomon

---

[12] In the apparatus to *Mos.* C-W also cite extracts from the *Catena in Numeros* and the *Catena in Psalmos*.

BARḤADBŠABBA ʿARBAYA, bishop of Ḥalwan (c. 600)
Cause of the Foundation of the Schools, 375.6–376.4 Scher: Philo the Jew was Director of the School of biblical exegesis in Alexandria[13]

ANASTASIUS SINAÏTA (c. 610– c. 700)
Duae Viae 13.10.1–96, CCG 8.251 Uthemann: cites Ammonius of Alexandria who cites a dialogue between Philo and Mnason, in which Philo attacks the divinity of Christ [C]

CHRONICON PASCHALE (c. 650)
PG 92.69A: quotes *Mos.* 2.222–224 on the vernal equinox and the Passover feast [M]

ANANIAS SHIRAKATZI (c. 650)
Armenian Easter treatise, containing extensive reference to Philo's interpretation of Ex. 12:2, p. 126–127 Strobel[14]

PS.SOPHRONIUS (7th century)
Ἱερωνύμου ἐπιστολὴ πρὸς Δέξτρον (= Greek translation of Jerome, *De viris illustribus*) 12, 21, 23 von Gebhardt [C]

JOHN OF DAMASCUS (c. 675– c. 750)
Prol. in Sacra Parallela, PG 95.1040B, 1044B: Philo (and Josephus) are cited, even though they are Jews, because they can make a valuable contribution [MC]

BEDA VENERABILIS (c. 673–735)
In Marci evangelium praefatio, CCL 120.431: citation from Jerome on the beginnings of the church of Alexandria

GEORGE SYNCELLUS (died after 810)
Ecloga chronographica 399.5, 402.14, 19 Mosshammer: Philo on the reign of Gaius (taken from Eusebius) [M]

ANONYMOUS Syrian commentator of the works of Gregory of Nazianzus (8th–9th century)
ms. London, Brit. Libr. Add. 17,147, fol. 98a and 144a: some quotations are found from other writers, among them two quotations from 'Philo the Hebrew'

IŠOʿDAD DE MERV (c. 850)
Commentary on Exodus 23:19, 56.5 van den Eynde: Philo is cited on the injunction not to boil a lamb in its mother's milk (cf. *Virt.* 143–144)
Commentary on Numbers 7:11, 120.28 van den Eynde: on the phases on the moon and the ten sacrifices (cf. *Spec.* 1.177–178)

---

13 This rather inaccessible text is printed at Runia *op. cit.* (n. 3) 269–270.
14 Further references to Philo in the Armenian tradition are not recorded in our list.

FRECULPHUS, Bishop of Lisieux from c. 825 to 851
Chronicon 2.1.11, PL 106.1126: On Philo and the fate of the Jews under Gaius [M]

PHOTIUS, bishop of Constantinople (c. 820–891)
Bibliotheca 103–105, 2.71–72 Henry: record of Philonic works read, with critical comments added, to which a biographical notice is appended [VMC]

GEORGE THE SINNER (OR THE MONK) (c. 830– c. 890)
Chronicon 9.4 1.324.17 de Boor: in the reign of Gaius Philo and Josephus, the Hebrew sages, were prominent

ANASTASIUS INCERTUS (9th century)
In hexaemeron 7, PG 89.961D: Philo among those Church fathers who allegorized paradise in terms of the church [C]

ARETHAS, archbishop of Caesarea (c. 850– c. 940)
Commentary on the Apocalypse 1, PG 106.504D: on the Hebdomad [MC]

ANONYMOUS COMPILER of Nestorian exegesis (10th century (?))
Exegesis Psalmorum 29.1 Vandenhoff: Philo as 'spiritual philosopher' in a long list of exegetes

SOUDA (c. 1000)
1.10.14 Adler: s.v. 'Αβραάμ, Philo's book on the life of the πολιτικός will testify to Joseph [M]
1.18.32: on the term ἀγαλματοφορούμενος [M]
1.472.3: on the term βίος (reference mistaken, actually Eusebius, *Suppl. min. ad quaest. ad Marinum* PG 22.1008)
2.146.9: s.v. δύναμις, two powers enter into every soul [M]
2.655.3: in the notice on Josephus it is mentioned that Apion accused Philo
2.698.27: s.v. θεός, an extract from Isidore of Pelusium *Ep.* 2.143 on Philo's doctrine of God (see above under Isidore) [M]
2.705.29: s.v. θεραπευταί, Philo's account mentioned and name explained [M]
4.737–8: s. v. Φίλων, biographical notice. with list of writings [TVCM][15]

Leiden University

[15] Other Byzantine references printed by Mangey and Cohn and also two intriguing Jewish texts in Mangey are later than 1000 AD.

BIBLIOGRAPHY SECTION

PHILO OF ALEXANDRIA
AN ANNOTATED BIBLIOGRAPHY 1991

D. T. RUNIA, R. M. VAN DEN BERG,
R. RADICE, K. G. SANDELIN, D. SATRAN

1991*

M. ALEXANDRE JR., 'The Art of Periodic Composition in Philo of Alexandria', in D. T. RUNIA, D. M. HAY and D. WINSTON (edd.), *Heirs of the Septuagint. Philo, Hellenistic Judaism and Early Christianity: Festschrift for Earle Hilgert*, BJS 230 [= *The Studia Philonica Annual* 3 (1991)] (Atlanta 1991) 135–150.

Rhetoric for Philo is not merely the art of speaking well or a technique of persuasion. It has a crucial role in the interpretation of wisdom. Philo's method of writing lengthy and complex periods should be seen in the context of ancient rhetoric. Alexandre thus first briefly outlines the theory of the period in Greco-Roman rhetoric. He then proceeds to analyse a number of examples of Philonic periods, dividing them into cola and demonstrating Philo's love for various rhetorical techniques such as the use of isocolic phrases, *gradatio*, *amplificatio*. The examples given are *Legat.* 53–56, *Mos.* 2.253–255, *Flacc.* 123-124, *Ebr.* 157–159. In Philo's rhetoric structure is the key to meaning, but that meaning is placed in the service of the interpretation of scripture. (DTR)

J. N. BAILEY, '*Metanoia* in the Writings of Philo Judaeus', *Society of Biblical Literature Seminar Papers* 30 (1991) 135–141.

This study examines the use of μετάνοια and cognate terms in the writings of Philo, especially in the tractate *On Repentance*, a part of the work *On the virtues*. Philo is almost the only author of Greek philosophy who endorses μετάνοια as a virtue. It is concluded that the aims of this treatise were: (1) to show that repentance as part of Jewish religion is rational and virtuous, in an attempt to enhance adherence to the Law

* The principles on which this annotated bibliography is based have been outlined in *SPhA* 2 (1990) 141–142, and are largely based on those used to compile the 'mother work', R-R. One deviation is that all language restrictions have been abandoned. The division of the work has been as follows: material in English and Dutch by D. T. Runia (DTR) and R. M. van den Berg (RvdB); in French, German, Italian, Spanish by R. Radice (RR); in Hebrew by D. Satran (DS); in Scandinavian languages by K. G. Sandelin (KGS). Other scholars who have given valuable assistance are P. Borgen, P. W. van der Horst, H. J. de Jonge, K. A. Morland, T. Seland, D. Sly, G. Sterling, T. Seland.

The Studia Philonica Annual 6 (1994) 122-159

among an educated Hellenistic audience and to respond to philosophers who denigrated it; (2) to encourage proselytes to recognise the importance of their conversion, while at the same time urging ethnic Jews to fully accept them. (RvdB)

L. L. BELLEVILLE, *Reflections of Glory: Paul's Polemical Use of the Moses-doxa Tradition in 2 Corinthians 3:1–18*, JSNTSupp 52 (Sheffield 1991), esp. 31–35

The author examines the Jewish and Hellenistic Moses-doxa tradition in order to explain the differences that occur between 2 Cor. 3:7, 12–18 and Exod. 34:28–35, paying some attention to Philo, and especially to his *De Vita Moses*. As various parallels show, Philo and Paul both made use of the same Moses-doxa tradition concerning the prophet's changed appearance after he had descended from Mt. Sinai. (RvdB)

B. L. BLACKBURN, *Theios Anēr and the Markan Miracle Traditions*, WUNT 2.36 (Tübingen 1991), esp. 64-69.

In his survey of divine miracle workers of the pre-Christian period the author examines the treatment of Moses by Philo. He refutes the claim that for Philo Moses was a deity, although he admits that Philo saw him as a divine man on more intimate terms with God than the Moses that occurs in Exodus. (RvdB)

G. BOCCACCINI, *Middle Judaism: Jewish Thought 300 B.C.E. – 200 C.E.* (Minneapolis 1991), esp. 189–212.

To demonstrate the methods of Philo's exegesis of the Torah, the author discusses his treatment of two themes, memory and virginity. Philo follows the Aristotelian distinction between memory and recollection, but where Aristotle uses these terms for indicating functions of the mind only, Philo extends them to religious concepts used in describing the mind's path to the mystical encounter with God. In his reflection on virginity Philo accepts the negative perception of sexuality prevalent in Middle Judaism. New, however, is that he sees in virginity, as a part of continence, a way to regain the felicity of Eden. See further the review of this study by D. Winston at *SPhA* 5 (1993) 233–237. (RvdB)

P. BORGEN, 'The Sabbath Controversy in John 5:1–18 and Analogous Controversy Reflected in Philo's Writings', in D. T. RUNIA, D. M. HAY and D. WINSTON (edd.), *Heirs of the Septuagint. Philo, Hellenistic Judaism and Early Christianity: Festschrift for Earle Hilgert*, BJS 230 [= *The Studia Philonica Annual* 3 (1991)] (Atlanta 1991) 209–221.

Comparisons between Philo and John show that John 5:1–18 is a specifically christianized version of a conflict on the sabbath that was also present in the Jewish community in Alexandria. In both Philo and John exegesis of Gen. 2:2–3 plays a central role. (DTR)

A. P. BOS, *In de greep van de Titanen: Inleiding tot een hoofstroming van de Griekse filosofie*, Verantwoording 5 (Amsterdam 1991), esp. 89-96.

In this book, which concentrates on the views of the origin and destination of man as gvien in Greek pre-philosophical and philosophical thought, a chapter is devoted to Philo. After Philo, his Jewish background and his allegorical mode of interpretation have been introduced, attention is paid to his doctrine of the double creation of both the universe and man and to the destination of man, viz. his return to his divine origin. In order to illustrate the doctrine of the soul's journey, allegorical interpretations of various Pentateuchal passages are listed and briefly discussed. (RvdB)

S. B. Bowman, 'Art. Philo', in A. P. Kazdhan (ed.), *Oxford Dictionary of Byzantium*, 3 vols. (New York–Oxford 1991) 3.1655.

Disappointly brief and superficial notice on the fate of Philo in the Byzantine period. (DTR)

H. Burkhardt, 'Inspiration der Schrift durch weisheitliche Personal-inspiration: zur Inspirationslehre Philos von Alexandrien', *Theologische Zeitschrift* 47 (1991) 214–225.

A modern theological orientation regards inspiration as a veritable dictation by God of the contents of revelation, so that the prophet can be considered as a kind of secretary or as God's quill. This brings inspiration close to mantic, and in a certain sense this association is present in Philo, for it is true that there are a considerable number of passages, e.g. *Spec.* 1.65 and 4.49,—almost certainly inspired by Plato—, which express the notion of inspiration with concepts and terms derived from the terminology of mantic. Nevertheless this analogy does not go beyond the level of terminology, and is used exclusively to demonstrate the divine origin of Mosaic wisdom. In this sense, the author concludes, Philo cannot be regarded as the spiritual father of the doctrine of the mechanical inspiration of scripture, as he is often regarded. (RR)

C. Carlier, *La* μητρόπολις *chez Philon d'Alexandrie: le concept de colonisation appliqué à la Diaspora juive* (Mémoire pour l'Académie des Inscriptions et Belles-Lettres, Ecole Biblique et Archéologique Française, Jerusalem 1991).

Taking *Legat.* 281 as starting point, the author presents a detailed study of Philo's use of the terms μητρόπολις and ἀποικία, also comparing it with what is found in the LXX. Behind Philo's seemingly Greek use of the term μητρόπολις lies a resurgence of the problem of the relation between the centre (Jerusalem) and the periphery (Jewish communities in the diaspora, described as ἀποικίαι). On the other hand Philo uses the term πάτρις to describe the city where the Jews live in the diaspora. This usage must be seen as being in opposition to the role of the μητρόπολις. (DTR)

A. Chester, 'Jewish Messianic Expectations and Mediatorial Figures', in M. Hengel and U. Heckel (edd.), *Paulus und das antike Judentum*, WUNT 58 (Tübingen 1991), esp. 48–50.

Sketching the main features and significance of mediatorial figures from the second century BC to the first century AD, the author turns to Philo's mediatorial concepts. The most important of these is the Logos which, as a figure separate from God, represents God's activity towards and relation with the world. (RvdB)

A. D. DE CONICK and J. FOSSUM, 'Stripped before God: a New Interpretation of Logion 37 in the Gospel of Thomas', *Vigilae Christianae* (1991) 123-150.

The authors reject the widely accepted interpretation of Logion 37 in the Gospel of Thomas as baptismal. In their view the message of the Logion is that encratitism was a requirement for salvation and the return to the pre-lapsarian condition of paradise. To support their alternative interpretation the authors make use of relevant passages in Philo. (RvdB).

J. D. CROSSAN, *The Historical Jesus: The Life of a Mediterranean Jewish Peasant* (San Francisco 1991).

In his assessment of the evidence for the historical Jesus, Crossan draws on Philonic material in three contexts. First, he weighs the evidence from Josephus and Philo (*Legat.*) for the aniconic shields and Caligula's statue (pp. 129–32), preferring the Josephan version where they differ. Second, he uses Philo as a representative of a sapiential understanding of the kingdom of God (pp. 288-89). Third, he draws on the Carabas episode and a governor's attitude toward a criminal condemned to crucifixion during feasts in *Flacc.* in his treatment of the passion narrative (pp. 380-81, 390-91). (DTR; based on summary supplied by G. Sterling)

S. DANIEL-NATAF [ס. דניאל-נטף] (ed.), פילון האלכסנדרוני. כתבים [Philo of Alexandria: *Writings*]: vol. 2, *Exposition of the Law, Part One*, Bialik Institute and Israel Academy of Sciences and Humanities (Jerusalem 1991).

This is the second in a projected five-volume presentation of the (Greek) Philonic corpus in modern Hebrew translation. The volume before us in no way departs from the high standard set by its predecessor in the series (see *SPhA* 2 (1990) 182-184). In accord with the guidelines set forward clearly in the introduction to the series (vol.1, xxii-xxiii), this volume presents the Hebrew reader with the initial portion of the general Exposition of the Law: *De opificio mundi*, *De Abrahamo*, *De Iosepho*, *De Decalogo*, and *De specialibus legibus* 1. This volume is the handiwork of the general editor of the series in conjunction with C. Schur, who contributed the translations of *Abr.* and *Spec.* 1. (DS)

E. DASSMANN *et al.*, *Reallexikon für Antike und Christentum*, Band XV = Lieferungen 113–120 (Stuttgart 1991).

Articles with special sections on Philo are: G. O'Daly, Art. 'Hierarchie', 41–73, esp. 50–51 (hierarchy); A. Lumpe–H. Bietenhard, Art. 'Himmel', 173–212, esp. 196–197 (heaven); J. Engemann, Art. 'Hirt', 577–607, esp. 589 (shepherd); J. Procopé, Art. 'Hochmut', 795–858, esp. 824–825 (pride, arrogance); F. K. Mayr, Art. 'Hören', 1023–1111, esp. 1071–1074 (hearing); A. Dilhle–B. Studer–F. Rickert, Art. 'Hoffnung', 1159–1250, esp. 1177–1178 (hope). (DTR)

E. DASSMANN *et al.*, *Reallexikon für Antike und Christentum*, Lieferung 121 (Stuttgart 1991).

Articles with special sections on Philo are: F.-L. Hossfeld–G. Schöllgen, Art. 'Hohepriester' 4–58, esp. 19–23 (High priest); G. J. M. Bartelink, Art. 'Homer' 117–147, esp. 125–126 (Homer). (DTR)

B. DECHARNEUX, 'Le temps et l'espace dans la double création philonienne du monde', in *L'espace et le temps: Actes du XXIIe congrès de l'Association des Sociétés de Philosophie de Langue Française (Dijon, 29–31 août)* (Dijon-Paris 1991) 142–144.

The conception of time appears to be a common element between *Aet.* and *Opif.*, even if in the two texts the same definition is used in order to reach opposed conclusions (in the one case the eternity of the cosmos, in the other its origin in creation). For Decharneux the difference is to be explained through the differing contexts, abstract and theoretical in *Aet.*, mythical in *Opif.* (RR)

L. H. FELDMAN, 'Nodet's New Edition of Josephus' *Antiquities*', *JSJ* 22 (1991) 88–113, esp. 90f.

In his extensive review of Nodet's new edition of the first three books of Josephus' *Antiquitates*, Feldman argues against the editor that there is more than a coincidental resemblance between the works by Philo and Josephus, listing a large number of parallel passages. (RvdB)

F. FENDLER, *Studien zum Markusevangelium: zur Gattung, Chronologie, Messiasgeheimnistheorie und Überlieferung des zweiten Evangeliums*, Göttinger theologische Arbeiten 49 (Göttingen 1991), esp. 62–68.

Even if we do not posses sufficient material to define the chronology of the Philonic writings in a precise manner, it can be maintained that the *De vita Moysis* is a late work. Fendler reaches this conclusion on the basis of a brief but articulated analysis of the treatise from diverse perspectives—linguistic, stylistic, compositional (confirming the division into two books), thematic, and finally from the viewpoint of its origin and the purpose for which it was written. The final part of the discussion (66–68) is devoted to an examination of the relations between *Mos.* and Mark's Gospel. (RR)

S. D. FRAADE, *From Tradition to Commentary: Torah and its Interpretation in the Midrash Sifre to Deuteronomy* (Albany 1991), esp. 7–13.

In his introductory chapter the author compares the Dead Sea scroll *pesarim*, the commentary of the *Sifre* and those by Philo to each other. Three structural features of Philo's commentaries, shared with the *Sifre*, distinguish them from the *pesarim*: (1) their dialectical style; (2) the enchaining of interpretations; (3) multiple interpretations. An important difference between the multiple interpretation of the *Sifre* and Philo's commentaries, however, is that the first lacks a standard hierarchical plan, in contrast to Philo, for whom the allegorical interpretation is the more important one in comparison with the literal one. (RvdB)

Y. FRANKEL [י. פרנקל], דרכי האגדה והמדרש [= *The Methods of the Aggadah and the Midrash*] (Jerusalem 1991), esp. 2.473-475.

In the course of this comprehensive investigation of rabbinic literature, the author briefly discusses possible connections with Philo's method. He relies on the study of Heinemann (R-R 5006) and concludes that 'even if in the general perception of Torah and its exegesis there are qualitative differences between the Jewish-Hellenistic philosopher and the Rabbis, there exists, nevertheless, a proximity in the sort of interpretative questions which they address to the biblical text' (473). (DS)

G. GILBERT, 'The making of a Jew: "God-fearer" or convert in the story of Izates [Josephus' JA 20.34-38]', *Union Seminary Quarterly Review* 44 (1991) 299–313, esp. 303–305.

In arguing that Izates was a Jew and not a 'God-fearer', the author adduces Philo as evidence of a Judaism in which there were Jews who were not circumcised. Passages discussed are *Migr.* 89–93, *QE* 2.2. (DTR)

I. GOBRY, 'La ténèbre (γνόφος): l'héritage alexandrin de Saint Grégoire de Nysse', *Diotima: Revue de Recherche Philosophique* 19 (1991) 79–89, esp. 79–81.

A passage in Book II of the *De vita Moysis* of Gregory of Nyssa (162ff.), in which it is stated that in order to obtain the *visio Dei* Moses had to enter into the darkness, certainly has Philonic precedents (*Post.* 13–16). This would explain the predominantly metaphysical character of the passage. Gregory, however, probably did not receive it directly from Philo, but made use of Clement of Alexandria as intermediary. (RR)

L. L. GRABBE, 'Philo and Aggada: a Response to B. J. Bamberger', in D. T. RUNIA, D. M. HAY and D. WINSTON (edd.), *Heirs of the Septuagint. Philo, Hellenistic Judaism and Early Christianity: Festschrift for Earle Hilgert*, BJS 230 [= *The Studia Philonica Annual* 3 (1991)] (Atlanta 1991) 153–166.

Grabbe notes that the question of the relation between Philo and the Aggada is important, but has never received an adequate treatment. He commends the study of Bamberger (= R-R 7703) for its methodological awareness, as distilled in six cautionary rules. But an analysis of the 41 examples of parallels that Bamberger collected between Philo and the Aggada reveals that he very often transgressed his own rules. Indeed only 6 of the original 41 examples survive as possibly valid, and even these are not compelling. Grabbe concludes the article by adding 4 more rules to Bamberger's list and briefly making some suggestions for a 'proper study'. (DTR)

P. GRAFFIGNA, 'Un hapax di Filone d'Alessandria: ἀγαλματοφορεῖν', *Maia* 43 (1991) 143–148.

This study undertakes a semantic analysis of the term ἀγαλματοφορέω. The term is an original Philonic creation, and it plays an important in his theory of the image. The essay examines the passage where Philo uses this verb, and compares this usage with several other similar terms and phrases in sources close to Philo. On the basis of this examination it is concluded that Philo coined the term to signify that an idea 'bears form' in the divine and human intellect. In Philo the specific term ἄγαλμα denotes an idea that reflects a higher model. Together with other phrases such as θεὸν περιφέρειν

(Epictetus *Diatr.* 137.17–18), τὸ θεῖον ἔχειν ἐν νῷ (Zeno, SVF 1.146 (25)), τῷ νῷ ἐνοικεῖν (Porphyry, *Ad Marc.* 11.20), τὴν εἰκόνα ἔχειν (*CH* I, *Poimandres*), ἀγαλματοφορέω constitutes a semantic 'paratactic' field, where the terms ἄγαλμα–εἰκών–τὸ θεῖον and the verbs περιφέρω–φέρω–ἐνοικέω can be interchanged. ἀγαλματοφορέω represents a synthesis of that field, unifying the various elements in it. (RR)

J. GRONDIN, *Einführung in die philosophische Hermeneutik* (Darmstadt 1991), esp. 33-36.

In the context of the history of philosophical hermeneutics attention is drawn to Philo's allegorical model of interpretation. (RvdB)

J. M. HALLMAN, *The Descent of God: Divine Suffering in History and Theology* (Minneapolis 1991), esp. 23–29.

Philo's views on the immutability or mutability of God are examined as part of an investigation into the viability of an incarnational Christology. The author argues that Philo's adherence to a doctrine of divine immutability (esp. in *Deus*) must be carefully analysed. It is suggestive, for example, that he never uses the concept of *apatheia* of God. It is concluded that Philo does not completely absorb the Greek notion of divine immutability and impassibility. The scriptural portrait of God remains dominant. (DTR)

R. G. HAMERTON-KELLY, 'Allegory, Typology and Sacred Violence: Sacrificial Representation and the Unity of the Bible in Paul and Philo', in D. T. RUNIA, D. M. HAY and D. WINSTON (edd.), *Heirs of the Septuagint. Philo, Hellenistic Judaism and Early Christianity: Festschrift for Earle Hilgert*, BJS 230 [= *The Studia Philonica Annual* 3 (1991)] (Atlanta 1991) 53–70.

This article approaches Philo's thought from a broad theological perspective, honouring him for interpreting the Bible for his time, just as we must do for ours. First four methods of biblical interpretation are outlined: allegory, typology, Bultmannian theology, Biblical theology of Sacred History (*Heilsgeschichte*). In opposition to these theologies the author presents the hermeneutic of Sacred Violence as proposed by R. Girard, which is then related to the Pauline theology of the cross. Hamerton-Kelly concludes that Philo was right to seek the universal meaning of the biblical text, but 'was wrong to find that meaning in a form of Platonism rather than in the Gospel of the Cross (70).' (DTR)

D. M. HAY (ed.), *Both Literal and Allegorical: Studies in Philo of Alexandria's* Questions and Answers on Genesis and Exodus, BJS 232 (Atlanta 1991).

First collective study devoted to the subject of Philo's *Quaestiones*, based in part on a seminar held in Anaheim in 1985. Individual contributions are summarized under the names of the authors. The volume concludes with a bibliography and four indices. See further the review by S.-K. Wan in this Annual, vol. 5 (1993) 222–227. (DTR)

D. M. HAY, 'References to Other Exegetes', in IDEM (ed.), *Both Literal and Allegorical: Studies in Philo of Alexandria's* Questions and Answers on Genesis and Exodus, BJS 232 (Atlanta 1991) 81–97.

Collects, analyses, and reflects on those passages in the *Quaestiones* in which Philo refers to other exegetes. Of the 47 references 9 may be purely hypothetical, while another 9 have parallels in other Philonic writings. Some of these are so close that Hay suggests there may not have been a great time gap between the *Quaestiones* and other exegetical works. The last part of the article makes interesting observations on the purpose of the treatises. The actual questions posed may well in many cases have come from previous or contemporary exegetes. Philo does not name them in order to lend his own work greater authority. The very form of the *Quaestiones*, Hay concludes, suggests that Philo saw himself as belonging to a community and succession of exegetes. (DTR)

D. M. HAY, 'Philo's View of Himself as an Exegete: Inspired, but not Authoritative', in D. T. RUNIA, D. M. HAY and D. WINSTON (edd.), *Heirs of the Septuagint. Philo, Hellenistic Judaism and Early Christianity: Festschrift for Earle Hilgert*, BJS 230 [= *The Studia Philonica Annual* 3 (1991)] (Atlanta 1991) 41–53.

The evidence on which Hay's discussion is based on is the collection of all those passages in Philo in which he uses the pronoun ἐγώ and/or the first person singular to describe his own exegetical activity. This yields interesting observations on Philo's perception of the inspiration he received as exegete and on the potential audience he may have had in mind. Philo may have avoided being specific on the nature of his audience because he expected (or at least hoped) that he would have a wide and continuing audience. (DTR)

E. HILGERT, 'A Review of Previous Research on Philo's *De Virtutibus*', *Society of Biblical Literature Seminar Papers* 30 (1991) 103–115.

Gives a survey of scholarship specifically devoted to the treatise *De virtutibus*. Hilgert first discusses the question of its structure and contents, then lists the mss. in which the treatise is found, followed by an account of printed editions and translations. He concludes with brief references to discussions on the relation between the treatise and Classical thought and New Testament studies. It would seem that much study has been devoted to Philo's teaching on the virtues, but little to his specific treatise *On the Virtues*. The article concludes with the challenging words: 'The door of opportunity stands open.' (DTR)

E. HILGERT, 'The *Quaestiones*: Texts and Translations', in D. M. HAY (ed.), *Both Literal and Allegorical: Studies in Philo of Alexandria's* Questions and Answers on Genesis and Exodus, BJS 232 (Atlanta 1991) 1–15.

Gives a thorough survey of the various traditons of the *Quaestiones*. The fragmentary Greek tradition is very complex, and we may be certain that not all fragments have yet been located. The Latin translation has been well edited by F. Petit. In the case of the Armenian translation the lack of a critical edition is keenly felt. Substantial work remains to be done on this tradition, but at least we have good translations . (DTR)

D. W. HURLEY, *A Historical and Historiographical Commentary on Suetonius' 'Life Of C. Caligula'* (diss. Columbia University 1991).

This commentary is a close reading of Suetonius' *Life of Caligula*, which is compared to accounts in other authors, including Philo. (RvdB, based on DA 52-08A, p. 2912)

N. JANOWITZ, 'The Rhetoric of Translation: Three Early Perspectives on Translating Torah', *Harvard Theological Review* 84 (1991) 129–140.

The article argues that the reports given by Aristobulus, Aristeas and Philo on the translation of the Torah into Greek differ, because the authors adapted the story to their personal situation. Philo's version, in which it is stated that the translators were under inspiration and that each word was translated literally, has to be understood against the background of his exegetical model. His exegesis was based on the premiss that each word of the Torah was inspired by God, and this had to be case for the Greek translation as well. (RvdB)

D. N. JASTRAM, 'Philo's Concept of Generic Virtue', *Society of Biblical Literature Seminar Papers* 30 (1991) 323–347.

Based on research carried out by the author for his Wisconsin Ph.D. (1989), this article tackles the complex but important use that Philo makes of the philosophical terminology of γένος (genus), εἶδος (species) and ἰδέα (form, idea) in his ethical theory in order to describe various aspects of virtue. Two patterns are followed: (1) a simple contrast between generic and specific virtue; (2) a tripartite framework comprising generic virtue, specific virtues, and particular concrete acts of instances of specific virtues. Two key allegorical examples are used for these distinctions, the rivers in Paradise and the Ten Commandments. In two other key passages the genus-species hierarchy is fused with the Platonic forms: the double creation of man, and the change of name from Sarai (perishable virtue) to Sarah (imperishable virtue). Philo regards imperishable virtue (generic and specific) as the archetype of perishable virtue (also generic and specific), thus equating the former in many respects with Platonic forms. This means that the terms 'generic' and 'specific' receive a double sense: (1) what is more or less general in the classificatory hierarchy of genus, species, particular; (2) what is imperishable or perishable. This duality lies behind Philo's use of homonymous ethical terms (e.g. prudence can be imperishable or perishable) and the structure of his allegories. (DTR)

R. A. KRAFT, 'Philo and the Sabbath Crisis: Alexandrian Jewish Politics and the Dating of Philo's Works', in B. A. PEARSON *et al.* (edd.), *The Future of Early Christianity: Essays in Honour of Helmut Koester* (Minneapolis 1991) 131–141.

This essay is described by the author as a report on work in progress concentrating on chronological clues in Philo's writings. It is argued that the anonymous authority who tried to destroy the sabbatical tradition mentioned at *Somn.* 2.123–132 is likely to have been Philo's nephew Tiberius Julius Alexander. This is an economical hypothesis in two respects. (1) It helps to count for the negative treatment of the figure of Joseph in *Somn.* contrary to the positive depiction of him in other works such as *Ios.* Initially Philo treated Joseph sympathetically, but after the Sabbath crises he made him into a prototype of Alexander. (2) Since the negative Joseph is especially found in the allegorical treatises and since Alexander was prefect of Egypt in the late sixties, it may be suggested that these treatises were written considerably later than is generally thought, i.e. when Philo was in his seventies or eighties. This is chronologically not impossible. (RvdB)

J. LAPORTE, 'The High Priest in Philo of Alexandria', in D. T. RUNIA, D. M. HAY and D. WINSTON (edd.), *Heirs of the Septuagint. Philo, Hellenistic Judaism and Early Christianity: Festschrift for Earle Hilgert*, BJS 230 [= *The Studia Philonica Annual* 3 (1991)] (Atlanta 1991) 71–82.

Examines the role of the high priest in the thought of Philo both from the literal and the allegorical perspective. Though idealized, the high priest is not deprived of his human reality. His most important task is the liturgical act of propitiation on Yom-Kippur. But in Philo's view the priesthood of the high priest is also combined with the priesthood of the faithful in a movement of interiorization made possible through the doctrine of the logos as human reason related to the divine Logos. The Sage is thus the chief symbol of healing. But this does not mean that the practice of ritual forgiveness as practised by the human high priest becomes spiritually meaningless. (DTR)

S. LEVARIE, 'Philo on Music', *Journal of Musicology* 9 (1991) 124–130.

Philo makes many references to music throughout his voluminous writings, but these have hitherto received little attention. Though not a professional musician, Philo is well acquainted with the basic facts of music theory and practice. After dealing with examples of musical metaphor, analogy and actual praxis in Philo (the most important is found at *Contempl.* 64ff.), the author concludes that Philo, unlike later generations, still recognised music as a spiritual force. (RvdB)

D. LÜHRMANN, 'The Godlessness of Germans Living by the Sea according to Philo of Alexandria', in B. A. PEARSON *et al.* (edd.), *The Future of Early Christianity: Essays in Honour of Helmut Koester* (Minneapolis 1991) 57–63.

Reflections on the curious account given by Philo at *Somn.* 2.120–121 about Germans living by the sea and trying to keep back the incoming tides with their swords. Philo calls this an action of 'godlessness' (ἀσέβεια). The accusation may in fact have a political rather than a religious background, i.e. these German tribes were godless because they did not accept the Roman order of peace. Philo might have known better if he had read the account of the Germans in Strabo, as derived from Posidonius. (DTR)

B. L. MACK, 'Wisdom and Apocalyptic in Philo', in D. T. RUNIA, D. M. HAY and D. WINSTON (edd.), *Heirs of the Septuagint. Philo, Hellenistic Judaism and Early Christianity: Festschrift for Earle Hilgert*, BJS 230 [= *The Studia Philonica Annual* 3 (1991)] (Atlanta 1991) 21–39.

Examines the theme of the relation between wisdom and apocalyptic eschatology in Philo's thought, arguing against the position of P. Borgen in his article '"There Shall Come Forth a Man": Reflections on Messianic Ideas in Philo' (published in 1992, but available earlier in typescript). The final words of the article summarize Mack's thesis trenchantly (39): 'Philo was a child of wisdom and the diaspora synagogue. He was hardly a strong candidate for an apocalyptic persuasion. Because he was not, the turn he took with its language in *De praemiis et poenis* is singularly unconvincing. Wisdom in Philo? Yes. Apocalyptic? No.' (DTR)

S. MacKnight, *A Light among the Nations: Jewish Missionary Activity in the Second Temple Period* (Minneapolis 1991), esp. 68–70.

Dealing with Jewish missionary activity in the Second Temple period, the author pays attention to the propaganda techniques used by Philo, of which his depiction of Moses is perhaps the best example. Notwithstanding Philo's skill in apologetics, polemics and propaganda, the author concludes that Philo was not so much interested in proselytising gentiles as in bolstering Jewish self-identification. This is shown by the lack of direct speech to gentiles in Philo's *œuvre*. (RvdB)

J. A. Martens, *A Second Best Voyage: Judaism and Jesus on Oaths and Vows* (diss. McMaster University (Canada) 1991).

The carelessness in swearing oaths and taking vows leading to swift regret at the end of the Second temple period confronted the leaders within Judaism with two problems: (1) which formulae of oaths and vows are binding? (2) how can one gain release from an oath or a vow? The dissertation proposes and defends the independent integrity of the stands on oaths and vows by Philo, Qumran, and the Pharisees. Their positions are compared to that of Jesus. (RvdB, based on DA 54-02A, p. 561)

J. W. Martens, *The Superfluity of the Law in Philo and Paul: a Study in the History of Religions* (diss. McMaster University (Canada) 1991).

Martens investigates how Graeco-Roman discussions of 'higher' law—viz. the law of nature (*nomos physeos*), the unwritten law (*agraphos nomos*), and the living law (*nomos empsychos*)—influenced or might have influenced Philo and Paul in their attempts to understand the Mosaic law in an Hellenistic environment. Each of these forms of Graeco-Roman law, it is argued, implied a depreciation of the written or civil law. Did Philo, who adopted each of these forms of law, imply such a depreciation of the Mosaic law? The author concludes that for Philo this was not the case. Contrary to Paul, he upheld the Mosaic law. (RvdB, based on DA 54-02A, p. 562)

J. W. Martens, 'Philo and the Higher Law', *Society of Biblical Literature Seminar Papers* 30 (1991) 309–322.

In facing the problem of the relation between the written law of Moses and the 'higher' law, i.e. non-arbitrary law, demanded by Greek philosophy, Philo was confronted by a dilemma. If he accepted the existence of a kind of 'higher' law he was in danger of rendering the law of Moses superfluous; if he did not accept its existence the law of Moses would be arbitrary. In an attempt to find a way out, Philo linked together all forms of higher law (the law of nature, the unwritten law, the *nomos empsychos*) so that they almost became one. The law of Moses is then conceived as a 'true copy' of this higher law. It helps to guide the weak and the ordinary people who are not by themselves in a position to be an unwritten law or a *nomos empsychos*. In this way the law of Moses is clearly linked with the higher law without becoming superfluous or only of secondary importance. It is a vision of law unique in the ancient world. (RvdB)

E. MARTIN MORALES, '*De Fuga et Inventione*: Filon de Alejandria', *Notizario Centro di Studi sul Guidaismo Ellenistico* 2bis (1991) 1–7.

An occasional paper presented in the context of the research centre for Hellenistic–Jewish studies in Rome (see *SPhA* 2 (1990) 228). *De fuga* is one of Philo's most systematic treatises because it has a clearly defined didactic-methodological goal. Its function becomes clear if it is read in conjunction with *Congr.* and *Mut.* in a sequence which is not only determined by the continuity of the biblical text (Gen. 16:1–6 in *Congr.*, Gen. 16:6–14 in *Fug.*, Gen. 17:1–11 in *Mut.*), but also by the complementarity of themes dealt with, which are presented as stages in the same formative-educative process, i.e. propaedeutics represented by Abraham, ascesis represented by Jacob, contemplation represented by Isaac. The author emphasizes the great influence that *Fug.* had in Christian thought, and mentions as concrete example the *De doctrina christiana* of Augustine. (RR)

J. P. MARTÍN, 'El *Sofista* de Platón y el platonismo de Filón de Alejandría', *Methexis* 4 (1991) 81–99.

The analysis carried out in this article focuses especially on the history of Platonism and Philo's place therein. Martín holds that the relation between Plato and Philo should be evaluated from at least four points of view: topological (i.e. the citations of Plato found in Philo), epistemological, comparative/historical, and systematic or properly philosophical. In the case of the fourth area, which is particulary broad in its connotations, he intends not to furnish definitive results, but rather simply to indicate some lines of research. His basic thesis is that, 'just as the *Timaeus* is central for the theme of creation and the *Phaedrus* for the doctrine of man, so the *Sophist* has this place for ontology and dialectic' (83). A detailed analysis of the Platonic text and the corresponding passages in Philo leads to the conclusion that Philo's synthesis of the *Timaeus* and Genesis is systematically incompatible with Plato's *Sophist*. This is so because in the latter the Absolute is constituted through a movement of relations between supreme genera, where in the former relations are constituted through the action of an Absolute which is transcendent and inscrutable. (RR)

J. P. MARTÍN, 'Philo and Augustine, *De civitate Dei* XIV 28 and XV: Some Preliminary Observations', in D. T. RUNIA, D. M. HAY and D. WINSTON (edd.), *Heirs of the Septuagint. Philo, Hellenistic Judaism and Early Christianity: Festschrift for Earle Hilgert*, BJS 230 [= *The Studia Philonica Annual* 3 (1991)] (Atlanta 1991) 283–294.

Argues on the basis on an examination of 14 conceptual pairs of themes that the nucleus of Augustine's idea of the two cities goes back to Philo. Biblical pairs such as Abel and Cain, Sarah and Hagar etc. are not only related to themselves, but also to the themes of two citizenships and two moral paths in history. Both in Augustine and in Philo there is a tendency to confuse two schemes, that of evil versus good and nature versus grace. Martín declines to answer the question whether there was a direct dependence of Augustine on Philo, but does assert that so far scholarship has not asked the right questions on this issue. (DTR)

B. C. MCGING, 'Pontius Pilate and the Sources', *Catholic Biblical Quarterly* 53 (1991) 416–438.

It is generally agreed that there is a divergence between Philo and Josephus on the one hand and the Gospel authors on the other in their portrayal of Pontius Pilate. In the view of the author, however, there is no flagrant contradiction between our three sources. Although not specially incompetent and not a monster, Pilate was unable and unwilling to avoid situations of serious friction with the Jews. (RvdB)

B. McGINN, *The Presence of God: a History of Christian Mysticism*, vol. 1 *The Foundations of Mysticism* (New York–London 1991), esp. 35–41.

A section is devoted to Philo as part of a comprehensive account of the foundations of Western, i.e. Christian, mysticism. Philo is regarded as one of 'central philosophers whose thought is both representative of the time and also directly relevant to Latin Christian mysticism (35)' (the others are Plotinus and Proclus). (DTR)

A. MÉASSON and J. CAZEAUX, 'From Grammar to Discourse: a Study of the *Questiones in Genesim* in Relation to the Treatises', in D. M. HAY (ed.), *Both Literal and Allegorical: Studies in Philo of Alexandria's Questions and Answers on Genesis and Exodus*, BJS 232 (Atlanta 1991) 125–225.

The title of this long and important analysis of the relation between the *Quaestiones* and the Treatises (i.e. primarily the Allegorical Commentary) is explained through the authors' conviction that the Treatises have a fully developed dynamic quality which gives them force and movement, whereas the *Quaestiones* are static and fragmented, like 'note-cards'. The difference is compared to that between grammar and the style of a masterpiece. Chronological considerations are of secondary importance. It is the literary genre that differentiates them. The authors illustrate their thesis with extensive analyses of Philonic texts which can be subdivided as follows: (a) a profile of *QG* 1 (including a list of parallel of passages); (b) reflections on the structure of *Leg.*, allowing comparison between the two works; (c) comparison of *Leg.* 3.75–104 with *QG* 1.47–48; (d) comparison of *QG* 1.57–99 with *Gig.-Deus*; (e) analyses of *QG* 2–3; (f) extensive analyses of *QG* 4 (note esp. long passages on §1, 2, 8), including extensive comparison with parallel passages in other Philonic works; (g) brief remarks on *QG* 5–6 (i.e. 4.71–245 Aucher). The article is concluded with a final analogy. The *Quaestiones* are not to be viewed as notes containing preliminary materials for a treatise. They are to be compared with a *catechism*, solid and elementary, allowing the meaning to be preserved and Faith to be guarded. The Treatises in contrast form a *theology*, more ambitious and more suited for infusing the truth of Reason into the human mind, but at the same time making maximum demands on the reader. The two series are unequal in value, for '"Philo" is himself only in the Treatises (225).' (DTR)

J. MÉLÈZE MODRZEJEWSKI, *Les Juifs d'Egypte de Ramses II à Hadrien*, Collection des Nereides (Paris 1991), esp. 135–144 and *passim*.

A study on Jews in Egypt from the time of Joseph until the 2nd century CE can hardly avoid making frequent reference to Philo, even if in the foreword the author declares that he will place the emphasis on documents less well known than the LXX and Philo. From p. 131 onwards the story of the Jews under Roman rule is told, with interesting information on Philo's family at 150–151. (DTR)

A. MENDELSON, 'Two glimpses of Philo in Modern English Literature: Works by Charles Kingsley and Francis Warner', in D. T. RUNIA, D. M. HAY and D. WINSTON (edd.), *Heirs of the Septuagint. Philo, Hellenistic Judaism and Early Christianity: Festschrift for Earle Hilgert*, BJS 230 [= *The Studia Philonica Annual* 3 (1991)] (Atlanta 1991) 328–343.

Philo appears on the stage in at least two works of modern English literature, in Charles Kingsley's novel *Hypatia* (1853), and Francis Warner's play *Light Shadows* (1979). Mendelson examines the role that Philo plays in both works and draws some conclusions on his role as a Jew. Kingley uses systematic stereotyping, in which social and theological views coincide. In Warner social stereotyping has disappeared, but Philo and his co-religionists are still regarded as theologically immature. (DTR)

K. A. MORLAND, *The Galatian Choice. Galatians 1:6–12 and 3:8–14 in the Light of Jewish Curse-Texts and Antique Rhetoric* (diss. Oslo–Trondheim 1991), esp. Part I.

In this book the Philonic references with a few exceptions are confined to Part I: Curse and anathema—the Jewish horizon. After a semantic field analysis of the Pauline passages studied, the author looks for Jewish parallel material which he finds also in Philo's writings. Lists of the Philonic texts pertaining to the concept of 'curse' are given on pp. 347–348, 352–357, 361–62 and 369–70. *Praem.* 79–172 is analyzed on pp. 49–52. According to the author the paraenetic feature of Deut 27–30, commented upon in the passage, has been sharpened. The aim of the treatise seems to be to exhort the fellow Jews to follow the law 'in order to prepare for the turning of the ages, with the curse and blessing motif as an important element' (p. 52). *Leg.* 3 is basically an exposition of the curses in Gen 3. 'By relating the curse to pleasure, sense-perception and actions, Philo manages to establish the curses...as exhortations toward covenantal obedience' (p. 87). Several texts are found in Philo where curse and blessing form antitheses (p. 96–97). Philo also refers to texts (e.g. Gen 12:3) containing promises to the Gentiles (e.g. *Migr.* 118–126, p. 107). When Philo in *Spec.* 1.315–318 refers to Deut. 13:1–11 demanding the putting to death of the prophet who propagates apostasy, this killing 'seems to take the form of lynching' (p. 135). See further the provisional bibliography 1994 below for the published version of this thesis. (KGS)

J. H. C. NEEB, *Genesis 28:12: The Function of a Biblical Text in Early Jewish and Christian Communities (Origen)* (diss. St. Michael's College (Canada) 1991).

Chapter 4 situates Origen within his Greek philosophical context (Plato, Philo). In chapter 5 Origen's dependence on Philo's *De Somniis* is also discussed. (RvdB, based on DA 53-08A, p. 2856)

J. VAN OORT, *Jerusalem and Babylon: a Study into Augustine's* City of God *and the Sources of his Doctrine of the Two Cities*, Supplements to Vigiliae Christianae 14 (Leiden 1991), esp. 234–254.

In his exhaustive study on the sources of Augustine's doctrine of the two cities Van Oort examines the claim that Augustinus had been influenced in this respect by (Neo)-

Platonism, esp. Philo and Plotinus. It is concluded that there is some superficial resemblance between (Neo)-platonic thought and Augustine. But no parallels are found for the most characteristic elements of Augustine's doctrine, namely (1) that the two societies are absolutely antithetical, and (2) that they have an origin and a progress in time. Augustine must have derived these elements from another source. (RvdB)

J. PANAGOPOULOS, Ἡ ἑρμηνεία τῆς ἁγίας Γραφῆς στήν ἐκκλησία τῶν πατέρων: οἱ τρεῖς πρῶτοι αἰώνες καί ἡ Ἀλεξανδρινή ἐξηγητική παράδοση ὡς τόν πέμπτο αἰῶνα, [*The Interpretation of Holy Scripture in the Patristic Church: the First Three Centuries and the Alexandrian Exegetical Tradition up to the Fifth Century*] vol. 1 (Athens 1991), esp. 79–85.

A section is devoted to Philo as part of a comprehensive account of biblical exegesis during the first three centuries of the Church and of Alexandrian exegesis up to the fifth century. (DTR)

R. J. QUINONES, *The Changes of Cain: Violence and the Lost Brother in Cain and Abel Literature* (Princeton 1991), esp. 23–29.

Philo plays an extremely important role in the history of the Cain–Abel theme, because through his exegetical commentaries the biblical brothers are transformed into universal rival and contending principles. This approach is followed by Ambrose and Augustine. (DTR)

R. RADICE, 'Observations on the Theory of the Ideas as the Thoughts of God in Philo of Alexandria', in D. T. RUNIA, D. M. HAY and D. WINSTON (edd.), *Heirs of the Septuagint. Philo, Hellenistic Judaism and Early Christianity: Festschrift for Earle Hilgert*, BJS 230 [= *The Studia Philonica Annual* 3 (1991)] (Atlanta 1991) 126–134.

Radice offers arguments against the conventional view that Philo cannot possibly have played a role in the development of the Middle Platonist doctrine of the ideas as thoughts of God, even though he is the first to record it. He postulates a double Platonist tradition, one purely Greek, the other Jewish-Alexandrian. Philo developed the notion of the ideas as thoughts of God as the result of his exposition of Mosaic thought. His location in Alexandria at the cross-roads of various philosophical tendencies meant that Greek philosophers must have been acquainted with his works, and so he was able to act as a *catalyst* in the development of Middle Platonist thought. Radice refers for further details to his monograph reviewed by D. Winston in *SPhA* 4 (1992) 159–164. (DTR)

J. RIAUD, 'Quelques réflexions sur les Thérapeutes d'Alexandrie à la lumière de *De vita Mosis* II, 67', in D. T. RUNIA, D. M. HAY and D. WINSTON (edd.), *Heirs of the Septuagint. Philo, Hellenistic Judaism and Early Christianity: Festschrift for Earle Hilgert*, BJS 230 [= *The Studia Philonica Annual* 3 (1991)] (Atlanta 1991) 184–191.

Various reflections on the portrait of the theoretic or contemplative life of the Therapeutae such as it is presented in *Contempl*. According to Riaud their perfect way of life represents the goal of philosophy such as Philo conceived it. (DTR)

S. D. ROBERTSON, *The Account of the Ancient Israelite Tabernacle and First Priesthood in The 'Jewish Antiquities' of Flavius Josephus* (diss. Annenberg Research Institute 1991), esp. chap. 2.

In chapter 2 the author compares the description of the Tabernacle court and superstructure by Flavius Josephus to, among others, Philo. It is concluded that Josephus shows close acquaintance with Philo's *Life of Moses*. (RvdB, based on DA 53-07A, p. 2504)

J. R. ROYSE, *The Spurious Texts of Philo of Alexandria: a Study of Textual Transmission and Corruption with Indexes to the Major Collections of Greek Fragments*, Arbeiten zur Literatur und Geschichte des Hellenistischen Judentums 22 (Leiden 1991).

Important monograph, produced as part of the preparations for an edition of the Fragments of Philo. Royse sifts out all those fragmentary texts that have been erroneously attributed to Philo in modern scholarship. At the same time he furnishes much valuable information about the transmission of less well-known parts of the Philonic corpus. For a more detailed account of the book's contents the reader is referred to the review article in *SPhA* 4 (1992) 78–86. In an Appendix Royse gives tables for all the major collections of Greek fragments so far published. This has now been complemented by a reverse index in *SPhA* 5 (1993) 156–179. (DTR)

J. R. ROYSE, 'Philo's *Quaestiones in Exodum* 1.6', in D. M. HAY (ed.), *Both Literal and Allegorical: Studies in Philo of Alexandria's* Questions and Answers on Genesis and Exodus, BJS 232 (Atlanta 1991) 17–27.

Taking his cue from L. Früchtel, Royse shows that the original Greek text of the passage can be almost entirely reconstructed on the basis of two quotations in the *Sacra Parallela*. On the basis of this text he makes comments on the Armenian translation and argues against Petit that, when Philo states that τὸ ἱερὸν γράμμα contains the Greek adage μηδὲν ἄγαν (nothing to excess), he is referring to Mosaic scripture. (DTR)

J. R. ROYSE, 'Philo, Κύριος, and the Tetragrammaton', in D. T. RUNIA, D. M. HAY and D. WINSTON (edd.), *Heirs of the Septuagint. Philo, Hellenistic Judaism and Early Christianity: Festschrift for Earle Hilgert*, BJS 230 [= *The Studia Philonica Annual* 3 (1991)] (Atlanta 1991) 167–183.

Printed editions of the LXX, based primarily on Christian mss., render the Tetragrammaton יהוה as κύριος, and אלהים as θεός. But evidence of Jewish practice accumulated during the last century indicates that there was considerable variety in the way the Tetragrammaton was dealt with in written form. Royse examines the evidence allowing us to determine what Philo read in his mss. and what he himself wrote, and comes to the following conclusions: (1) in the biblical texts he read the Tetragrammaton was written in palaeo-Hebrew or Aramaic letters and not translated by κύριος; (2) his own written use of κύριος is consistent with having read such texts and having pronounced the Tetragrammaton as κύριος; (3) his remarks at *Mos.* 2.114 and 2.132 can be explained if we suppose that he saw the Tetragrammaton untranslated in the text he had before him. (DTR)

C. RUIZ-MONTERO, 'Aspects of the Vocabulary of Chariton of Aphrodisias', *Classical Quarterly* 41 (1991) 484–489.

Compares vocabulary of the novelist with, *inter alia*, Philo. Finds that it coincides more with Plutarch, Josephus and Philo than with Diodorus of Sicily and Dio of Prusa, the other authors used. This leads to a dating c. 100 AD. (DTR)

D. T. RUNIA, 'Secondary Texts in Philo's *Quaestiones*', in D. M. HAY (ed.), *Both Literal and Allegorical: Studies in Philo of Alexandria's* Questions and Answers on Genesis and Exodus, BJS 232 (Atlanta 1991) 47–79.

Philo's *Quaestiones* answer exegetical questions posed on Genesis and Exodus taken in the sequence of the biblical text. The paper addresses the question to what extent other biblical texts are referred to in the course of the exegesis (a practice that is fundamental to Philo's method in the Allegorical Commentary). In total 100 examples of such 'secondary texts' are found. These are analysed from various points of view. It is concluded that the use of such texts in the *Quaestiones* is strictly limited. They are used primarily to illustrate or confirm interpretations that Philo puts forward. For only about two-thirds of the examples parallels can be found elsewhere in the Philonic corpus. This shows that the *Quaestiones* have an independent position among Philo's writings, and do not have a merely preparatory character. (DTR)

D. T. RUNIA, 'Philo of Alexandria in Five Letters of Isidore of Pelusium', in D. T. RUNIA, D. M. HAY and D. WINSTON (edd.), *Heirs of the Septuagint. Philo, Hellenistic Judaism and Early Christianity: Festschrift for Earle Hilgert*, BJS 230 [= *The Studia Philonica Annual* 3 (1991)] (Atlanta 1991) 295–319.

Gives text and translation, together with detailed commentary, of the four letters of the desert father Isidore of Pelusium (370–435) in which Philo is explicitly named (*Ep.* 2.143, 270, 3.19, 3.81), and also of a fifth letter (4.176), the contents of which is clearly based on *Mos*. It emerges that Isidore possessed a more than superficial acquaintance with Philo's thought and writings. In two letters Philo's status as a Jew is emphasized. Isidore uses him as an effective weapon in his contest with contemporary Judaism. (DTR)

D. T. RUNIA, 'Witness or Participant? Philo and the Neoplatonic Tradition', in A. VANDERJAGT and D. PÄTZOLD (edd.), *The Neoplatonic Tradition: Jewish, Christian and Islamic Themes*, Dialectica Minora 3 (Köln 1991) 36–56.

As everyone knows, Philo gives much valuable information as a witness on the beginnings of Middle Platonism. But did he participate in and contribute to that tradition himself? The paper makes a start on examining the extent to which Philo may have played a role in the development of Neoplatonism. In the first part a *status quaestionis* is given, particularly on the relation between Philo and Plotinus. In the second part a survey is given on the survival of Philo's writings. The third part concentrates on a specific example, namely the theme of God as ὁ ἑστώς ('the standing one'). It is argued that Plotinus' use of the concept goes back to Philo probably via Numenius. In conclusion it is asserted that the entire question is very difficult, but that the burden of proof in this question must lie with those who argue that Philo had no influence on the Neoplatonic tradition whatsoever. (DTR)

D. T. RUNIA, 'Underneath Cohn and Colson: the Text of Philo's *De Virtutibus*', *Society of Biblical Literature Seminar Papers* 30 (1991) 116–134.

How reliable are the texts of Cohn-Wendland and Colson which almost all Philonists use? This question is posed in the case of *De virtutibus*. This treatise has a complex mss. history. The paper examines the evidence of the direct and indirect tradition, and also looks at the problems surrounding the title and the structure of the work (i.e. which parts did it originally consist of). It is concluded that Philonists may consider themselves fortunate that the job of editing has been competently done, but that there are no grounds for complacency. Serious research cannot just be based on translations, but must take text and critical apparatus into account. (DTR)

D. T. RUNIA, D. M. HAY and D. WINSTON (edd.), *Heirs of the Septuagint. Philo, Hellenistic Judaism and Early Christianity: Festschrift for Earle Hilgert*, BJS 230 [= *The Studia Philonica Annual* 3 (1991)] (Atlanta 1991).

The third volume of *The Studia Philonica Annual* deviates from earlier volumes in that it almost entirely consists of articles written by scholars in honour of Earle Hilgert, former editor of *Studia Philonica*, who in 1991 retired from his professorship at McCormick Theological Seminary. A photo of the honorand is placed opposite the title page. All but two of the articles focus on Philo, and thus are summarized in this bibliography. (DTR)

D. T. RUNIA, R. RADICE and P. A. CATHEY, 'Philo of Alexandria: an Annotated Bibliography 1987-88', in D. T. RUNIA, D. M. HAY and D. WINSTON (edd.), *Heirs of the Septuagint. Philo, Hellenistic Judaism and Early Christianity: Festschrift for Earle Hilgert*, BJS 230 [= *The Studia Philonica Annual* 3 (1991)] (Atlanta 1991) 347–374.

Bibliography of Philonic studies primarily for the year 1988 (68 items), with addenda for 1987 (9 items). As the introductory blurb states (347): what ... would be a more suitable way to conclude a Festschrift for Earle Hilgert than with a bibliography of Philonic studies?' (DTR)

K. G. SANDELIN, 'The Danger of Idolatry According to Philo of Alexandria', *Temenos* 27 (1991) 109–150.

Pagan religion had an attractive force on many Jews in the Hellenistic and Imperial era. Philo wrestles with the question in several texts. This shows that it was a real problem among Jews in Alexandria. To Philo idolatry is a deification of created things and it is also closely connected with passions. It is dangerous because those who have invented the pagan myths have had the intention to make the God who really exists to be consigned to oblivion. Jews in Alexandria confronted idolatry in several contexts: gymnasia, sportive contests and the theatre. Philo made actualizations of different Biblical passages which gave him the opportunity to take a warning stand against idolatry in its various forms. (KGS)

E. P. SANDERS, *Judaism: Practice and Belief, 63 BCE – 66 CE* (London–Philadelphia 1991).

Extensive use is made of Philonic evidence for the reconstruction of what the author calls 'common Judaism', and esp. for the role of diaspora Judaism therein. For further details see the review article by A. Mendelson in this volume. (DTR)

G. SCARPAT, 'La Torre di Babele in Filone e nella Sapienze (Sap. 10, 5)', *Rivista Biblica* 39 (1991) 167–173.

The author concentrates especially on the term σύγχυσις (confusion) which Philo deals with in *Conf.* 187 in relation to the bibical episode of the construction of the tower of Babel. The term in question shows a semantic affinity with Sap. 10:5, and particularly with the concept of ὁμόνοια πονηρίας (the concord of evil). For this reason the σύγχυσις of which Philo speaks can be interpreted as the confusion which God arouses in the planning of evil by malevolent men. Such confusion is necessary so that the good will triumph. (RR)

J. M. SCHOLER, *Proleptic Priests: Priesthood in the Epistle to the Hebrews* JSNTSupp 49 (Sheffield 1991), esp. 63–71.

In the chapter on priesthood in the literature outside the New Testament a section is devoted to Philo's views on priesthood. A distinction is made between Philo's description of actual priesthood and his symbolic interpretation of it. In his description Philo does not diverge significantly from the Old Testament tradition. In his symbolic interpretation the high priest symbolises the Logos that is the mediator between God and man. The universal priesthood of the people of Israel during the Passover is interpreted as a portrayal of the soul's progress towards God. This spiritual priesthood requires a spiritual sacrifice in the form of prayer. Although Philo does not discard animal sacrifice, he values prayer as the superior form of sacrifice. (RvdB)

A. B. SCOTT, *Origen and the Life of the Stars*, Oxford Early Christian Studies (Oxford 1991), esp. 63–75.

As part of the background to Origen's views on the life and nature of the stars a short chapter is included on Philo. Scott lists and briefly discusses the more important Philonic passages on his subject. Philo does much to accommodate himself to the prevailing philosophical climate, and so comes close to regarding the stars as divine. 'He follows the conventions of his day in honouring the stars, but he both too good a Jew and too good a Platonist to take this to its logical consequences (74).' Differently than Origen, however, Philo does not recognize the possibility of evil in heaven. (DTR)

J. P. SCULLION, *A Traditio-Historical Study of the Day of Atonement (Yom Kippur, Purification)* (diss. Catholic University of America 1991), esp. chap. 2.

In aiming to further an understanding of the soteriological significance of the Christ event through a traditio-historical study of Yom Kippur, chapter 2 examines the understanding of Yom Kippur in various Second Temple authors, including Philo. (DTR; based on DA 52–02A p. 569)

R. Skarsten, 'Some Applications of Computers to the Study of Ancient Greek Texts: a Progress Report', *Symbolae Osloenses* 66 (1991) 203–220.

A brief introduction to the possibilities that computers offer for studying ancient Greek texts, written at a non-specialist level. For Philonists two aspects are particularly interesting: Skarsten furnishes further information on the KWIC-concordance to Philo's works being produced in Norway (see further *SPhA* 2 (1990) 112–115); various examples are given to support his conviction that the work *De aeternitate mundi* is pseudo-Philonic. The author refers to the unpublished version of his doctoral thesis, which was missed in our earlier bibliographies: *Forfatterproblemet ved De aeternitate mundi i Corpus Philonicum* (diss. Bergen 1987). (DTR)

T. Seland, *Jewish Vigilantism in the First Century C.E.: a Study of Selected Texts in Philo and Luke on Jewish Vigilante Reactions against Nonconformers to the Torah* (diss. Trondheim 1991).

In order to investigate and understand some Jewish texts dealing with violence against non-conformers to the Torah, the author applies the model of vigilantism as a heuristic device. The specific texts dealt with are Philo *Spec.* 1.54–57; 1.315–318, 2-252–254, and the Lukan Acts 6:8ff; 21:15–36 and 23:12–15. The study contains three chapters. In the first it is argued that the selected texts of Philo confirm the hypothesis that, when central aspects of the Jewish constitution were endangered by fellow-Jews, Philo endorsed that they should be taken away on the spot. No court procedures are to be invoked, the zealous persons are to consider themselves as performing all the duties of a court and should kill the perpetrator without further delay. In the second chapter several aspects of the first century Mediterranean world are pointed out as probable bases of plausibility for apostasy and vigilantism. In the third and last chapter, the selected texts from the Acts of the Apostles are investigated and found to provide evidence of zealotic vigilantism in Jerusalem in the first century, and that Stephen and Paul should be considered as victims of such vigilantism. In the cases against both Stephen and Paul Diaspora Jews were involved, increasing the relevance of the Philonic texts. But the scenario in Jerusalem was also heavily influenced by the social situation of the Jews in general and of the Christian Jews in Jerusalem in particular resulting from the growing tendencies of pervasive factionalism. The study has a bibliography, but no indexes. (Abstract supplied by author)

D. I. Sly, '1 Peter 3:6b in the Light of Philo and Josephus', *Journal of Biblical Literature* 110 (1991) 126-129.

This short article attempts to explain the inconsistency between the depiction of Sarah's relation to her husband Abraham in Genesis and in 1 Pet 3:6b by the fact that the author, shocked by the behaviour of Sarah, tried to turn her into an ideal Hellenistic wife. The treatment of Sarah by Philo and Josephus is discussed in order to show that this ambiguity of feelings towards Sarah was shared by contemporaries. (RvdB)

D. I. Sly, 'Philo's Practical Application of δικαιοσύνη', *Society of Biblical Literature Seminar Papers* 30 (1991) 298–308.

To Philo justice (τὸ δίκαιον) is the overarching ethical principle and at the same time identical with God's covenant. Given the hierarchical view of existence maintained by both Greeks and Jews alike, Philo thinks it δίκαιον when the better rules and the worse is ruled. This principle of justice determines the relations of man to God, man to man and man to nature. The appropriate form of δικαιοσύνη for a man in his relation to inferior beings is φιλανθρωπία in combination with mercy (τὸ ἔλεον) and pity (τὸ οἶκτον), unless one has broken the law. Such an action means that one has acted deliberately against the best interest of Israel as God's covenant people. This helps us to understand Philo's attitude to women, which seems rather inconsistent at first sight. Women, lacking reason, are inferior to men. As long as they allow to be ruled by men and do not break the law, men should show philanthropy, mercy and pity to them. As soon as women start to be assertive or immodest however, not accepting their inferior role, they should be punished most severely, because they threaten the greater good. (RvdB)

D. I. SLY, 'Changes in the Perception of the Offence in Numbers 25:1', *Proceedings of Eastern Great Lakes & Midwest Biblical Society* 11 (1991) 200–209, esp. 204–206.

Philo's perception is included in this survey of references and allusions to the Phineas story, which concentrates on the implications concerning the nature of the offence which triggered Phineas' heroic reaction. For Philo Phineas and the Midianite women represent moral paradigms of universal significance, i.e. good versus evil. (DTR)

G. E. STERLING, 'Philo's *Quaestiones*: Prolegomena or Afterthought?', in D. M. HAY (ed.), *Both Literal and Allegorical: Studies in Philo of Alexandria's* Questions and Answers on Genesis and Exodus, BJS 232 (Atlanta 1991) 99–123.

Argues that if we are to understand the *raison d'être* of the *Quaestiones*, we have to determine their place within the Philonic corpus and especially their relation to the Allegorical Commentary. Sterling bases his verdict on a detailed examination of the first book of *QG*, which is compared with the corresponding sections of the Allegorical Commentary. He concludes that the undoubted difference in emphasis between the two is to be explained through the fact that in the *Quaestiones* Philo wanted to present all the options, where in the Allegorical Commentary he wrote from a definite perspective. This means that the *Quaestiones* can be regarded as the prolegomena to the *Allegoriae*, and that they should therefore be intensively used in intepreting the latter. (DTR)

L. TELESCA, 'Filone e Ambrogio: due testi a confronto', *Notizario Centro di Studi sul Guidaismo Ellenistico* 2 (1991) 1-13.

Telesca examines the text of *Fug*. 157–160 and the parallel passage of Ambrose, *Ep*. III (67) 3–7 in order to demonstrate by means of the method of 'schematic' analysis the structural analogy that exists between them. On the basis of this confrontation, which takes into account various levels of significance, i.e. biblical/exegetical, symbolic, and theological, it is concluded that Philo, despite appearances to the contrary, was able to express his own doctrinal contributions in a much more ordered way than Ambrose. The same comparison also reveals the remarkable ability of the allegorical method to express new kinds of meaning—in Ambrose's case in the area of christology—even though it makes use of the same symbolic elements. (RR)

A. TERIAN, 'The Priority of the *Quaestiones* among Philo's Exegetical Commentaries', in D. M. HAY (ed.), *Both Literal and Allegorical: Studies in Philo of Alexandria's* Questions and Answers on Genesis and Exodus, BJS 232 (Atlanta 1991) 29–46.

In order to determine the chronology of the *Quaestiones* within the Philonic corpus it is necessary to make a careful examination of the internal cross-references given by Philo himself. Terian examines such passages, many of which had been adduced by earlier scholars, and concludes that 'textual arguments that do not allow the *Quaestiones* to stand at the beginning of Philo's exegetical commentaries can no longer be maintained. Except for references to the Περὶ ἀριθμῶν, Philo is altogether silent in the *Quaestiones* about his other works. These should thus be regarded as the earliest of his exegetical commentaries (46).' (DTR)

A. TERIAN, 'Strange Interpolations in the Text of Philo: the Case of the the *Quaestiones in Exodum*', in D. T. RUNIA, D. M. HAY and D. WINSTON (edd.), *Heirs of the Septuagint. Philo, Hellenistic Judaism and Early Christianity: Festschrift for Earle Hilgert*, BJS 230 [= *The Studia Philonica Annual* 3 (1991)] (Atlanta 1991) 320–327.

Eight interpolations in the Armenian text of the *Quaestiones in Exodum* are identified and analysed. Five of these were already present in the Greek text translated by the Armenian translator. Terian argues that these betray the same hand as three interpolations in the text of *De animalibus*. This scribe seems to have become frustrated by the extremes of Philo's allegorical practice, and so from time to time could resist undermining the text he was copying out. (DTR)

T. H. TOBIN, 'Romans 10:4: Christ the Goal of the Law', in D. T. RUNIA, D. M. HAY and D. WINSTON (edd.), *Heirs of the Septuagint. Philo, Hellenistic Judaism and Early Christianity: Festschrift for Earle Hilgert*, BJS 230 [= *The Studia Philonica Annual* 3 (1991)] (Atlanta 1991) 272–280, esp. 277ff.

Philo uses the term τέλος very extensively in his writings and in a variety of contexts. Two of these can be adduced to illuminate Paul's usage in Rom. 10:4: (1) the context of metaphors of seeking or striving toward a goal; (2) the context that speaks more specifically about the goal of the Law. (DTR)

N. UMEMOTO, 'Die Königsherrschaft Gottes bei Philon', in M. HENGEL and A. M. SCHWEMER (edd.), *Königsherrschaft Gottes und himmlischer Kult im Judentum, Urchristentum und in der hellenistischen Welt*, WUNT 55 (Tübingen 1991) 207–256.

Even though the possibility that man has to know, and therefore also to speak, about God is limited in absolute terms, he is at least able to recognize God's unicity and, in consequence thereof, also his sovereignty. In this description philosophical principles of Platonic and Stoic doctrine are expressed: from Platonism the affirmation that God is cause of good alone; from Stoicism the conception of God as king of the cosmic megalopolis. It is possible to derive from these two philosophical orientations respectively the transcendent role of God-king and the immanent aspects of his sovereignty. The meeting point of these two tendencies is the Jewish conception of the monarch who shows justice, mercy and sollicitude for his subjects. From the theological viewpoint the view is translated into the doctrine of the two powers, one beneficent/creative, the other royal/sovereign (pp. 226ff.). Philo holds that the royalty of God stands at the basis of every form of human monarchy, including the empire of Rome (cf. 241ff.), and also, in particular, the superiority of the wise man, of whom Abraham and Moses are examples (pp. 252ff.). (RR)

J. Romney WEGNER, 'Philo's Portrayal of Women—Hebraic or Hellenic?', in A.-J. LEVINE (ed.), *"Women like this": New Perspectives on Jewish Women in the Greco-Roman World*, Early Judaism and its Literature 1 (Atlanta 1991) 41–66.

The author returns to the subject she dealt with earlier at R-R 8250. Philo has no interest in women as a subject for sustained discussion, yet he expresses his opinions on 'the female' at every turn. This depiction owes far more to Greek ideas, mediated through Hellenistic culture, than to the Jewish Scripture he inherited from his ancestors. His views on mind as a male attribute and sense-perception as a female attribute can be traced back to Aristotelian science and Pythagorean dichotomies. Moreover Philo often insults women beyond the needs of the context or describes their positive traits as male rather than female, contradicting the 'Jewish' interpretations of these texts. But Philo does assign a positive value to women in his treatment of procreation, and it may be suggested that 'Philo's true attitude to women was one of ambivalence —perhaps even cognitive dissonance—rather than the misogyny that seems to inform most of his theoretical statements about the female (50-51).' (DTR)

H. WEISS, 'Philo on the Sabbath', in D. T. RUNIA, D. M. HAY and D. WINSTON (edd.), *Heirs of the Septuagint. Philo, Hellenistic Judaism and Early Christianity: Festschrift for Earle Hilgert*, BJS 230 [= *The Studia Philonica Annual* 3 (1991)] (Atlanta 1991) 83–105.

The Sabbath functioned for Philo in diverse important theological, cosmological, philosophical, religious and social roles. Weiss collects all the evidence that he can muster in Philo's writings and discusses it under the headings of (a) the significance of the observance, (b) the significance of the number, and (c) the significance of the Sabbath (i.e. as a period of rest). In the final section nine conclusions are drawn, of which we mention only the last: Philo did not consider the Sabbath 'a cornerstone of Jewish practice' (Mendelson). (DTR)

H. F. WEISS, *Der Brief an die Hebräer*, Kritisch-exegetischer Kommentar über das Neue Testament 15 (Göttingen 1991), esp. 100–103 and *passim*.

Further material in the on-going discussion on Philo's relation to the Epistle to the Hebrews. (DTR)

D. WINSTON, 'Aspects of Philo's Linguistic Theory', in D. T. RUNIA, D. M. HAY and D. WINSTON (edd.), *Heirs of the Septuagint. Philo, Hellenistic*

Judaism and Early Christianity: Festschrift for Earle Hilgert, BJS 230 [= *The Studia Philonica Annual* 3 (1991)] (Atlanta 1991) 109–125.

Winston gives a synoptic account of Philo's views on the origin and status of language. Philo has a general theory of language which is derived from Greek philosophical speculation, but is nonetheless marked by various adaptations made in order to suit it to the scriptural account. Philo thus follows his philosophical master Plato in having a deep distrust of language and the written word. On the other hand his praise of the accuracy of the Septuagint translation seems informed by propagandistic motives. And when he claims that Mosaic names differ in no way from the external object they represent, this can only be read as an exaggerated attempt to emphasize the absolute precision of Mosaic name-making, for this statement clearly transgresses the bounds of his own epistemological principles. (DTR)

D. WYRWA, 'Über die Begegnung des biblischen Glaubens mit dem griechischen Geist', *Zeitschrift für Theologie und Kirche* 88 (1991) 29–67, esp. 39–47.

The Hebrew expression translated in ἐγώ εἰμι ὁ ὤν (Ex. 3:14) certainly did not have a philosophical content in the original biblical version, but simply expressed God's presence and his freedom. Nevertheless this expression concerning God, when combined with the other divine characteristics of unity, majesty and transcendence, was open to a metaphysical interpretation (in the sense of a spiritual Being who is pure and absolute) which is first historically realized in Philo. Philo deals with this biblical text about thirty times and builds on it a theology with a transcendent orientation. Its principal doctrines are the distinction between the existence of God and his essence, which is unknowable for man, and the theory of the Logos as creator, in which biblical, Stoic and Platonic themes flow together (41ff.). Philo's contribution, broadly speaking, consisted in the translation of the foundations of the Jewish faith into the dualistic-transcendent ontology of Plato. (RR)

A. XAVIER, *A Study of* Theodidaktoi *(I Thessalonians 4,9)* (diss. Pontifical Gregorian University (Vatican) 1991).

This thesis is devoted to the *hapax legomenon* in 1 Thess. 4:9 *theodidaktoi*. Within this scope attention is paid to the use of *autodidaktos* by Philo. (RvdB, based on DA 53-04C, p. 627)

J. ZANDEE, *The Teachings of Silvanus: a Commentary (Nag Hammadi Codex VII, 4): Text, Translation, Commentary*, Egyptologische uitgaven 6 (Leiden 1991), esp. 516–522.

Frequent reference is made to Philo throughout this massive commentary on an anti-Gnostic document found at Nag Hammadi. Various threads are drawn together in the concluding section at pp. 516–522. The connections of Silvanus with Philo are paralleled in his relation to Clement and Origen, so that one may speak of an 'Alexandrian' type of theology. (DTR)

Addenda 1989–90

Manuel ALEXANDRE Jr, *Argumentação Retórica em Fílon de Alexandria*, Bibliotheca Euphrosyne 4 (Lisbon 1990).

A comprehensive study on Philo's rhetorical argumentation and the role that rhetoric plays in the composition of his treatises. In the first part Alexandre gives a full account of the background of rhetorical theory and practice in the Greco-Roman world and of Philo's own theory of rhetorical argumentation. In the second part he focusses on how these theories are put into practice in Philo's own writings, organizing his examples under three headings: (a) formal structure of a discourse; (b) structures of a complete argument; (c) rhythmic and periodic structures (for this section see also the 1991 article summarized above). An English summary of the main theses is provided at pp. 339–346. See further the review by J. P. Martín at *SPhA* 4 (1992) 156–157. (DTR)

P. J. BEKKEN, 'Apropos jødedommens mangfold i det fønste ærkunre: observasjoner til debatten om jødisk kultus hos Filo, i Acta og Johannis-evangelis' [in Norwegian = On the Variety of Judaism in the First Century A.D.: Observations on the Debate on Jewish Cult in Philo, Acts and the Gospel of John], *Tidsskrift for Teologi og Kirke* 59 (1988) 161-173.

The Judaism in the first century AD was diverse. The topic of this essay is an analysis of various practices and views on temple and sabbath which existed in the Alexandrian Jewish community reflected in Philo's writings. Moreover, an examination of the debate and conflicts on temple and sabbath among Jews in Alexandria may throw light upon similar debates and conflicts reflected in Acts and the Gospel of John. Accordingly, this essay illustrates how debate and conflicts reflected in Philo's writings can throw light upon aspects of the New Testament, just as the New Testament can illuminate aspects of Philo's writings. (KGS, based on author's abstract)

J. DILLON, *The Golden Chain: Studies in the Development of Platonism and Christianity*, Variorum Collected Studies Series (London 1990).

Five of the 28 studies reprinted in this volume refer to Philo in the title: IX (The Transcendence of God in Philo: Some Possible Sources, = R-R 7513); X (Philo and the Stoic Doctrine of Eupatheiai, written in collaboration with A. Terian, = R-R 7713; XI Ganymede as the Logos: Traces of a Forgotten Allegorisation in Philo? = R-R 8011); XVIII Plotinus, Philo and Origen on the Grades of Virtue = R-R 8328); XX (The Theory of Three Classes of Men in Plotinus and in Philo, cf. *SPhA* 4 (1992) 103). Philo is also mentioned in some other studies; see index p. 3 at the end of the volume. (DTR)

T. L. DONALDSON, 'Proselytes or 'Righteous Gentiles'? The Status of Gentiles in Eschatological Pilgrimage. Patterns of Thought', *Journal for the Study of Pseudepigrapha and Related Literature* 7 (1990) 3–27, esp. 1–16.

Eschatological pilgrimage in the terminology of this study has to do with the view that on the day of judgment those scattered in exile will return to Zion. The study deals in particular with the question whether the gentiles that turn to the God of Israel in the end times are fully regarded as proselytes or rather as 'righteous gentiles'. Two texts by Philo, *Praem.* 164-72 and *Mos.* 2.43-44 are discussed and it is concluded that it is unlikely that Philo's text provides any solid evidence for a proselyte view of eschatological pilgrimage on the part of gentiles. 'Language apparently 'proselyte' in form is used to describe something closer to 'righteous gentiles' in substance (16).' (RvdB)

E. FLEISCHER [ע. פליישר], לקדמוניות תפילות החובה בישראל [= 'On the Beginnings of Obligatory Jewish Prayer'] *Tarbiz* 59 (1990) 397–441, esp. 410–411.

In the course of a wide-ranging argument against the existence of communal, fixed prayer prior to age of the Rabbis, the author surveys a range of ancient authors, including Philo, in order to demonstrate that during the period of the Second Temple the synagogue served not as a place of prayer but as a forum for public gathering and for the study of Law. (DS)

J. GLUCKER, 'Κριτικαὶ παρατηρήσεις εἰς κείμενα τοῦ Φίλωνος' [= Critical Observations on texts of Philo], *Platon* 42 (1990) 128–135.

Critical notes on *Sacr.* 102, *Sacr.* 123; *Det.* 135, *Det.* 138; *QG* 1.79, *Agr.* 25, *Agr.* 97. A list in English of the proposed emendations is given on p. 135. (DTR)

M. HADAS-LEBEL, *Jerusalem contre Rome*, Patrimoines Judaïsme (Paris 1990), esp. 61–64, 344–347.

There is an undoubted tendency to idealize Rome and its Empire in both Philo and Josephus, even if they give accurate denunciations of abuses that take place (61ff.). This appreciation is due to the realization that Rome's military and political power, together with its judicial organization, was in a position to guarantee freedom of worship, which in the time of Philo was more important to Jews than political freedom. (RR)

J.-G. KAHN [י. כהן-ישר], על משמעות בלילת הלשונות במשנתו של פילון האלכסנדרוני [= 'The Meaning of the Confusion of Tongues according to Philo of Alexandria'], *Proceedings of the Tenth World Congress of Jewish Studies* (Jerusalem 1990) A.127–134.

The author examines briefly Philo's attitude toward language and concludes that he saw human language by its very nature as an obstacle to thought and the multiplicity of languages as yet a further encumbrance. Despite the title of the article, very little space is devoted to the story of Babel and its exegesis. (DS)

S. R. C. LILLA, 'Die Lehre von den Ideen als Gedanken Gottes im griechischen patristischen Denken', in H. EISENBERGER (ed.), *EPMHNEYMATA: Festschrift für Hadwig Hörner zum sechzigsten Geburtstag*, Bibliothek des klassischen Altertumswissenschaften 2.79 (Heidelberg 1990) 27–50, esp. 29–32.

Philo's thoughts on the Ideas as God's thoughts need to be included in this survey of the theme in the Greek Church Fathers, the author argues, because he so clearly influenced later developments. A short presentation of Philonic texts is given, with the chief emphasis on *Opif.* With regard to the sources of Philo's usage, Lilla sees a coalescence of Platonic and Stoic elements which go back to both Antiochus and Posidonius. (DTR)

J. MANSFELD, 'Doxography and Dialectic: the *Sitz im Leben* of the 'Placita'', in W. HAASE (ed.), *ANRW* II 36.4 (Berlin–New York 1990) 3056-3229, esp. 3117–22.

Somn. 1.30ff is analysed as part of a wide-ranging examination of doxographies on the nature and parts of the soul. Philo used either an academic source or a source of the Placita older than the Vetusta Placita postulated by Diels. (DTR)

L. E. NAVIA, *Pythagoras: an Annotated Bibliography* (New York–London 1990).

Five references to Philo are taken up in this comprehensive bibliography on Pythagoras and Pythagoreanism in the ancient world; see index on p. 378. (DTR)

H. W. NEUDORFER, 'Das Diasporajudentum und der Kanon', in G. MAIER, *Der Kanon der Bibel* (Giessen-Basel-Wuppertal 1990) 83–101, esp. 89–92.

Although Philo does not possess the concept of the Canon as a technical term with reference to Scripture, there can be no doubt that he regards the Pentateuch as of superior status to the rest of the Hebrew bible, as is evidenced by the fact that of the 1161 citations of the Bible in Philo only 41 do not deal with the Pentateuch. Tied to this is Philo's mechanical conception of prophetic inspiration, in which the personality of the prophet is reduced to zero and he is regarded as nothing but the instrument of God. (RR)

P. J. RASK, *The Lists of the Twelve Tribes of Israel* (diss. The Catholic University Of America 1990).

In investigating the differences between the lists of of the sons of Jacob/tribes of Israel in the OT, the author also pays attention to other, extra-biblical, sources containing such lists, among which Philo is included. (RvdB, based on DA 51-05A p.1663)

A. RESCIGNO, 'Nota a Filone, *De praemiis et poenis*, 1,1', in I. GALLO (ed.), *Contributi di filolofia greca*, Università degli Studi di Salerno: Quaderni de Dipartimento di Scienze dell'Antichità 6 (Naples 1990) 127–136.

The article concentrates on the final part of the text under discussion: τὰ μὲν γενόμενα ὡς ἡγεμονικά, τὰ δ' ὡς ὑπήκοα καὶ γενησόμενα. The author's starting point is the emendation of the text suggested by Cohn and the defence of the traditional text by Colson, with which she agrees. Philo's text is then interpreted in the light of his general doctrine of creation, and particularly his view of matter, which sometimes seems to have been created, but at other times pre-exists the same creation process. (RR)

K. G. SANDELIN, 'Dragning till hednisk kult bland judar under hellenistisk tid och tidig kejsartid [in Swedish = Attraction towards Pagan Cults among Jews during the Hellenistic and Early Imperial Era]', *Scandinavian Jewish Studies [Nordisk Judaistik]* 10 (1989) 11–26.

There exists evidence that some Jews did participate in pagan cult during the time of the Greek and the Roman hegemonies in the eastern Mediterranean area. Examples may be shown of clear deviations from the basic Jewish principle not to mingle with heathen devotional activities both inside the Jewish realm (Maccabees) and outside it (papyri and inscriptions). In some instances Jews were forced to join pagan cult, in other cases they did it without external pressure. In Wisdom and in Philo we find a polemical attitude towards such behaviour. Jews were also in a more indirect way brought under pagan influence by athletic contests and theatre, education in the gymnasia and adjustment to architectural and artistic endeavours. (KGS)

D. A. SAPP, *An Introduction to Adam Christology in Paul: a History of Interpretation, the Jewish Background, and an Exegesis of Romans 5:12–21* (diss. Southwestern Baptist Theological Seminary 1990).

Argues that approaches to Paul's Adam Christology in terms of Gnostic or Philonic thought are inadequate. (RvdB, based on DA 51-07A, p. 2427)

D. R. SCHWARTZ, 'On Drama and Authenticity in Philo and Josephus', *Scripta Classica Israelica* 10 (1989-90) 113-129.

'Philo's histories [in *Flacc.* and *Legat.*] are frequently quite enjoyably read or heard read, but this enjoyment sometimes results from a willingness to depart from the facts in order to make the story more dramatic. This, apparently, did not bother Philo, because he was out to write enjoyable and didactic historical historical novels (119).' Apologetic aims too frequently interfere with Philo's historiography. (DTR)

N. WILLERT, *Pilatusbilledet i den antike jødedom og kristendom* [in Danish = *The Image of Pilate in Ancient Judaism and Christianity*] (Aarhus 1989), esp. 25-60.

The book contains a series of detailed analyses of texts from Antiquity describing the figure of Pontius Pilate. The basic authors analyzed are Philo, Josephus and the writers of the Gospels of the New Testament. The Philonic text given special attention is *Legat.* 298-305. Willert here like in the writings of Josephus detects political as well as religous tendencies. In his book, probably meant for Emperor Claudius, Philo wants to denounce the political order of having a Roman prefect stationed in Palestine. According to Willert neither Tiberius nor Pilate were anti-Semitic or anti-Jewish by principle. In some of their actions disapproved of by the Jews we may see examples of a nascent Emperor-cult instead. (KGS)

D. WINSTON, 'The Sage as Mystic in the Wisdom of Solomon', in J. G. GAMMIE and L. G. PURDUE (edd.), *The Sage in Israel and the Ancient Near East* (Winona Lake 1990) 383–397, esp. 386–388.

Attention is devoted to similarities and differences between the author of the Wisdom of Solomon and Philo on the theme of the sage as mystic. (DTR)

B. P. WOLFE, *The Place and Use of Scripture in the Pastoral Epistles*, (diss. Aberdeen 1990).

The author claims among other things that the traditions of II Peter and Philo on the doctrine of Scripture are not as different from Paul as is often supposed. (RvdB, based on DA 53-03A, p. 846)

A. ZOUMPOS, ''Ἀνάλεκτα' [= 'Readings'], *Platon* 42 (1990) 85–92.

25 textual notes, of which two on Philo. (DTR, based on *APh* 62 (1991) no. 14635)

SUPPLEMENT

A Provisional Bibliography 1992–94

The user of this supplementary bibliography of very recent articles on Philo is again reminded that it will doubtless contain inaccuracies and red herrings, because it is not in all cases based on autopsy. It is merely meant as a service to the reader. Scholars who are disturbed by omissions or keen to have their own work on Philo listed are strongly encouraged to take up contact with the bibliography's compilers.

1992

ANONYMUS, 'Philo of Alexandria. 'On the life of the Therapeutae [ancient contemplative Jewish sect; excerpt from *On the contemplative life*]' *Parabola* 17 (1992) 57–60.

J. ARIETI, 'Man and God in Philo: Philo's Interpretation of Genesis 1:26', *Lyceum* 4 (1992) 1–18.

M. BARKER, *The Great Angel: a Study of Israel's Second God* (Westminster 1992), esp. chap. 7.

P. BILDE, T. ENGBERG-PEDERSEN, L. HANESTAD AND J. ZAHLE (edd.), *Ethnicity in Hellenistic Egypt* (Aarhus 1992).

E. BIRNBAUM, *The Place of Judaism in Philo's Thought* (diss. Columbia 1992).

G. BOCCACCINI, *Portraits of Middle Judaism in Scholarship and Arts: a Multimedia Catalog from Flavius Josephus to 1991*, Quaderni di Henoch (Turin 1992).

P. BORGEN, Art. 'Philo', in D. FREEDMAN (ed.), *Anchor Bible Dictionary* (New York 1992) 5.333–342.

P. BORGEN, 'Filo fra Aleksandria: Joedisk filosof og Jesu samtidige', *Midtoesten Forum* 7 (1992) 40–46.

P. BORGEN, Art. 'Judaism in Egypt', in D. FREEDMAN (ed.), *Anchor Bible Dictionary* (New York 1992) 3.1061–1072.

P. BORGEN, 'Philo and the Jews in Alexandria', in P. BILDE *et al.* (edd.), *Ethnicity in Hellenistic Egypt* (Aarhus 1992) 122–138.

P. BORGEN, '"There Shall Come Forth a Man": Reflections on Messianic Ideas in Philo', in J. H. CHARLESWORTH (ed.), *The Messiah* (Minneapolis 1992) 341–361.

D. BOYARIN, 'Behold Israel According to the Flesh: on Anthropology and Sexuality in Late Antique Judaism', *Yale Journal of Criticism* 5 (1992) 27–57.

D. BOYARIN, 'This we know to be the Carnal Israel', *Critical Inquiry* 18 (1992).

F. E. BRENK, 'Darkly beyond the Glass: Middle Platonism and the Vision of the Soul', in S. GERSH and C. KANNENGIESSER (edd.), *Platonism in Late Antiquity*, Christianity and Judaism in Antiquity 8 (Notre Dame 1992) 39–60, esp. 46–51.

D. I. BREWER, *Techniques and Assumptions in Jewish Exegesis before 70 C. E.*, TSAJ 30 (Tübingen 1992), esp. 198–212.

G. L. BRUNS, *Hermeneutics Ancient and Modern* (New Haven-London 1992), esp. 83–103.

R. and C. CLARK KROEGER, *I Suffer not a Woman: Rethinking 1 Timothy 2:11–15 in Light of Ancient Evidence* (Grand Rapids 1992), esp. 146–148.

N. G. COHEN, 'Review of S. BELKIN, *The Midrash of Philo*: vol. 1', *JSJ* 23 (1992) 100–105.

E. DASSMANN *et al.*, *Reallexikon für Antike und Christentum*, Lieferung 122 (Stuttgart 1992).

K. THRAEDE, Art. 'Homonoia (Eintracht), 176–289, esp. 238–239 (concord); K. HOHEISEL, Art. 'Homosexualität', 289–364, esp. 334–335 (homosexuality).

J. D. DAWSON, *Allegorical Readers and Cultural Revision in Ancient Alexandria* (Berkeley 1992)

D. DELIA, *Alexandrian Citizenship During the Roman Principate*, American Classical Studies 23 (Atlanta 1992).

C. DOGNIEZ and M. HARL, *La Bible d'Alexandrie: Le Deuteronome* (Paris 1992).

C. A. EVANS, *Non-canonical Writings and New Testament Interpretation* (Peabody 1992), esp. 80–86.

L. H. FELDMAN, 'Was Judaism a Missionary Religion in Ancient Times?', in M. MOR (ed.), *Jewish Assimilation, Acculturation and Accommodation: Past Traditions, Current Issues and Future Prospects* (Lanham 1992) 24–37.

R. FELDMEIER, *Christen als Fremden in 1 Petrusbrief*, WUNT 64 (Tübingen 1992).

W. W. FORTENBAUGH, P. M. HUBY, R. W. SHARPLES and D. GUTAS, *Theophrastus of Eresus: Sources for his Life, Writings, Thought, and Influence*, 2 vols., Philosophia Antiqua 54 (Leiden 1992), esp. 1.342–355.

G. H. GILBERT, *Pagans in a Jewish world: Pagan Involvment in Jewish Religious and Social Life in the First Four Centuries* CE (diss. Colombia 1992).

J. GLUCKER, 'Critolaus' Scale and Philo (Evidence for Critolaus' Scale Metaphor in Passages by Philo of Alexandria)', *CQ* 42 (1992) 142–146.

M. GOODMAN, 'Jewish Proselytizing in the First Century', in J. LIEU, J. NORTH and T. RAJAK (edd.), *The Jews among Pagans and Christians in the Roman Empire* (London 1992) 53–78.

L. GRABBE, *Judaism from Cyrus to Hadrian: Sources, History, Synthesis*, 2 vols. (Minneapolis 1992).

P. GRAFFIGNA, *Filone di Alessandria, La vita contemplativa*, Opuscula 47 (Genoa 1992).

P. GRAFFIGNA, 'Osservazioni sull'uso del termine φαντασία in Filone d'Alessandria', *Koinonia* 16 (1992) 5–19.

J. T. GREENE, *Balaam and His Interpreters: a Hermeneutical History of the Balaam Traditions*, BJS 244 (Atlanta 1992), esp. 145–147.

D. M. HAY, 'Things Philo Said and Did not Say about the Therapeutae', *SBLSP* 31 (1992) 673–684.

A. HILHORST, 'Was Philo Read by Pagans? The Statement on Heliodorus in Socrates *Hist. Eccl.* 5.22', *SPhA* 4 (1992) 75–77.

P. HOFRICHTER, 'Logoslehre und Gottesbild bei Apologeten, Modalisten und Gnostikern: Johanneische Christologie im Lichte ihrer frühesten Rezeption', in H.-J. KLAUCK (ed.), *Monotheismus und Christologie: zur Gottesfrage im hellenistischen Judentum und im Urchristentum*, Quaestiones Disputatae 138 (Freiburg 1992) 186–217, esp. 187–193.

L. P. HOGAN, *Healing in the Second Temple Period*, NTOA 21 (Freiburg–Göttingen 1992), esp. 168–207.

P. W. VAN DER HORST, ''Gij zult van goden geen kwaad spreken': de Septuaginta-vertaling van Exodus 22:27 (28), haar achtergrond en invloed', *Nederlands Theologisch Tijdschrift* 46 (1992) 192–198; reprinted in *Studies over het Jodendom in de Oudheid* (Kampen 1992) 142–151.

R. S. KRAEMER, *Her Share of the Blessings: Women's Religions among Pagans, Jews, and Christians in the Greco-Roman World* (Oxford 1992), esp. 114–117, 126–127.

P. V. LEGARTH, *Guds tempel. Tempelsymbolisme og kristologi hos Ignatius af Antiokia* [God's Temple. Temple Symbolism and Christology in Ignatius of Antioch] (Århus 1992), esp. 38-43.

C. LÉVY, 'Le concept de doxa des Stoïciens à Philon: essai d'étude diachronique', in J. BRUNSCHWIG and M. NUSSBAUM (edd.), *Passions and Perceptions: Proceedings of the Fifth Symposium Hellenisticum* (Cambridge 1992) 251–284.

J. MANSFELD, *Heresiography in Context: Hippolytus' Elenchos as a Source for Greek Philosophy*, Philosophia Antiqua 56 (Leiden 1992), esp. 313–315.

C. MARKSCHIES, *Valentinus Gnosticus? Untersuchungen zur valentinianischen Gnosis mit einem Kommentar zu den Fragmenten*, WUNT 65 (Tübingen 1992).

J. MARTENS, 'Unwritten Law in Philo: a Response to Naomi G. Cohen', *JJS* 43 (1992) 38–46.

J. P. MARTÍN, 'El platonismo medio y Filón según un estudio de David Runia', *Methexis (Argentina)* 5 (1992) 135–144.

G. MAY, *Creatio ex nihilo: the Idea of Creation in Early Christian Thought* (Edinburgh 1992).

P. A. MEIJER, *Plotinus On the Good or the One (Enneads VI,9),* Amsterdam Classical Monographs 1 (Amsterdam 1992), esp. 326–328.

M. NIEHOFF, *The Figure of Joseph in Post-Biblical Jewish Literature*, AGJU 16 (Leiden 1992), esp. chap. 3.

F. PETIT, *La Chaîne sur la Genèse: Édition intégrale chapitres 1 à 3*, Traditio Exegetica Graeca 1 (Louvain 1992).

A. REINHARTZ, 'Philo on Infanticide', *SPhA* 4 (1992) 42–58.

C. J. ROETZEL, '*Oikoumene* and the Limits of Pluralism in Alexandrian Judaism', in J. A. OVERMAN and R. S. MACLENNAN (edd.), *Diaspora Jews and Judaism: Essays in Honor of, and in Dialogue with, A. Thomas Kraabel*, University of Florida Studies in the History of Judaism 41 (Atlanta 1992) 163–182, esp. 174–179.

J. L. RUBENSTEIN, *The History of Sukkot during the Second Temple and Rabbinic Periods: Studies in the Continuity and Change of a Festival* (diss. Columbia University 1992).

D. T. RUNIA, *Platonisme, Philonisme en het begin van het christelijk denken*, Quaestiones Infinitae 2 (inaugural lecture, Utrecht 1992).

D. T. RUNIA, 'The Language of Excellence in Plato's *Timaeus* and Later Platonism', in S. GERSH and C. KANNENGIESSER (edd.), *Platonism in Late Antiquity*, Christianity and Judaism in Antiquity 8 (Notre Dame 1992) 11–37, esp. 11–12, 34.

D. T. RUNIA, 'An Index to Cohn-Wendland's *Apparatus Testimoniorum*', *SPhA* 4 (1992) 87–96.

D. T. RUNIA, ''Where, tell me, is the Jew...?': Basil, Philo and Isidore of Pelusium', *VC* 46 (1992) 172–189.

D. T. RUNIA, 'A Note on Philo and Christian Heresy', *SPhA* 4 (1992) 65–74.

D. T. RUNIA, 'Confronting the Augean stables: Royse's *Fragmenta Spuria Philonica*', *SPhA* 4 (1992) 87–96.

D. T. RUNIA, 'Philo and Origen: a Preliminary Survey', in R. J. DALY (ed.), *Origeniana Quinta: Papers of the 5th International Origen Congress Boston College 14–18 August 1989*, Bibliotheca Ephemeridum Theologicarum Lovaniensium 105 (Leuven 1992) 333–339.

D. T. RUNIA, 'Verba Philonica, ΑΓΑΛΜΑΤΟΦΟΡΕΙΝ, and the authenticity of the *De Resurrectione* attributed to Athenagoras', *VC* 46 (1992) 313–327.

D. T. RUNIA (ed.), *The Studia Philonica Annual Volume 4*, BJS 264 (Atlanta 1992).

D. T. RUNIA, R. RADICE, and D. SATRAN, 'Philo of Alexandria: an Annotated Bibliography 1988–89', *SPhA* 4 (1992) 97–124.

D. R. SCHWARTZ, *Studies on the Jewish Background of Christianity*, WUNT 60 (Tübingen 1992).

G. SELLIN, 'Gotteserkenntnis und Gotteserfahrung bei Philo von Alexandria', in H.-J. KLAUCK (ed.), *Monotheismus und Christologie: zur Gottesfrage im hellenistischen Judentum und im Urchristentum*, Quaestiones Disputatae 138 (Freiburg 1992) 17–40.

F. SIEGERT, *Drei hellenistisch-jüdische Predigten: Ps.-Philon, 'Über Jona', 'Über Jona' (Fragment) 'Über Simson'. II. Kommentar nebst Beobachtungen zur hellenistische Vorgeschichte der Bibelhermeneutik*, WUNT 61 (Tübingen 1992).

D. SILLS, 'Vicious Rumours: Mosaic Narratives in First Century Alexandria', *SBLSP* 31 (1992) 684–694.

M. SIMONETTI, *The Early Church and the Word of God: an Historical Outline of Patristic Exegesis* (Edinburgh 1992).

G. E. STERLING, '*Creatio Temporalis, Aeterna, vel Continua*? an Analysis of the Thought of Philo of Alexandria', *SPhA* 4 (1992) 15–41.

A. TERIAN, *Quaestiones et Solutiones in Exodum I et II e versione armeniaca et fragmenta graeca*, Les Œuvres de Philon d'Alexandrie 34c (Paris 1992).

M. THEOBALD, 'Gott, Logos und Pneuma: Trinitarische Rede von Gott im Johannesevangelium', in H.-J. KLAUCK (ed.), *Monotheismus und Christologie: zur Gottesfrage im hellenistischen Judentum und im Urchristentum*, Quaestiones Disputatae 138 (Freiburg 1992) 41–87, esp. 79ff.

T. H. TOBIN, Article 'Logos', in D. FREEDMAN (ed.), *The Anchor Bible Dictionary* (New York 1992) 4.348–356.

G. M. VIAN, 'Le Quaestiones di Filone', *Annali di Storia dell' Esegesi* 9 (1992) 365–388.

S. K. WAN, *The* Quaestiones et solutiones in Genesim et in Exodum *of Philo Judaeus: a Synoptic Analysis* (diss. Harvard 1992).

J. WHITTAKER, 'Catachresis and Negative Theology: Philo of Alexandria and Basilides', in S. GERSH and C. KANNENGIESSER (edd.), *Platonism in Late Antiquity*, Christianity and Judaism in Antiquity 8 (Notre Dame 1992) 61–82.

E. WILL and C. ORRIEUX, *"Prosélytisme juif"?: histoire d'une erreur*, Histoire (Paris 1992), esp. 81–101.

D. WINSTON, 'Philo's Conception of the Divine Nature', in L. E. GOODMAN (ed.), *Neoplatonism and Jewish Thought*, Studies in Neoplatonism Ancient and Modern 7 (Albany 1992) 21–42.

C. K. WONG, 'Philo's Use of Chaldaioi', *SPhA* 4 (1992) 1–14.

1993

Y. de Andia, *Henosis: l'union à Dieu chez Denys l'Aréopagite* (diss. Paris-Sorbonne 1993), esp. Part IV Chapter I.

K. Armstrong, *A History of God* (London 1993), esp. 81–86.

L. Berk, 'Logos bij Johannes en Philo', *Interpretatie* 1.4 (1993) 17–19, 1.6 (1993) 23–24.

A. E. Berstein, *The Formation of Hell: Death and Retribution in the Ancient and Early Christian Worlds* (Ithaca 1993).

E. Birnbaum, 'The Place of Judaism in Philo's Thought', *SBLSP* 32 (1993) 54–69.

P. Borgen, 'Heavenly Ascent in Philo: an Examination of Selected Passages', in J. H. Charlesworth and C. A. Evans (edd.), *The Pseudepigrapha and Early Biblical Interpretation*, JSPSup14 (Sheffield 1993) 246–268.

D. Carabine, *The Unknown God: Apophasis from Plato to Eriugena* (1993).

G. P. Carras, 'Dependence or Common Tradition in Philo *Hypothetica* viii 6.10 – 7.20 and Josephus *Contra Apionem* 2.190–219', *SPhA* 5 (1993) 24–47.

G. Casadio, 'Gnostische Wege zur Unsterblichkeit', in E. Hornung and T. Schabert (edd.), *Auferstehung und Unsterblichkeit*, Eranos N.F. 1 (München 1993) 203–254, esp. 214–218.

J. Cohen, *The Origins and Evolution of the Moses Nativity Story*, Numen Book series 58 (Leiden 1993), esp. chap. 2.

N. G. Cohen, 'The Greek Virtues and the Mosaic Laws in Philo: an Elucidation of *De Specialibus Legibus* IV 133–135', *SPhA* 5 (1993) 9–23.

J. Dillon, 'Philo and Middle Platonism: a Response to Runia and Sterling', *SPhA* 5 (1993) 151–155.

P. Ellingworth, *Commentary on Hebrews*, New International Greek Testament Commentary (Grand Rapids 1993).

E. E. Ellis, 'Christos in 1 Corinthians 10.4-9', in M. C. De Boer (ed.), *From Jesus to John: Essays on Jesus and New Testament Christology in Honor of Marinus de Jonge*, JSNTSup 84 (Sheffield 1993) 168-73.

D. Farias, *Studi sul pensiero sociale di Filone di Alessandria*, Pubblicazioni degli Istituti di Scienze giuridiche, economiche, politiche e sociali della facoltà di giurisprudenza della Università di Messina 180 (Milan 1993).

L. H. Feldman, *Jew and Gentile in the Ancient World* (Princeton 1993).

L. H. Feldman, 'Palestinian and Diaspora Judaism in the First Century', in H. Shanks (ed.), *Christianity and Rabbinic Judaism: a Parallel History of their Origins and Early Development* (Washington 1993) 1–39, 327–336 (notes), esp. 27ff.

R. A. J. Gagnon, 'Heart of Wax and a Teaching that Stamps: τύπος διδαχῆς (Rom. 6:17b) once more', *JBL* 112 (1993) 667–687, esp. 682ff.

A. C. GELJON, 'De goddelijke Logos bij Philo', *Interpretatie* 1.8 (1993) 28–29.

J. GLUCKER, 'Piety, Dogs and a Platonic Reminiscence: Philo, *Quod deterius* 54–56 and Plato, *Euthrypo* 12e–15a', *Illinois Classical Studies* 18 (1993) 131–138.

V. GUIGNARD, *Le rapport d'Israel à l'histoire dans l'œuvre de Philon d'Alexandrie* (D.E.A. d'histoire ancienne, Poitiers 1993).

M. HARL, 'La Bible d'Alexandrie et les études sur la Septante: réflexions sur une première expérience', *VC* 47 (1993) 313–340, esp. 330–334.

H. W. HOLLANDER and J. W. HOLLEMAN, 'The Relationship of Death, Sin and Law in 1 Cor. 15:56', *NT* 35 (1993) 270–291, esp. 275–8, 286.

P. W. VAN DER HORST, 'Philo van Alexandrinus over de toorn Gods', in A. DE JONG and A. DE JONG (edd.), *Kleine Encyclopedie van de toorn*, Utrechtse Theologische Reeks 21 (Utrecht 1993) 77–82.

P. W. VAN DER HORST, 'Thou shalt not Revile the Gods': the LXX Translation of Ex. 22:28 (27), its Background and Influence', *SPhA* 5 (1993) 1–8.

A. KAMESAR, *Jerome, Greek Scholarship, and the Hebrew Bible*, Oxford Classical Monographs (Oxford 1993) esp. 91–93.

J. -Y. LELOUP, *Prendre soin de l'Être: Philon et les thérapeutes d'Alexandrie* (Paris 1993).

D. LINDSAY, *Josephus and Faith: "Pistis" and "Pisteuein" as Faith Terminology in the Writings of Flavius Josephus and the New Testament*, AGJU 19 (Leiden 1993).

F. PETIT, *La Chaîne sur la Genèse: Édition intégrale chapitres 4 à 11*, Traditio Exegetica Graeca 2 (Louvain 1993).

S. M. POGOLOFF, *Logos and Sophia: the Rhetorical Situation of 1 Corinthians*, SBL dissertation series (Atlanta 1993).

R. RADICE, '*Didaskalikos* 164, 29–30 e la probabile influenze di Filone di Alessandria', *Archivio di Filosofia* 61 (1993) 45–63.

A. REINHARTZ, 'Parents and Children: a Philonic Perspective', in S. J. D. COHEN (ed.), *The Jewish Family*, Brown Judaic Series 289 (Atlanta 1993).

A. REINHARTZ, 'Philo's *Exposition of the Law* and Social History: Methodological Considerations', *SBLSP* 32 (1993) 6–21.

J. R. ROYSE, 'Reverse Indexes to Philonic texts in the Printed Florilegia and Collections of Fragments', *SPhA* 5 (1993) 156–179.

D. T. RUNIA, *Philo in Early Christian Literature: a Survey*, Compendia Rerum Iudaicarum ad Novum Testamentum III 3 (Assen–Minneapolis 1993).

D. T. RUNIA, 'God of the Philosophers, God of the Patriarchs: Exegetical Backgrounds in Philo of Alexandria', in F. J. HOOGEWOUD and R. MUNK (edd.), *Joodse Filosofie tussen Rede en Traditie: Feestbundel ter ere van de tachtigste verjaardaag van Prof. dr. H. J. Heering* (Kampen 1993) 13–23.

D. T. RUNIA, 'Was Philo a Middle Platonist? a Difficult Question Revisited', *SPhA* 5 (1993) 112–140.

D. T. Runia (ed.), *The Studia Philonica Annual,* Volume 5, BJS 287 (Atlanta 1993).

D. T. RUNIA and R. RADICE, 'Philo of Alexandria: an Annotated Bibliography 1990', *SPhA* 5 (1993) 180–208.

N. SCHUMAN, *Gelijk om gelijk* (diss. VU Amsterdam 1993).

G. E. STERLING, 'Platonizing Moses: Philo and Middle Platonism', *SPhA* 5 (1993) 96–111.

H. TARRANT, *Thrasyllan Platonism* (Ithaca 1993).

A. TERIAN, 'Two Unusual Uses of aṙn in the Armenian Version of Philo's *Quaestiones*', *Annual of Armenian Linguistics* 14 (1993) 49–54.

T. H. TOBIN S.J., 'Was Philo a Middle Platonist? Some suggestions', *SPhA* 5 (1993) 147–150.

P. J. TOMSON, *'Voor één dag genoeg' (Matt 6:34): het brood, het Woord en de wetenschap*, In Caritate 3 (inaugural address Brussels 1993).

W. C. VAN UNNIK, *Das Selbstverständnis der jüdischen Diaspora in der hellenistisch-römischen Zeit: aus dem Nachlaß herausgegeben und bearbeitet von P. W. van der Horst*, AGJU 17 (Leiden 1993).

S. K. WAN, 'Philo's *Quaestiones et Solutiones in Genesim*: a Synoptic Approach', *SBLSP* 32 (1993) 22–53.

R. McL WILSON, 'Philo and Gnosticism', *SPhA* 5 (1993) 84–92.

D. WINSTON, 'Philo and Middle Platonism: Response to Runia and Sterling', *SPhA* 5 (1993) 141–146.

C. D. YONGE, *The Works of Philo Complete and Unabridged,* with a Foreword by D. M. SCHOLER (Peabody Mass. 1993).

D. ZELLER, 'Notiz zu den "immerfließenden Quellen der göttlichen Wohltaten"', *SPhA* 5 (1993) 93–94.

1994

P. W. VAN DER HORST, 'Silent Prayer in Antiquity', *Numen* 41 (1994) 1–25, esp. 13.

P. GARNSEY, 'Philo Judaeus and Slave Theory', *Scripta Classica Israelica* 13 (1994) 30–45.

P. GRAFFIGNA, 'Tra il doppio e l'unita: parentela (συγγένεια) tra uomo e Dio in Filone d'Alessandria', *Koinonia* 19 (1994).

H. -J. KLAUCK, 'Ein Richter im eigenen Innern: das Gewissen bei Philo von Alexandrien', in Idem, *Alter Welt und neuer Glaube: Beiträge zur Religionsgeshcichte, Forschungsgeschichte und Theologie des Neuen Testaments*, NTOA 29 (Freiburg–Göttingen 1994) 33–58.

K. A. Morland, *The Rhetoric of Curse in Galatians: Paul Confronts another Gospel*, Emory Studies in Early Christianity (Atlanta 1994).

R. Radice, *La filosofia di Aristobulo e i suoi nessi con il De Mundo attribuito ad Aristotele*, Pubblicazoini del Centro di Ricerche di Metafisica: Collana Temi metafisici e problemi del pensiero antico. Studi e Testi 33 (Milan 1994).

G. J. Schils, *Stoic and Platonist Readings of Plato's* Timaeus (diss. Berkeley 1994), esp. chap. 4 'Philo Judaeus, on a Cruise to Alexandria'.

Leiden, Luino, Åbo, Jerusalem

REVIEW ARTICLE

'DID PHILO SAY THE SHEMA?' AND OTHER REFLECTIONS ON E. P. SANDERS' *JUDAISM: PRACTICE AND BELIEF* [1]

Alan Mendelson

By the time this paper appears in print, the first reviews of E. P. Sanders' most recent book, *The Historical Figure of Jesus* (1994), will already have appeared.[2] Yet, since Sanders' work is both controversial and thought-provoking at any time, the reader will bear with me if I consider in more than a cursory fashion Sanders' 1992 offering to scholarship:

> *Judaism: Practice and Belief, 63*BCE – *55*CE, SCM Press, London, and Trinity Press International, Philadelphia 1992, xix + 580 pages, $29.95 (*not* on acid-free paper). ISBN 1-56338016-1 (UK), 0334-02469-2 (U.S.A.)

A consideration of *Judaism: Practice and Belief* is not out of place in a journal primarily devoted to Philo of Alexandria because, as the title of this book implies, the author sets himself the task of covering both Palestine and the Diaspora.

How, then, does Philo fare in *Judaism: Practice and Belief*? We cannot begin to answer that question without taking into account the core concept of the book, what Sanders calls Common Judaism. A comment made by Sanders on the first page of his Preface sheds some light on what he means by Common Judaism:

> I have by no means lost confidence in the common-denominator theology that I described in *Paul and Palestinian Judaism*; on the contrary, I am more convinced than ever that a broad agreement on basic theological points characterized Judaism in the Graeco-Roman period. Now I wish to place theology into its proper historical context, religious practice (ix).

---

[1] I wish to thank Adele Reinhartz, Eileen Schuller, and especially the indefatigable Editor of this journal, David Runia, for reading and commenting on previous drafts of this paper. Except where otherwise noted, all quotations of Philo are taken from the Loeb Classical Library edition.

[2] Cf. Geza Vermes' review of *The Historical Figure of Jesus* in the *Times Literary Supplement*, March 25, 1994, p.4.

***The Studia Philonica Annual* 6 (1994) 160–170**

Common Judaism thus refers to a body of agreed-upon beliefs and practices which bound Graeco-Roman Jews, wherever they lived, together in a religious community. Although it may have been Palestinian in origin, between 63 BCE and 55 CE Common Judaism does not appear exclusively on Palestinian soil.

To some extent, Sanders uses Philo to broaden the geographical base of the consensus which he (Sanders) finds in Judaism of the Graeco-Roman period. If Sanders finds a passage in Philo which agrees with Palestinian practice, he seizes on it because it supports his contention that a community of belief extended beyond Palestine. As Sanders himself realizes, one must be highly selective in the use of Philo because Philo cannot be imported lock, stock, and barrel into a concept such as Common Judaism. Although I do not want to belabor this point, we need only think back to the efforts in a previous generation to subsume Philo under the grander concepts of Native Judaism (Wolfson) or even Hellenistic Mysteries (Goodenough).

Many contemporary scholars have commented on the ways in which Philo's concept of Judaism differed from the Judaisms practiced in Palestine. In my view, Philo was guided by his own distinctive agenda. He often spoke as an Alexandrian Jew who was trying to solve Alexandrian Jewish problems. To find the lowest common denominator between divergent forms of Judaism without being reduced to the level of truisms—this is the delicate task which Sanders sets for himself. Does Sanders manage to conjoin the evidence of a particular Alexandrian writer (a writer known for subtlety, nuance, and a philosophical disposition) to more systematic demands of a book on the universal theme of Common Judaism? I hope to show in what follows that we can answer this question with a qualified yes.

We should note, first of all, that *Judaism: Practice and Belief* is composed of three parts:

I Context (3–43)
II Common Judaism (47–303)
III Groups and Sects (317–494)

Those who are interested in the Diaspora will find Part II the most relevant section of the book. A glance at the first half of Part II reveals that it is almost exclusively concerned with the Temple. But, in the second half of Part II, Sanders turns to topics related to the observance of the law of God; there are chapters on worship, the sabbath, circumcision, purity, food, charity and love. Part II concludes with reflections on theology and hopes for the future.

Very early in Part II, Sanders recalls a 'memorable' sentence from

Morton Smith. Since I discern the spirit of this sentence throughout *Judaism: Practice and Belief*, I would like to cite it also:[3]

> Down to the fall of the Temple, the normative Judaism of Palestine is that compromise of which the three principal elements are the Pentateuch, the Temple, and the *amme ha'arez*, the ordinary Jews who were not members of any sect.

There are any number of interesting parallels between Smith and Sanders. Sanders' own definition of Common Judaism owes much to Smith's comment. Both Smith and Sanders stress compromise and the active role of ordinary Jews. This is a fine beginning, and I commend the effort, which is so clear in Sanders' definition and throughout his book, to uncover the religious experience of 'the people.' For too long, historians of this and other periods have concentrated on the elite, as if they alone existed and lived noteworthy lives.

Sanders is well aware that the experience of Greek-speaking Jews cannot simply be grafted onto his concept of Common Judaism. Indeed Sanders addresses this problem as soon as he defines his key concept. Thus Sanders' crucial Chapter 5 begins in this way:

> Within Palestine, 'normal' or 'common' Judaism was what the priests and the people agreed on. We shall see that in general Jews of the Greek-speaking Diaspora shared in this normal Judaism, although their participation in temple worship, which was an important ingredient, was restricted (47).

It is significant to note here that one of Smith's three pillars, the Temple, is of 'restricted' use when it comes to the Greek-speaking Diaspora. This is not the place to discuss at length Philo's attitudes toward the Temple. We should recall, however, what Philo wrote in *Spec.* 1.66–67:[4]

> The highest and true temple of God is, we must believe, the whole universe, having for its sanctuary the holiest part of all existence, namely heaven, for its votive offerings the stars, for its priests the angels, who are servitors of his powers, unbodied souls, not mixtures of rational and irrational nature as ours are, but with the irrational eliminated, completely mind, pure intelligences, in the likeness of the monad. The other temple is made by hand...

Given Philo's tendency to spiritualize both the Temple and sacrifices, it is even more problematic than Sanders realizes to include Philo's views on these subjects in a supposed Jewish consensus in the Graeco-Roman period. That is, Philo's divergences from other Jewish writers on these

---

[3] M. Smith, 'The Dead Sea Sect in Relation to Ancient Judaism,' *NTS* 7 (1960–61) 356, quoted in Sanders, *Judaism: Practice and Belief* 48.

[4] The translation of this passage is that of D. Winston, *Philo of Alexandria: The Contemplative Life, The Giants, and Selections* (New York 1981) 279.

particular topics may be more significant than his apparent convergences.[5]

If Sanders is right about the Jews of the Greek-speaking Diaspora sharing in 'normal' Judaism, what elements of Common Judaism can we discern in Philo? Let us begin with Sanders' notion of compromise. Here I think that Sanders points in a useful direction. For although Philo's Judaism does not appear to be a compromise between the priests and the people, it does seem to occupy a middle ground between the claims of the literalists, on the one hand, and the extreme allegorists, on the other.[6]

To this point, we have found one element of Sanders' Common Judaism—the notion of compromise—which finds a rough parallel in Philo. It seems to me that if someone were to explore the implications of this parallel in more detail, the results may well prove to be valuable. At the same time, I should stress that the kind of compromise which might be attributed to Philo is qualitatively different from that which characterizes Common Judaism. Sanders' notion of Common Judaism has a very human, populist edge. Most scholars, I think, would agree that this aspect is lacking in Philo. After all, aside from a few details in *In Flaccum* and *De Legatione*, what do we know of ordinary people from the works of Philo? Philo's Judaism is more rarified, the product of one man's (or one group's) philosophical imagination.

While I do not wish to dwell any further on the contrasts between Common Judaism and Philo's Judaism, they must be borne in mind as we proceed. There is, to put it gently, a mis-match between the framework which Sanders sets out at the beginning of *Judaism: Practice and Belief* and the work of Philo, the main witness to the Greek-speaking Diaspora. This fundamental disparity may help to explain several problematic discussions involving Philo in Part II of Sanders' book.

In his discussion of annual festivals, Sanders maintains that 'all Jews, whether in Jerusalem or not, could gather in companies and participate in the Passover sacrifice.' From this he concludes that 'some Jews in the Diaspora sacrificed at Passover' (134). To support his claim, Sanders cites some inconclusive evidence from Josephus (*AJ* 14.260). The evidence from Philo concerning the Passover is found in *Spec.* 2.146–48. Let us examine the crucial parts of that passage in more detail:

---

[5] Cf. V. Nikiprowetzky, 'La spiritualisation des sacrifices et le culte sacrificiel au temple de Jérusalem chez Philon d'Alexandrie,' *Sem* 17 (1967) 97–116; and H. J. Klauck, 'Die heilige Stadt: Jerusalem bei Philo und Lukas,' *Kairos* 28 (1986) 129–51.

[6] My comments here are dependent on the important article of M. J. Shroyer, 'Alexandrian Jewish Literalists,' *JBL* 55 (1936) 261–84.

> (146) [Passover] is a reminder and thank-offering for that great migration from Egypt which was made by more than two millions of men and women in obedience to the oracles vouchsafed to them....These are the facts as discovered by the study of ancient history. (147) But to those who are accustomed to turn literal facts [*ta rhēta*[7]] into allegory, the Crossing-festival suggests the purification of the soul. They say that the lover of wisdom is occupied solely in crossing from the body and the passions, each of which overwhelms him like a torrent, unless the rushing current be dammed and held back by the principles of virtue. (148) On this day every dwelling-house is invested with the outward semblance and dignity of a temple. The victim is then slaughtered and dressed for the festive meal which befits the occasion....

My problem with using this passage in a discussion of actual religious practice lies in the fact that some of the passage is clearly allegorical. In *Spec*. 2.147, Philo speaks of those who are accustomed to turn literal statements into allegory. According to Philo, such allegorists see in the Passover a purification of the soul. This passage makes me think, first, of those who embellished the West Wall of the Dura Synagogue and, then, of Goodenough's interpretation of the scene of the Migration from Egypt in his *Jewish Symbols*.[8] It does not prepare me for the idea which Sanders finds in it that Jews in the Diaspora actually slaughtered lambs at their homes on the first night of Passover. Sanders' position depends on a reading of a passage in which Philo suddenly ceases his reflections on the allegorical meaning of the Crossing-festival (in *Spec*. 2.147) and, without another word, begins to talk about the actual practices of Alexandrian Jews (in *Spec*. 2.148). Of course, Sanders may be right about what 'some Jews' did on the Passover. I cannot prove that Jews in the Diaspora did not offer pascal sacrifices any more than Sanders can prove that they did. But in assessing the issue in Philo, one must take into account all the passages in the Philonic corpus in which Philo spiritualizes sacrifice. When these passages are considered, I think we arrive at a final verdict of *ignoramus*: we do not know.[9]

After many years of reading Philo, I have (with some reluctance) come to the conclusion that Philo's testimony about realia is never completely above suspicion. Sanders wants to know what the priests at the Temple wore. Philo presumably can tell us; after all he was an eye-witness. And yet, even a straightforward question such as this involves Sanders in some convolutions:

---

[7] David Runia rightly suggested to me that one could translate these words as 'literal statements.'

[8] Reference here is to Plate 14 in E. R. Goodenough's *Jewish Symbols in the Greco-Roman Period* (New York 1964) Vol. 11 and his discussion of it in Vol. 10, 125–39.

[9] Cf. my discussion of this in *Philo's Jewish Identity* (Atlanta, 1988) 62–67.

> [Philo's] statement that the priests wore only a short tunic and visible breeches is eminently reasonable, and he is quite definite about it; nevertheless, he seems to be wrong. This passage almost, not quite, shakes my general view that, at the time he wrote the *Special Laws*, he had made a pilgrimage. Possibly he had forgotten precisely what he had seen and unconsciously 'dressed' the priests in costumes that he thought were reasonable; perhaps his view of priestly garments was shaped by having seen pagan priests in short tunics (94).

Even at my most sceptical, I do not doubt that Philo made at least one pilgrimage to Jerusalem. But I do not know when he made that trip, and it does not surprise me that he got the details 'wrong'. Sanders has an obvious flair for the realia of life. Unfortunately, Philo did not share that ability and therefore is not a reliable recorder of this mundane level of things.

In discussing Philo's knowledge of sacrifices in *Judaism: Practice and Belief*, Sanders writes:

> Philo had visited the temple, and some of his statements about it (e.g.the guards) seem to be based on personal knowledge. But his discussion of the sacrifices is 'bookish,' and at some important points it reveals that he is passing on information derived from the Greek translation of the Hebrew Bible (the Septuagint), not from observation (104).

The question which this raises is the following: how do we know when Philo is being 'bookish' and when he is faithfully recording his observations? Could Philo himself distinguish between these two modes of acquiring information? Was Philo perhaps also being 'bookish' when he talked about paschal sacrifices?

In his discussion of ancient observance, Sanders states that the Shema was 'fundamental to Jewish life and worship' (195). Sanders considers the Shema in two sections: first there is Deut. 6:4–5; this is followed by Deut.6.6–9. According to Sanders, 'the mishnaic rabbis simply took it for granted, as something that did not require debate or proof, that every Jew said the Shema (along with daily prayers) twice a day, morning and evening (*Berakhot* I.1–3)' (196). Having noted this, Sanders goes on to say that the recitation of the Shema 'seems to have been very widespread' (196). Widespread enough to include Philo?

Sanders' dicussion of the Shema raises two related questions. Did Philo have a set liturgy and did that liturgy include at the very least Deut. 6:4–5? I think Sanders would like to answer these questions in the affirmative, but he is too good an historian to yield to the temptation of assuming what needs to be proved. Sanders, of course, is not the first modern scholar who has wished to see the Shema as a universal Jewish prayer before the destruction of the Second Temple. According to

Wolfson, in Palestine the belief in the unity of God expressed itself in the recitation of Deut. 6:4 twice a day. Then Wolfson moves from Palestine to the Diaspora:[10]

> Undoubtedly the same confession of the belief in the unity of God was also followed twice daily by Hellenistic Jews. It is probably because this principle was so commonly well known among those of his contemporaries to whom he addressed himself in his works that Philo never directly quotes in support of it that classical scriptural proof-text.

To be frank, I do not think that we can accept the arguments of Wolfson or the suggestions of Sanders. In the works of Philo which have survived, there is, as Wolfson admits, no reference to this crucial text. Philo had ample opportunities to refer to Deut. 6:4–5. For instance, in his presentation of the 'creed' at the end of *De Opificio* the issue of the unity of God is front and center. Yet Philo does not refer to the Shema. Nor does he mention it in the numerous passages which refer to prayer. Most scholars today agree that at least some of Philo's works were not written for an inner circle, but rather for marginal Jews or learned pagans. We certainly cannot explain Philo's failure to cite the Shema in these largely apologetic works as a case of the Shema being too well known. In the absence of any concrete evidence, we cannot trace the role of the Shema as the centerpiece of Jewish liturgy back to Philo.

For purposes of argument, let us glance at Winston's collection of passages which have to do with worship.[11] From this sample, it is evident that prayer for Philo consists of personal supplications or hymns of praise to God who actually needs nothing from us (though we might think we need something from Him). Prayer does not seem to be regularized as it was for Philo's Therapeutae in *Contempl.* 89.[12] (In fact, Philo seems to regard the prayers of the Therapeutae as one of their distinguishing marks.) Prayer for Philo seems to be a spontaneous, spiritual activity of the soul, not the recitation of set texts. What takes place at the *proseuktērion*, a word which is usually translated as 'place of prayer'? Philo answers this in his treatise on Moses. In that work, Philo explains that on the Sabbath Jews congregate for the purpose of pursuing 'the study of wisdom.' He continues (*Mos.* 2.216):

> For what are our places of prayer [*proseuktēria*] throughout the cities but schools of prudence and courage and temperance and justice and also of piety, holiness and every virtue by which duties to God and men are discerned and rightly performed.

---

[10] H. A. Wolfson, *Philo* (Cambridge 1947) II, 95.

[11] Winston, *Selections*, 157–63.

[12] Cf. D. M. Hay, 'Things Philo Said and Did Not Say About the Therapeutae,' *SBLSP* 31 (1992) 681–82.

The same picture emerges from *Spec.* 2. 61–62.[13] What is clear from these passages is that on the subject of prayer Philo cannot be easily subsumed under the general notion of Common Judaism.

The apparent difficulty of including Philo under Common Judaism raises a more general problem for Philonists. Many of us have assumed in our writings that Philo was a unique individual in whom different theological and cultural streams came together. Philo may have been influenced by Platonists, Stoics, Neo-Pythagoreans, allegorists, earlier Hellenistic Jewish authors, and others. Yet Philo can never be reduced to one of these sources. For many of us, the streams which came together in Philo converged once and only once in a *hapax phainomenon*.

My comments in the previous paragraph took as their premise the idea, shared by many Philonists today, that Philo was a unique individual. Sanders' use of Philo in *Judaism: Practice and Belief* challenges that assumption. In other words, Sanders may be challenging us to stop regarding Philo as a *hapax phainomenon*. Philo belonged to a people who were spread out across the Mediterranean World. Sanders seems to be saying that Philo, for all his reading of Plato, was a Jew—a Jew in many ways like other Jews. For all his learning, Philo's religious identity can also be seen in terms of five areas of ultimate concern: worship of God, Sabbath observance, circumcision, purity observance, and support of the Temple. Sanders is eloquent in describing what he calls 'orthopraxy in worldwide Judaism' (237).[14] To support his idea, he appropriately cites Philo's claim that the Jews 'would even endure to die a thousand deaths sooner than accept anything contrary to the laws and customs which [God] had ordained (*Hypothetica* 6.9)' (239). Even though placing Philo in the ranks of the Jewish population of the Mediterranean involves a flattening of Philo as an individual, I think that the exercise ultimately is salutary, and the results are instructive.

In his preface to *Judaism: Practice and Belief*, Sanders acknowledges that he has not lost confidence in the 'common-denominator theology' which he first described in *Paul and Palestinian Judaism* (1977). Indeed he is explicit about extending the common-denominator method in the book under review here (p. ix). As long as we are aware that this approach results in some blurring of the marks of identity by which we have come to know Philo, there is a great deal to be learned from Sanders about Judaism in the Graeco-Roman period.

In a book which is replete with thought-provoking analyses, it is

---

[13] See my discussion of Sabbath activities in *Secular Education in Philo of Alexandria* (Cincinnati 1982) 32–33.

[14] Sanders puts his case very compellingly on pp. 236–40.

difficult to isolate one for special attention. Yet Sanders' treatment of the Theodotus inscription is short enough to be manageable and typical enough to be instructive. The Theodotus inscription, from a Greek-speaking synagogue in Jerusalem,[15] has sparked a certain amount of scholarly debate. Hengel has declared that Theodotus was a Pharisee.[16] Sanders disagrees in the following insightful passage:

> Martin Hengel assumes that the Theodotus inscription, which says that a family of priests built and maintained a synagogue in Jerusalem, is an indication of Pharisaic activity. The Pharisees were generally responsible for the development of synagogues in Palestine, and so he 'assume[s] that this foundation, too, had a Pharisaic background.'... Yet the inscription says that the supporting family was priestly, and evidently it was rich. Priests as priests cared about the law. They did not have to be Pharisees to do so. They believed in it and they taught it. The assumption that the Pharisees were the only ones committed to the law, and that whenever anyone else showed commitment it was because of Pharisaic influence, pervades scholarly descriptions of second-temple Judaism, and consequently Pharisees crop up everywhere. But if people will put that assumption aside and look again at the literature, they will see things in a truer light, and they will not be compelled to insert the Pharisees into every narrative. One of the main ambitions of this book is to encourage readers to see common Judaism and common Jews as devoted to the law (450–51).

I have quoted this passage at great length—for which I should offer some apology. While not mentioning Philo, this passage lays out in a clear way the conditions under which Philo and others in the Hellenistic world could and did thrive as Jews. Philo, to use a formulation from Sanders, 'cared about the law.' He cared—not because of Pharisaic influence, not because of Native (rabbinic) Judaism, but because of his Common Judaism. Sanders' concept of Common Judaism has made the entire phenomenon of ancient Jewish practice and belief much more coherent. For having the tenacity to work out his complex ideas in such rewarding detail, we owe him our gratitude.

At this point, I would like to recall a few words written by Professor Jacob Neusner concerning the author of this impressive book:[17]

> Let us not forget that Sanders is constructing a vast apologia for rabbinic Judaism in the framework of Protestant Evangelical theology. His is a major contribution to the defense and rehabilitation of Judaism in contemporary Christian theology, and I think massive goodwill informs his work...

---

[15] Sanders reproduces the actual inscription on p.176.

[16] The reference which Sanders gives is to Hengel's *Between Jesus and Paul* (trans. J. Bowden; Philadelphia 1983) 16–18.

[17] J. Neusner, 'The Mishna in Philosophical Context and Out of Canonical Bounds,' *JBL* 112 (1993) 295, n.10.

Whether 'evangelical' is the appropriate word to use here is for others to decide, but Neusner's point is well taken. For *Judaism: Practice and Belief* is a masterly addition to Professor Sanders' *oeuvre*. Not only is the book guided by 'worthy motives' as Neusner would admit; it is also informed by an almost insatiable curiosity into every detail of Jewish life in the early Roman period. What really guides Sanders is a profound passion and love for everything connected to first-century Judaism.

I do not use the words 'passion' or 'love' lightly; certainly they cannot be routinely applied to all books written about this period. But what else could lie behind Sanders' valiant attempts to picture the microcosm of everyday life? What else would induce Sanders to move, almost minute by minute, through 'a day in the life of the temple' (116)? The ambiguity of the last phrase is significant: for Sanders the Temple as well as everyone and everything connected to it are alive.

Sanders' basic commitments may be revealed by glancing at the titles of several chapters of *Judaism: Practice and Belief.* Consider the following, taken almost at random: Chapter 6, 'The Ordinary Priests and the Levites: At Work in the Temple'; Chapter 8, 'The Common People: Daily Life and Annual Festivals'; and, finally, Chapter 10, 'The Priests and Levites Outside the Temple'. Sanders' commitment, then, is both to the concrete realia of life and to the ordinary people who lived that life. If there is a bias here, it may be summed up in Sanders' remark that social reality is 'more important than Pharisaic debates' (131). For while that remark is made with regard to the presence of women and children in the Temple, I think it applies to many topics that he raises.

Like almost every important book, *Judaism: Practice and Belief* has its detractors. Neusner, in the same article I have just quoted, says the following:

> As to Sanders's most recent statement of his opinions, *Judaism: Practice and Belief*, his use of the Mishna as a handbook of facts on how things really were in the first centuries BCE and CE is of course indefensible. He picks and chooses what is historical and what is not, as though he were a firsthand witness.[18]

What historian, we might ask, does not pick and choose? For Neusner, the only alternative to writing the sort of book which Sanders has written seems to be to write a 43-volume commentary on the Mishna. This, according to Neusner, somehow would form the basis for showing 'how everything holds together.'[19] In my view, Neusner is merely being rhetorical when he suggests this option. The production of a

[18] *Idem*.
[19] *Ibid*., 296.

commentary on the Mishna, however desirable, is not a prerequisite for, and does not guarantee the quality of a convincing book on first-century Judaism. Indeed, if scholars of good will and worthy motives wait until they have completed multi-volume commentaries on the Mishna before venturing an opinion, we shall all be denied the challenging hypotheses and reconstructions of the sort found in *Judaism: Practice and Belief.*

In concluding, I would like to turn to the second giant (Morton Smith being the first) whose spirit permeates *Judaism: Practice and Belief.* I am referring, of course, to Erwin R. Goodenough, whom Sanders mentions in the Preface:

> In 1966, I decided to study what I then thought of as 'practical piety'. I was fascinated by E.R. Goodenough's depiction of Judaism: rabbinic Judaism was a small island in a sea of another form of Judaism, which shared the general characteristics of Hellenistic mysticism. I thought that a study of pious practices, such as prayer, purifications and offerings to the temple, might help to clarify the relationship between Palestinian and Diaspora Judaism (ix).

The more I think about this intellectual lineage, the more sense it makes. Sanders does not concur with the idea of a Judaism impregnated with Hellenistic mysticism. But, like Goodenough, Sanders has explored the sea as widely and thoroughly as it is possible to do. What he has found there are forms of Jewish piety which have a legitimacy and a power formerly accorded only to rabbinic Judaism itself.

McMaster University
Hamilton, Canada

REVIEW ARTICLE

PHILO
IN A SINGLE VOLUME

David T. Runia

The publication of an English translation of the complete works of Philo in a single volume last year is certainly a landmark in the history of Philonic studies, and it is only fitting that our Annual devote attention to this event, which will surely have significant repercussions for the study of Philo in the English-speaking world and beyond. It is not the first time that Philo has been available in a single volume. The *editio princeps* of Philo by Adrian Turnebus (Paris 1552) was in a single volume, as were three bilingual editions (Greek and Latin) published in the 17th century (Geneva 1613, Paris 1640, Frankfurt 1691, reissued with additions 1729). But these were monumental folio volumes, cumbersome to use and beyond the reach of all but libraries and wealthy patrons of the arts. Since then Philo has only been available in multi-volumed editions and translations. Now the situation has changed dramatically. A compact, handsomely produced single-volumed edition has been made available at a price that cannot possibly be a deterrent for any prospective buyer. Full details of this volume are as follows:

> *The Works of Philo Complete and Unabridged: New Updated Version*, translated by C. D. Yonge, with a foreword by David M. Scholer. Hendrickson Publishers, Peabody, Massachusetts, 1993. xx + 918 pages + 6 maps. Hardbound with dust jacket, size 16 x 24 x 4.5 cm. Price $29.95.[1] ISBN 0-943575-93-1.

What I wish to do in this review article is introduce the reader to the background of the new publication, describe what the volume offers, and reach a verdict on its value and usability.

Let me say at the outset that the chief aim of the publisher and the team responsible for the project's realization is highly laudable. They were concerned about the availability of Philo's writings for a broader public. In the publisher's preface we read: 'The only other English text of

[1] Official price. Discounts available from the publisher for teachers and libraries.

Philo exists in ten volumes plus two supplementary volumes in the prestigious (and expensive) Loeb Classical Library published by Harvard University Press. The Loeb edition includes the Greek and is particularly prized by the scholarly community. Unfortunately, however, this series has been largely out of the reach of most students of Jewish and Christian antiquity.' There can be no disagreement with this statement. The Loeb Philo, published from 1929 to 1962 and mainly the work of F. H. Colson, is still in print, but now costs $252.[2] The new Philo, although lacking the Greek text, covers almost the same ground at a fraction of the price. In his foreword the leader of the project, David Scholer, compares the situation in Josephan studies. Here too there is a highly competent Loeb text and translation (in 9 volumes). But biblical and classical scholars have the alternative of purchasing the single-volume translation of William Whiston, first published in 1736. Literally hundreds of thousands of copies of Whiston have been sold during the last 250 years. We may expect that tens of thousands of copies of the new Philo will find their way onto scholars' shelves. Is the appearance of this volume not an occasion for rejoicing, and also for gratitude towards Hendrickson, the enterprising publisher who has made the project possible?

Before we can answer that question we have to take a good look at what is being offered us, and this will constrain us to explore some rather unfamiliar byways of Philonic scholarship. The translation that is now being republished was for the most part made some 140 years ago, first having been printed in 4 volumes in Bohn's Ecclesiastical Library in 1854–55. It is thus by now firmly in the public domain, which no doubt has helped to keep the price down to its very reasonable level.[3] Both the publisher and the translator are fascinating 19th century figures.

Henry G. Bohn (1796–1884) was a successful English publishing entrepreneur, who according to his biographer 'discovered in the cheap issue of works of a solid and instructive kind' a notable way of making very considerable amounts of money.[4] In 1846 he founded his Standard

---

[2] For further details see R-R pp. 22–24. Even at this price, the Loeb Philo is the cheapest way to acquire a new copy of the Greek text. The *editio maior* of Cohn-Wendland was reprinted in 1962 and costs about $400 (including the 2 volumes of indices by Leisegang). Perhaps it would be a good idea to reprint the *editio minor*.

[3] G-G 475 notes reprints in 1894, 1899 (New York), 1900 (London). Already in 1929 Colson and Whitaker in the preface to vol. 1 of the Loeb edition say that copies of Yonge 'appear to be scarce'. Leiden University library has two copies. The one I am using used to belong to the influential Dutch Hegelian, G. J. P. J. Bolland (1854–1922), and is full of interesting pencil annotations.

[4] *Dictionary of National Biography* vol. 36 (London 1893) 304–306.

Library, augmented soon thereafter by 15 other Libraries, including the Classical Library (1848) and the Theological Library (1851). By 1896 these totalled 748 volumes, which could be purchased for the sum of £160. In the early years of the enterprise he recruited the services of Charles Duke Yonge (1812–1891), who contributed 19 volumes to three different Libraries.[5] The son of an Eton schoolmaster, Yonge attended the Universities of Cambridge and Oxford, and graduated from the latter with first-class honours in Classics in 1835. For the next 30 years he appears to have supported himself by means of private teaching activities and literary work, until in 1866 he was appointed to the Regius professorship of Modern History and English Literature in Queen's College, Belfast, a position which he retained until his death. In the elegant wording of his biographer: 'Yonge was a most prolific writer. From 1844 till his death his pen was seldom idle.'[6] Today we might describe him as a 'graphoholic'. In addition to the 19 volumes already mentioned he published 36 other works.[7] Until 1855 these are all in the area of the Classics. Thereafter he branched out into History, English literature and Grammar.

On the basis of these facts it is reasonable to suppose that Yonge did his work for Bohn's Libraries in order to provide financial support for himself and his wife.[8] In the period 1852 to 1855 there must have been a flurry of activity. In 1853 two volumes of Diogenes appeared, in 1854 three volumes of Athenaeus, in 1854–55 four volumes of Philo. It would seem that a total of nearly 4000 pages of Greek text (now spread out over 20 Loeb volumes) were translated in less than four years. One must suspect that the translation of Philo occupied him for a year at the most.[9] Naturally we have to admire the incredible industry of the man, but one cannot help wondering how thoroughly the task was carried out.

In the final sentence of his preface (reprinted in the present volume) Yonge informs the reader that 'the text which has been used in this translation has been generally that of Mangey'. He refers here to the great edition of Thomas Mangey in two volumes, published in London in 1742, which contained all the works of Philo preserved in Greek, together with a Latin translation. The numbering of Mangey's edition is

---

[5] Classical Library: Ammianus Marcellinus 2 vols., Athenaeus 3 vols., Cicero 6 vols., Diogenes Laertius 2 vols. Ecclesiastical Library: Philo 4 vols. Antiquarian Library: Matthew of Westminster 2 vols.

[6] *Dictionary of National Biography* vol. 63 (London 1900) 324.

[7] In 42 volumes, making 61 volumes in all.

[8] He married his wife Anne in 1837, but the couple remained childless.

[9] Compare the Loeb edition which took Colson (together with Whitaker) at least two decades to complete the Loeb edition (which actually involved less translation).

still given in the margin of the Loeb edition (which is useful since it is still—*mirabile dictu*—the numbering referred to by LSJ), but has been dropped in the new single-volume publication. Mangey's edition was a remarkable achievement for its time, and far surpassed its predecessors. But it is important to realize that it was not a critical edition in the modern sense of the term. Mangey certainly did do some investigation of the manuscript tradition of Philo's works—he collated various mss. that were available to him in England—, but working a century before the so-called Lachmannian revolution in textual criticism,[10] he did not carry out this task systematically and comprehensively. For this reason his edition, for all its merits, is vastly inferior to the truly critical edition of Cohn and Wendland, which is based on the scientific method of textual criticism developed in 19th-century Germany. Moreover many of the features of the *corpus Philonicum* which we simply take for granted, e.g. in the organization and the ordering of the various treatises, were the work of Cohn (and to a lesser degree Wendland),[11] and so were not present in the text that Yonge had at his disposal.

But Yonge did not only use Mangey's edition. In a number of footnotes, reprinted in the volume under review, we learn that he also made use of the editions of A. F. Pfeiffer (1785–92) and C. E. Richter (1828–30), both of which were largely based on Mangey's work.[12] The second of these is important, for it allowed Yonge to include material which had not yet been discovered at the time of Mangey's edition. Firstly he could include two small sections of *Spec.* II discovered by Cardinal Mai and first published in 1818. More importantly, Richter (who was commendably up-to-date in his knowledge of what happening in the study of Philo) had added to Mangey's corpus the Latin translation of the Philonic treatises only preserved in Armenian which had been published by J. B. Aucher in 1822–26. Here, however, we encounter a puzzle. Yonge only translates the first three books of *QG* and ignores the other nine treatises printed by Richter (including some Ps.Philonica). Why did he do this? The publisher of the present volume suggests he 'lacked access' to these works. But this solution is cannot be right.

[10] K. Lachmann (1793–1851) was the first classical scholar to insist that it was necessary when editing texts to make an analysis (*recensio*) of the available mss. and to determine their interrelationships in a *stemma* which ideally should reveal the *archetypus* of the tradition and also determine which textual variants are preferred.

[11] Particularly important here was Cohn's long article 'Einteilung und Chronologie der Schriften Philos', *Philologus* Supplbd. 7 (1899) 385–437. In his preface to the German translation of Philo's works Cohn says that in the critical edition Mangey's traditional order was followed to the extent possible.

[12] See notes to *Leg.* 2.9, *Sacr.* 20, *Spec.* 2.214. The latter was published by E. B. Schwickert (though Yonge refers to it as Schwickest). For these editions see G-G 407, 413.

Book 3 is included with book 4 and the two books of *QE* in vol. VII of Richter's edition. It he could translate book 3, then he could have included the remaining treatises as well. It is more likely that Yonge got tired of the drudgery of translating a translation of a translation and said to his publisher 'enough is enough'.[13]

Let us now examine with more precision what is presented to us in this new volume. After the publisher's preface which we have already mentioned, it commences with an eight-page foreword by the leader of the project, David Scholer. We are briefly told about Yonge's life, the background to his translation and the method used in the current adaptation of his work. Personally I would have liked to have read a lot more about these matters, but no doubt they are of minor interest to most of the prospective buyers of the book. Scholer gives a brief account of Philo's life and writings,[14] and then goes on to show how interesting a source he is for various subjects that will interest modern readers: Hellenistic Judaism, Greek philosophy, New Testament writings (e.g. the question of circumcision that is so important for Paul, and the background to the Epistle to the Hebrews), the position of women in Second Temple Judaism, lexical and conceptual terms relevant to the New Testament, and so on. An alphabetical list of Philo's works is then given. The abbreviations recommended appear to be based on usage in the Loeb edition. To my mind it would have been better if the list used in this Annual and in Radice-Runia had been recommended.[15] Finally we are presented with an admirably up-to-date list of references to further literature on Philo. If the reader pursues these references, he or she will be thoroughly initiated into English-speaking scholarship on Philo.[16]

If we turn now to the presentation of the translation itself, the method used in the project becomes very clear. Every effort has been made to adapt Yonge's work as much as possible to what in North America has

---

[13] Another consideration is that all four volumes are about 500 pages. It is possible that the publisher set aside the remainder of the Armenian material for the sake of uniformity (there was a standard price for all volumes in the Ecclesiastical Library).

[14] Here two inaccuracies should be noted. It is suggested that perhaps a million Jews lived in Alexandria, which is impossible, since the total population of the city is estimated to have been about 600,000. At *Flacc.* 43 Philo states (perhaps with some exaggeration) that there were at least a million Jews resident in the whole of Egypt. Secondly it is wrongly concluded from *Prov.* 2.107 (not 2.64; on the references to this treatise see further below) that Philo visited the Temple *only* once. All we can conclude from this text, however, is that he went *at least* once.

[15] Some of the abbreviations are clumsily long (*Quaest. in Gen.*, *Quaest. in Ex.*, *Quis Heres*, *Quod Deus*, *Quod Omn. Prob.*). I prefer *Legat.* to *Leg.* for *Legatio ad Gaium*, because it prevents confusion with *Legum Allegoriae*, for which Scholer suggests *Leg. All.*

[16] All non-English contributions are ignored, but this is excusable in the introduction to an English translation.

become the standard presentation of Philo's writings, the Loeb Classical Library edition. With a few exceptions the titles Yonge gives to Philo's treatises are altered to conform to the Loeb titles.[17] In two cases this leads to the prolongation of titles that are rather unsatisfactory: 'Allegorical Interpretation' for *Legum Allegoriae*, and especially the absurd 'On mating with the preliminary studies' for *De congressu quaerendae eruditionis gratia*.[18] The old Roman paragraph numbering of Yonge has been retained, but most importantly the Arabic numbers of Cohn-Wendland and the Loeb edition have been added, making the translation fully compatible with modern references to Philonic writings. The resultant adaptation is thus rather successful for the part of Philo's *œuvre* covered in the first eight of the twelve Loeb volumes. Various changes had to be made to treatises such as *Sacr.*, *Spec.* II, *Virt.* on account of significant differences between Mangey and the modern edition (including the need to add freshly translated passages on a number of occasions),[19] but these have been intelligently and efficiently carried out.[20]

Unfortunately at vol. IX of the Loeb edition problems commence. The treatises *Prob.*, *Contempl.*, *Aet.* and *Flacc.* furnish no difficulties. But then *Flacc.* is artificially separated from *Legat.* merely for the sake of following the order of the Loeb edition.[21] The fragments of *Hypoth.* are separately listed (Yonge had included them in a larger section of fragments), as are those from *Prov.* This last move, however, is very questionable, since the Greek fragments in Colson represent only a small part of the entire treatise, which is preserved in two books in the Armenian. Moreover Colson's numbering of paragraphs in these fragments has been taken over, which is bound to exacerbate the already rampant confusion between the numbering systems of Aucher and Colson.[22] As noted above, in the case of the *Quaestiones* Yonge translated only the first three books of *QG*. The treatise *De animalibus* and the fragment *De Deo* are also not included. We do receive two appendices of lesser value: (1) Yonge's translation of the *De mundo*, a non-authentic cento of passages drawn

---

[17] In the case of a few treatises (e.g. *Cher.*, *Mut.*, *Spec.* III) translations are given of the shorter Latin titles rather than the longer titles used by the Loeb.

[18] The Greek title should be translated 'On intercourse for the purpose of preliminary studies'. The title in the new Yonge contains a serious misprint (*studies* instead of *gratia*).

[19] The new translations were made by Gregory Sterling and James Ernest. Their contributions to the project might have been given more publicity.

[20] It was inconsistent, however, to preserve the subtitles in parts of *Spec.* II–IV.

[21] In the case of the Loeb this was doubtless motivated for pragmatic reasons in order to stretch the main body of the translation out to ten volumes. Yonge had kept them together.

[22] See the example of confusion above in n. 14.

mainly from *Aet.*; (2) his translation of the fragments collected together by Mangey at the end of the second volume of his edition.[23] Finally two indices of subjects and biblical passages—the former taken over from the original, the latter newly compiled—complete the volume (the maps do not seem to be of any great relevance to Philo).

From the previous paragraph it will be apparent that the publisher's claim that we here have a 'complete and unabridged' edition of Philo's writings is somewhat misleading. For the sake of clarity I draw up a list of those parts of Philo that are not included.

(a) *Quaestiones in Genesim* IV;
(b) *Quaestiones in Exodum* I and II;
(c) Most of *De Providentia* I and II;
(d) *De animalibus*;
(e) various fragments, including *De Deo*.

It is a pity that no solution was found for the inclusion of these works. But even if the volume is not entirely what it promises, it does have much to offer, and certainly more than has ever previously been included in a single volume Philo, which in itself is quite an achievement.

The translation is printed in two columns. The size of the type is relatively small, but the text is very readable indeed. The margins of the pages are kept to an absolute minimum, allowing more than a thousand words per page, and so making it possible to include almost all of Philo's writings on less than 900 pages. This combination of compactness and clarity makes it a fine example of the printer's art. It was decided to include the scanty footnotes that Yonge had included in his original version. These are arguably of some value because they give us insight into the translator's interests. Most of them refer to those aspects of Philo that are of concern to a classical scholar (quite a few Greek etymologies are given[24] and many lines of Dryden's *Aeneid* and Pope's *Homer* are cited). Yonge's knowledge of exegetical and theological subjects seems to have been very limited. For example at *QG* 1.43, 1.100 and 2.3 he makes remarks about the Hebrew bible that are quite irrelevant to Philo's Septuagint-based exegesis. Yonge's notes could have easily been deleted without any loss to all but the most historically-minded reader.

---

[23] These will surely be a very little use to anyone because most fragments are insufficiently identified, and the references that are given are totally out of date. For example at 886–894 'Fragments from a monkish manuscript' are printed, without further any indication of what the source is. It is in fact the Codex Rupefucaldi, on which see J. R. Harris, *Fragments of Philo Judaeus* (Cambridge 1886) xx, 4 (under δ′). On the current state of affairs regarding the fragments of Philo see further *SPhA* 4 (1992) 80.

[24] It is a pity that his Greek has been transliterated. Here modern technology seems to lead to retrogressive results.

The notes added by the publisher are confined to informing the user which changes have been made to Yonge's original presentation. References to the biblical sources alluded to or commented on by Philo are retained.[25] These might have been better placed in the text, and could have been considerably expanded.

What, then, about the translation itself? This of course is the most important question of all, because the purpose of the volume is to present Philo's own words and thoughts to the reader, and the more accurately this is done the better. In the preface to the first volume of the Loeb edition the translators describe the translation in the following terms: 'Yonge's work has considerable merits, but there is much that requires correction, and he had before him a less trustworthy text than that which is available at the present day. Moreover, his way of reproducing Philo's long and involved sentences in the exact form of the Greek seems to us to make the treatises duller and heavier than they need be.' This is not, however, the impression I gained from my perusal of the text. The translation seems surprisingly lacking in archaic features, and in some respects it seems more fluent than Colson and Whitaker's own version (but this compliment could of course be double-edged).

There remains the question of how accurate and reliable the translation is. We may assume that Yonge's training at Eton, Cambridge and Oxford gave him a knowledge of Greek that would be envy of many today.[26] But, as we already noted when discussing Yonge's biographical details, the translation was in all likelihood produced in some haste. The best we can do now is to check what we have before us. For the purposes of this review I have made a study of three short passages in Yonge's translation chosen at random. In order to present the results of my test-cases I cannot avoid delving into the details of text and translation. Impatient readers may skip the next few paragraphs and turn to the conclusions that I reach.

(i) *De opificio mundi* 170–172

§170 'from whom one should keep aloof': translates ὧν ἄξιον ἀπέχεσθαι which Cohn excised (on dubious grounds) from his edition.
'but this is affirmed only by men...': Yonge fails to see that this clause continues

---

[25] Bible references were taken over by Yonge from Richter, who in turn was strongly dependent on Mangey. For example at *Det.* 18 Yonge refers to Deut. 16:20, as does Richter, but Mangey erroneously refers to Deut. 21:20. Richter was also the first to introduce the chapter divisions with Roman numbers.

[26] As noted above, between 1844 and 1855 he published a number of works on Greek grammer and lexicography.

the position of the atheists, i.e. that God is a man-made concept.
§171 'no glory': not in the text; cf. Colson 'no superiority'.
'essence': a strange translation of ὕλη, = matter or material.
'boundless in extent': ἄπειροι refers not to the size but to the number of cosmoi; moreover the pun with ἄπειροι meaning 'inexperienced' in this way remains unclear (as Whitaker in the Loeb manages to do quite well).
§172 'it follows of necessity': the words φύσεως νόμοις καὶ θέσμοις are left untranslated.
'subject of so much contention': περιμάχητα means 'priceless' here.

In sum we have six mistakes/inaccuracies, of which 2 seriously affect the meaning.

(ii) *De confusione linguarum* 168–179

§169 'a number of creators': the Greek says merely πλῆθος, a 'plurality'.
§170 'to whom [God] alone it is granted to govern': Philo would never write this, since who would be the one to grant anything to God? θέμις should be translated 'right' or 'legitimate'.
'arrange': διοικεῖν means 'administer'.
§173 'no shame': Colson's 'no reverence' is better.
'their design': in C-W the conjecture ἀπόνοιαν (stupidity) has rightly replaced the weak ἐπίνοιαν. Yonge still translates the old text.
§174 quotation marks at beginning of the paragraph otiose.
'heavenly souls': οὐρανίων should be translated 'celestial beings'.
'impossible': not a good translation for οὐ θέμις (see above on §170).
§175 'at once': not in the Greek.
§176 'portion': we would now translate μοῖρα as 'part'.
§179 'intellect': as Colson points out, the ms. reading νοῦ retained by Yonge may well be right; Mangey's and Wendland's emendation ἀνθρώπου is probably unnecessary.
'subordinate power': the text reads 'to others' (plural).
'to those about him': τοῖς μετ' αὐτόν means 'to those after him', i.e. inferior to him in status.

There are no really serious mistakes in this passage, but a number of renderings that do not bring out Philo's meaning clearly.

(iii) *De vita contemplativa* 83–90

§84 'at another [time] moving': the antithesis between τῇ μὲν (plainsong) and τῇ δὲ (harmony) is not adequately rendered.
'all necessary strophes': C-W's emendation ἐν χορείᾳ, based on the Armenian version, is to be preferred.
§85 'each chorus of the men and each chorus of the women': Colson's 'each choir' is simpler and better.
§86 'level and dry road': ξήραν πᾶσαν (sc. γῆν) should be translated separately, i.e. broad highway and land that was completely dry.
§87 both 'Israelites' and 'miracle' are introduced by the translator.
§88: this section goes rather badly wrong.
μάλιστα not 'as far as possible' but 'especially', 'above all'.
'humorous': should be 'harmonious'! (this mistake, also found in the original,

can only be explained through the fact that the printer did not read Yonge's handwriting correctly).
'shrill': 'high-pitched' would be friendlier.
μέλεσιν ἀντήχοις καὶ ἀντιφώνοις: these words are not translated
σέμνοι does not mean 'beautiful' but 'reverent' or 'solemn' (simply a careless mistake by the translator).
'the end of ... was piety': this only makes sense if we realize that 'end' here (τέλος) means 'goal' or 'purpose'.
§89 'but being even more awake than when they came to the feast, as to their eyes and their whole bodies, and standing there till morning': this makes little sense, and makes the nightly vigil even more demanding than it was. Compare Colson's translation: 'but more alert and wakeful than when they came to the banquet, they stand with their faces and whole body turned to the east...'
εὐημερία does not mean 'tranquillity' but 'prosperity', or in this context 'well-being'.
γεωργήσοντες: this verb (part of a doublet) is not translated.
§90 τῶν ἐν αὐτῇ is best taken with φύσεως ('and nature's parts) rather than with καὶ ψυχῇ μόνῃ βιωσάντων as Yonge takes it.
The final sentence is difficult. Yonge makes things easier for himself by ignoring καλοκἀγαθίας προσθεῖσα, but his translation is superior to that of Colson, who construes wrongly.
Philo's meaning is obscured in this passage on about six occasions.

We may conclude on the basis of this sample, I believe, that the results are not too distressing. We note that (1) various careless errors are made; (2) on a number of occasions Yonge's use of an inferior text leads to a less meaningful rendering (but at least twice he is saved from unnecessary emendations); and (3) rather often Philo's meaning is not as clearly and exactly rendered as one would like (often the result of the tendency to smooth over difficulties in the text). For the most part, however, the translation manages to give a reasonable indication of the contents of Philo's text. It is clear enough for a first orientation, but is quite insufficient to guarantee a precise idea of what Philo meant to say when he wrote his works. In short it would be most unwise to base a serious discussion on Yonge's translation without reference to the Greek text or to other translations.

It is time to reach a verdict. Naturally the first thing one has to do is banish all notions of scholarly purism. For the most part this book represents the state of Philonic studies in the 1830's, when Andrew Jackson was President of the United States and Queen Victoria had yet to ascend the English throne. The updating of Yonge's translation has been limited to the serviceable Introduction and the adaptation of the original version to the contents and sequence of works in the Loeb edition (without *QG* 3–4 and *QE*). Fortunately this has been competently done (even if we had a few quibbles). Where this newly published version scores well is in its presentation and its price. The fact that everything is in one volume and that it can be purchased for such a modest sum will mean that Philo can become much more widely available than hitherto. Henry G. Bohn would be very proud of Hendrickson Publishers (and could probably teach them a trick or two). But the limitations of Yonge's version should be squarely faced. It was a product of haste based on a pre-critical edition. Even where its text was sound, it still abounds in inaccuracies and unclarities. The team that produced this present volume did not take the more difficult route of revising the entire translation in conformity with modern standards. For this reason it is fervently to be hoped that this new edition will be used *only for purposes of consultation*, i.e. in order to gain access to Philo's writings, and *not* for the attempted furtherance of scholarship. If the volume is indeed put to the restricted use which I recommend, then we have every reason to be grateful to the publisher and his team for the hard work that they put into this project.

The reviewer may be forgiven, however, if he does not end his discussion at this point. After all there is no law against dreaming a dream. What would it require to make a really first-rate singe-volume Philo? The first suggestion that springs to mind is a thorough revision of the classic Loeb translation. One might compare Jonathan Barnes' revision of the Oxford Aristotle Translation that was published in two volumes 10 years ago.[27] Copyright problems make this project impracticable.[28] So the only alternative is a fresh translation produced *ab novo* by a team of scholars working in close cooperation. (The task is too great and too broad in scope for a single individual. Moreover projects that take half a life-time have in recent years very distinctly gone out of fashion.) Every effort would need to be made to ensure that this volume did indeed represent the complete Philo. This would mean that an Armenologist would have to join the team, and that the situation of the fragments would need careful attention. Extensive annotation would not be necessary. Philo's references to scripture ought to be very fully given (and are best placed in the margin). Apart from this only his allusions to other sources need be noted. It would, however, given the complexities of many of Philo's writings, be very useful to commence every treatise with a summary of its contents. Finally a scriptural index and a very detailed subject index could complete the volume. The price could not

[27] By Princeton University Press in the Bollingen series

[28] Harvard University Press was approached with this idea, but the proposal was rejected, even when it was suggested that they themselves publish the resultant volume. I am most puzzled by this response in light of the tremendous market possibilities of a really first-rate complete Philo.

match that of the volume under review, but could surely be kept to about $50–$60. It would attract fewer buyers, but those who invested in it would be able to do a lot more with it.

Will all this remain a dream? I fear that for the time being it will. The adage *ars longa vita brevis* is as true as ever, and we have the additional handicap of living in an age that likes to see quick results. It looks as if for the foreseeable future the new Yonge will have the field to itself. But I sincerely hope I am proved wrong.

University of Leiden

BOOK REVIEW SECTION

William A. HORBURY and D. NOY. *Jewish Inscriptions of Graeco-Roman Egypt: With an index of the Jewish inscriptions of Egypt and Cyrenaica*. Cambridge 1992. xxiv + 378 pages + 32 plates. ISBN 0-521-41870-4. $110.

The last two decades have witnessed a major shift in our understanding of Judaism in the Graeco-Roman period from normative Judaism with significant aberrations to a pluriform Judaism or even Judaisms. It is not accidental that Jewish epigraphy has come of age during this same period.[1] From the comprehensive collection of J.-B. Frey,[2] we have now moved to specific collections. While geographical regions or cities have been used as categories for grouping inscriptions in the past, the shift in perspective has made such groupings a requirement rather than a convenience. The Cambridge Divinity Faculty Jewish Inscriptions Project is one of leaders in the emergence of Jewish epigraphy. This volume represents their first publication.

W. Horbury and D. Noy have edited all known Jewish inscriptions from Egypt during the Graeco-Roman period, i.e., from the third century BCE to the sixth century CE. Their work is based on the earlier collections of Frey and the revisions of D. M. Lewis in *Corpus Papyrorum Judaicarum*.[3] They did not, however, simply reissue the work of their predecessors: they added sixteen new inscriptions from Egypt,[4] eliminated six which are probably not Jewish,[5] and included two additional sets: one of inscriptions outside of Egypt but which deal with Egyptian Jews and another of non-Jewish inscriptions which contain Jewish names.[6] Four criteria governed the decision for inclusion or exclusion: the presence of Jewish names, distinctively Jewish vocabulary, Hebrew, and the provenance of the inscription in the case of Tell el-Yehoudieh (Leontopolis).[7] The differences between Horbury and Noy and their pre-

[1] For a brief survey of recent developments see the comments of P. W. van der Horst and J. W. van Henten (edd.), *Studies in Early Jewish Epigraphy*, AGJU 21 (Leiden 1994) 1–4.

[2] *Corpus Inscriptionum Judaicarum. Recueil des inscriptions juives qui vont du IIIe siècle avant Jésus-Christ au VIIe siècle de notre ère* (2 vols.; Rome 1936–52). B. Lifshitz provided a prolegomenon with corrections and additions to volume one (New York 1975) 21–107.

[3] The Jewish Inscriptions of Egypt', in V. A. Tcherikover, A. Fuks, and M. Stern (edd.), *Corpus Papyrorum Judaicarum* 3 vols.; (Cambridge, MA 1957–64) 3.138–66.

[4] Nos. 10, 11, 12, 18, 23, 26, 102, 103, 104, 105, 123, 124, 126, 131, 132, 134.

[5] Appendix 1 (nos. 135–40).

[6] Appendixes 2 (nos. 141–53) and 3 (nos. 154–56) respectively.

[7] These are the same basic criteria used in *CPJ*. See 1.xvii.

decessors is not, however, merely quantitative. Their work represents a significant advance in our understanding of the inscriptions. For example, they argue that the inscriptions found at Demerdash, a suburb of ancient Heliopolis, provide evidence of a Jewish community at that site rather than displaced inscriptions from Leontopolis.[1]

The collection opens with a preface in which the editors set out their principles and division of labor. This is followed by an introduction to the major sites where the inscriptions were discovered (the necropoleis of Alexandria [16% of the collection] and the sites of Tell el-Yehoudieh [57%] and Demerdash [9%]) and to the surprisingly large number of metrical inscriptions (10% mainly in elegiac diptichs). The inscriptions come next. They are arranged geographically from north to south with those of uncertain provenance placed last. The inscriptions for each locale are arranged in rough chronological sequence. Each entry assigns a new number to the inscription along with a cross-reference to the plates and to *CIJ* where possible. The entry proper provides the place of origin, date, and class of inscription; the present location; the source for the printed text; the text; a critical apparatus; a fresh translation; a dual bibliography beginning with works which reproduce the entire inscription followed by other publications—both arranged in chronological order; commentary in the form of notes; and descriptions of the stone (where appropriate) with notes on the forms of the letters. There are two exhaustive sets of computer-based indices for the Jewish material (all non-Jewish material is excluded): Noy's indices of the Egyptian material and G. Lüderitz's and J. M. Reynolds' indices of the Jewish inscriptions of Cyrenaica. These are arranged into nine and eight categories respectively and transform the collection into a wonderfully useful reference work. The volume concludes with a bibliography, list of abbreviations, a concordance cross-listing the numbering systems of the present volume with *CIJ* and thirty-two plates.

Philonic material is used in three ways. First, most of the references are to linguistic parallels. Second, on several occasions Philo is cited for the existence of a Jewish practice.[2] Third, on rare occasions Philonic material is developed in connection with a theological conviction expressed in an epitaph.[3]

The limited use of the Philonic material is not unique. The intro-

---

[1] Nos. 106–14 and pp. xviii–xix.

[2] No 20 (p. 33), on images; no 28 (p. 50), on teaching in the synagogue; and no 39 (p. 100), on the Jews as an ἔθνος.

[3] E.g., p. xxiv, where Philo's hope of immortality is contrasted with the absence of an expectation of future existence in the majority of epitaphs; and no 36 (p. 85), where 'good hope' is common to Philo and an epitaph.

duction and notes do not attempt to develop a synthesis as Frey did for his edition or as V. Tcherikover did for the papyri.[1] This appears to have been a conscious decision on the part of the editors who have both subsequently published broader analyses.[2] A second limitation of the notes is that a number of terms which appear early in the collection are not discussed in detail until later. For example, ἄωρε or some form of the adjective appears several times in the collection before the discussion in the notes.[3] I found this a bit frustrating. Another area where I was a bit disappointed was in the indices: there are omissions in a set of otherwise superb indices. For example, I checked the index listing epitaphs and found that it omitted n. 4. Similarly, n. 105 although problematic, is wanting in the index for προσευχή inscriptions: it warrants a question mark but should be included. Readers should also note—as the editors do in the preface—that this work went to press before the release of P. W. van der Horst's work on epitaphs.[4] Since 76% of the present collection are epitaphs, users will find Van der Horst's work a useful companion.

I do not intend for these observations to suggest a lack of appreciation for a very fine and needed edition of Jewish inscriptions from Egypt. Everyone who works in Egyptian Judaism or Judaism in the Graeco-Roman world is indebted to Horbury and Noy. As the ἀρραβών of The Cambridge Divinity Faculty Jewish Inscriptions Project, this edition makes the future bright.

Gregory E. Sterling
University of Notre Dame

---

[1] Frey, *CIJ* liii–cxliv and Tcherikover, *CPJ* 1.1–111.

[2] W. Horbury, 'Jewish Inscriptions and Jewish Literature in Egypt, with Speical Reference to Ecclesiasticus', in *Studies in Jewish Epigraphy* 9–43 and D. Noy, 'The Jewish Communities of Leontopolis and Venosa', in *ibid.* 162–82.

[3] It appears in nos. 12, 31, and 35, but is not discussed in detail until no 41. Cf. also πασίφιλος which appears as early as no 30 but is not discussed until no 41 or φιλάδελφος which is in no 86 but not discussed until no 113.

[4] *Ancient Jewish Epitaphs: An introductory Survey of a Millenium of Jewish Funerary Epigraphy (300* BCE– *700* CE*)* (Kampen 1991).

Clara KRAUS REGGIANI, *4 Maccabei*. Commentario storico ed esegetico all'Antico e al Nuovo Testamento, Supplementi 1. Marietti, Genova 1992. 166 Seiten. ISBN 88-21-18040-9.

In der italienischen Kommentarreihe, die offensichtlich nicht nur für Theologen, sondern auch für andere Gebildete und kulturgeschichtlich Interessierte gedacht ist, legt die italienische Erforscherin der jüdisch-hellenistischen Literatur eine Erklärung des 4 Makkabäerbuchs vor, das auch nach römisch-katholischer Sicht nicht unter die 'deuterokanonischen', sondern unter die 'apokryphen' Schriften des Alten Testaments gehört, da es im Unterschied zum 1 und 2 Makk in der Vulgata nicht enthalten ist. Es ist m. E. dennoch erfreulich, daß der interessierte Leser auch mit diesem Buch vertraut gemacht wird, zumal da die makkabäischen Märtyrer von der katholischen Kirche auch als Heilige angesehen werden und da aus dem 4 Makk mancherlei zum Verständnis der Vorstellung von heiligen Märtyrern deutlich wird, auch wenn die Schilderungen des Martyriums literarisch nicht eben modernem Geschmack entsprechen. Kulturgeschichtlich ist das Interessanteste an diesem Buch freilich wohl die Mischung von biblischer Überlieferung samt unzweideutigem Aufruf zum Festhalten am Gesetz des Mose mit einer weitgehenden Offenheit für hellenistisches Denken.

Diese Zwitterstellung betont auch Frau Kraus Reggiani von Anfang an (p. 8), indem sie mehrere Aspekte nennt, unter denen das Büchlein beachtenswert ist: es handelt sich um eine der wenigen erhaltenen religiösen Reden aus dem hellenistischen Judentum (höchstens die in armenischer Übersetzung erhaltenen, dem Philon von Alexandrien untergeschobenen Predigten *Über Samson* und *Über Jona* wären hier noch zu nennen); es ist das erste Beispiel eines Martyrologiums, auf die fromme christliche Literatur von großem Einfluß. Literarisch ist es interessant in seiner Kombination von (angeblichem) philosophischem Traktat über die stoisch klingende These, daß die fromme Urteilskraft (oder 'Vernunft') Absolut-Herrscherin über die Leidenschaften ist, und erzählerischer, gar nicht mehr 'philosophischer' Entfaltung des Grundmotivs. Dieses wird freilich auch innerhalb der Erzählung mehrfach wiederholt, womit aber die innere Fremdheit der beiden Komponenten gegeneinander eher noch unterstrichen wird.

So ergibt sich auch die Struktur des Büchleins, die sich bei Frau Kraus Reggiani so darstellt: Exordium (4 Makk 1,1–12): Die philosophische These; 1. Hauptteil (1:13 –3:18): Entfaltung der These unter Bezugnahme auf die Tora sowie auf das Beispiel des Königs David; 2. Hauptteil (3:19–17:6): Das exemplarische Martyrium des Eleazar, der sieben Brüder und ihrer Mutter (nach 2 Makk 7); Epilog (17:7–18:24): Folgerungen und

Abschluß—nach einer nochmaligen Rede der Mutter, deren Tod freilich schon in 17:1 erzählt worden war.

In der Allgemeinen Einleitung (pp. 9–71) wird nach Einleitenden Bemerkungen (zur Frage des Autors und des ursprünglichen Titels, der handschriftlichen und editorischen Tradition, einer Liste der benutzten modernen Kommentare, die leider im Literaturverzeichnis (pp. 147–52) nicht noch einmal aufgeführt werden, und Bemerkungen zu Sprache und Stil des 4 Makk) die Struktur des Büchleins anhand einer gegliederten, ausführlichen Inhaltsübersicht verdeutlicht (pp. 16–19). Danach folgen eine 'analytische Interpretation', die ebenfalls der Abfolge von 4 Makk nachgeht (pp. 20–41; der Epilog [17:7–18:24] wird hier nicht erwähnt bzw. in den 2. Hauptteil mit einbezogen), sowie 'Einleitungsfragen' zu 4 Makk. Frau Kraus Reggiani plädiert für Antiochien (nicht Alexandrien) als Entstehungsort, diskutiert die Frage der Einheitlichkeit oder Verteilung auf zwei Autoren bzw. Schichten (erzählerischer Hauptteil—philosophischer 'Rahmen') und behandelt ausführlich die Frage der Datierung, für die in der Forschung verschiedene Ansätze zwischen dem ersten Drittel des ersten und dem ersten Drittel des zweiten Jh. n. Chr. vorliegen (in diesem Falle käme 4 Makk ganz in die Nähe der ersten christlichen Martyrologien zu stehen). Die Frage sei nicht eindeutig zu klären, doch bevorzugt Kraus Reggiani offenbar die frühere Ansetzung (p. 51).

An theologisch-eschatologischen Themen werden dann vor allem die stellvertretende Sühne für fremde Schuld und die Hoffnung auf jenseitigen Lohn für das Martyrium (einschließlich der Unsterblichkeit der Seele) behandelt (pp. 52–61). Der letzte Abschnitt der Einleitung (pp. 62–68) nimmt die schon oben erwähnte Frage der hebräischen und der griechischen Komponenten in 4 Makk auf, während ein Appendix (pp. 69–71) mögliche Beziehungen zwischen 4 Makk und der frühchristlichen Literatur diskutiert, unter anderem die von H.-J. Klauck ('Hellenistische Rhetorik im Diasporajudentum. Das Exordium des vierten Makkabäerbuchs (4 Makk 1.1–12)', *NTS* 35 (1989) 451–65) beobachteten Analogien zwischen dem Exordium (4 Makk 1:1–12) und dem Proömium des Lukas-Evangeliums (1:1–4). Bei der Gelegenheit sei angemerkt, daß der Autorin die deutsche Übersetzung und Kommentierung von 4 Makk durch Klauck (*JSHRZ* III/6; (Gütersloh 1989)) seinerzeit offenbar noch nicht zugänglich war.[1]

---

[1] Eine Kleinigkeit zum Literaturverzeichnis (p.151f.) sei noch angemerkt: Auch für die englische Neubearbeitung des 'klassischen' Werkes von Emil Schürer (von dessen drittem Band wohl besser die 4. Auflage von 1909 zu zitieren wäre, die doch wohl 1970 nachgedruckt wurde) sollte der Name des Ur-Autors weiterhin genannt werden; die Aufführung nur unter den Namen der verdienstvollen englischen Überarbeiter von Band III

Die zweite Hälfte des vorliegenden Bandes (pp. 77–146) nimmt die Übersetzung und Kommentierung des Textes von 4 Makk ein, worauf hier nicht mehr im einzelnen eingegangen werden kann; es folgen Literaturverzeichnis (pp. 147–52) und Register der Stellen aus Bibel und antiker Literatur sowie der biblischen Namen und der zitierten modernen Autoren (pp. 153–66). Insgesamt ist es sehr begrüßenswert, daß mit diesem Buch dem modernen Leser auch in Italien der interessante Text an der Schnittstelle zweier Kulturen in kompetenter Weise nahegebracht wurde.

Nikolaus Walter
Naumburg/Jena

Louis H. FELDMAN, *Jew and Gentile in the Ancient World: Attitudes and Interactions from Alexander to Justinian.* Princeton University Press, Princeton 1993. xii + 679 pages. ISBN 0-691-07416-X. $59.50.

Throughout the expansion of research into Second Temple Judaism in the last score of years, most studies have focused on specific issues or geographical locales. This is a result of both pragmatic as well as theoretical concerns: not only has the expanding body of evidence inversely constricted the scope of works, but the recognized diversity of that material has made syntheses very difficult. This is clear from the number of labels currently competing as arches: Second Temple Judaism, Early Judaism, Middle Judaism. On the basis of a lifetime of research, Louis Feldman offers an integrative interpretation of Judaism in both the Hellenistic and Roman worlds in the form of his erudite *magnum opus*.

Feldman begins with the question: How should we explain Judaism's ability to attract proselytes and sympathizers in spite of popular opposition (pp. ix, 416)? His answer is that 'Judaism was internally strong and was, for this reason, admired by many, even its detractors' (p. 416; cf. also 445). He organizes this response in four major units: the first two chapters sketch the inner strength of Judaism in Palestine (1) and the Diaspora (2); chapters three-five assess the alleged hostility toward the Jews from governments (3), the populace (4), and intellectuals (5); chapters six-eight present the attractiveness of Judaism through its antiquity (6), embodiment of the cardinal virtues (7), and ideal founder (8); chapters nine-eleven squarely address the issue of Jewish missionary

(Vermes-Millar-Goodman) ist irreführend, auch wenn sich leider noch keine kurze, aber eindeutige Bezeichnung dafür eingebürgert hat.

activity with respect to proselytes (9), sympathizers or 'God-fearers' (10), and continued activity in the third, fourth, and fifth centuries (11). He concludes with a helpful summary which is worth reading as both an introduction and a conclusion (12).

Feldman's portrait of a self-sufficient and unified Judaism in the first two chapters faces several major difficulties. The first chapter is an attempt to overturn the thesis of Martin Hengel that Judaism was significantly hellenized in Palestine as early as the second century BCE. Feldman counters: 'The question, then, is not how thoroughly Jews and Judaism in the Land of Israel were Hellenized, but how strongly they resisted Hellenization' (p. 44). In order to make his case, Feldman must deny the Jewish identity of Hellenistic Jewish authors like Eupolemus who lived and wrote in Palestine in the second century BCE.[1] I find it incredible to believe that anyone but a Jew would write a history of Judaism on the basis of both the Hebrew text and the LXX in the second century BCE.[2] In short, I do not think that Feldman has overturned Hengel. Feldman does accept Jewish appropriation and assimilation of Hellenism in the Diaspora, yet counters by pointing out that there is very little evidence for apostasy. While he is undoubtedly correct in arguing for the resilience of Judaism, he again argues against the grain of the *communis opinio* by minimizing the diversity of Judaism.[3] For example, he dismisses the literalists and allegorists mentioned by Philo as insignificant (pp. 74–76, 421). I find the marginalization of divergent perspectives disconcerting. It is true that outsiders did not generally distinguish among Jewish groups; however, they were not all reacting to the same form of Judaism. This is a point which Feldman does not adequately address.

The second unit of his argument, the analysis of the prejudice against the Jews, argues that governments which dealt with the Jews generally

---

[1] The indices are woefully inadequate, e.g., the index lists the following references to Eupolemus, pp. 28–29, 131, 207, 242, 471 no 34, 527 nos. 33, 34. It omits the following: pp. 317, 419, 426, 431, 534 no 22. The same is true for other authors whom I consulted, e.g,, the Egyptian Jewish author Artapanus who appears on pp. 211, 267, 283, 426–27, 431, 532 no 11, 534 no 22, 536 no 40, 586 no 71 in addition to the references of the index.

[2] I have examined the work of Eupolemus in my *Historiography and Self-definition: Josephos, Luke-Acts and Apologetic Historiography*, NovTSup 64 (Leiden 1992) 207–22.

[3] Statements reflecting the current consensus include Robert A. Kraft and George W. E. Nickelsburg, 'The Modern Study of Early Judaism', in *Early Judaism and Its Modern Interpreters,* The Bible and Its Modern Interpreters (Philadelphia 1986) 2; Jacob Neusner, William Scott Green, and Ernest S. Frerichs (edd.), *Judaisms and Their Messiahs at the Turn of the Christian Era* (Cambridge 1987); J. Andrew Overman and William Scott Green, 'Judaism (Greco-Roman Period)', *ABD* 3 (1992) 1038; and Shaye J. D. Cohen and Ernest S. Frerichs (edd.), *Diasporas in Antiquity,* BJS 288 (Atlanta 1993).

treated them with favor. By way of contrast, the populace often found economic reasons for attacking the Jews. This opposition was not, according to Feldman, widespread among the intellectuals as most have maintained. He works through the basic charges leveled against Jews and offers the most favorable interpretation of the charge. For example, he thinks that Horace's barb on Jewish credulity (*Credat Iudaeus Apella, non ego*) is not 'vicious but more in a spirit of wonder at their naiveté' (p. 171).[1] While Jews were not the only group for whom gullibility proved proverbial, it is difficult for me to see how this is anything but an expression of contempt. It is true that early reports on Jews by pagans are favorable (e.g., Hecataeus of Abdera); however, I find Feldman's reading of the later evidence strained. I am still inclined to think that Josephus was closer to the mark when he wrote: 'The Lysimachuses and Molons and certain other writers of that ilk rail at us as the most worthless of humanity.'[2]

The third unit of his argument presents the attractions of the Jews. Feldman opens with a brief but helpful analysis of the significance of antiquity for the Jews.[3] Here again he offers the most favorable reading without considering the negative thrust of some statements. For example, he notes that even the bitterest opponents of the Jews conceded their antiquity (pp. 178–81, 429). What he fails to note is that there is a discernible tendency on the part of some of these authors to move the date down in time as a polemic against Jewish antiquity. The dating of the exodus among ancient authors is confused: Manetho, Ptolemy of Mendes, and Apion all know the tradition which associates the exodus with the expulsion of the Hyksos by the native eighteenth dynasty[4]; Manetho also knows of a much later—518 years according to Josephus—exodus during the eighteenth dynasty which Chaeremon follows[5]; Apion appears to offer his own position by synchronizing it with the founding of Carthage[6]; Lysimachus and Tacitus think that it

---

[1] *Sermones* 1.5.101–01 (M. Stern, *Greek and Latin Authors on Jews and Judaism,* 3 vols. (Jerusalem 1974–84) 1.323 no 128 (Hereafter *GLAJJ*)).

[2] *CA* 2.236.

[3] He omits the important work of Peter Pilhofer, *Presbyteron Kreitton: Der Alterbeweis der jüdischen und christlichen Apologeten und seine Vorgeschichte,* WUNT 2.39 (Tübingen 1990).

[4] Sources which associate the exodus with Amosis are Ptolemy of Mendes in Tatian, *Or.* 38 (*GLAJJ* 1.380 no 157a) and in Clement, *Strom.* 1.21.101.5 (*GLAJJ* 1.380–81 no 157b) and Apion in Eusebius, *PE* 10.10.16 (*GLAJJ* 1.392 no 163c; see also no 163a–b). Manetho associates it with Tethmosis III and IV in Josephus, *CA* 1.75–90 (*GLAJJ* 1.66–74 no 19).

[5] Manetho in Josephus, *CA* 1.227–53 (*GLAJJ* 1.78–86 no 21) and Chaeremon in Josephus, *CA* 1.288–92 (*GLAJJ* 1.419–21 no 178).

[6] Josephus, *CA* 2.17 (*GLAJJ* 1.395–97 no 165).

belongs in the time of Bocchoris in the twenty-fourth dynasty[1]; and finally, Josephus himself exclaims in exasperation that Apollonius Molon and others date it as they wish.[2] While these dates are early by Greek standards, they are relatively late by Near Eastern measurements. More important is the tendency of the later authors to move the date down in time—a move I understand to be a polemic against Jewish antiquity but which Feldman does not even consider. Feldman's treatment of the incarnation of the central virtues among Jews is more balanced: he alternates the presentation between pagan evidence and Josephus for σοφία, ἀνδρεία, σωφροσύνη, δικαιοσύνη, and εὐσέβεια. The lack of balance, however, appears again in his analysis of Moses where he accentuates the positive and ignores the negative. For example, he highlights several details about the Osarsiph story in Manetho and ignores the scurrilous nature of the report as a whole (p. 237).

The final unit of Feldman's major argument addresses an area which has been the focal point of a recent debate: Was Judaism an active missionary religion or did it passively welcome those who were attracted to it? Feldman makes a strong case for the former. While I am sympathetic to his view, he again tends to accept material which suits his perspective too quickly. For example, he argues that Alexander Polyhistor knew the LXX since he wrote a Περὶ Ἰουδαίων. His evidence is the assumption that such a work 'could hardly have been composed without access to the major source of early biblical history, the Bible, presumably in the Greek translation' (p. 317). Unfortunately, there is no solid evidence to substantiate this statement. I have tried in vain to find some specific textual connection. It appears that Polyhistor culled his information from Jewish, Samaritan, and pagan sources but did not consult the LXX itself.[3] It is this repeated tendency which I find troubling.

I fear that the extent of these critical remarks will mask my appreciation for a very learned work from a scholar to whom I am indebted. Feldman's tome displays vast learning and strikes a note which needs to be heard repeatedly: Judaism was a vibrant and powerful force in these periods. I found it impossible to avoid the impression that this note harmonized with the ancient *apologia* for Judaism. Philonists will, accordingly, not find it surprising that *Spec.* and *Mos.* receive the bulk of attention with significant nods at *Virt*, *Flacc.*, and *Legat.* However,

---

[1] Lysimachus in Josephus, *CA* 1.304–11 (*GLAJJ* 1.383–86 no 158); 2.16 (*GLAJJ* 1.386–87 no 159) and Tacitus, *Hist.* 5.3.1 (*GLAJJ* 2.17–63 no 281).

[2] *CA* 2.16 (*GLAJJ* 1.151–52 no 47).

[3] *Historiography and Self-definition*, 147–48.

Josephus not Philo is the major inspiration for Feldman. In many ways Feldman has done for ancient Judaism in the twentieth century what Josephus did in the first. While I am more skeptical than Feldman about this symphony, I greatly appreciate his industry.

Gregory E. Sterling
University of Notre Dame

Willem Cornelis VAN UNNIK, *Das Selbstverständnis der jüdischen Diaspora in der hellenistisch-römischen Zeit.* Aus dem Nachlaß herausgegeben und bearbeitet von Pieter Willem VAN DER HORST. AGJU 17. E.J. Brill, Leiden 1993. 200 Seiten. ISBN 90-04-09693-0. $63.

Dieses Buch enthält fünf Vorträge des bekannten niederländischen Gelehrten (1910–78), die dieser im Jahre 1967 am *Swedish Theological Institute* in Jerusalem gehalten hat. Sein letzter Doktorand, P. W. van der Horst, hat dem Vortragsmanuskript die Fußnoten hinzugefügt, dabei auch neueste Literatur berücksichtigt;[1] er hat hierdurch und durch die Anhänge und Register das ganze zu einem lesenswerten Buch gemacht—eine entsagungsvolle, dankenswerte Arbeit.

Die Frage, die sich der Verfasser stellte, ist keineswegs veraltet; sie war auch damals nicht durch eine bloß ephemere 'Forschungslage' bedingt. Es ist die folgende Frage: Wie haben die Juden der Diaspora ihre Situation selbst empfunden (1. Vortrag, S. 51–68)? —Zu Recht korrigiert der Verfasser einige unbedachte Bemerkungen des *ThWNT*, die einen gewissen Stolz in der Selbstdarstellung des Diasporajudentums identifizieren mit dessen Lebensgefühl (S. 58ff.). Van Unniks durchgehende Antwort ist: 'Zerstreutsein' war für die davon betroffenen Juden eine Strafe Gottes und eine schwer zu ertragende Situation, im politischen wie im theologischen Sinne. Nur apologetische Flucht nach vorn hat in den Schriften eines Philon und Josephus einen gewissen Stolz hinzugebracht—Stolz nicht über das Zerstreutsein, sondern über die durchgehaltene Gesetzestreue (so S. 159, im Schlußkapitel).

Soviel zunächst zum Buch als ganzem. Van Unniks Argumentation erhält im 2. Kapitel ('Der Ausdruck 'Diaspora'', S. 69–88) das Fundament einer sorgfältigen Begriffsexegese, vorgenommen nicht nur am Wort διασπορά, sondern am Wortfeld von διασπείρειν und seinen wichtigsten Synonymen (v.a. διασκορπίζειν). Es liegt keine einheitliche hebräische Wurzel zugrunde; wir haben es mit einem Diaspora-

[1] Wichtig ist der Hinweis auf Gerhard Delling, *Die Bewältigung der Diasporasituation durch das hellenistische Judentum* (Berlin 1987) S. 126 Anm. 156.

Theologumenon zu tun, faßbar erstmals in der LXX-Übersetzung des Pentateuchs. Beherrschend sind Lev 26:3–13 und Dtn 28:15ff.; 30:1ff. Das sind die Kapitel, die dem Volk Israel die Alternative zwischen Segen und Fluch vorhalten. 'Zerstreutwerden' ist der Gipfel des *Fluchs*; nur die eschatologische Aussicht auf erneute Sammlung mildert ihn. Bei allen Verschiedenheiten der Kontexte ist also klar, daß διασπορά nicht 'Ausbreitung' meint, sondern 'Zerstreuung'. So auch S. 158.

Man kann sich das Verfahren van Unniks mit einem Blick verdeutlichen, wenn man in Henri Estiennes *Thesaurus Graecae linguae* den Artikel διασπορά aufschlägt. Was Stephanus schon richtig bot und ordnete,[1] das *ThWNT* jedoch verzeichnete, wird hier im Detail nachgeprüft und dargestellt, unter Aufweis des Bekenntnischarakters der jüdischen Texte (Juden geben zu, von Gott gestraft zu sein) und der theologischen Probleme.

Sachbezug des Ausdrucks διασπορά, so erfahren wir, war in der jüdischen und christlichen Literatur bis ins 4.Jh. n. Chr. ausschließlich Israel; von einer kirchlichen 'Diaspora' ist noch keine Rede. Joh 7:35 ist ein Beispiel: διασπορά τῶν Ἑλλήνων meint die in der griechischsprachigen Welt verteilten Juden (im Gegensatz zu denen in Babylonien). Auch Jak 1:1 und 1.Pt 1:1 wenden sich an—nunmehr Christen gewordene—Glieder der jüdischen Diapsora (S. 79f.). So war jedenfalls die Auffassung noch bei den Kirchenvätern. Appendix II bietet hierzu die Texte.

Verwendungen des Substantivs διασπορά außerhalb der Septuaginta und der von ihr abhängigen jüdisch-christlichen Literatur sind äußerst selten. Die drei Stellen (zwei von Epikur, eine von Aristoteles; alle drei durch Plutarch überliefert) bestätigen den pejorativen Charakter: 'Zerstreuung' von Atomen, die nicht mehr zusammenfinden; 'Zerstreuung' der Seelenteile, die eine Hoffnung auf Unsterblichkeit zunichte macht; 'Zerstreuung' von Solons Asche.[2]

Was das Judentum betrifft, so geht 'Zerstreuung' als Ereignis über in 'Zerstreuung' als Dauerzustand, der aber seine pejorative theologische Wertung behält. Die Christen haben sie nicht erst erfunden, jedoch am deutlichsten das Problem benannt. Auf S. 77–79 finden sich hierzu die Zitate aus Justin, Hippolyt, der syrischen *Didascalia Apostolorum*, den *Constitutiones Apostolicae*, Origenes und Eusebius. 'Verflucht sind sie, die das Gebotene nicht tun können... Es ist nämlich unmöglich, daß sie in

---

[1] Sein Hinweis auf das lat. *dispersu* (als Ablativ von *dispersus*) ist eine wenig plausible Textvariante zu Cicero, *Ad Atticum* 9.9.3; sie wird vom Verfasser zu Recht übergangen.

[2] Diesen letzten Beleg hat van der Horst aus dem elektronischen *Thesaurus linguae Graecae* hinzugefügt (Appendix II, S. 167).

der Zerstreuung unter den Heiden alles befolgen, was das Gesetz befiehlt.'[1] Schon Paulus hatte den Finger darauf gelegt (Gal 3:10).

Das 3. Kapitel ist auch argumentativ das Zentrum des Buches. Es behandelt die Septuaginta, die in ihrer Qualität als Heilige Schrift des Diasporajudentums dessen Theologie bestimmt: ''Diaspora' in der griechischen Übersetzung von 'Gesetz, Propheten und Schriften'' (S. 89–107). Bekanntlich dominiert in dieser Sammlung das Gesetz; und dort wiederum sind es die Flüche von Lev 26 und Dtn 28 bzw. 30 (S. 94ff.), von denen sich die Propheten (S. 98ff.), in geringerem Maße auch die Schriften (S. 104ff.)[2] als abhängig erweisen—d.h. selbst wenn moderne literarkritische Analyse das Gegenteil behaupten sollte, so haben sie doch in der Antike ihr Gewicht aus der Übereinstimmung mit der Tora bezogen. Meist, wenn auch nicht immer, ist es das Volk Israel, das für den Fall seines Ungehorsams mit 'Zerstreuung' bedroht wird.

Philon, dem wir nun unser Interesse zuwenden, begegnet hauptsächlich im 4. Kapitel: 'Diaspora in der jüdischen Literatur der hellenistischen und römischen Zeit' (S. 108–47; dort v.a. 127–37). Als Kontrast geht ihm sein alexandrinischer Antipode, das 3. Makkabäerbuch, voraus (S. 125f.). Dort findet sich eine der klarsten Beteuerungen, daß die ἀποικία (diesen Ausdruck verwendet 3 Makk anstelle von διασπορά) in Gottlosigkeit verstricke: 'Unser Leben (ist) infolge des Aufenthalts in der Ferne in Gottlosigkeiten verstrickt worden' (3:10).[3] Der Kontext zitiert, kein Wunder, Lev 26.

Wie sieht Philon die Lage?—Insofern ähnlich, als das jüdische Volk, und zwar insgesamt, ihm wie 'Waisen' in der Welt vorkommt (*Spec.* 4.179;[4] S. 130). Jedoch findet sich das Schema 'Vertreibung (als Strafe)—Zerstreuung—Sammlung' bei ihm 'fast nicht' (128). Er kennt es zwar, stimmt ihm auch gelegentlich bei (134), legt es jedoch nicht zugrunde. Was das Wort διασπορά betrifft, so ist bezeichnend, daß es in den von Mayers Index erfaßten Schriften nur zweimal begegnet: einmal metaphorisch (διασπορὰ ψυχῆς, *Praem.* 115), und einmal, um den *Segen* aus Dtn 30:4 aufzunehmen (*Conf.* 197). Der diesbezügliche Fluch ist verschwunden, auch da, wo Philon vorgibt, die Segnungen und Flüche

---

[1] *Const. Apost.* 6.25.1, griechisch zitiert auf S. 77, Fußnote 69.

[2] Aus dem erweiterten Kanon der Septuaginta ist der auf S. 117f. (also erst im 4. Vortrag) zitierte Baruch-Text 1.15–3.8 aufschlußreich, eine Aufnahme von Lev 26 und Dtn 28 in einem Gebet, das laut V. 14 Bestandteil der (synagogalen?) Liturgie war. Van Unnik, S. 117 und 155, nimmt den Vermerk Bar 1.14 für bare Münze, wovor jedoch der neue Schürer III/2, 739–40 (van der Horst verweist auf ihn in der Fußnote) zu recht warnt.

[3] Im Urtext. ἀσεβείαις κατὰ τὴν ἀποικίαν ὁ βίος ἡμῶν ἐνέσχηται. Das 'worden' in der Übersetzung sollte besser fehlen; es handelt sich um einen Dauerzustand.

[4] Σχεδὸν δὲ καὶ τὸ σύμπαν Ἰουδαίων ἔθνος ὀρφανοῦ λόγον ἔχει συγκρινόμενον τοῖς ἁπανταχοῦ πᾶσι.

von Dtn 28 vollständig behandelt zu haben (*Praem.* 162–66; S. 132f.).

Die Diasporasituation wird von Philon als schwierig erlebt—wie könnte es anders sein?—sie gilt aber nicht als Strafe Gottes. *De praemiis et poenis,* sein eschatologischer Abschluß des großen Pentateuch-Kommentars, wo zitatartig allerlei Elemente der jüdischen Eschatologie auftauchen, die sonst bei Philon fehlen, stellt immerhin eine zu erwartende Rückkehr der Zerstreuten (σποράδες) in Aussicht (§ 165; S. 133).

Philon ist derjenige, der wenigstens andeutet, daß zu große Bevölkerungsdichte bzw. mangelnde Erträge Juden zur Auswanderung gezwungen hätten (*Flacc.* 45; S. 135f.). Während in Bar 3.7f. ἀποικισμός und ἀποικία Ausdrücke für 'Verbannung' waren (S. 118), läßt Philons Gebrauch von ἀποικία eher an 'Kolonien' im griechischen Sinne denken (S. 128, 136).[1] Damit verwischt er ein theologisches Problem, dem auch van der Horst nicht weiter nachdenkt. Wir werden darauf zurückkommen. Auf den Schlußseiten des Buches (wir greifen vor) bemerkt der Verfasser, wie stark, aber auch aussichtslos, Philons Versuche waren, ein Einvernehmen herzustellen zwischen den für sich lebenden Juden und einer 'Welt, die mehr und mehr zu einer größeren Einheit anwuchs' (S. 163).[2]

Wir überspringen die übrigen Analysen des 4. Kapitels, die die Spätschriften der Septuaginta, *Die Testamente der zwölf Patriarchen* und Josephus zum Gegenstand haben. Gelegentlich klingt an (was das *ThWNT* übertrieben hat), daß die Zerstreuungssituation eine Gelegenheit sei, Gott unter den Heiden bekannt zu machen (S. 112 f.). Tob 13:3f. geht in diese Richtung, besonders im Vulgata-Text, Weish. Sal. 18.4 (auf S. 61 zitiert), und natürlich Philon, *Mos.* 2.17–21[3] sowie einige anonyme jüdischen Äußerungen des 3. Jh. (S. 145–47). Was Josephus betrifft, so vermeidet er, ganz wie Philon, den pejorativen Ausdruck διασπορά. Der theologische Hintergrund ist derselbe: Auch er hat 'der Gerichtspredigt der Bibel, die im nachbiblischen Judentum noch sehr gut verstanden wurde, die Spitze abgebrochen' (144).

Die Schlußvorlesung (S. 148–65) behandelt 'Das theologische Verständnis von Diaspora'. Die Gründe und Motive, aus denen Juden

---

[1] Entscheidend ist, was der jeweilige Kontext als Ursache des 'Wohnsitzwechsels' angibt.

[2] Der Rezensent möchte jedoch van Unniks Worten, daß ein solches Einvernehmen—er spricht von einer 'Verschmelzung' der Anschauungen—'zutiefst unmöglich' war, widersprechen. Philon ist, wie Josephus ja auch, am politischen Messianismus seiner Zeit gescheitert. Es ist *diese* Gefahr, bei deren Analyse sie versagten. Sie war mit schlichtem Verschweigen der Messiaserwartung und mit ständigem Verweis auf das Walten der Vorsehung noch nicht gebannt, bezog die doch ihren Zündstoff aus extremen sozialen Ungleichheiten.

[3] Aus Josephus wäre vergleichbar *C. Ap.* 2.282–84.

(mehrheitlich!)[1] außerhalb des Gelobten Landes wohnten, waren vielfältig und keineswegs auf die dramatischen Fälle von *galuth*='Verbannung' zu reduzieren. Wie konnten sie dennoch durchgehend als Strafe Gottes empfunden werden? Was motivierte die nicht selten sogar verschärfende Ausdrucksweise der LXX-Übersetzer? Die Frage ist wichtig, selbst wenn sich keine einheitliche und auch keine befriedigende Antwort finden läßt. In der Mischna (*Megilla* 3.6) sind die Segnungen und Flüche als liturgische Lesung für alle Fasttage belegt (S. 155): van Unnik rechnet mit einer Eigenmacht dieser Texte, die sie über Jahrhunderte hat wirksam sein lassen.

Dies ist eine stimulierende und gründliche Untersuchung, wenngleich es ungerecht wäre, die Lösung aller in ihr berührten Probleme zu erwarten. Dem Rezensent sei erlaubt, an einer Stelle einen eigenen Faden anzuknüpfen. Philon, so stellte van Unnik fest, hat eine Tendenz, die 'Zerstreuung' umzustilisieren zur 'Kolonie' im griechischen Sinne. Hierin steckt ein Problem, von dem man nicht erwarten kann, daß ein jüdischer Schriftsteller es ausdrücklich nennt. Offenbar riskierte niemand auszusprechen, daß das Gelobte Land nicht derart 'von Milch und Honig floß', wie nötig gewesen wäre, um den Segen einer unübersehbar zahlreichen Nachkommenschaft Abrahams zu ernähren. Das Problem wird dadurch noch verschärft, daß die Tora (Lev 25; vgl. Dtn 15) verheißt, das Land werde in jedem siebten Jahr sogar ohne Bebauung seine Bewohner ernähren. Dieser Segen ist, soweit die Geschichte erkennen läßt, ausgeblieben.[2] Hat man den Verheißungen nicht getraut? Oder soll der hellenistischen Wirtschaft sowie den Römern und ihren Steuerpächtern die Schuld gegeben werden? Das wäre aber keine Antwort auf die Ernährungsfrage.

Wir berühren hier das Ungesagte der jüdischen Theologie.[3] Um es an Philon zu veranschaulichen: Könnte ein Motiv für sein Verbleiben in Alexandrien—obwohl der Boden dort ja heiß war—ein Ausweichen vor der vollen Gesetzeslast gewesen sein? Die Agrargesetze, darunter das vom 7. Jahr und das vom 50. Jahr, galten ja nicht außerhalb des

---

[1] S. 54 erwähnt S. W. Barons Schätzung, 'daß die Judenschaft 7 bis 10% der Bevölkerung des Römerreichs ausmachte'!

[2] Vgl. 1. Makk 6:49, 53. Weitere Versuche, wenigstens das Sabbatjahr einzuhalten (wir schweigen vom Jobeljahr), sind bekannt: s. J. Jeremias, *Jerusalem zur Zeit Jesu*, (Göttingen 1958[2]) 206. Aus derselben Zeit wie Jeremias' Belege datiert jedoch Hillels Einrichtung des *prozbol*; sie ist eine förmlich-rechtliche Umgehung von Pflichten des Sabbatjahrs. Irgendwie war das Judentum gespalten, gerade im Mutterland.

[3] Paulus hätte gesagt: das ἀδύνατον τοῦ Νόμου (Röm 8:3). Bis heute hat sein Volk ihm diese Schonungslosigkeit nicht verziehen, wenngleich er nicht in der Tora selbst, sondern im 'Fleisch' den Schuldigen ausmacht.

Gelobten Landes.[1] Das Deuteronomium steigert die Lage ins Unerträgliche, wenn es in 27:26 proklamiert: 'Verflucht (LXX: 'zusätzlich verflucht') ist jeder, der nicht in allen Worten dieses Gesetzes bleibt, daß er sie tut!' Wie sollte man außerhalb des Landes Israel diesem Fluch entgehen? Oder war man ihm eben dadurch ferner gerückt? Gerade einem Mann von der Ernsthaftigkeit Philons sind solche Fragen zuzutrauen.

Auf S. 60 lesen wir: 'Es könnte eben auch so sein, daß das Leben in einer Umgebung, wo die richtige Gesetztestreue so gehemmt wurde, nicht als eine Befreiung, sondern als eine Last empfunden wurde.' Sicherlich! Und könnte es auch anders sein—für Philon z.B.?

Van Unnik vermerkt, daß Philons *De praemiis et poenis,* sein Kommentar zu Dtn 28, eine Auslegung des V. 64 schuldig bleibt. Gehen wir weiter: es gibt auch keine Stellungnahme Philons zu jenem Fluch im Kapitel vorher, Dtn 27:26.[2] An die Stelle einer Erfüllung des *ganzen* Gesetzes tritt bei Philon stillschweigend eine Theologie des guten Willens: wir können sagen, es ist Philons Rechtfertigungslehre. Sie läßt die gute Absicht für die Tat gelten. In *Virt.* 184f. findet sich die Versicherung, Gott werde 'der guten Absicht zuvorkommen': προαπαντᾶν τῷ βουλήματι.[3] So suchte, auf seine typisch nicht-konfrontative Art, Philon den Ausweg aus dem 'Fluch des Gesetzes', Dtn 27:26. Van Unnik hätte es bemerken können, tut es jedoch nicht, und sei es aus Rücksicht auf sein Jerusalemer Auditorium.

Die Grenzen seines Buches kommen jedoch hauptsächlich aus einer engen Begrenzung des untersuchten Wortfeldes. Van Unnik hat παροικία nicht einbezogen, kommt also auf Stellen wie Sir 29.22–28 und Arist 249 nicht zu sprechen.[4] Bei letzterer—einem Lob des Zuhause-Seins—wüßte man wahrhaft gerne, was sein jüdischer Autor dachte, d.h. ob und mit welchem politischen und theologischen Recht er sich in Alexandrien 'zu Hause' fühlte. Philon geht wiederum einen weichen Weg mit der Kompromißauskunft, Jerusalem sei 'Metropole' aller

---

1 Der Unterschied zwischen dem *Talmud des Landes Israel* ('Jerusalemer Talmud') und dem Babylonischen Talmud gibt davon Zeugnis: in letzterem hat der *Seder Zera'im* ('Saaten'), außer in seinem ersten Traktat (*Berakoth* 'Segnungen'), keine *gemara.*

2 So nach *Biblia Patristica, Supplement.*

3 Hier liegt möglicherweise die Wurzel der patristischen Theologie von der Entscheidungsfreiheit und den—letztlich Gott zuzuschreibenden—guten Werken. Denn eben jenes προαπαντᾶν wird von Basilius (Melanchthon zitiert ihn in den *Loci theologici* von 1559, *locus* 4, S. 271 Stupperich) zur Benennung der göttlichen Hilfe gebraucht.

4 Bezüglich Philons kann empfohlen werden: R. Feldmeier, *Die Christen als Fremde. Die Metapher der Fremde in der antiken Welt, im Urchristentum und im 1.Petrusbrief* (WUNT 64; Tübingen 1992) 60–74.

Juden; ihr jeweiliges Land aber sei ihre 'Heimat' (πατρίς; *Flacc.* 46).[1] Daneben aber—wir erweitern nochmals den Horizont des Buches van Unniks—betrachtet Philon den ganzen Kosmos als seine Heimat und schreibt sich bereitwillig in dessen πολίτευμα ein (*Jos.* 69). Auch damit nicht genug; er zählt sich zu denjenigen, die sich der ἰδεῶν πολιτεία (sc. der Kontemplation)[2] eingeschrieben haben (*Gig.* 61; nochmals ἐγγράφειν). Diese *realized eschatology* läßt an des Paulus himmlisches Bürgerrecht denken (Phil 3:20).

Wenn also die gegenwärtige Rezension irgendetwas an van Unniks schönem Buch auszusetzen hat, dann in Bezug auf die Philon-Verwendung. Der Verfasser hätte genauer sagen können, welche Theologie bei Philon das beklommene 'Diaspora'-Gefühl überwinden hilft. Es ist wahrlich kein Zufall, daß jenes häßliche Wort bei ihm fehlt. Darüber hinaus wird jetzt noch um ein Stück verständlicher, warum Philons Wirkungsgeschichte ausschließlich im Christentum liegt.

Van Unniks deutscher Stil liest sich sehr angenehm und läßt staunen über die Sprachbeherrschung des Verfassers. Gewisse Redundanzen[3] wird man dem mündlichen Vortrag zugute halten. Freilich wäre es gut gewesen, wenn das Manuskript vor dem Druck von einem Lektor mit Deutsch als Muttersprache gelesen worden wäre; das hätte häufige Verwechslungen von ü und u[4] (schwere Unterscheidung für Deutschlands nördliche Nachbarn), falsche Verwendungen von ß, sz und ss,[5] sowie grammatische Fehler[6] vermeiden helfen. Doch bleibt, daß dieses

---

[1] Der Verfasser verweist einmal auf diese Stelle (S. 157). Indirekt, vielleicht ohne es zu wissen, hatte er sie auf S. 65 schon zitiert.

[2] Dem Rezensent will scheinen, daß Philon dieser Tätigkeit in seinem alexandrinischen Studierzimmer besser nachgehen konnte als in den Debatten der Jerusalemer Rechtsgelehrten.

[3] Z.B. S. 73, zweite Hälfte, sowie vieles vom Schlußkapitel.

[4] Die Wörter 'drücken' und 'drucken' werden verwechselt (S. 62 (zweimal), 71). Ebenso steht Fünde (54) statt Funde.

[5] ß sollte stehen für ss in 'schliessen' (72), 'besassen' (90), 'Verheissungen' (123), 'heisse' (154), 'Bundesschliessung' (155), für sz in 'groszer' (53).—Umgekehrt sollte ss stehen für ß in 'überflüßig' (52), 'müßen' (81, 82, 128). S. 55, statt 'beeinflüßen', lies: beeinflussen; S. 57 'abstößenden' lies: abstoßenden.—Ein s statt ss oder ß steht auf S. 69 'ein bischen'; S. 85 'bewuste'; S. 151 'bewust'. *Das* statt *daß* ist verwendet auf S. 109, Z. 8. Andere orthographische Fehler: S. 86 'representativ'; S. 93 'ausschwermen'; S. 114 'Restoration'; S. 125 Anm. 155 'Konsekwenzen'. Druckfehler im Griechischen: κατὰ τοῦ (statt τὸ) ῥῆμα (71); οἱ (104) lies οἵ; το (119) lies τὸ.

[6] Beispiele: 'unsere Zerstreute' (65) lies: unsere Zerstreuten; 'Bösewichten' (126) lies: Bösewichter; 'keine Kontakt' (87) lies: keinen Kontakt; 'unheilsvolle' (88) lies: unheilvolle; 'Sündenhaftigkeit' (109) lies: Sündhaftigkeit; 'auf Verdiensten' (118) lies: auf Verdienste; 'die Unvernünftige' (131) lies: die Unvernünftigen; 'des Wiederkehrs' (132) lies: der Wiederkehr; nach 'einschließlich' (133 unten) müßte Genitiv stehen, usw. Gelegentlich fehlen Kommas; und es begegnen kuriose Worttrennungen.

Buch sich besser liest als manches von Deutschen geschriebene.

Die Beigaben des Herausgebers bestehen in einem Vorwort, einer Einleitung (S. 13–28), einer Bibliographie der wissenschaftlichen Arbeiten van Unniks (S. 29–50), einer 'Appendix I: 'Diaspora' im Pseudophilonischen *Liber Antiquitatum Biblicarum*' (S. 167f.), einer 'Appendix II: Διασπορά: der TLG-Bestand' (S. 169–91) und einem dreifachen Register (Stellen,[1] Namen, Stichworte). Der Band ist in der bei Brill gewohnten Qualität hergestellt.[2]

Folker Siegert
Neuchâtel

David DAWSON, *Allegorical Readers and Cultural Revision in Ancient Alexandria*. University of California Press, Berkeley–Los Angeles–Oxford 1992. xi + 341 pp. ISBN 0-520-07102-6. $35.00.

Nowhere has the method of allegorical interpretation been more extensively developed than in the Alexandrian tradition. The study under review, which has its origins in a Yale dissertation directed by Bentley Layton, argues that this tradition has been viewed too much as a single, even monolithic, whole. Concentrating on three major Alexandrian figures in the Jewish-Christian tradition, Philo, Valentinus and Clement, the author examines the role that allegory plays in their thought and argues that on this question they adopt strongly divergent positions.

The study is admirably structured. In the Introduction Dawson makes clear that he does not want to examine allegory in a traditionalist mode (whether sacred of secular). Not only does he take into account late modernist and post-modernist perspectives on allegorical discourse. He is also particularly concerned with the social and cultural functioning of allegory. Allegorical interpretation is undertaken as a challenge to the accepted meaning of a text (which Dawson identifies with the literal meaning, whether it is literally literal or not). It can thus have a conservative or 'domesticating' tendency, when accepted cultural values are defended (e.g. Hellenistic allegorization of Homer the all-wise poet). Equally, however, it can have a 'revisionary' or 'counter-hegemonic'

---

[1] Leider ist nur der Haupttext verzettelt worden, sodaß z.B. die Nennungen von Dtn 27:26 und Gal 3:10 auf S. 79, Anm. 75 im Register nicht erscheinen.

[2] Ein Hinweis nur betr. den elektronischen Satz: Die SuperGreek-Typen haben einen größeren Leerraum als die der verwendeten Lateinschrift: es stört optisch, wenn griechische Wörter rechts von sich einen solchen großen Leerraum haben (z.B. auf S. 85 unten).

impulse, when the revised meaning challenges accepted cultural patterns. Dawson argues that this occurs with all three Alexandrian writers that he focuses on, but differently in each case.

Although at first the reader is treated to a good deal of literary theory, thereby gaining valuable insights into the current state of debate, Dawson's method is basically diachronic. He first takes a closer look at the Hellenistic background, examining the methods of Cornutus (who is hardly an allegorist in his view) and Heraclitus Allegoricus, as well as other authors such as Plutarch who are rather ambivalent towards the allegorical method. Philo's use of allegory is summarized under the not entirely clear title 'the reinscription of reality'. What this means is that for Philo the *text* is of primary importance, i.e. the Mosaic text which is regarded as 'rewritten' in two ways, firstly through Moses who has incorporated in his books the dominant culture of Hellenism *avant la lettre*, and secondly through Philo the allegorical interpreter himself, who reads the text in such a way as to claim that it represents the sum total of authentic intellectual wisdom and culture, as well as the plot of world history. For Valentinus the slogan is the 'apocalypse of mind'. In the case of the Christian Gnostic the boundary between text and commentary becomes deliberately blurred. Dawson compares the way in which the Mosaic text is *commented* on by Philo, but *re-composed* by the author of the prologue to John's Gospel. In the same way Valentinus takes the basic Gnostic myth and rewrites it, so that the narrative element of the myth is detemporalized and transformed into the interior vision of the interpreter.[1] Truth is found within, and the goal and outcome is spiritual perfection. What is the revisionary impulse behind this vision? Dawson argues that Valentinus is offering a subversion of Judaism even more radical than that previously attempted by Gnostic thinkers (in so-called Jewish Gnosticism). The third figure is Clement and the chapter on his allegorism is entitled 'the new song of the *Logos*'. Clement remains more loyal to the biblical text than Valentinus, but textuality cannot mean the same to him as it does to Philo, because he listens above all to the divine Voice that speaks through the text. In the Bible this Voice becomes less and less mediated, until it speaks through the Saviour himself, and since his death through the apostolic tradition. The revisionary aspect in Clement's allegory involves his 'taking the high ground' in the context of other competing groups (including 'heretics') in the pluriform situation of the Alexandrian church. Clement stays closer to Philo than Valentinus because he privileges the

[1] Note that the *Gospel of Truth* is considered an authentic work of Valentinus himself, and so supplies Dawson with most of his material.

textual above the experiential hermeneutic. Truth is the 'will to hermeneutical power' in response to the voice of the Logos speaking through the text.

The above summary attempts to give the main line of Dawson's argument, which he himself presents with great clarity. It cannot possibly do justice to the details of his discussion, which not only grapple with the hermeneutical aspects of the subject, but also have much to say on epistemological and exegetical issues (note especially the discussions on catachrestic and apophatic approaches to theology). I have no hesitation in recommending the book to everyone interested in these central aspects of the Alexandrian tradition.

One aspect of Dawson's approach which I found intriguing was his view on the nature of allegory. As was already apparent in the summary given above, he takes a *broad* view of what allegory is. Valentinus' rewriting of Gnostic myth is regarded as allegory, even though it is quite different to Heraclitus' interpretation of Homer or Philo's reading of Moses. In one respect, however, he restricts the use of the term, and this I found thought-provoking. He insists that allegory—whether composed or interpreted—must involve a *narrative* dimension, i.e. a story that has a beginning, middle and end. For this reason an etymology or even a series of etymologies such as we find in Cornutus should not be regarded as allegory. Is this necessarily so? Certainly Genesis has a story, and Philo's allegory of the soul can be conceived as having a narrative component, the quest of the soul for her origin and goal in God. But what about physical allegory, such as the interpretation of the Cherubim in terms of two hemispheres or two divine powers (cf. *Cher.* 25–29, *Mos.* 2.98–100)? Does this have a story line? Is it not possible to give an allegorical interpretation of a legal injunction such as the interpretation of the dietary laws in Ps.Aristeas 143–154? It is by no means easy to give a description of allegory that covers all cases, since the term is used to denote both a limited trope and an extended method of composing or reading texts. Dawson's requirement of narrativity seems to me too stringent. Allegorical interpretation involves reading a text in terms of or in relation to a complex and usually systematic conception or theory. A single etymology on its own is not allegory, as Dawson rightly argues, but if that etymology has its place among other etymologies within a systematic whole (as we find in Philo, but also in Cornutus), then it should be regarded as an allegorical technique. Dawson's suggestion is constructive, however, if it is taken less stringently, since he draws our attention to the fact that allegory is very often connected to a narrative account, most notably in the allegory of the soul. In the chapter on Philo the role of the allegory of the soul is in fact rather underplayed. Instead

Dawson concentrates on the Exposition of the Law, the overall structure of which he interprets as an attempt at universal history, in which the Jewish people will play the decisive role (cf. *Mos.* 2.44). In the chapters on Valentinus and Clement the insistence on the narrative aspect of allegory gives rise to problems. The *Gospel of Truth* has a 'curious non-linear "antinarrative" quality' (149) in which sequential progression from origin to goal is abandoned. We do not read, however, that this means Valentinus no longer practises allegory. As for Clement, Dawson emphasizes the conception of a grand progression from law (Old Testament) to gospel (New Testament), but this is not related to the formal characteristics of allegorization in the *Stromateis* and his other works.

What then should we think of the main theses of this book? The examination of Alexandrian allegorical practice against the background of its social and cultural context is surely a most worthwhile exercise. With regard to the theory of three different methods of practising allegory I am somewhat more ambivalent. The distinctions that are made seem to me basically persuasive, but then extended so far that they become overdrawn. Too often Dawson turns a contrast into an antithesis. The emphasis on textuality in the case of Philo seems to me to be quite right. But the antithesis established between him and Valentinus is too strong. Philo subordinates himself to the text of Moses, but as exegete he too claims inspiration for his insights (compare the passages studies by Sze-kar Wan in this volume). Dawson concentrates on Philo's view of universal history, whereas for his profoundest thought the allegory of the soul is more important, and this brings him much closer to Valentinus. It is certainly true that the personified Logos plays a more important role in Clement than in Philo. But the practice of Clement's allegory only makes sense if it is read against the background of a reading of the Bible in the light of philosophy which is strongly indebted to Philo. Dawson argues that both Philo and Clement read inter-textually, i.e. the explain one text by adducing parallel texts from elsewhere in scripture.[1] This is of course entirely correct. He then goes on to make an antithesis (213): 'the essential difference between the intratextual character of Clement's and Philo's allegorical readings can be summarized

[1] Cf. the distinction between primary and secondary biblical lemmata which I tried to introduce in my research on the subject; cf. studies IV and V in Exegesis and Philosophy: Studies on Philo of Alexandria (London 1990), first published in 1984–87. It is a pity that Dawson does not take studies by Cazeaux, Radice, Goulet, Burkhardt into account. He refers to Robert Hamerton-Kelly's seminal article published in *SPhA* 1 (1972), but research has surely moved on since then. Also Van den Hoek's monograph on Clement's use of Philo could have been consulted with profit (it is referred to, but its results are not exploited).

this way: Clement gives meaning control over lexical details, whereas Philo gives scripture's lexical expression control over meaning.' The formulation is too sharp to be convincing. Philo does both and Clement does both. The fact that Philo often gives a running commentary, whereas Clement's *Stromateis* are more systematically (but still very associatively) structured needs to be taken into account (Clement's practice in the *Hypotyposeis* may well have been quite different). To my mind the attempted hermeneutic antithesis does not work. On the last page of the chapter Dawson refers to the exegesis of Gen. 22:3–4 at *Str.* 5.73.1 and states that 'unlike Philo [in *Somn.* 1.64] Clement remains seemingly untroubled by the lexical peculiarities of this sentence and confidently interprets it according to one reading'. He seems unaware, however, that Clement is following Philo exactly here, but this time it concerns the use of the same text at *Post.* 17–18.[1]

In the long run I found that the study shows a tendency to become too ambitious and too schematic. In its Afterword it relates the three forms of revisionary allegorical practice to later hermeneutical models in western thought: the Philonic paradigm is taken up by Augustine and the North American Puritans (rewriting the world in terms of the biblical text); Valentinus' approach anticipates Hegel, Emerson and the transcendentalists; Clement leads the way to Schleiermacher, Heidegger and Gadamer. The contrasts that are drawn are very stimulating, to be sure, but to my mind they have an unfortunate consequence. They break up the historical and ideological unity of the Alexandrian tradition to a greater degree than is warranted.

David T. Runia
University of Leiden

Theo K. Heckel, *Der Innere Mensch: Die paulinische Verarbeitung eines platonischen Motivs*. WUNT 2.53. J. C. B. Mohr (Paul Siebeck), Tübingen 1993. x + 257 Seiten. ISBN 3-16-146026-X.

Zweifellos geht die Metapher auf Platon, *Rep.* 9.589a, zurück. Die Erlanger Dissertation stellt S. 12–26 diesen Text auf dem Hintergrund der Ideenlehre vor (S. 20, 3. Z. v. u. lies. ἡγεμονικόν statt λογιστικόν). Er habe aber in der Zeit vor Philon kaum Wirkung gezeigt. Erst im Mittelplatonismus (einführend S. 31–42), konkret bei Philon (einführend S. 42–50), beginne seine Rezeption. In der Sammlung philo-

---

[1] Cf. Van den Hoek, *op. cit.* 173.

nischer Belege S. 50–61 achtet Heckel auf die exegetische Funktion der Metapher und gewichtet dann—methodisch D. T. Runia folgend—den Einschlag des Platonismus bzw. die Eigenleistung Philons, durch den 'das Pneuma der Textreligion des Judentums' in 'die erst nach ihm besser belegbare Strömung des Mittelplatonismus' hineingepumpt worden sei (so das Fazit S. 76).

Heckel hat sich in die Philosophiegeschichte und in Philon hineingearbeitet. Und doch fehlt diesem Teil die nötige Umsicht. Philons Verwendung der Metapher steht isoliert in seiner Zeit. Es muß ja schon auffallen, daß er nie vom ἐντὸς ἄνθρωπος spricht (64), einige Male vom Menschen in uns, meistens aber vom 'wahren Menschen'[1] o. ä. Hier ist eben Platons 1. *Alkibiades* 130c wirksam geworden, den Philon nach Ausweis von *Opif.* 66 kennt. Er verbindet sich mit anderen Platonstellen, nicht nur *Rep.* 588–89, dem Phaidros-Mythos (S. 67 fehlen die einschlägigen Arbeiten von Boyancé, Méasson), sondern auch *Leges* 959ab, was im ἕκαστος ἡμῶν *Agr.* 9, 108; *Her.* 231 noch nachklingt. Das alles hätte Heckel bei J. Pépin, *Idées Grecques sur l'Homme et sur Dieu* (Paris 1971), nachlesen können, den er im Literaturverzeichnis führt. Dann ware ihm auch aufgegangen, daß die Bezeichnung des Geistes als des eigentlichen Menschen auch in der Stoa verbreitet ist und daß man die Äußerung des Kleanthes, *SVF* 1.123, durchaus ernst nehmen muß (gegen S. 30, 1ies dort ἄνθρωπο<u>ν</u>, S. 62), wobei ψυχή sicher die Vernunftseele meint.

In der 'von Paulus unabhängigen Nachgeschichte der Metapher vom 'Inneren Menschen'', die Heckel S. 76–88 beschreibt, hält m.E. der Einfluß des 1. *Alkibiades* zunächst an. So im *Corpus Hermeticum* (vgl. S. 81, wo man ἔννους nicht mit '*inner*vernünftig' übersetzen sollte). Erst bei Zosimos und an drei Stellen der NHC ist ausdrücklich vom 'Inneren Menschen' die Rede. Heckel führt das darauf zurück, daß man sich nun stärker des platonischen Ursprungs rückversicherte. Da aber die griechische bzw. lateinische Version der Sextussprüche bzw. des Asclepius die Metapher nicht hat,[2] kann man fragen, ob dies so unabhängig von Paulus geschieht, zumal das *Philippusevangelium* noch 'weitere Stichworte aus Röm 7' bietet. Die Nag-Hammadi-Belege wären dann ins Kapitel 'Das gnostische Exil der Metapher' (221–26) zu stellen. Dort meint Heckel, daß die von Eirenaios bzw. Epiphanios referierten Gnostiker wohl nicht von Paulus abhängig sind. Bei Basilides, der ja Röm 7 kommentiert hat, und seinem Schüler Valentin kann das m.E.

---

1 Hier läßt Heckel die Enos-Stellen *Det.* 138; *Abr.* 11f. weg.

2 S. 83 ist ein Zitat aus dem Asclepius verstümmelt. Es sollte nicht mit 'uulus' enden, sondern mit 'vultus similitudine figuraret'.

aber durchaus der Fall sein. Andererseits läßt sich das selbständige Weiterwirken der platonischen Metapher etwa bei Epiktet und Plotin beobachten.[1] Sie gehört eben zum Rüstzeug eines weit verbreiteten, nicht nur in Alexandria beheimateten, vulgären Platonismus, der — wie mir scheint — auch Paulus vertraut ist.

Für Heckel aber ist wichtig, daß der Kultur Alexandrias 'die entscheidenden Anstöße für den Aufstieg der Metapher vom 'Inneren Menschen' zu verdanken sind' (88). Denn in Gestalt der Gegner des Paulus schwappte die 'alexandrinische platonische Denkaura' (141) nach Korinth über. Dabei müssen die im 2. Korintherbrief greifbaren Gegner freilich stark der Front angeglichen werden, die G. Sellin durch die Weisheitstheologie des Apollos geprägt sieht.[2] So vertritt Heckel in Kap. IV die Hypothese, daß Paulus in 2 Kor 4:16 die Terminologie der Gegner — Apollos wird hier natürlich entbehrlich (144) — übernommen habe, um sie zu 'reinigen'. Nun ist nicht zu bestreiten, daß in dem Abschnitt 4:7–5:10 dualistische, platonische Motive anklingen.[3] Aber sperren sie sich so sehr gegen die sonstige paulinische Theologie? M.E. kann Heckel in 4.3.2 nur 'Tradition' und 'Redaktion' scheiden, indem er künstliche Gegensätze aufbaut. Dabei legt sich doch Paulus in dem V. 7 beginnenden Gedankengang im Wechsel von 'Gefäß' zu 'Leib' und 'Fleisch' zunächst einmal der 'äußere Mensch' nahe, dem er dann den 'inneren' entgegensetzt. In dem wenige Monate später geschriebenen Röm kann er problemlos auf diese Metapher zurückgreifen (7:22); er verwendet sie in nicht erst durch Gegner vermittelter Kenntnis des platonischen Sinns parallel zu νοῦς (7:23, 25b). Der νοῦς ist auch Röm 12:2 (vgl. 2 Kor 4:16) Ansatzpunkt der eschatologischen Erneuerung. Zu den Parallelbegriffen zählt auch πνεῦμα (Röm 8:10, vgl. 16; 1 Thess 5:23), worauf Heckel nicht eingeht, wie überhaupt die Ausführungen über den paulinischen Umgang mit der Metapher (146f., 147 lies in der 5. Z. 4:16; 206–08) zu knapp geraten sind.

In dem Röm 7 gewidmeten Kapitel meint Heckel den Stein der Weisen in der Frage, wie der geschilderte Konflikt einzuordnen ist, gefunden zu haben: Es handelt sich um einen unbewußten Konflikt. An diese These ist die Gretchenfrage zu stellen: Bestand die Sünde in einem Durchbrechen des Gebotes oder nicht? Wenn ersteres nicht zu leugnen ist, müßte das faktische Begehren dem Ich unbewußt gewesen sein. Das geht nur, wenn man es auf der Linie Käsemanns (dem Heckel 188

---

[1] Vgl. H. Windisch, *Der zweite Korintherbrief* (Göttingen 1970) 152f. Heckel erwähnt diese Philosophen nicht.

[2] *Der Streit um die Auferstehung der Toten* (Göttingen 1986).

[3] Vgl. auch περιφέρειν τὴν νέκρωσιν (4.10), dazu Windisch, a.a.O. 145, der Platon, *Phaidros* 250c und Philon, *Leg.* 3.69 vergleicht. Zu ergänzen ware περιφέρειν in *QG* 1.70.

zugeneigt scheint) als fromme Selbstverwirklichung faßt, eine Exegese, die ich seit Wilckens überholt glaubte. Außerdem gibt uns K. Berger[1] zu bedenken, ob die Kategorie des Unbewußten überhaupt antikem Selbstverständnis entspricht.

Fazit zur Paulusdeutung: Neben der Behandlung von Einleitungsfragen[2] und Kontextanalysen stellt Heckel zwei schwerlich überzeugende Hauptthesen zur Debatte. Seine Argumentation wird auch durch philologische Eigenwilligkeiten geschwächt: So gibt er 2 Kor 5:7 als 'Wandel gemäß (διά mit Genitiv!) dem Geschauten (!)' wieder (121f.). Die Unterscheidung von ποιεῖν und πράσσειν in Röm 7 (187f.) ist schon durch V. 15b, dessen Aufnahme in V. 19, dessen Weiterführung in V. 20 unwahrscheinlich (vgl. noch die synonyme Verwendung in 1:32; 2:3, 13f., 25; 13:4). In 7:21 gewinnt Heckel durch eine gezwungene Konstruktion ein 'Gesetz für mich' (191f). Dazu kommen noch relativ häufige Fehler im Griechischen: außer den genannten vgl. 81 ὄντος statt ὄντως; 178 Anm. 121 παλαιώτης; 191 τὸν καλόν statt τὸ καλόν; 222 οἰκτήριον statt οἰκητήριον.

Der Philonforscher wird in dem Buch kaum Weiterführendes finden. Mir ist allerdings neu, daß man die *expositio legis* als 'Nachschriften' bezeichnet (45 zweimal). Doch vielleicht ist das die schiefe Wiedergabe von 're-writing', womit der Gewährsmann Heckels, P. Borgen (den man freilich vergebens im Literaturverzeichnis sucht), in *ANRW* II.21.1 S. 117 diese Schriften Philons charakterisiert. Außerdem habe ich ein schönes deutsches Wort gelernt: Konkludenz (90 zweimal, 98f.). Sie fehlt leider dieser Dissertation in entscheidenden Punkten.

Dieter Zeller
Johannes GutenbergUniversität
Mainz

Gregory E. STERLING, *Historiography and Self-Definition: Josephos, Luke-Acts and Apologetic Historiography*. NovTSup 64. E. J. Brill, Leiden 1992. xv + 500 pages. ISBN 90-04-09501-2. $125.75.

Die 1989 abgeschlossene, danach nur noch leicht überarbeitete Dissertation (bei John R. Donahue, S.J., gearbeitet) hatte sich zum Ziel gesetzt, die Frage zu untersuchen, inwieweit die seit langem vertretene Auffassung, das lukanische Doppelwerk—insbesondere die Apostelgeschich-

1 *Historische Psychologie des Neuen Testaments* (Stuttgart 1991) 35–40.
2 S. 149 Anm. 5 finde ich mich fälschlich unter den Befürwortern einer Abtrennung von Röm 16 eingereiht.

te—trage apologetischen Charakter, zutreffend ist bzw. bei welchem Sinne von 'Apologie' sie gelten kann. Meist wurde die These in Verbindung mit der Verselbständigung der christlichen Kirche gegenüber der Synagoge gesehen, insbesondere mit der Befürchtung, daß die Kirche den Schutz des römischen Staates verlieren würde, der dem Judentum als einer *religio licita* galt. Man meinte, in der Apostelgeschichte die Bemühung des Lukas zu erkennen, gegenüber Rom die Kirche oder 'das Christentum' als eine politisch unbedenkliche Gemeinschaft darzustellen, die sich der Gesellschaft gegenüber wohlverhalten werde, so daß auch ihr jener Schutz einer *religio licita* zukommen könne.

Dieser sozial-politische Aspekt ist es aber nicht, von dem aus sich Sterling dem Problem nähert. Vielmehr stellt er die Frage nach der Gattung der Apg. im literaturgeschichtlichen Sinne, nämlich als Frage danach, ob sich der Apg. ein Platz innerhalb einer Serie von spätantiken apologetischen Schriften, näherhin in einer Reihe von apologetisch orientierten Geschichtsdarstellungen zuweisen läßt. Auch die Frage, inwieweit es sich in der Apg. um eine historisch 'glaubhafte' Darstellung der urchristlichen Geschichte handelt, steht also nicht im Vordergrund. Wenn Sterling das Problem behandeln will, inwiefern 'Luke-Acts is a historical work', dann stellt er sogleich klar, es gehe um die Stellung der Apg. innerhalb 'the framework of ancient historiography', womit ein 'settlement of the issue of veracity', also eine Erörterung der Frage nach der historischen Zuverlässigkeit der Apg., nicht beabsichtigt ist (ohne daß deshalb eine darauf zielende Fragestellung diskreditiert werden soll).[1] Somit muß zunächst die Existenz einer Gattung 'apologetische Historiographie' in der spätantiken Literatur erwiesen und beschrieben werden. Das hat zur Folge, daß nun die eigentlich neutestamentliche Arbeit, die Arbeit an der Apg. bzw. am lukanischen Doppelwerk, zu einem Schlußkapitel (Chap. VII) der vorgelegten Dissertation wird, das nur etwa ein Fünftel des Ganzen umfaßt, während der überwiegende Teil der Arbeit dazu dient, eine Traditionslinie antiker apologetischer Historiographie, und zwar nach Möglichkeit einer nahöstlichen apologetischen Historiographie,[2] darzustellen. Demnach gehört die Untersuchung in das Gebiet der 'Formgeschichte' oder 'Gattungsgeschichte', wobei von Sterling 'Form' und 'Funktion' von Werken einer Gattung ganz im Sinne der 'klassischen Formgeschichte' zusammengedacht werden.[3] Dabei wird sich ergeben, daß diese Gattung ihre Funktion insbesondere bei der Eigendarstellung der Geschichte von Völkern, die

---

[1] Alle Zitate: Sterling p. 3.
[2] Ebd. p.11.
[3] Ebd. p.14.

erst neu in den hellenistisch-römischen Kulturkreis eingetreten sind, besitzt (daher die geographische Komponente 'nahöstlich'). Zur formgeschichtlichen Fragestellung gehört insbesondere auch die Frage nach der vom Autor angezielten und erhofften bzw. für sein Werk zu erwartenden Leserschaft; bei der eingangs skizzierten These von der apologetischen Zweckbestimmung der Apg. war danach kaum gefragt worden (allenfalls soweit, daß man an Theophilos als Vermittler des Buchs an Regierende dachte).

Waren bisher einige wesentliche Leitlinien des methodologischen Chapter I (pp. 1–19) skizziert worden, so kann es hier nicht darum gehen, den Inhalt der weiteren Kapitel gleichmäßig in den Einzelheiten wiederzugeben. Sterling greift (Chap. II, pp. 20–54) weit zurück in die Geschichte der griechischen Historiographie, insbesondere der Ethnographie, die bei Hekataios von Milet und bei Herodotos noch ineinander übergehen. Dafür hat er sich intensiv in die Diskussion literaturgeschichtlicher Fragen der (Spät-)Antike außerhalb der Bibelwissenschaft eingearbeitet und vermag damit dem Theologen eine gute Erweiterung seines Horizonts zu geben. Er arbeitet gut heraus, wie auf Grund der Art und Weise der Wahrnehmung fremder Völker und Kulturen selbst ein 'Klassiker' des 'Wissenschaftstourismus' wie Herodotos das Wahrgenommene auf Grund der mitgebrachten Sichtweise notwendig teilweise verzeichnet, da sich der Autor nur auf Mitgeteiltes und von außen Gesehenes bezieht und nicht in der Lage ist, die fremde Welt von innen her zu sehen und sichtbar zu machen.[1]

Ein grundlegender Wandel in der Wahrnehmung fremder Länder und Völker vollzieht sich dann mit dem Wachsen der geschichtlichen Macht Persiens und der griechischen bzw. makedonischen Reaktion darauf, insbesondere in den Kriegszügen Alexanders des Großen. Erst jetzt bildet sich bei den Hellenen das Bewußtsein sowohl einer gemeinsamen griechischen Kultur wie auch einer Überlegenheit dieser Kultur über die der 'barbarischen' Völker aus. Das bedeutet auch, daß sich nun 'Ethnography in Transition' befindet (chap. III, pp. 55–102). Hier sind Hekataios von Abdera und Megasthenes die Autoren, an denen Sterling seine Sicht verdeutlicht; bei diesem (zweiten) Hekataios kommt übrigens zum ersten Mal ein Abschnitt in den Blick, der sich speziell mit den Juden befaßt.[2] Beide Autoren leben als Griechen längere Zeit in

---

[1] Auf p. 46 und 48 bietet Sterling kleine Tabellen, in denen er die umfangreicheren und kürzeren ethnographischen *Logoi* im Geschichtswerk des Herodotos auflistet und so veranschaulicht, wie dieser bei der Darstellung fremder ethnographischer Gegebenheiten schon ein Stück weit über Hekataios von Milet hinauskommt.

[2] Mit nahezu allen Gelehrten nimmt auch Sterling an, daß der berühmte 'Exkurs über die Juden' (F. Jacoby, *FGrHist* 264 F 6; M. Stern, *GLAJJ* I.26–35) nicht von dem (älteren)

den Ländern, von denen sie berichten, und infolgedessen können sie—als von außen Gekommene—schon weit besser von innen her darstellen, ja sogar sie als eine der hellenischen Geschichte und Kultur gegenüber ältere und idealere Kultur auffassen—in bemerkenswerter Spannung zu dem sonstigen griechischen Überlegenheitsgefühl. In der Neigung zum Idealisieren des Fremden deutet sich an, daß diese Autoren ihre Wahrnehmungen nicht nur als 'Historiker', sondern auch als Philosophen verarbeiten.

Chap. IV (pp. 102–36) stellt nun die Anfänge der (im eigentlichen Sinne) apologetischen Geschichtsschreibung dar, und zwar am Beispiel des Babyloniers Berossos und des Ägypters Manethon. Hier sind es nun Vertreter der fremden Völker selbst, die ihre eigene Tradition den Griechen bekanntmachen wollen, und das heißt nun zugleich: gegenüber Mißverständnissen und Falschdarstellungen verteidigen wollen. Freilich findet etwa das Werk des Berossos bei griechischen Lesern wenig Interesse, weil er ihnen zu wenig entgegenkommt, sondern seinen babylonischen Idealen zu sehr verhaftet bleibt.[1] Darin deutet sich eine Schwierigkeit auch auf seiten des jeweiligen Autors an: auch wenn es ihm primär um eine Darstellung seiner heimatlichen kulturellen Tradition ging, mußte er auf irgendeine Weise mit der hellenistischen Kultur zurande kommen. Indem er die Selbstbeschreibung eines politisch unterlegenen Volkes versuchte, durfte er seine eigene Kultur weder verleugnen, noch durfte er sie allzusehr propagandistisch überhöhen. Vermittelnd wirkte hier der Gedanke, daß die eigene Kultur die ältere und die griechische von ihr abhängig sei; von Seiten mancher Griechen (z. B. bei Hekataios) bestand ja bereits die Bereitschaft, das zu akzeptieren. So konnte man die eigene Kultur hochhalten und doch auch die griechische als gleichwertig anerkennen. 'The result was the creation of a new literary genre which *challenged* and *identified* with Hellenism at the same time'.[2] Die Einsicht in diesen doppelseitigen Prozeß scheint mir schon eine wichtige Erkenntnis der Arbeit von Sterling zu sein, die dann natürlich auch für das 'hellenistische Judentum' gilt.

Diesem widmet sich Chap. V (pp. 137–225): 'The Hellenistic Jewish Historians'. Damit sind zunächst die Autoren der zwei letzten Jahrhunderte v. Chr., von deren Werken uns nur Fragmente erhalten sind, gemeint, noch nicht Josephus. Sterling widmet sich ihnen ausführlich

---

Hekataios von Milet stammt (wie es die älteste Überlieferung wohl versehentlich darstellt), sondern von Hekataios von Abdera.

[1] Sterling, p. 117.

[2] Ebd., p. 103 (Kursivdruck im Original).

und stellt sie dem Leser gründlich vor (was übrigens auch für die in den vorangehenden Kapiteln behandelten antiken Autoren und ihre einschlägigen Werke gilt). Von den 'Historikern' behandelt er die vier, deren erhaltene Fragmente ein einigermaßen deutliches Bild ergeben, und zwar zwei, die (wahrscheinlich) in Alexandrien wirkten: Demetrios und Artapanos, sowie zwei aus Palästina: Pseudo-Eupolemos (den Samaritaner) und Eupolemos. Sie alle werden von Sterling mit Recht als 'hellenistisch-jüdische' (bzw. -samaritanische) Autoren angesehen, d. h. als solche, die ihre Schriften nicht nur quasi zufällig in griechischer Sprache (übrigens mit unterschiedlicher Gewandtheit) verfaßt haben, sondern sich auch—je in ihrer Weise—der hellenistischen Kultur offen zugewandt haben. Hinsichtlich der von ihnen gemeinten Adressaten gibt er eine differenzierte Beschreibung: sie richten sich grundsätzlich an jüdische Leser, aber 'there was always an eye turned out to the larger world', also zur Welt der hellenistischen Kultur.[1] Ich kann dem nur zustimmen, auch der dabei vorausgesetzten Bestimmung des Charakters der Schriften als 'apologetischer' Literatur, die—vielleicht entgegen dem, was man vor 100 Jahren (Bousset-Greßmann usw.) darunter verstand—primär als nach 'innen' gerichtete Verteidigung gegen mißverstandene oder gar bewußt unfreundliche Darstellung 'der Juden' und ihrer Geschichte von außen her gesehen werden muß, im allgemeinen wohl ohne die Erwartung, 'heidnische' Leser damit wesentlich beeinflussen zu können[2], sondern in erster Linie dazu, 'to give the Jewish people a new identity in a new world'.[3] Damit ist das zweite Stichwort des Buchtitels angesprochen: 'Self-Definition', das ich für sehr förderlich zur Beschreibung der Funktion dieser Literatur halte, und man kann allenfalls bedauern, daß der mit diesem Stichwort gemeinten Funktion 'apologetischer' Literatur nicht eine grundsätzliche Erörterung gewidmet wird.

Zu Einzelheiten der mit diesen Fragmenten gegebenen Probleme möchte ich nur bemerken, daß ich auch durch Sterling nicht davon überzeugt worden bin, daß es richtig wäre, Demetrios in erster Linie als 'chronographisch' interessierten Autor anzusehen, dem es darum ginge, durch genauen Nachvollzug der biblischen (konkret: in der

---

[1] Ebd., p. 224.

[2] Geschweige denn sie 'missionieren' oder zu Proselyten machen zu können! – Immerhin ist zu beachten, was auch Sterling in diesem Zusammenhang anmerkt (p. 224), daß uns die Fragmente aller dieser Werke nur durch einen 'heidnischen' Leser bzw. Benutzer erhalten worden sind, den römischen Hellenisten Alexander Polyhistor (zu ihm vgl. pp.144–152). Freilich: er bringt diese Zitate in seiner Schrift *Über die Juden* in buntem Wechsel mit Fragmenten aus nichtjüdischen, z. T. dem Judentum unfreundlich gesonnenen Autoren, ohne sich selbst auf irgendeine Bewertung einzulassen. Er ist also bereit, sich informieren, aber durchaus nicht missionieren zu lassen.

[3] Ebd., p. 224f.

Septuaginta vorausgesetzten) Chronographie das höhere Alter der jüdischen Kultur gegenüber der griechischen nachzuweisen.[1] Ein Vergleich, der dieses Ziel erkennen ließe, ist in seinen Fragmenten nicht überliefert. Gewiß, ihn interessiert *auch* der chronologische Zusammenhang *innerhalb* der biblischen Geschichte, wie F 2 (am Anfang und am Ende) sowie F 6 erkennen lassen. Aber ein recht umfangreicher Teil des übrigen F 2 (auf den Sterling aber nicht näher eingeht) befaßt sich in umständlichen und mehrfach abgesicherten Berechnungen zu dem ihn (oder bibelkritische Leser?) offensichtlich beschäftigenden 'Problem', wie es denn möglich sei, die biblischen Angaben so zu ordnen, daß Jakob in sieben Jahren von 2 + 2 Frauen tatsächlich in der von der Bibel vorgegebenen Abfolge 12 Kinder (also 11 Jungen—noch ohne Benjamin—und 1 Mädchen) habe bekommen können; der Nachweis gelingt dem präzisen Rechner, indem er die kürzest möglichen Abstände von Geburten (10 Monate!), je verteilt auf die verschiedenen Frauen und Mägde, ansetzt. Das ist staubtrockene, aber sehr präzise 'Exegese' nach der Devise '... und die Bibel hat doch recht!', aber keine Darstellung, die irgendeinen Leser von dem eindrucksvollen Alter und 'philosophischen' Inhalt biblischer Überlieferungen überzeugen könnte. Im übrigen weisen auch weitere Fragmente darauf hin, daß Demetrios sich mit *Aporiai* und *Lyseis* in der Bibelauslegung befaßt (was auch Sterling keineswegs leugnet). Auch hier hat wohl hellenistische Denkweise, etwa die Homer-Philologie, Pate gestanden, aber doch wohl nicht das chronographische Problem des verschiedenen Alters der Kulturen. In dieser Hinsicht steht Demetrios (der auch sonst wohl als der älteste dieser jüdischen 'Historiker' gelten muß) durchaus am Anfang einer Aufnahme und Verarbeitung neuer Sichtweisen des biblischen Textes.[2] Natürlich gilt auch für meine Darstellung dasselbe, was Sterling gelegentlich mit Blick auf seine eigene Sicht anmerkt: es muß offenbleiben, ob die uns erhaltene, doch nur kärgliche Auswahl aus dem Werk (z. B.) des Demetrios tatsächlich 'repräsentativ' ist und seine Interessen vollständig widerspiegelt; dazu muß dann noch berücksichtigt werden, daß es Eusebios ist, der diese Fragmente unter dem Gesichtspunkt des hohen Alters des Judentums (als der *Praeparatio Evangelica*) zitiert—diese spätere Verwendung der Texte durch den Kirchenvater darf nicht einfach als das Interesse der zitierten Autoren selbst gelten.

Auch zu Artapanos möchte ich nur eine Anmerkung machen: Es scheint mir möglich, hinsichtlich des Verhältnisses der Mose-Darstellung bei Artapanos zu der bei Josephus entschiedener zu urteilen, als Sterling es tut. Daß der originale Artapanos-Text uns in einer durch Alexander Polyhistor gekürzten Fassung vorliegt, ist sicher. Wenn sich in seinen Fragmenten erzählerische Lücken aufzeigen lassen, deren zu erwartender bzw. passender Inhalt sich bei Josephus findet, dann kann man doch ziemlich sicher folgern, daß Josephus den vollständigen Artapanos-Text vor sich hat (dessen Autor er freilich nirgends nennt) und ihn in etwas anderer Auswahl als der Polyhistor in seine Erzählung einarbeitet.[3] Wenn das gilt, dann sollte es übrigens auch dabei bleiben, daß Josephus das Werk des Polyhistor *Über die Juden* nicht gekannt hat (sondern nur die *Libyka*, die Josephus—wenn auch ohne Buchtitel—als Quelle für Kleodemos Malchas in *Ant.* 1.240 nennt).[4]

---

[1] Diese Sicht wird von manchen Autoren vertreten, auf die sich Sterling in diesem Zusammenhang berufen kann, z. B. E. Bickerman und C. Holladay.

[2] Es ist nicht ganz dieselbe Sichtweise wie etwa in den Jubiläen, in denen es um die Etablierung des rechten Kultkalenders geht.

[3] Eine sehr ausführliche und übersichtliche Tabelle mit den Parallelen der Mose-Erzählung nach Artapanos (in die Wiedergabe durch den Polyhistor) und Josephus (*Ant.* 2.239–256) gibt Sterling auf pp. 270–76.

[4] Natürlich behandelt Sterling auch diese Frage sehr genau (pp. 268–80), und sein Argument, daß Josephus, der sein Werk in Rom verfaßt hat, auch Zugang zu dem Werk des Polyhistor *Über die Juden* gehabt haben müsse (p. 283), ist an sich hörenswert—zumal er

Josephus als der bekannteste jüdische Geschichtsschreiber, der in der Literatur auch bisher immer schon als 'Apologet' charakterisiert worden ist, wird nun in chap. VI eingehend behandelt und in die Linie der 'apologetischen Historiographie' eingezeichnet, mit gutem Recht, wie mir scheint. Dafür ist die Frage, inwieweit er seine jüdisch-hellenistischen Vorgänger gekannt hat, an sich nicht entscheidend; auch sie wird aber von Sterling natürlich zu klären versucht (pp. 263–84). Weit wichtiger ist aber, daß Josephus mit den Werken des Hekataios von Abdera und vor allem mit denen des Berossos und Manethon bekannt ist (pp. 258–63). Die Annahme, daß er auch literaturgeschichtlich in der von ihnen vertretenen Linie steht, ist also nicht nur eine Hypothese. Die beiden letztgenannten Autoren sahen jeder sich selbst 'as a member of a misrepresented subgroup within the larger world. As custodians of the groups' traditions (priests), they undertook the task of setting their own story out before the Hellenistic world'.[1] Auch das Hauptanliegen des Josephus in seinen *Antiquitates Judaicae* läßt sich so beschreiben, und es ist wieder eine m. E. wichtige Konsequenz dieser Sicht, daß Sterling zeigt, daß Josephus die Heiligen Schriften der Juden in der gleichen Weise ins Spiel bringt, wie es Berossos oder Manethon mit ihren priesterlich-historischen Traditionen tun (es ist gewiß kein Zufall, daß sich auch Josephus von einer Priesterfamilie herleitet): mit einer für griechische bzw. römisch-hellenistische Leser gewissermaßen adaptierten Fassung der heiligen Überlieferung (Sterling spricht mehrfach geradezu von 'translation', obwohl natürlich auch er voraussetzt, daß Josephus die Septuaginta benutzt) will er Verständnis für Geschichte und Eigenart seines Volkes wecken. Damit ist übrigens gesagt, daß Josephus—doch wohl anders als seine jüdisch-hellenistischen Vorgänger—(auch) auf nichtjüdische Leser hofft, wie sich auch Berossos und Manethon an die Leser der ihnen fremden, hellenistischen Kultur richteten. Er bemüht sich um Respekt für sein Volk und dessen Geschichte. Mit 'missionarischen' Absichten hat das noch nichts zu tun. Etwas anders steht es dann in *Contra Apionem.* Hier kann man heimlich oder unterschwellig ('surreptitiously', p. 305) nun doch Werbung für das Judentum erkennen, wobei eventuell zu berücksichtigen ist, daß *Contra Apionem* erst der Periode nach Domitian angehört.[2] Was wiederum die *Antiquitates* im Verhältnis zum älteren *Bellum Judaicum*

---

den Autor ja doch jedenfalls kennt. Ich meine aber doch, daß Josephus von der Existenz eines solchen Standard-Werkes eines 'heidnischen' Autors über die Juden mit großer Begeisterung berichtet haben würde (etwa in *Contra Apionem*)—wenn er es denn gekannt hätte.

[1] Sterling, p. 262f.

[2] Ebd., p. 305f.

angeht, so bemerkt Sterling einen Wandel in der Wertung der Pharisäer durch Josephus zum Besseren. Weil Josephus das von ihm vertretene Judentum stets in Kontakt mit seiner Umwelt sieht, würdigt er in *Bellum* die politische Haltung der Pharisäer kritisch, dagegen in den *Antiquitates* ihre fromme Haltung gegenüber der Tora positiv. 'Josephos presents a Judaism that interacts with that world [i.e.: the Greco-Roman world]. For Josephos the issue is not Judaism or Hellenism, but Judaism in Hellenism.' So ist das Ziel seiner Darstellung in den *Antiquitates* eine 'self-definition of Judaism in historical terms', und zwar natürlich in einem Licht, das nichtjüdischen Lesern günstiger erscheinen sollte als in den Darstellungen durch Fremde. In der nach der Zerstörung des Zweiten Tempels für das jüdische Volk völlig neuen Lage setzte er sich mit seinen Mitteln dafür ein, daß der Respekt vor dem Judentum bei seinen Lesern erhalten oder wiederhergestellt würde.[1]

Insgesamt zielt die Arbeit Sterlings auf eine Einreihung des lukanischen Doppelwerks (im Deutschen haben wir nicht die praktische Kurzformel 'Luke-Acts'; sie sei im folgenden benutzt) in diese Traditionslinie orientalischer apologetischer Historiographie, wie sie nun in chap. VII (pp. 311–89) vollzogen wird. Dabei geht es wirklich um Luke-Acts insgesamt, also keineswegs nur um die Apostelgeschichte. Vielmehr erhält nun das Lukasevangelium als 'erstes Buch' die Rolle der 'heiligen Geschichte', die die junge christliche Gemeinde als Basisüberlieferung weitergibt, die aber ihrerseits betont als Verlängerung der Gechichte Gottes mit dem Volk Israel dargestellt wird, so daß auf diese indirekte Weise auch der Gesichtspunkt der 'uralten' Tradition mit ins Spiel gebracht werden kann. Hierhin rechnet Sterling auch die allgemein anerkannte Anlehnung des Lukas an die 'Septuaginta-Sprache' (vor allem in den den Akteuren in den Mund gelegten Reden), die den Eindruck der 'Altertümlichkeit' von Luke-Acts verstärken solle,[2] aber vor allem die Kurzfassungen alttestamentlicher Heilsgeschichte in Apg. 7 und 13.[3] Wenn Sterling also auch den Autor Lukas als Apolo-

---

[1] Ebd., p. 308f. Wenn auch Sterling somit Josephus ganz als Hellenisten (jüdischer Nationalität) sieht, so bleibt mir auch nach dieser Untersuchung für Josephus der Eindruck eines Chamäleons, das seine Farbe wechselt, je nachdem, ob man es mit der Brille des Hellenismus oder mit der des Judentums ansieht—und zwar in einer anderen Weise als bei Philon, über den man zunächst vielleicht dasselbe sagen möchte. Philon ist in seiner Zwitterrolle doch wohl 'echter' als Josephus, bei dem mir immer der etwas unangenehme Beigeschmack der Mimikry bleibt. Zu diesem Eindruck trägt sicher auch die Rolle bei, die Josephus immer wieder sich selbst in den politischen und den geistigen Auseinandersetzungen zuschreibt, die eben Apologetik immer auch im Blick auf ihn selbst enthält.

[2] Sterling, p. 368f. 372–75.

[3] Die fast als *opinio communis* geltende These, daß die dem Stephanus in den Mund

geten versteht, dann meint er damit nicht in erster Linie das Moment der politischen Absicherung gegenüber dem Imperium Romanum, sondern zuerst die Stellungnahme in der geistigen Auseinandersetzung mit der hellenistischen Welt, in die sich das (Heiden-)Christentum hinausgewagt hat. In der deutschen exegetischen Forschung war es in jüngerer Zeit vor allem Eckhard Plümacher, der Luke-Acts bzw. ihren Autor Lukas ganz in der Traditionslinie hellenistischer Historik sah, wobei es ihm allerdings speziell um eine Verbindung zum 'dramatischen Episodenstil' bzw. zur 'tragisch-pathetischen Historiographie' hellenistischer Autoren ging.[1] Auch Sterling erfaßt den Autor Lukas als einen sich ganz dem Hellenismus öffnenden Theologen, der die ihm überkommenen Traditionen aus der Frühzeit der Kirche bewußt hellenisiert habe. Theologisch *und* apologetisch wichtig ist seine These, daß Lukas mit der intensiven Bezugnahme auf die 'Schriften' Israels vor allem darauf zielt, die Geschichte des Volkes Israel als Vor-Geschichte der jungen Kirche zu erfassen und ihr damit eine Kontinuitäts-Linie von Adam bis zu Jesus zuzuordnen, die das neue 'Volk' der Christen mit dem allerersten Anfang der Menschheit verbindet. Dies ist für Sterling auch ein wichtiger Ertrag seines Studiums der 'heidnischen' Verfasser von apologetischen Geschichtsdarstellungen: diese Autoren treten stets für ein ganzes 'barbarisches' Volk (das der Babylonier oder der Ägypter usw.) ein. So tut es nun auch Lukas, indem er damit zugleich die christlichen Gemeinden als ein 'Volk'—wenn auch in 'Zerstreuung'—erfaßt.[2] Wen denkt sich Lukas als Leser seines Doppelwerks? In erster Linie Christen, vor allem auch solche, die schon als 'Gottesfürchtige' der Synagoge nahegestanden hatten, ehe sie Christen wurden. Nur Leser, die in den Traditionen Israels bewandert sind, können den von Lukas gebrauchten altertümelnden Stil überhaupt erkennen und würdigen.[3] Ihnen will Lukas die neue 'Self-Definition' als 'Volk' verdeutlichen, wobei Lukas nicht so sehr eine lokale Gemeinde, vielmehr alle im Imperium vorhandenen Christen-Gruppen zusammen ins Auge faßt. In diesem Sinne kann Sterling auch die Formulierung Bultmanns aufgreifen, wonach die Christenheit in Luke-

---

gelegte Rede (Apg. 7.2–50) bis auf einige lukanische Einschübe ihrerseits selbst aus jüdisch-hellenistischer Quelle stammt, erwähnt Sterling, wenn ich recht gesehen habe, nicht, obwohl er auf p. 363f. kurz davor steht, indem er Übereinstimmungen von Apg. 7 mit jüdisch-hellenistischen Autoren gegen den Bibeltext notiert. Die These würde seine Sicht natürlich noch verstärken.

[1] Vgl. etwa E. Plümacher, Art. Apostelgeschichte, TRE III (1978) 483–528: p. 509–513. – Der Bezug auf die 'tragisch-pathetische Historiographie' wird von St. (etwa p. 373f.) nicht eigens diskutiert.

[2] Ebd., p. 374.

[3] Ebd., pp. 374–77.

Acts als neue 'weltgeschichtliche Größe' ('as an entity of world history') verstanden werden soll.[1] Lukas weist der christlichen Gemeinde ihren Platz in der Weltgeschichte zu, indem er ihr eine neue 'Selbst-Definition' gibt—so wie Josephus seinem Volk nach der Zerstörung Jerusalems eine neue Identität geben möchte. Natürlich ist damit dann auch der Blick auf Menschen außerhalb der Gemeinde verbunden, aber nur in indirekter Weise. Lukas möchte den eigentlichen Lesern, also der christlichen Gemeinde, Hilfen geben zum Umgang mit den Instanzen des Imperiums. So zeigen vor allem die Reden des Paulus in seinen verschiedenen Verhören, wie man sich in solchen Situationen mutig und klug verhalten und selbst eine Apologie des Christentums bewirken kann. Auf diesem Umwege kann denn auch Sterling der verbreiteten '*religio-licita*-Deutung' von Luke-Acts noch ein wenig Wahrheitsgehalt abgewinnen.[2]

Das sind Ergebnisse, die m. E. starke Beachtung verdienen. Keine Erörterung der literarischen Gattung und Eigenart von Luke-Acts wird an ihnen künftig vorbeigehen dürfen. Trotzdem wird man nicht erwarten, daß damit die Diskussion schon abgeschlossen wäre. Die Frage, ob Lukas stärker in jüdischen Traditionen lebt bzw. aus ihnen schöpft oder ob er tatsächlich in dem von Sterling behaupteten und belegten Maße ein 'hellenistisch-christlicher' Autor ist, dürfte noch nicht erledigt sein. Man kann nicht umhin, zu sehen, daß die 'Fraktion' der 'Judaisierenden' in der Lukas-Exegese auch ihrerseits wieder neue Studien vorlegt, von denen ich hier nur zwei nach 1989 erschienene deutsche Arbeiten nennen will, zu denen Sterling noch nicht Stellung nehmen konnte: Jürgen Wehnerts Arbeit über *Die Wir-Passagen der Apostelgeschichte* mit dem sprechenden Untertitel *Ein lukanisches Stilmitel aus jüdischer Tradition*,[3] sowie Eckart Reinmuths Untersuchung *Pseudo-Philo und Lukas: Studien zum* Liber Antiquitatum Biblicarum *und seiner Bedeutung für die Interpretation des lukanischen Doppelwerks*,[4] in der Reinmuth auf eine nicht geringe Menge von sprachlichen, motivlichen und strukturellen Analogien zwischen Luke-Acts und *LAB* bis in die literarisch-kompositorische Gestaltung hinein verweist, woraus er auf eine jüdische Herkunft des Lukas und auf seine Verankerung in der jüdischen literarischen Tradition schließt. Wenn man die literaturgeschichtliche Zuordnung von Luke-Acts zum Hellenismus sieht (und bejaht, wie es Sterling mit guter Begründung tut), dann wird man doch auch seine

---

[1] Ebd., p. 378. Das Bultmann-Zitat stammt aus der *Theologie des Neuen Testaments* (in der deutschen Fassung seit der 3. Aufl. von 1958: p. 469).

[2] Ebd., pp. 381–86.

[3] (GThA 40; Göttingen 1989).

[4] (WUNT 74; Tübingen 1994).

Augen nicht vor dem Aufweis von Beziehungen zur jüdischen Literatur verschließen dürfen. Die Debatte um Lukas 'zwischen zwei Welten' wird also noch weitergehen. Es ist aber deutlich geworden, daß Sterling mit seiner Arbeit einen gewichtigen Beitrag zu dieser Debatte geliefert hat, den niemand ohne Schaden übergehen kann.[1]

Nikolaus Walter
Naumburg/Jena

Dennis R. LINDSAY, *Josephus and Faith: Πίστις and Πιστεύειν as Faith Terminology in the Writings of Flavius Josephus and in the New Testament.* Arbeiten zur Geschichte des antiken Judentums und des Urchristentums 19. Leiden 1993. xiv + 212 pages. ISBN 90-04-09858-5. $63.

This is an English translation of the author's 1990 German doctoral dissertation, prepared at Tübingen under the supervision of Professor Dr. Otto Betz. Dr. Lindsay is Principal and Lecturer in Biblical Studies at Springdale College in Birmingham, England. His book is the first book-length study of faith language in Josephus, and it makes a substantial contribution.

The first third of the book is devoted to chapters on πίστις and related words in literature prior to Josephus and the New Testament: chapter one deals with pagan authors from Sophocles to Lucian of Samosata, chapter two with the LXX, chapter three with Ben Sirach, and chapter four with Philo. Lindsay argues that πίστις and πιστεύειν, while not technical religious terms in the Classical period, became such in the Hellenistic era within and outside the Jewish tradition. The LXX (including Sirach, where the two terms appear more often than in other Greek OT books) often used πιστ- terms to translate words in the MT built on the root אמן, though that stem's association with truth and 'standing firm' sometimes causes its derivatives to be rendered with other Greek words. In a twenty-page discussion of Philo, Lindsay argues that the Alexandrian tended to use faith language to express a non-Hebraic intellectual belief ('orthodoxy') rather than a personal relationship with God. Philo also held, Lindsay argues, a superstitious or

[1] Es sei noch angemerkt, daß Sterlings Arbeit recht gut lesbar ist. Der Aufbau ist übersichtlich und der Stil sehr klar, so daß dem Leser eigentlich immer deutlich wird, mit welcher Begründung Sterling seine Argumentation vorantreibt. Dazu dienen ihm immer wieder Zwischenfragen sowie eine ganze Reihe von kleineren und größeren Tabellen, die dem Leser das Mitgehen sehr erleichtern. Auch differenziert er sehr besonnen seine Ergebnisse, indem er immer auch den jeweiligen Wahrscheinlichkeitsgrad reflektiert.

utilitarian notion of religious faith as a means of gaining happiness in the present life (*Abr.* 268 is cited as a proof-text)—in contrast to the Epistle to the Hebrews, Philo's faith concept is not shaped by the cross and eschatology.

The second half of this book offers a series of chapters analyzing the usage of faith terms in Josephus and the NT: a chapter on πίστις and ἀπιστία, one on πιστεύειν and ἀπιστεῖν, and one on πιστός and ἄπιστος. The Jewish historian uses πίστις about 200 times and πιστεύειν 225 times, mostly in non-religious ways. The religious uses, however, involve some interesting nuances: faith as trust in Moses and the prophets as well as in God, faith in a intellectual (or 'creedal') sense regarding God and immortality, and emphasis on the faithfulness of God (*pace* Ralph Marcus's Loeb translation, Lindsay translates πίστις τοῦ θείου in *Ant.* 17.179 and 284 as a subjective rather than objective genitive). In contrast to Philo and the NT, however, Josephus never links Abraham with πίστις or related terms; for him, Moses is 'the father of faith'. As he does with Philo, Lindsay uses the syntactical and content categories applied to Josephus in Adolf Schlatter's *Der Glaube im Neuen Testament* (1927 edition) as the basis for his own discussion and comparison with NT data. Josephus entirely lacks the NT's missionary concern, but (unlike Philo) he bases his religious usage of πιστ- terms solely on the Jewish religious tradition.

The monograph concludes with a lengthy discussion of Martin Buber's *Two Types of Faith* (1951): Lindsay finds the two-type distinction important but argues that Buber partly misrepresented the OT and seriously misinterpreted the NT (especially the writings of John and Paul). He contends that the NT and the OT (including the LXX) share a common Hebraic ('Biblical') concept of faith that emphasizes trust and personal commitment, whereas Josephus in part and Philo (almost wholly) presuppose a Greek faith concept that involves intellectual assent with little or no stress on personal commitment. The NT writers developed the πιστ- terminology beyond LXX patterns (as a result of the Christ event) so as 'to express the proper relationship of humankind to God' (189). There is an appendix listing Hebrew equivalents for πιστ- terms in Ben Sirach, a fairly extensive bibliography, and an index to ancient authors.

As a survey of Josephus's use of πίστις and congeners, this book makes an important contribution. I think Lindsay's interpretations of specific texts in the historian's oeuvre are often perceptive and always at least defensible (though one may disagree about details—for example, I prefer Marcus's rendering of πίστις τοῦ θείου as 'faith in God'). Actually the book would be a more satisfying contribution to scholarship if the author had limited himself to Josephus. The initial survey of the Greek pagan tradition is useful, but offers little new, and the same is true for the chapter on the LXX. The treatment of NT uses of faith terminology is sketchy and usually marked by an absence of reference (let alone, careful review) of significant secondary literature. Lindsay does devote four pages to the current hot scholarly debate about the meaning of πίστις Χριστοῦ in Paul, but he fails to discuss some of the most important participants in that debate (Erwin R. Goodenough, George Howard and Richard B. Hays). But the weakest section of the book is the treatment of Philo. Lindsay's assertions that Philo's concept of faith lacks the dimension of personal commitment and is tied to a 'utilitarian' notion that faith guarantees 'the good life' are made without significant exegesis of Philonic texts or consideration of alternative scholarly interpretations (e.g., Ronald Williamson, *Jews in the Hellenistic World: Philo* [Cambridge 1989] 209–10). Finally, given the author's desire to connect Josephus with broad linguistic and cultural traditions, it is a pity that he does not provide a fuller analysis of faith terminology in the later books of the LXX, in post-biblical Greco-Jewish documents and fragments, and in early Christian writings outside the NT.

David M. Hay
Coe College

NEWS AND NOTES

Some recent Philo meetings

The 48th General Meeting of the Studiorum Novi Testamenti Societas was held in Chicago, Illinois 9-13 August 1993. The Society's Seminar on 'Philo of Alexandria and Christian Beginnings' met for three sessions, which were chaired by David Hay. The following papers were presented and discussed: Peder Borgen, 'Some Hebrew and Pagan Features in Philo's and Paul's Interpretation of Hagar and Ishmael' (Dieter Zeller, respondent); Abraham Terian, 'A Stratum of Originality in Philo'; David Dungan, 'Non-Retaliation Traditions in Matthew and Luke' and 'Savior Gods in the Mediterranean World' (Gregory E. Sterling, respondent); and Gregory E. Sterling, 'Magister or Maverick? Philo of Alexandria and Egyptian Judaism' (David Hay, respondent). The final session concluded with a discussion of the current research of the persons attending the Seminar and plans for the 1994 meeting. This meeting will be held in Edinburgh at the beginning of August, and will probably be the final meeting of this particular seminar.

The Philo of Alexandria Seminar of the Society of Biblical Literature met at the Society's national meeting in Washington, D. C. on 20-21 November 1993. Gregory E. Sterling presided at the first session, while Robert A. Kraft presided at the second. Five papers were summarized and discussed on the first day: Adele Reinhartz, 'Philo's Exposition of the Law and Social History: Methodological Considerations'; Sze-kar Wan, 'Philo's *Quaestiones et solutiones in Genesim*: A Synoptic Approach'; Ellen Birnbaum, 'The Place of Judaism in Philo's Thought: Israel, Jews, and Proselytes,'; Angela V. Askew, 'Philo of Alexandria on Genesis, Eternity, and Time,'; and Carl R. Holladay, 'Aristobulus and the Beginnings of the Jewish Philosophical Tradition'. On the second day a panel of reviewers discussed David T. Runia's book, *Philo in Early Christian Literature; A Survey* (CRINT III.3; Fortress, 1993). The panel members were Abraham Terian, Annewies van den Hoek, Robert L. Wilken, and David Winston. Dr. Runia responded to their comments. The papers of the panel have been published in this volume (see pp. 90–110 above). A short business meeting followed. The next meeting of the seminar will be held in Chicago in November 1994.

David M. Hay

NOTES ON CONTRIBUTORS

R. M. van den Berg is studying Classical Philology and Philosophy at the University of Leiden. His postal address is Burggravenlaan 9, 2313 HM Leiden, The Netherlands.

David Hay is McCabe Professor of Religion, Coe College, Cedar Rapids, Iowa. His postal address is Department of Religion and Philosophy, Coe College, Cedar Rapids IA 52402, U.S.A.; his electronic address is dhay@coe.edu.

Annewies van den Hoek is Lecturer in Greek and Latin at the Harvard Divinity School, Harvard University, and also Fellow for Research at the Boston Museum of Fine Arts. Her address is 26 Common Street, Dedham, MA 02026, U. S. A.

Pieter W. van der Horst is Professor of New Testament, Faculty of Theology, Utrecht University. His postal address is Faculty of Theology, Utrecht University, Postbus 80.105, 3508 TC Utrecht, The Netherlands; his electronic address is vdhorst@cc.ruu.nl.

John R. Levison is Research Scholar in Residence at Duke Divinity School and Associate Professor of Biblical Studies at North Park College. During the 1993–94 academic year he was an Alexander von Humboldt Research Fellow at the Institut für antikes Judentum und hellenistische Religionsgeschichte in Tübingen. His postal address is The Divinity School, Duke University, Durham NC 27708, U. S. A.

Alan Mendelson is Professor of Religious Studies at McMaster University, Hamilton, Canada. His postal address is Department of Religious Studies, McMaster University, Hamilton, Ontario, L8S 4C8, Canada; his e-mail address is: mendelsn@mcmail.cis.mcmaster.ca.

Roberto Radice is Lecturer in Ancient Philosophy at the Sacred Heart University, Milan. His postal address is Via XXV Aprile 4, 21016 Luino, Italy.

David T. Runia is Professor of Ancient and Medieval Philosophy, Leiden University, and also C. J. de Vogel Professor Extraordinarius in Ancient Philosophy at Utrecht University. His postal address is

Rijnsburgerweg 116, 2333 AE Leiden, THE NETHERLANDS; his electronic address is runia@rulcri.leidenuniv.nl.

Karl-Gustav SANDELIN is Lecturer in Biblical Exegesis and Acting Professor of New Testament at the Åbo Akademi University. His postal address is Palomäkigatan 26 C 3, 20540 Åbo, FINLAND; his electronic address is ksandeli@finabo.abo.fi.

David SATRAN is Senior Lecturer in the Department of Comparative Religion, Hebrew University, Jerusalem. His postal address is Department of Comparative Religion, Hebrew University, Mt. Scopus, Jerusalem 91905, ISRAEL; his electronic address is Satran@hum.huji.ac.il.

Folker SIEGERT is Professor of New Testament, Faculté de Théologie, Université de Neuchâtel, Switzerland. His postal address is Faculté de Théologie, Faubourg de l'Hôpital 41, CH-2000 Neuchâtel, SWITZERLAND (fax 41 38 240920).

Gregory E. STERLING is Assistant Professor in New Testament, Department of Theology, University of Notre Dame. His postal address is Department of Theology, University of Notre Dame, Notre Dame IN 46556, U.S.A.; his electronic address is gregory.e.sterling.1@nd.edu.

Richard STONEMAN is Senior Editor for Classics and Biblical Studies at Routledge. His postal address is 105 Lennard Road, Beckenham, Kent BR3 1QR, UNITED KINGDOM; his electronic address is rstonema@routlond.mhs.compuserve.com.

Abraham TERIAN is Professor of Religion and Philosophy at Sterling College. His postal address is Department of Religion and Philosophy, Sterling College, Sterling, Kansas 67579, U. S. A.

Sze-Kar WAN is Assistant Professor of New Testament, Andover Newton Theological School, Boston. His address is Department of New Testament, Andover Newton Theological School, 210 Herrick Road, Newton Centre, MA 02145, U.S.A.; his e-mail address is: andovrb@bcvms.bc.edu.

Nikolaus WALTER is Professor of New Testament, Faculty of Theology, Friedrich-Schiller University of Jena, Germany. His postal address is Wilhelm-Wagner-Straße 7, 06618 Naumburg (S), DEUTSCHLAND.

Robert L. WILKEN is Professor of the History of Christianity, Department of Religious Studies, University of Virginia. His postal address is Department of Religious Studies, University of Virginia, Charlottesville, Virginia 22903, U.S.A.

David WINSTON is Professor of Hellenistic and Jewish Studies, Graduate Theological Union, Berkeley. His postal address is 1220 Grizzly Peak, Berkeley CA 94708, U.S.A.

Dieter ZELLER is Professor für Religionswissenschaft des Hellenismus at the Johannes-Gutenberg University of Mainz and Honorar-Professor at the Ruprecht-Karls University of Heidelberg. His postal address is Schillerweg 4, 6228 Eltville (Erbach), DEUTSCHLAND.

INSTRUCTIONS TO CONTRIBUTORS

Authors of articles and book reviews in *The Studia Philonica Annual* are asked to conform to the following guidelines.

1. *The Studia Philonica Annual* accepts articles for publication in the area of Hellenistic Judaism, with special emphasis on Philo and his *Umwelt.* Articles on Josephus will be given consideration if they focus on his relation to Judaism and classical culture (and not on primarily historical subjects). The languages in which the articles may be published are English, French and German. Translations from Italian or Dutch into English can be arranged at a modest cost to the author.

2. Since the Annual is being produced with a minimum of secretarial assistance, the editors request with some insistence that all articles and reviews be submitted on microdiskette. In the case of longer articles, contributions submitted as typescript will only be accepted by way of exception. For the formatting of submitted material the editors have the following order of preference:

(a) Apple Macintosh, formatted in MS-Word, using SMK Greek (or Super-Greek) and SuperHebrew;

(b) MS-DOS on 5.25" (360K or 1.2M) or 3.5" (720K or 1.44M) diskettes, formatted in MS-Word or Word Perfect (preference for 5.1, 4.2 and 5.0 also accepted, preferably not 6.0 or Word for Windows unless in export format to WP 5.1 or Word 5.0); users of Nota Bene are requested to submit a copy exported to DCA format.

In all cases it is **imperative** that a hard copy accompany the text on diskette, and that authors gives full details of the word processor used. No handwritten Greek or Hebrew can be accepted. Authors are requested not to vocalize their Hebrew and to keep their use of this language to a reasonable minimum. It should always be borne in mind that not all readers of the Annual can be expected to read Greek or Hebrew. Transliteration is permissible for incidental terms.

3. With regard to the citation of scholarly references the Annual will henceforth subscribe to the conventions embodied in the following examples (note (i) that no publishers' names are given, (ii) for article single quotation marks are used, and (iii) that books and journals are italicized, series are not):

A. Mendelson, *Secular Education in Philo of Alexandria,* Monographs of the Hebrew Union College 7 (Cincinnati 1982) 15–27.

Y. Amir, 'The Transference of Greek Allegories to Biblical Motifs in Philo', in F. E. Greenspahn, E. Hilgert, B. L. Mack (edd.), *Nourished with Peace: Studies in Hellenistic Judaism in Memory of Samuel Sandmel*, Scholars Press Homage Series 9 (Chico, California 1984) 15–25.

J. P. Martín, 'El encuentro de exégesis y filosofia en Filón Alejandrino', *Revista Biblica* 46 (1984) 199–211.
Mendelson *op. cit.* (n. 0) 23ff.
Amir, *art. cit.* (n.0) 16–18 **or** Martín 'El encuentro' 199–201.

It is also possible to give references by author and date in the footnotes only, with full details presented in a bibliography at the end of the article (see the example on pp. 295–319 of volume 3). Contributors are asked to follow these guidelines very closely, since mss. that deviate significantly cannot be accepted.
For the abbreviations to be used, see further below. A sound guide to the way that Philonic scholarship should be cited will be found in R. Radice and D. T. Runia, *Philo of Alexandria: an Annotated Bibliography 1937–1986*, VCSup 8 (Leiden 1988). Note that with regard to the use of capitals in citing English references, both English-American and continental European conventions are permissible.

4. It is suggested that the following abbreviations be used (this **replaces** the guidelines set out in *SPh* 1 (1971) 92–96, 2 (1972) 77–80).
(a) Philonic treatises are to be abbreviated according to the following list. Numeration is according to Cohn and Wendland's edition, using Arabic numbers only (e.g. *Spec.* 4.123). Note that *De Providentia* should be cited according to Aucher's edition, and not the LCL translation of the fragments by F. H. Colson.

Abr.	*De Abrahamo*
Aet.	*De aeternitate mundi*
Agr.	*De agricultura*
Anim.	*De animalibus*
Cher.	*De Cherubim*
Contempl.	*De vita contemplativa*
Conf.	*De confusione linguarum*
Congr.	*De congressu eruditionis gratia*
Decal.	*De Decalogo*
Deo	*De Deo*
Det.	*Quod deterius potiori insidiari soleat*
Deus	*Quod Deus sit immutabilis*
Ebr.	*De ebrietate*
Flacc.	*In Flaccum*
Fug.	*De fuga et inventione*
Gig.	*De gigantibus*
Her.	*Quis rerum divinarum heres sit*
Hypoth.	*Hypothetica*
Ios.	*De Iosepho*
Leg. 1–3	*Legum allegoriae* I, II, III
Legat.	*Legatio ad Gaium*
Migr.	*De migratione Abrahami*

Mos. 1–2	*De vita Moysis* I, II
Mut.	*De mutatione nominum*
Opif.	*De opificio mundi*
Plant.	*De plantatione*
Post.	*De posteritate Caini*
Praem.	*De praemiis et poenis, De exsecrationibus*
Prob.	*Quod omnis probus liber sit*
Prov. 1–2	*De Providentia* I, II
QE 1–2	*Quaestiones et solutiones in Exodum* I, II
QG 1–4	*Quaestiones et solutiones in Genesim* I, II, III, IV
Sacr.	*De sacrificiis Abelis et Caini*
Sobr.	*De sobrietate*
Somn. 1–2	*De somniis* I, II
Spec. 1–4	*De specialibus legibus* I, II, III, IV
Virt.	*De virtutibus*

(b) Standard works of Philonic scholarship are abbreviated:

Aucher	*Philonis Judaei sermones tres hactenus inediti* (Venice 1822), *Philonis Judaei paralipomena* (Venice 1826)
G-G	H. L. Goodhart and E. R. Goodenough, 'A General Bibliography of Philo Judaeus', in E. R. Goodenough, *The Politics of Philo Judaeus: Practice and Theory* (New Haven 1938, reprinted Hildesheim 1967²) 125–321
PCH	*Philo von Alexandria: die Werke in deutscher Übersetzung*, edited by L. Cohn, I. Heinemann *et al.*, 7 vols. (Breslau, Berlin 1909–64)
PCW	*Philonis Alexandrini opera quae supersunt*, ediderunt L. Cohn, P. Wendland, S. Reiter, 6 vols. (Berlin 1896–1915)
PLCL	*Philo in Ten Volumes (and Two Supplementary Volumes)*, English translation by F. H. Colson, G. H. Whitaker (and R. Marcus), 12 vols., Loeb Classical Library (London 1929–62)
PAPM	*Les œuvres de Philon d'Alexandrie*, French translation under the general editorship of R. Arnaldez, J. Pouilloux, C. Mondésert (Paris 1961–)
R-R	R. Radice and D. T. Runia, *Philo of Alexandria: an Annotated Bibliography 1937–1986*, VCSup 8 (Leiden 1988)
SPh	*Studia Philonica*
SPhA	*The Studia Philonica Annual*

(c) Biblical books, Pseudepigraphical, Qumran, Rabbinic and Gnostic literature are to be abbreviated as recommended in the 'Instructions to Contributors' in the *Society of Biblical Literature Membership Directory and Handbook 1993*, pp. 383–400 (copies available on request). Note that biblical books are not italicized and that between chapter and verse a colon is placed (placement of a full stop after the abbreviation is optional, provided the author is consistent). Authors writing in German or French should follow their own conventions for biblical citations.

(d) Classical and Patristic authors should be cited in the manner recommended by the three Oxford lexica:

H. G. Liddell, R. Scott , H. S. Jones (edd.), *A Greek-English Lexicon* (Oxford 1940[9]);
P. G. W. Glare (ed.), *The Oxford Latin Dictionary* (Oxford 1982);
G. W. H. Lampe (ed.), *A Patristic Greek Lexicon* (Oxford 1961).

Preferred abbreviations for Josephus, however, are *AJ*, *BJ*, *c. Ap.*, and *Vita*, but English abbreviations (*Antiquities*, *War*, etc.) are permitted. Once again consistency is the first requirement.

(e) Journals, monograph series, source collections and standard reference works are to be be abbreviated in accordance with the recommendation listed in the 'Instructions to Contributors' in the *Society of Biblical Literature Membership Directory and Handbook 1992*, pp. 217–226. The following list contains a selection of the more important abbreviations (adding a few abbreviations of Classical and philosophical journals and standard reference books not furnished in the list mentioned above.

ABD	*The Anchor Bible Dictionary* , 6 vols. (New York etc. 1992)
AC	*L'Antiquité Classique*
ACW	Ancient Christian Writers
AGJU	Arbeiten zur Geschichte des antiken Judentums und des Urchristentums
AJPh	*American Journal of Philology*
AJSL	*American Journal of Semitic Languages*
ALGHJ	Arbeiten zur Literatur und Geschichte des hellenistischen Judentums
ANRW	*Aufstieg und Niedergang der römischen Welt*
AP	*L'Année Philologique (founded by Marouzeau)*
BAGD	*A Greek-English Lexicon of the New Testament and other Early Christian literature*, edited by W. Bauer, W. F. Arndt, F. W. Gingrich, F. W. Danker (Chicago 1979[2])
BDB	*Hebrew and English lexicon of the Old Testament*, edited by F. Brown, S. R. Driver, C. A. Briggs (Oxford 1952)
BibOr	Bibliotheca Orientalis
BJRL	*Bulletin of the John Rylands Library*
BJS	Brown Judaic Studies
BZAW	Beihefte zur Zeitschrift für die alttestamentliche Wissenschaft
BZNW	Beihefte zur Zeitschrift für die neutestamentliche Wissenschaft
CAH	*The Cambridge Ancient History*, edited by J. B. Bury *et al.*, 16 vols. (Cambridge 1923–)
CBQ	*The Catholic Biblical Quarterly*
CBQMS	The Catholic Biblical Quarterly. Monograph Series
CChr	Corpus Christianorum, Turnhout
CIG	*Corpus Inscriptionum Graecarum*, edited by A. Boeckh, 4 vols. in 8 (Berlin 1828–77)

CIJ	*Corpus Inscriptionum Judaicarum*, edited by J. B. Frey, 2 vols. (Rome 1936–52)
CIL	*Corpus Inscriptionum Latinarum* (Berlin 1862–)
CIS	*Corpus Inscriptionum Semiticarum* (Paris 1881–1962)
CP	*Classical Philology*
CPJ	*Corpus Papyrorum Judaicarum*, ed. by V. Tcherikover and A. Fuks, 3 vols. (Cambrige Mass. 1957–64)
CQ	*The Classical Quarterly*
CR	*The Classical Review*
CRINT	Compendia Rerum Iudaicarum ad Novum Testamentum
CPG	*Clavis Patrum Graecorum*, edited by M. Geerard, 5 vols. (Turnhout 1974–87)
CPL	*Clavis Patrum Latinorum*, edited by E. Dekkers (Turnhout 1954)
CSCO	Corpus Scriptorum Christianorum Orientalium
DA	Dissertation Abstracts
DBSup	*Dictionnaire de la Bible*, Supplément (Paris 1928–)
DSpir	*Dictionnaire de Spiritualité*
EncJud	*Encyclopaedia Judaica*, 16 vols. (Jerusalem 1972)
EPRO	Études préliminaires aux religions orientales dans l'Empire romain
FrGH	*Fragmente der Griechische Historiker*, edited by F. Jacoby
GCS	Die griechischen christlichen Schriftsteller, Leipzig
GLAJJ	M. Stern, *Greek and Latin authors on Jews and Judaism*, 3 vols. (Jerusalem 1974–1984)
GRBS	*Greek, Roman and Byzantine Studies*
HKNT	Handkommentar zum Neuen Testament, Tübingen
HNT	Handbuch zum Neuen Testament, Tübingen
HR	*History of Religions*
HThR	*Harvard Theological Review*
HUCA	*Hebrew Union College Annual*
JAAR	*Journal of the American Academy of Religion*
JAOS	*Journal of the American Oriental Society*
JbAC	*Jahrbuch für Antike und Christentum*
JBL	*Journal of Biblical Literature*
JHI	*Journal of the History of Ideas*
JHS	*The Journal of Hellenic Studies*
JJS	*The Journal of Jewish Studies*
JQR	*The Jewish Quarterly Review*
JR	*The Journal of Religion*
JRS	*The Journal of Roman Studies*
JSHRZ	*Jüdische Schriften aus hellenistisch-römischer Zeit*
JSJ	*Journal for the Study of Judaism (in the Persian, Hellenistic and Roman Period)*
JSNT	*Journal for the Study of the New Testament*
JSNTSup	Journal for the Study of the New Testament. Supplements Series
JSOT	*Journal for the Study of the Old Testament*
JSP	*Journal for the Study of the Pseudepigrapha and Related Literature*
JSS	*Journal of Semitic Studies*
JThS	*The Journal of Theological Studies*
KB	L. Koehler and W. Baumgartner, *Lexicon in Veteris Testamenti libros*, 3 vols. (Leiden 1967-83³)

KJ	*Kirjath Sepher*
LCL	Loeb Classical Library
LSJ	*A Greek-English lexicon*, edited by H. G. Liddell, R. Scott , H. S. Jones (Oxford 1940⁹)
MGWJ	*Monatsschrift für Geschichte und Wissenschaft des Judentums*
Mnem	*Mnemosyne*
NCE	*New Catholic Encyclopedia*, 15 vols (New York 1967)
NHS	Nag Hammadi Studies
NovT	*Novum Testamentum*
NTA	*New Testament Abstracts*
NTOA	Novum Testamentum et Orbis Antiquus
NTS	*New Testament Studies*
OLD	*The Oxford Latin dictionary*, edited by P. G. W. Glare (Oxford 1982)
OTP	J. H. Charlesworth (ed.), *The Old Testament Pseudepigrapha*, 2 vols. (New York-London 1983–85)
PAAJR	*Proceedings of the American Academy for Jewish Research*
PAL	*Philon d'Alexandrie: Lyon 11–15 Septembre 1966* (Paris 1967)
PG	Patrologiae cursus completus: series Graeca, edited by J. P. Migne, 162 vols. (Paris 1857–1912)
PGL	*A Patristic Greek lexicon*, ed. by G. W. H. Lampe (Oxford 1961)
PhilAnt	Philosophia Antiqua
PL	Patrologiae cursus completus: series Latina, edited by J. P. Migne, 221 vols. (Paris 1844–64)
PW	Pauly-Wissowa-Kroll, *Real-Encyclopaedie der classischen Altertumswissenschaft*, Stuttgart
PWSup	Supplement to PW
RAC	*Reallexikon für Antike und Christentum*
RB	*Revue Biblique*
REA	*Revue des Études Anciennes*
REArm	*Revue des Études Arméniennes*
REAug	*Revue des Études Augustiniennes*
REG	*Revue des Études Grecques*
REJ	*Revue des Études Juives*
REL	*Revue des Études Latines*
RGG	*Die Religion in Geschichte und Gegenwart*, 7 vols. (Tübingen 1957–65³)
RhM	*Rheinisches Museum für Philologie*
RQ	*Revue de Qumran*
RSR	*Revue des Sciences Religieuses*
SB	H. L. Strack and P. Billerbeck, *Kommentar zum Neuen Testament aus Talmud und Midrasch*, 6 vols. in 7 (Munich 1922–61)
SBLDS	Society of Biblical Literature. Dissertation Series
SBLMS	Society of Biblical Literature. Monograph Series
SBLSPS	Society of Biblical Literature. Seminar Papers Series
SC	Sources Chrétiennes
Sem	*Semitica*
SHJP	E. Schürer, *The history of the Jewish people in the age of Jesus Christ*, revised edition, 3 vols. in 4 (Edinburgh 1973-87)
SJLA	Studies in Judaism in Late Antiquity
SNTSMS	Society for New Testament Studies. Monograph Series
SR	*Studies in Religion*

StUNT	Studien zur Umwelt des Neuen Testaments
SVF	Stoicorum veterum fragmenta, edited by J. von Arnim
TDNT	*Theological Dictionary of the New Testament*, 10 vols. (Grand Rapids 1964–76)
THKNT	Theologischer Handkommentar zum Neuen Testament, Berlin
TRE	*Theologische Realenzyklopädie*, Berlin
TSAJ	Texte und Studien zum Antike Judentum
TU	Texte und Untersuchungen zur Geschichte der altchristlichen Literatur, Berlin
TWNT	*Theologisches Wörterbuch zum Neuen Testament*, 10 vols. (Stuttgart 1933–79)
VC	*Vigiliae Christianae*
VCSup	Supplements to Vigiliae Christianae
VT	*Vetus Testamentum*
WUNT	Wissenschaftliche Untersuchungen zum Neuen Testament
ZAW	*Zeitschrift für die alttestamentliche Wissenschaft*
ZKG	*Zeitschrift für Kirchengeschichte*
ZKTh	*Zeitschrift für Katholische Theologie*
ZNW	*Zeitschrift für die neutestamentliche Wissenschaft*
ZRGG	*Zeitschrift für Religions- und Geistesgeschichte*

Brown Judaic Studies

140001	*Approaches to Ancient Judaism I*	William S. Green
140002	*The Traditions of Eleazar Ben Azariah*	Tzvee Zahavy
140003	*Persons and Institutions in Early Rabbinic Judaism*	William S. Green
140004	*Claude Goldsmid Montefiore on the Ancient Rabbis*	Joshua B. Stein
140005	*The Ecumenical Perspective and the Modernization of Jewish Religion*	S. Daniel Breslauer
140006	*The Sabbath-Law of Rabbi Meir*	Robert Goldenberg
140007	*Rabbi Tarfon*	Joel Gereboff
140008	*Rabban Gamaliel II*	Shamai Kanter
140009	*Approaches to Ancient Judaism II*	William S. Green
140010	*Method and Meaning in Ancient Judaism I*	Jacob Neusner
140011	*Approaches to Ancient Judaism III*	William S. Green
140012	*Turning Point: Zionism and Reform Judaism*	Howard R. Greenstein
140013	*Buber on God and the Perfect Man*	Pamela Vermes
140014	*Scholastic Rabbinism*	Anthony J. Saldarini
140015	*Method and Meaning in Ancient Judaism II*	Jacob Neusner
140016	*Method and Meaning in Ancient Judaism III*	Jacob Neusner
140017	*Post Mishnaic Judaism in Transition*	Baruch M. Bokser
140018	*A History of the Mishnaic Law of Agriculture: Tractate Maaser Sheni*	Peter J. Haas
140019	*Mishnah's Theology of Tithing*	Martin S. Jaffee
140020	*The Priestly Gift in Mishnah: A Study of Tractate Terumot*	Alan. J. Peck
140021	*History of Judaism: The Next Ten Years*	Baruch M. Bokser
140022	*Ancient Synagogues*	Joseph Gutmann
140023	*Warrant for Genocide*	Norman Cohn
140024	*The Creation of the World According to Gersonides*	Jacob J. Staub
140025	*Two Treatises of Philo of Alexandria: A Commentary on* De Gigantibus *and* Quod Deus Sit Immutabilis	Winston/Dillon
140026	*A History of the Mishnaic Law of Agriculture: Kilayim*	Irving Mandelbaum
140027	*Approaches to Ancient Judaism IV*	William S. Green
140028	*Judaism in the American Humanities I*	Jacob Neusner
140029	*Handbook of Synagogue Architecture*	Marilyn Chiat
140030	*The Book of Mirrors*	Daniel C. Matt
140031	*Ideas in Fiction: The Works of Hayim Hazaz*	Warren Bargad
140032	*Approaches to Ancient Judaism V*	William S. Green
140033	*Sectarian Law in the Dead Sea Scrolls: Courts, Testimony and the Penal Code*	Lawrence H. Schiffman
140034	*A History of the United Jewish Appeal: 1939-1982*	Marc L. Raphael
140035	*The Academic Study of Judaism*	Jacob Neusner
140036	*Woman Leaders in the Ancient Synagogue*	Bernadette Brooten
140037	*Formative Judaism I: Religious, Historical, and Literary Studies*	Jacob Neusner
140038	*Ben Sira's View of Women: A Literary Analysis*	Warren C. Trenchard
140039	*Barukh Kurzweil and Modern Hebrew Literature*	James S. Diamond
140040	*Israeli Childhood Stories of the Sixties: Yizhar, Aloni, Shahar, Kahana-Carmon*	Gideon Telpaz
140041	*Formative Judaism II: Religious, Historical, and Literary Studies*	Jacob Neusner
140042	*Judaism in the American Humanities II: Jewish Learning and the New Humanities*	Jacob Neusner

140043	*Support for the Poor in the Mishnaic Law of Agriculture: Tractate Peah*	Roger Brooks
140044	*The Sanctity of the Seventh Year: A Study of Mishnah Tractate Shebiit*	Louis E. Newman
140045	*Character and Context: Studies in the Fiction of Abramovitsh, Brenner, and Agnon*	Jeffrey Fleck
140046	*Formative Judaism III: Religious, Historical, and Literary Studies*	Jacob Neusner
140047	*Pharaoh's Counsellors: Job, Jethro, and Balaam in Rabbinic and Patristic Tradition*	Judith Baskin
140048	*The Scrolls and Christian Origins: Studies in the Jewish Background of the New Testament*	Matthew Black
140049	*Approaches to Modern Judaism I*	Marc Lee Raphael
140050	*Mysterious Encounters at Mamre and Jabbok*	William T. Miller
140051	*The Mishnah Before 70*	Jacob Neusner
140052	*Sparda by the Bitter Sea: Imperial Interaction in Western Anatolia*	Jack Martin Balcer
140053	*Hermann Cohen: The Challenge of a Religion of Reason*	William Kluback
140054	*Approaches to Judaism in Medieval Times I*	David R. Blumenthal
140055	*In the Margins of the Yerushalmi: Glosses on the English Translation*	Jacob Neusner
140056	*Approaches to Modern Judaism II*	Marc Lee Raphael
140057	*Approaches to Judaism in Medieval Times II*	David R. Blumenthal
140058	*Midrash as Literature: The Primacy of Documentary Discourse*	Jacob Neusner
140059	*The Commerce of the Sacred: Mediation of the Divine Among Jews in the Graeco-Roman Diaspora*	Jack N. Lightstone
140060	*Major Trends in Formative Judaism I: Society and Symbol in Political Crisis*	Jacob Neusner
140061	*Major Trends in Formative Judaism II: Texts, Contents, and Contexts*	Jacob Neusner
140062	*A History of the Jews in Babylonia I: The Parthian Period*	Jacob Neusner
140063	*The Talmud of Babylonia: An American Translation XXXII: Tractate Arakhin*	Jacob Neusner
140064	*Ancient Judaism: Debates and Disputes*	Jacob Neusner
140065	*Prayers Alleged to Be Jewish: An Examination of the Constitutiones Apostolorum*	David Fiensy
140066	*The Legal Methodology of Hai Gaon*	Tsvi Groner
140067	*From Mishnah to Scripture: The Problem of the Unattributed Saying*	Jacob Neusner
140068	*Halakhah in a Theological Dimension*	David Novak
140069	*From Philo to Origen: Middle Platonism in Transition*	Robert M. Berchman
140070	*In Search of Talmudic Biography: The Problem of the Attributed Saying*	Jacob Neusner
140071	*The Death of the Old and the Birth of the New: The Framework of the Book of Numbers and the Pentateuch*	Dennis T. Olson
140072	*The Talmud of Babylonia: An American Translation XVII: Tractate Sotah*	Jacob Neusner
140073	*Understanding Seeking Faith: Essays on the Case of Judaism II: Literature, Religion and the Social Study of Judiasm*	Jacob Neusner
140074	*The Talmud of Babylonia: An American Translation VI: Tractate Sukkah*	Jacob Neusner
140075	*Fear Not Warrior: A Study of 'al tira' Pericopes in the Hebrew Scriptures*	Edgar W. Conrad

140076	*Formative Judaism IV: Religious, Historical, and Literary Studies*	Jacob Neusner
140077	*Biblical Patterns in Modern Literature*	Hirsch/Aschkenasy
140078	*The Talmud of Babylonia: An American Translation I: Tractate Berakhot*	Jacob Neusner
140079	*Mishnah's Division of Agriculture: A History and Theology of Seder Zeraim*	Alan J. Avery-Peck
140080	*From Tradition to Imitation: The Plan and Program of Pesiqta Rabbati and Pesiqta deRab Kahana*	Jacob Neusner
140081	*The Talmud of Babylonia: An American Translation XXIII.A: Tractate Sanhedrin, Chapters 1-3*	Jacob Neusner
140082	*Jewish Presence in T. S. Eliot and Franz Kafka*	Melvin Wilk
140083	*School, Court, Public Administration: Judaism and its Institutions in Talmudic Babylonia*	Jacob Neusner
140084	*The Talmud of Babylonia: An American Translation XXIII.B: Tractate Sanhedrin, Chapters 4-8*	Jacob Neusner
140085	*The Bavli and Its Sources: The Question of Tradition in the Case of Tractate Sukkah*	Jacob Neusner
140086	*From Description to Conviction: Essays on the History and Theology of Judaism*	Jacob Neusner
140087	*The Talmud of Babylonia: An American Translation XXIII.C: Tractate Sanhedrin, Chapters 9-11*	Jacob Neusner
140088	*Mishnaic Law of Blessings and Prayers: Tractate Berakhot*	Tzvee Zahavy
140089	*The Peripatetic Saying: The Problem of the Thrice-Told Tale in Talmudic Literature*	Jacob Neusner
140090	*The Talmud of Babylonia: An American Translation XXVI: Tractate Horayot*	Martin S. Jaffee
140091	*Formative Judaism V: Religious, Historical, and Literary Studies*	Jacob Neusner
140092	*Essays on Biblical Method and Translation*	Edward Greenstein
140093	*The Integrity of Leviticus Rabbah*	Jacob Neusner
140094	*Behind the Essenes: History and Ideology of the Dead Sea Scrolls*	Philip R. Davies
140095	*Approaches to Judaism in Medieval Times III*	David R. Blumenthal
140096	*The Memorized Torah: The Mnemonic System of the Mishnah*	Jacob Neusner
140097	*Knowledge and Illumination*	Hossein Ziai
140098	*Sifre to Deuteronomy: An Analytical Translation I: Pisqaot 1-143. Debarim,Waethanan, Eqeb*	Jacob Neusner
140099	*Major Trends in Formative Judaism III: The Three Stages in the Formation of Judaism*	Jacob Neusner
140101	*Sifre to Deuteronomy: An Analytical Translation II: Pisqaot 144-357. Shofetim, Ki Tese, Ki Tabo, Nesabim, Ha'azinu, Zot Habberakhah*	Jacob Neusner
140102	*Sifra: The Rabbinic Commentary on Leviticus*	Neusner/Brooks
140103	*The Human Will in Judaism*	Howard Eilberg-Schwartz
140104	*Genesis Rabbah I: Genesis 1:1 to 8:14*	Jacob Neusner
140105	*Genesis Rabbah II: Genesis 8:15 to 28:9*	Jacob Neusner
140106	*Genesis Rabbah III: Genesis 28:10 to 50:26*	Jacob Neusner
140107	*First Principles of Systemic Analysis*	Jacob Neusner
140108	*Genesis and Judaism*	Jacob Neusner
140109	*The Talmud of Babylonia: An American Translation XXXV: Tractates Meilah and Tamid*	Peter J. Haas
140110	*Studies in Islamic and Judaic Traditions I*	Brinner/Ricks

140111	*Comparative Midrash: The Plan and Program of Genesis Rabbah and Leviticus Rabbah*	Jacob Neusner
140112	*The Tosefta: Its Structure and its Sources*	Jacob Neusner
140113	*Reading and Believing*	Jacob Neusner
140114	*The Fathers According to Rabbi Nathan*	Jacob Neusner
140115	*Etymology in Early Jewish Interpretation: The Hebrew Names in Philo*	Lester L. Grabbe
140116	*Understanding Seeking Faith: Essays on the Case of Judaism I: Debates on Method, Reports of Results*	Jacob Neusner
140117	*The Talmud of Babylonia: An American Translation VII: Tractate Besah*	Alan J. Avery-Peck
140118	*Sifre to Numbers: An American Translation and Explanation I: Sifre to Numbers 1-58*	Jacob Neusner
140119	*Sifre to Numbers: An American Translation and Explanation II: Sifre to Numbers 59-115*	Jacob Neusner
140120	*Cohen and Troeltsch: Ethical Monotheistic Religion and Theory of Culture*	Wendell S. Dietrich
140121	*Goodenough on the History of Religion and on Judaism*	Neusner/Frerichs
140122	*Pesiqta deRab Kahana I: Pisqaot 1-14*	Jacob Neusner
140123	*Pesiqta deRab Kahana II: Pisqaot 15-28 and Introduction to Pesiqta deRab Kahana*	Jacob Neusner
140124	*Sifre to Deuteronomy: Introduction*	Jacob Neusner
140126	*A Conceptual Commentary on Midrash Leviticus Rabbah: Value Concepts in Jewish Thought*	Max Kadushin
140127	*The Other Judaisms of Late Antiquity*	Alan F. Segal
140128	*Josephus as a Historical Source in Patristic Literature through Eusebius*	Michael Hardwick
140129	*Judaism: The Evidence of the Mishnah*	Jacob Neusner
140131	*Philo, John and Paul: New Perspectives on Judaism and Early Christianity*	Peder Borgen
140132	*Babylonian Witchcraft Literature*	Tzvi Abusch
140133	*The Making of the Mind of Judaism: The Formative Age*	Jacob Neusner
140135	*Why No Gospels in Talmudic Judaism?*	Jacob Neusner
140136	*Torah: From Scroll to Symbol Part III: Doctrine*	Jacob Neusner
140137	*The Systemic Analysis of Judaism*	Jacob Neusner
140138	*Sifra: An Analytical Translation I*	Jacob Neusner
140139	*Sifra: An Analytical Translation II*	Jacob Neusner
140140	*Sifra: An Analytical Translation III*	Jacob Neusner
140141	*Midrash in Context: Exegesis in Formative Judaism*	Jacob Neusner
140142	*Sifra: An Analytical Translation IV*	Jacob Neusner
140143	*Oxen, Women or Citizens? Slaves in the System of Mishnah*	Paul V. Flesher
140144	*The Book of the Pomegranate*	Elliot R. Wolfson
140145	*Wrong Ways and Right Ways in the Study of Formative Judaism*	Jacob Neusner
140146	*Sifra in Perspective: The Documentary Comparison of the Midrashim of Ancient Judaism*	Jacob Neusner
140147	*Uniting the Dual Torah: Sifra and the Problem of the Mishnah*	Jacob Neusner
140148	*Mekhilta According to Rabbi Ishmael: An Analytical Translation I*	Jacob Neusner
140149	*The Doctrine of the Divine Name: An Introduction to Classical Kabbalistic Theology*	Stephen G. Wald
140150	*Water into Wine and the Beheading of John the Baptist*	Roger Aus
140151	*The Formation of the Jewish Intellect*	Jacob Neusner
140152	*Mekhilta According to Rabbi Ishmael: An Introduction to Judaism's First Scriptural Encyclopaedia*	Jacob Neusner

140153	*Understanding Seeking Faith: Essays on the Case of Judaism III: Society, History, and Political and Philosophical Uses of Judaism*	Jacob Neusner
140154	*Mekhilta According to Rabbi Ishmael: An Analytical Translation II*	Jacob Neusner
140155	*Goyim: Gentiles and Israelites in Mishnah-Tosefta*	Gary P. Porton
140156	*A Religion of Pots and Pans?*	Jacob Neusner
140157	*Claude Montefiore and Christianity*	Maurice Gerald Bowler
140158	*The Philosophical Mishnah III: The Tractates' Agenda: From Nazir to Zebahim*	Jacob Neusner
140159	*From Ancient Israel to Modern Judaism I: Intellect in Quest of Understanding*	Neusner/Frerichs/Sarna
140160	*The Social Study of Judaism I*	Jacob Neusner
140161	*Philo's Jewish Identity*	Alan Mendelson
140162	*The Social Study of Judaism II*	Jacob Neusner
140163	*The Philosophical Mishnah I: The Initial Probe*	Jacob Neusner
140164	*The Philosophical Mishnah II: The Tractates' Agenda: From Abodah Zarah Through Moed Qatan*	Jacob Neusner
140166	*Women's Earliest Records*	Barbara S. Lesko
140167	*The Legacy of Hermann Cohen*	William Kluback
140168	*Method and Meaning in Ancient Judaism*	Jacob Neusner
140169	*The Role of the Messenger and Message in the Ancient Near East*	John T. Greene
140171	*Abraham Heschel's Idea of Revelation*	Lawerence Perlman
140172	*The Philosophical Mishnah IV: The Repertoire*	Jacob Neusner
140173	*From Ancient Israel to Modern Judaism II: Intellect in Quest of Understanding*	Neusner/Frerichs/Sarna
140174	*From Ancient Israel to Modern Judaism III: Intellect in Quest of Understanding*	Neusner/Frerichs/Sarna
140175	*From Ancient Israel to Modern Judaism IV: Intellect in Quest of Understanding*	Neusner/Frerichs/Sarna
140176	*Translating the Classics of Judaism: In Theory and In Practice*	Jacob Neusner
140177	*Profiles of a Rabbi: Synoptic Opportunities in Reading About Jesus*	Bruce Chilton
140178	*Studies in Islamic and Judaic Traditions II*	Brinner/Ricks
140179	*Medium and Message in Judaism: First Series*	Jacob Neusner
140180	*Making the Classics of Judaism: The Three Stages of Literary Formation*	Jacob Neusner
140181	*The Law of Jealousy: Anthropology of Sotah*	Adriana Destro
140182	*Esther Rabbah I: An Analytical Translation*	Jacob Neusner
140183	*Ruth Rabbah: An Analytical Translation*	Jacob Neusner
140184	*Formative Judaism: Religious, Historical and Literary Studies*	Jacob Neusner
140185	*The Studia Philonica Annual 1989*	David T. Runia
140186	*The Setting of the Sermon on the Mount*	W.D. Davies
140187	*The Midrash Compilations of the Sixth and Seventh Centuries I*	Jacob Neusner
140188	*The Midrash Compilations of the Sixth and Seventh Centuries II*	Jacob Neusner
140189	*The Midrash Compilations of the Sixth and Seventh Centuries III*	Jacob Neusner
140190	*The Midrash Compilations of the Sixth and Seventh Centuries IV*	Jacob Neusner
140191	*The Religious World of Contemporary Judaism: Observations and Convictions*	Jacob Neusner
140192	*Approaches to Ancient Judaism VI*	Neusner/Frerichs
140193	*Lamentations Rabbah: An Analytical Translation*	Jacob Neusner
140194	*Early Christian Texts on Jews and Judaism*	Robert S. MacLennan
140196	*Torah and the Chronicler's History Work*	Judson R. Shaver

140197	*Song of Songs Rabbah: An Analytical Translation I*	Jacob Neusner
140198	*Song of Songs Rabbah: An Analytical Translation II*	Jacob Neusner
140199	*From Literature to Theology in Formative Judaism*	Jacob Neusner
140202	*Maimonides on Perfection*	Menachem Kellner
140203	*The Martyr's Conviction*	Eugene Weiner/Anita Weiner
140204	*Judaism, Christianity, and Zoroastrianism in Talmudic Babylonia*	Jacob Neusner
140205	*Tzedakah: Can Jewish Philanthropy Buy Jewish Survival?*	Jacob Neusner
140206	*New Perspectives on Ancient Judaism I*	Neusner/Borgen/Frerichs/Horsley
140207	*Scriptures of the Oral Torah*	Jacob Neusner
140208	*Christian Faith and the Bible of Judaism*	Jacob Neusner
140209	*Philo's Perception of Women*	Dorothy Sly
140210	*Case Citation in the Babylonian Talmud: The Evidence Tractate Neziqin*	Eliezer Segal
140211	*The Biblical Herem: A Window on Israel's Religious Experience*	Philip D. Stern
140212	*Goodenough on the Beginnings of Christianity*	A.T. Kraabel
140213	*The Talmud of Babylonia: An American Translation XXI.A: Tractate Bava Mesia Chapters 1-2*	Jacob Neusner
140214	*The Talmud of Babylonia: An American Translation XXI.B: Tractate Bava Mesia Chapters 3-4*	Jacob Neusner
140215	*The Talmud of Babylonia: An American Translation XXI.C: Tractate Bava Mesia Chapters 5-6*	Jacob Neusner
140216	*The Talmud of Babylonia: An American Translation XXI.D: Tractate Bava Mesia Chapters 7-10*	Jacob Neusner
140217	*Semites, Iranians, Greeks and Romans: Studies in their Interactions*	Jonathan A. Goldstein
140218	*The Talmud of Babylonia: An American Translation XXXIII: Temurah*	Jacob Neusner
140219	*The Talmud of Babylonia: An American Translation XXXI.A: Tractate Bekhorot Chapters 1-4*	Jacob Neusner
140220	*The Talmud of Babylonia: An American Translation XXXI.B: Tractate Bekhorot Chapters 5-9*	Jacob Neusner
140221	*The Talmud of Babylonia: An American Translation XXXVI.A: Tractate Niddah Chapters 1-3*	Jacob Neusner
140222	*The Talmud of Babylonia: An American Translation XXXVI.B: Tractate Niddah Chapters 4-10*	Jacob Neusner
140223	*The Talmud of Babylonia: An American Translation XXXIV: Tractate Keritot*	Jacob Neusner
140224	*Paul, the Temple, and the Presence of God*	David A. Renwick
140225	*The Book of the People*	William W. Hallo
140226	*The Studia Philonica Annual 1990*	David Runia
140227	*The Talmud of Babylonia: An American Translation XXV.A: Tractate Abodah Zarah Chapters 1-2*	Jacob Neusner
140228	*The Talmud of Babylonia: An American Translation XXV.B: Tractate Abodah Zarah Chapters 3-5*	Jacob Neusner
140230	*The Studia Philonica Annual 1991*	David Runia
140231	*The Talmud of Babylonia: An American Translation XXVIII.A: Tractate Zebahim Chapters 1-3*	Jacob Neusner
140232	*Both Literal and Allegorical: Studies in Philo of Alexandria's Questions and Answers on Genesis and Exodus*	David M. Hay
140233	*The Talmud of Babylonia: An American Translation XXVIII.B: Tractate Zebahim Chapters 4-8*	Jacob Neusner

140234	*The Talmud of Babylonia: An American Translation XXVIII.C: Tractate Zebahim Chapters 9-14*	Jacob Neusner
140235	*The Talmud of Babylonia: An American Translation XXIX.A: Tractate Menahot Chapters 1-3*	Jacob Neusner
140236	*The Talmud of Babylonia: An American Translation XXIX.B: Tractate Menahot Chapters 4-7*	Jacob Neusner
140237	*The Talmud of Babylonia: An American Translation XXIX.C: Tractate Menahot Chapters 8-13*	Jacob Neusner
140238	*The Talmud of Babylonia: An American Translation XXIX: Tractate Makkot*	Jacob Neusner
140239	*The Talmud of Babylonia: An American Translation XXII.A: Tractate Baba Batra Chapters 1 and 2*	Jacob Neusner
140240	*The Talmud of Babylonia: An American Translation XXII.B: Tractate Baba Batra Chapter 3*	Jacob Neusner
140241	*The Talmud of Babylonia: An American Translation XXII.C: Tractate Baba Batra Chapters 4-6*	Jacob Neusner
140242	*The Talmud of Babylonia: An American Translation XXVII.A: Tractate Shebuot Chapters 1-3*	Jacob Neusner
140243	*The Talmud of Babylonia: An American Translation XXVII.B: Tractate Shebuot Chapters 4-8*	Jacob Neusner
140244	*Balaam and His Interpreters: A Hermeneutical History of the Balaam Traditions*	John T. Greene
140245	*Courageous Universality: The Work of Schmuel Hugo Bergman*	William Kluback
140246	*The Mechanics of Change: Essays in the Social History of German Jewry*	Steven M. Lowenstein
140247	*The Talmud of Babylonia: An American Translation XX.A: Tractate Baba Qamma Chapters 1-3*	Jacob Neusner
140248	*The Talmud of Babylonia: An American Translation XX.B: Tractate Baba Qamma Chapters 4-7*	Jacob Neusner
140249	*The Talmud of Babylonia: An American Translation XX.C: Tractate Baba Qamma Chapters 8-10*	Jacob Neusner
140250	*The Talmud of Babylonia: An American Translation XIII.A: Tractate Yebamot Chapters 1-3*	Jacob Neusner
140251	*The Talmud of Babylonia: An American Translation XIII.B: Tractate Yebamot Chapters 4-6*	Jacob Neusner
140252	*The Talmud of Babylonia: An American Translation XI: Tractate Moed Qatan*	Jacob Neusner
140253	*The Talmud of Babylonia: An American Translation XXX.A: Tractate Hullin Chapters 1 and 2*	Tzvee Zahavy
140254	*The Talmud of Babylonia: An American Translation XXX.B: Tractate Hullin Chapters 3-6*	Tzvee Zahavy
140255	*The Talmud of Babylonia: An American Translation XXX.C: Tractate Hullin Chapters 7-12*	Tzvee Zahavy
140256	*The Talmud of Babylonia: An American Translation XIII.C: Tractate Yebamot Chapters 7-9*	Jacob Neusner
140257	*The Talmud of Babylonia: An American Translation XIV.A: Tractate Ketubot Chapters 1-3*	Jacob Neusner
140258	*The Talmud of Babylonia: An American Translation XIV.B: Tractate Ketubot Chapters 4-7*	Jacob Neusner
140259	*Jewish Thought Adrift: Max Wiener (1882-1950)*	Robert S. Schine
140260	*The Talmud of Babylonia: An American Translation XIV.C: Tractate Ketubot Chapters 8-13*	Jacob Neusner

140261	*The Talmud of Babylonia: An American Translation XIII.D: Tractate Yebamot Chapters 10-16*	Jacob Neusner
140262	*The Talmud of Babylonia: An American Translation XV. A: Tractate Nedarim Chapters 1-4*	Jacob Neusner
140263	*The Talmud of Babylonia: An American Translation XV.B: Tractate Nedarim Chapters 5-11*	Jacob Neusner
140264	*Studia Philonica Annual 1992*	David T. Runia
140265	*The Talmud of Babylonia: An American Translation XVIII.A: Tractate Gittin Chapters 1-3*	Jacob Neusner
140266	*The Talmud of Babylonia: An American Translation XVIII.B: Tractate Gittin Chapters 4 and 5*	Jacob Neusner
140267	*The Talmud of Babylonia: An American Translation XIX.A: Tractate Qiddushin Chapter 1*	Jacob Neusner
140268	*The Talmud of Babylonia: An American Translation XIX.B: Tractate Qiddushin Chapters 2-4*	Jacob Neusner
140269	*The Talmud of Babylonia: An American Translation XVIII.C: Tractate Gittin Chapters 6-9*	Jacob Neusner
140270	*The Talmud of Babylonia: An American Translation II.A: Tractate Shabbat Chapters 1 and 2*	Jacob Neusner
140271	*The Theology of Nahmanides Systematically Presented*	David Novak
140272	*The Talmud of Babylonia: An American Translation II.B: Tractate Shabbat Chapters 3-6*	Jacob Neusner
140273	*The Talmud of Babylonia: An American Translation II.C: Tractate Shabbat Chapters 7-10*	Jacob Neusner
140274	*The Talmud of Babylonia: An American Translation II.D: Tractate Shabbat Chapters 11-17*	Jacob Neusner
140275	*The Talmud of Babylonia: An American Translation II.E: Tractate Shabbat Chapters 18-24*	Jacob Neusner
140276	*The Talmud of Babylonia: An American Translation III.A: Tractate Erubin Chapters 1 and 2*	Jacob Neusner
140277	*The Talmud of Babylonia: An American Translation III.B: Tractate Erubin Chapters 3 and 4*	Jacob Neusner
140278	*The Talmud of Babylonia: An American Translation III.C: Tractate Erubin Chapters 5 and 6*	Jacob Neusner
140279	*The Talmud of Babylonia: An American Translation III.D: Tractate Erubin Chapters 7-10*	Jacob Neusner
140280	*The Talmud of Babylonia: An American Translation XII: Tractate Hagigah*	Jacob Neusner
140281	*The Talmud of Babylonia: An American Translation IV.A: Tractate Pesahim Chapter I*	Jacob Neusner
140282	*The Talmud of Babylonia: An American Translation IV.B: Tractate Pesahim Chapters 2 and 3*	Jacob Neusner
140283	*The Talmud of Babylonia: An American Translation IV.C: Tractate Pesahim Chapters 4-6*	Jacob Neusner
140284	*The Talmud of Babylonia: An American Translation IV.D: Tractate Pesahim Chapters 7 and 8*	Jacob Neusner
140285	*The Talmud of Babylonia: An American Translation IV.E: Tractate Pesahim Chapters 9 and 10*	Jacob Neusner
140286	*From Christianity to Gnosis and From Gnosis to Christianity*	Jean Magne
140287	*Studia Philonica Annual 1993*	David T. Runia
140288	*Diasporas in Antiquity*	Shaye J. D. Cohen, Ernest S. Frerichs
140289	*The Jewish Family in Antiquity*	Shaye J. D. Cohen
140290	*The Place of Judaism in Philo's Thought*	Ellen Birnbaum

140291	*The Babylonian Esther Midrash, Vol. 1*	Eliezer Segal
140292	*The Babylonian Esther Midrash, Vol. 2*	Eliezer Segal
140293	*The Babylonian Esther Midrash, Vol. 3*	Eliezer Segal
140294	*The Talmud of Babylonia: An American Translation V. A: Tractate Yoma Chapters 1 and 2*	Jacob Neusner
140295	*The Talmud of Babylonia: An American Translation V. B: Tractate Yoma Chapters 3-5*	Jacob Neusner
140296	*The Talmud of Babylonia: An American Translation V. C: Tractate Yoma Chapters 6-8*	Jacob Neusner
140297	*The Talmud of Babylonia: An American Translation XXII.D: Tractate Baba Batra Chapters Seven and Eight*	Jacob Neusner
140298	*The Talmud of Babylonia: An American Translation XXII.E: Tractate Baba Batra Chapters Nine and Ten*	Jacob Neusner
140299	*The Studia Philonica Annual, 1994*	David T. Runia

Brown Studies on Jews and Their Societies

145001	*American Jewish Fertility*	Calvin Goldscheider
145002	*The Impact of Religious Schooling: The Effects of Jewish Education Upon Religious Involvement*	Harold S. Himmelfarb
145003	*The American Jewish Community*	Calvin Goldscheider
145004	*The Naturalized Jews of the Grand Duchy of Posen in 1834 and 1835*	Edward David Luft
145005	*Suburban Communities: The Jewishness of American Reform Jews*	Gerald L. Showstack
145007	*Ethnic Survival in America*	David Schoem
145008	*American Jews in the 21st Century: A Leadership Challenge*	Earl Raab

Brown Studies in Religion

147001	*Religious Writings and Religious Systems I*	Jacob Neusner, et al
147002	*Religious Writings and Religious Systems II*	Jacob Neusner, et al
147003	*Religion and the Social Sciences*	Robert Segal